# Microsoft Office 97 Professional 6 in 1

by Peter Aitken, Jennifer Fulton, Sue Plumley, and Faithe Wempen

Compiled by Faithe Wempen

A Division of Macmillan Computer Publishing
201 West 103rd Street, Indianapolis, Indiana 46290 USA

*To Margaret and J.P., my family. F.W.*

International Standard Book Number: 0-7897-0957-0

Library of Congress Catalog Card Number: 96-70772

99 98 97   8 7 6 5 4 3 2

Interpretation of the printing code: the rightmost double-digit number is the year of the book's first printing; the rightmost single-digit number is the number of the book's printing. For example, a printing code of 97-1 shows that this copy of the book was printed during the first printing of the book in 1997.

Screen reproductions in this book were created by means of the program Collage Complete from Inner Media, Inc., Hollis, NH.

*Printed in the United States of America*

**Publisher**
Roland Elgey

**Publishing Manager**
Lynn E. Zingraf

**Editorial Services Director**
Elizabeth Keaffaber

**Managing Editor**
Michael Cunningham

**Director of Marketing**
Lynn E. Zingraf

**Acquisitions Editor**
Martha O'Sullivan

**Product Development Specialist**
Lorna Gentry

**Technical Editor**
Herb Feltner

**Production Editor**
Audra Gable

**Editors**
Tom Lamoureux
Theresa Matthias
Linda Seifert

**Technical Specialist**
Nadeem Muhammed

**Book Designer**
Glenn Larsen

**Cover Designer**
Nathan Clement

**Production Team**
Marcia Brizendine
Jason Carr
Brian Grossman
Christy Hendershot
Tony McDonald
Kaylene Riemen
Donna Wright

**Indexer**
Robert Long

## Acknowledgments

Que Corporation would like to acknowledge the contributing authors of this book: Peter Aitken, Jennifer Fulton, Sue Plumley, and Faithe Wempen. Thanks also to Faithe Wempen for coordinating the fourth edition of this book.

And finally, thanks to our hard-working Que production team:

Marcia Brizendine, Jason Carr, Brian Grossman, Christy Hendershot, Robert Long, Tony McDonald, Kaylene Riemen, and Donna Wright.

## Trademarks

# We'd Like to Hear from You!

As part of our continuing effort to produce books of the highest possible quality, Que would like to hear your comments. To stay competitive, we *really* want you, as a computer book reader and user, to let us know what you like or dislike most about this book or other Que products.

You can mail comments, ideas, or suggestions for improving future editions to the address below, or send us a fax at (317) 581-4663. For the online inclined, Macmillan Computer Publishing has a forum on CompuServe (type **GO QUEBOOKS** at any prompt) through which our staff and authors are available for questions and comments. The address of our Internet site is **http:// www.mcp.com/que** (World Wide Web).

In addition to exploring our forum, please feel free to contact me personally to discuss your opinions of this book: I'm **75703,3251** on CompuServe, and I'm **lgentry@que.mcp.com** on the Internet.

Thanks in advance—your comments will help us to continue publishing the best books available on computer topics in today's market.

Lorna Gentry
Product Development Specialist
Que Corporation
201 West 103rd Street
Indianapolis, Indiana 46290
USA

# Contents

# Part III: Excel                                                   213

# Part IV: PowerPoint                                    339

# Introduction

"There aren't enough hours in the day." It's a common complaint. Time is a commodity everyone could use more of.

The Microsoft Corporation has packaged five of their most powerful and useful software products into one impressive package called Microsoft Office Professional. These programs run with the help of a sixth product: Microsoft Windows (95 or NT 3.51 and higher). With these software products, you can save time as you create impressive business documents, financial statements, and presentations, and you can manage your daily schedule.

Windows is a graphical user interface (GUI) that allows you to organize and run your software packages in a graphical operating system instead of using prompts and obscure commands (like you do with DOS). Windows comes with several useful applications, including a word processor (Write), a graphics painting program (Paint), and a communications program (HyperTerminal). It also features many accessories (such as a clock, a calendar, and a phone dialer) that will help organize and simplify your work.

The five software packages in Microsoft Office are:

- **Word for Windows**   Arguably the best Windows-based word processing program on the market. Word has features that enable you to create a one-page memo, a newsletter with graphics, or even a 500-page report.
- **Excel**   A powerful yet easy-to-maneuver spreadsheet program. Excel can be used to generate impressive financial statements, charts and graphs, and databases, and to share the information with other software packages.
- **PowerPoint**   An easy-to-use presentation program that lets you create impressive slides and overheads or print out presentations.
- **Outlook**   A daily planner, calendar, and to-do list that helps you get the most out of your day through careful schedule management.
- **Access**   A database program that's quickly become a leader in the industry because of its powerful capabilities and ease of use. Access is included only in the Professional edition of Office, not the Standard version.

# Using This Book

*Microsoft Office 97 Professional 6 in 1* is designed to help you learn these six programs (Office's five programs plus Windows) quickly and easily. You don't have to spend any time figuring out what to learn. All the most important tasks are covered in this book. There's no need for long classes or thick manuals. Learn the skills you need in short, easy-to-follow lessons.

The book is organized into seven parts—one for each of the six software packages, with approximately 20 lessons in each part, and a final part that helps you integrate the various programs to work seamlessly together. Because each of these lessons takes 10 minutes or less to complete, you can quickly master the basic skills you need to navigate Windows; create documents, financial statements, or slide shows; or send and reply to mail messages.

If this is the first time you've ever used Windows 95 (or NT 3.51) or a dependent product, begin with the Windows part of this book. What you learn in that part will help you navigate your way through the other software packages.

# Conventions Used in This Book

Each of the short lessons in this book includes step-by-step instructions for performing specific tasks. The following icons (small graphic symbols) are included to help you quickly identify particular types of information:

 **TIP**  These icons indicate ways you can save time when you're using any of the Microsoft Office products.

 **TERM**  These icons point out definitions of words you'll need to know in order to understand how to use a software package.

**CAUTION**  Caution icons help you avoid making mistakes.

In addition to the icons, the following conventions are also used:

**On-screen text**            On-screen text appears in bold type.

**What you type**             Information you type appears in bold type.

**Items you select**          Items you select or keys you press appear in bold type.

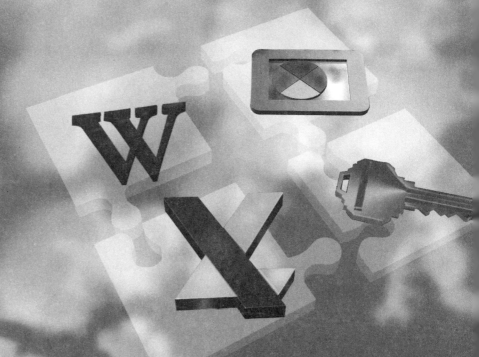

# Windows

# Understanding Windows

*In this lesson, you learn what Windows is and how to start it. You also learn the parts of the Windows desktop and find out how to use a mouse to manipulate items on the desktop.*

## The What and Why of Windows

Microsoft Windows is a program that sets up an "environment" for you to work in at your computer, based on colorful pictures (called *icons*) and menus. This friendly environment is called a *Graphical User Interface* (GUI).

**Graphical User Interface** A GUI (pronounced "GOO-ey") provides a picture-based way of interacting with your computer. Instead of typing commands at a prompt, you select from menus and pictures to tell the computer what you want.

Windows comes with many useful accessory programs, including a no-frills word processor (WordPad), a graphics program (Paint), and a communication program (HyperTerminal). It also provides several handy tools such as a Calculator and a Notepad. Some users never need more features than these simple programs provide. However, those who do need more features often turn to the Microsoft Office suite of *applications*, which you'll learn about in later parts of this book.

**Application** A computer program that does something useful, like enable you to compose a letter (Word) or create a spreadsheet (Excel). Sometimes the small accessory applications that come with Windows are called "applets."

Because this book is about Microsoft Office, I'll assume that you have purchased the more powerful Windows-based Microsoft Office applications, which do everything the simple programs do and more. That's why this book doesn't cover applications like WordPad; I'll assume you're using the Office products. If you are interested in learning more about WordPad, Paint, and the other free Windows applications, check out *The Complete Idiot's Guide to Windows 95* by Paul McFedries.

# Starting Windows

Once Windows is installed on your system (see the introduction for instructions on how to do this), you go directly to the Windows desktop each time you start your computer. There's no need to issue a special startup command. If you see a DOS prompt on the screen (something like **C:\>**), try typing **EXIT** and pressing **Enter**.

If Windows does not appear, turn your computer off and back on again. If Windows still does not appear, the program is not yet installed.

# Understanding the Windows Desktop

As you can see in Figure 1.1, the Windows desktop is made up of several components. These components are used throughout Windows and Windows applications to make it easy for you to get your work done.

The components of the desktop include the following:

**Icons**   Icons are pictures that represent programs (Microsoft Excel, WordPerfect, and so on), files (documents, spreadsheets, graphics), printer information (setup options, installed fonts), and computer information (hard and floppy disk drives). Although when you first see the Windows desktop, you have only two icons (My Computer and the Recycle Bin), icons are used throughout Windows and Windows applications. Icons come in large and small sizes, and Windows uses four types of icons: program, file, printer, and computer. I will point out each type of icon when it is introduced in the book.

**Desktop**   This is the area that takes up the entire background of the screen.

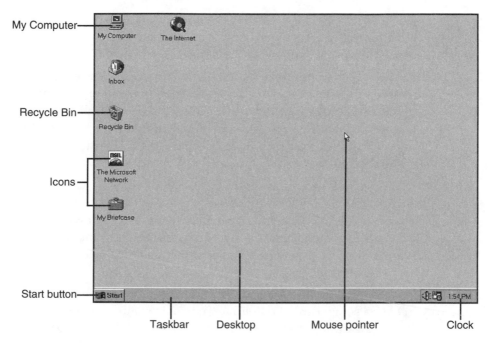

**Figure 1.1**   The Windows desktop.

**Mouse pointer**   The on-screen pointer (usually an arrow) that you use to select items and choose commands. You move the pointer by moving the mouse across your desk or mouse pad. You'll learn how to use the mouse later in this lesson.

**My Computer**   The My Computer icon gives you access to a window in which you can browse through the contents of your computer or find out information about the disk drives, control panel, and printers that you have on your computer.

**Recycle Bin**   The Recycle Bin serves as your electronic trash can. You drag unwanted files, folders, or other icons to the Recycle Bin, and the Recycle Bin appears to have papers spilling over the top of it. To permanently delete the items, first double-click the **Recycle Bin** icon to open its window. Select the items you want to delete, pull down the **File** menu, and choose **Empty Recycle Bin**. Windows asks you for confirmation.

**Start button**   You click the Start button to display the Start menu, which contains a list of commands that enable you to get to work quickly and easily. The Start menu contains commands for launching programs,

**5**

opening the most recently used files, changing settings, finding files or folders, accessing Help topics, running a program by entering a specific command line, and shutting down Windows.

**Taskbar**   Click a button on the taskbar to either launch a program or switch to a different task. For each application that you open, a button appears on the taskbar. When you use more than one application at a time, you can see the names of all the open applications on the taskbar. At any time, you can click the appropriate button on the taskbar to work with an open application.

Initially, the taskbar appears at the bottom of the screen. However, you can move it to the top, left, or right side of the screen to suit your needs. For example, if you were using the Microsoft Word for Windows program and the taskbar appeared above the status bar, you might want to drag the taskbar to the top of the screen and position it below the toolbars, where it is more convenient for use.

**Clock**   A clock at the right end of the taskbar displays the current time; if you have a sound card, the Volume Control icon appears next to the clock. The Volume Control feature enables you to control the volume for sounds played through your computer speaker and multimedia devices.

**Taskbar/Task List**   The Windows taskbar is different from the Windows 3.1 task list because the taskbar is accessible at all times. In Windows 3.1, you had to press Ctrl+Esc to access the Task List and press Alt+Tab to switch between tasks.

**Network Neighborhood**   If your computer is on a network, you have another icon on the desktop called Network Neighborhood. Double-click the **Network Neighborhood** icon to browse through your network and see what it contains. This icon also provides information on mapped drives and interfaces. (This icon isn't shown in Figure 1.1.)

**Inbox**   If you installed Microsoft Exchange during setup, you have the Inbox icon on the desktop. The Inbox functions as a central place to get information from various information services, such as The Microsoft Network, electronic mail systems, and Microsoft Fax software. Double-click the **Inbox** icon to send and receive mail and faxes on your network.

**My Briefcase**   If you chose the Portable or Custom option to install Briefcase, you have the My Briefcase icon on your desktop. You can use Briefcase to keep copies of your files updated at home on your main computer or on the road on your portable computer.

# Using the Mouse

You can use the mouse to quickly select any object on-screen, such as an icon or a window. (You'll learn about windows in the next lesson.) The process involves two steps: pointing and clicking.

To *point* to an object (icon, window title bar, and so on), move the mouse across your desk or mouse pad until the on-screen mouse pointer touches the object. You might have to pick up the mouse and reposition it if you run out of room on your desk.

To *click*, point the mouse pointer at the object you want to select, and quickly press and release the left mouse button. If the object is an icon or window, it becomes highlighted.

When you're pointing at an object, you can also click the right mouse button (*right-click*) it to bring up a menu of actions you can perform on the object (a shortcut menu). These shortcuts are mentioned throughout the book.

To *double-click* an item, you point to the item and press and release the left mouse button twice in rapid succession. Double-clicking performs an action; if you double-click an icon or a file, it opens.

You can also use the mouse to move an object (usually a window, dialog box, or icon) to a new position on-screen. You do this by *dragging* the object. To drag an object to a new location on-screen, point to the object, press and hold the left mouse button, move the mouse to a new location, and release the mouse button. The object moves with the mouse cursor.

In this lesson, you learned about the Windows desktop, and you learned how to use the mouse to manipulate items on the desktop. In the next lesson, you'll learn how to work with windows, the main building blocks of the Windows program.

# Working with a Window

*In this lesson, you learn how to open a window, use scroll bars, resize a window, move a window, and close a window.*

## What Is a Window?

A window is a rectangular area of the screen in which you view program folders, files, or icons. The window is made up of several components (see Figure 2.1) that are the same for all windows in Windows and Windows applications and make it easy for you to manage your work.

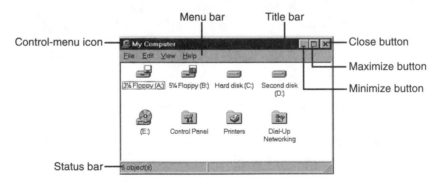

**Figure 2.1**   The My Computer window.

**Same Controls, New Look**  For the most part, the components in the Windows 95 and Windows 3.1 windows are the same. The main difference is that the title bar, the Minimize, Maximize, and Restore buttons, and the Control menu have new looks in Windows 95. In addition, Windows 3.1 windows don't have Close buttons, and the Minimize command varies slightly in that it reduces the window to a button on the taskbar, whereas in Windows 3.1 it reduces the window to an icon on the desktop.

# Opening Windows

To open a window from an icon, double-click the icon. For example, point at the My Computer icon on the desktop and double-click. If you do it correctly, the My Computer icon opens up to the My Computer window, as in Figure 2.1.

You can also use a shortcut menu to open a window. Just point to the icon and click the right mouse button, and a shortcut menu appears. Select **Open** on the shortcut menu, and the icon opens into a window.

# Using Scroll Bars

Scroll bars appear along the bottom and right edges of a window when text, graphics, or icons in a window take up more space than the area shown. Using scroll bars, you can move up, down, left, or right in a window.

Figure 2.2 shows an example. Because this window's content is not fully visible in the window, scroll bars are present on the bottom and right sides of the window.

The following steps show you one way to use the scroll bars to view items outside the window:

1. To see an object that is down and to the right of the viewable area of the window, point at the down arrow located on the bottom of the vertical scroll bar.
2. Click the arrow, and the window's contents scroll up.
3. Click the scroll arrow on the right side of the horizontal scroll bar, and the window's contents move left.

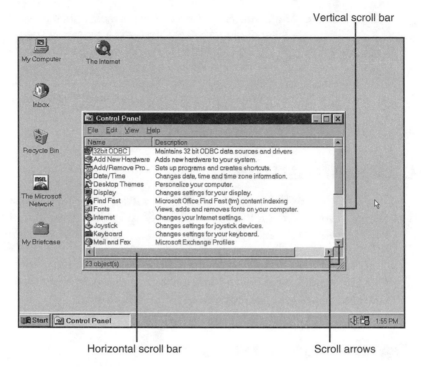

Vertical scroll bar

Horizontal scroll bar

Scroll arrows

**Figure 2.2** Scroll bars.

By its size within the scroll bar, the scroll box indicates how much of a window is not visible. In Figure 2.2, the scroll box size indicates that the portion visible in the window now is slightly more than half of the length of the file and about three-quarters of the width of the file.

If you know approximately where something is in a window (maybe two-thirds of the way down, for example), you might want to drag the scroll box. To drag a scroll box and move quickly to a distant area of the window (top or bottom, left or right), use this technique:

1. Point to the scroll box in the scroll bar and hold down the left mouse button.
2. Drag the scroll box to the new location.
3. Release the mouse button.

Sometimes you might need to move slowly through a window. You can move the contents of a window one window full at a time by clicking in the scroll bar on either side of the scroll box.

# Sizing a Window with Maximize, Minimize, and Restore

You may want to increase the size of a window to see its full contents, or you may want to decrease a window's size (even down to button form on the taskbar) to make room for other windows. One way to resize a window is to use the Maximize, Minimize, and Restore commands. If you use the mouse, you will use the Maximize, Minimize, and Restore buttons located on the right side of the window's title bar. If you use the keyboard, you can use the Maximize, Minimize, and Restore menu commands on the Control menu. The following list defines the purpose of each of these buttons and commands:

- Select the **Maximize** button or command to enlarge the window to its maximum size.
- Select the **Minimize** button or command to reduce the window to a button on the taskbar.
- Select the **Restore** button or command to return a window to the size it was before it was maximized. (The Restore button and command are available only after a window has been maximized.)

Figure 2.3 shows the My Computer window maximized to full-screen size. At full size, the Minimize and Restore buttons are available. At any other size, you see the Maximize button instead of the Restore button.

To maximize, minimize, or restore a window with the mouse, click the appropriate button. To maximize, minimize, or restore a window with the keyboard, follow these steps:

1. Press **Alt+Spacebar** to open the window's Control menu.
2. Select the **Restore**, **Minimize**, or **Maximize** command from the menu.

Minimize button    Restore button

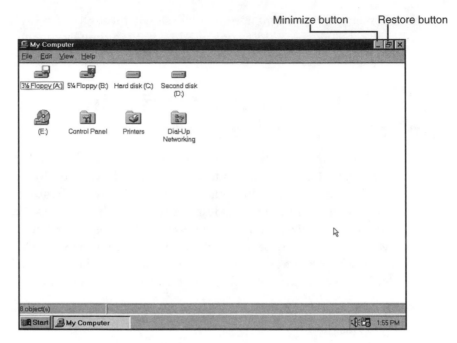

**Figure 2.3**   The My Computer window maximized to full-screen size.

 **TIP**   **Document Windows Are Different**   Later in this book when you are working with Office components, you will open documents within application windows. To access the Control menu for a document window, press **Ctrl+−** (minus sign).

# Sizing a Window's Borders

At some point, you may need a window to be a particular size to suit your needs. If so, simply drag the window border to change the size of the window.

To use the mouse, follow these steps:

**1.** Place the mouse pointer on the portion of the border (vertical, horizontal, or corner) that you want to resize. When the mouse pointer is positioned correctly, it changes into one of the shapes described here:

The vertical double-headed arrow appears when you position the mouse pointer over the top or bottom window border. It enables you to resize the window's height by dragging the border up or down.

The horizontal double-headed arrow appears when you position the mouse pointer over either side of the window border. It enables you to resize the window's width by dragging the border left or right.

The diagonal double-headed arrow appears when you position the mouse pointer over any of the four corners of the window border. It enables you to resize the window's height and width proportionally by dragging the corner diagonally.

**2.** Press the mouse button and drag the border. A faint line appears, indicating where the border will be when you release the mouse button.

**3.** Once the border is in the desired location, release the mouse button. The window is resized.

To resize a window using the keyboard, follow these steps:

**1.** Press **Alt+Spacebar** (or **Alt+–** for a document window in an application) to open the window's Control menu.

**2.** Press **S** to choose the Size command. The pointer becomes a four-headed arrow.

**3.** Use the arrow keys to move the pointer to the border or corner you want to resize. The mouse pointer turns into a different shape.

**4.** With the pointer on the border or corner, press the arrow keys to resize the window. A faint line appears showing the new border location.

**5.** When the faint line appears to be the size you want, press **Enter**. To cancel the operation, press **Esc**.

# Moving a Window

When you start working with multiple windows, moving a window becomes as important as sizing one. For example, you may need to move one or more windows to make room for other work on your desktop.

You can move a window with the mouse or keyboard. To move a window using the mouse, point at the window's title bar, press and hold the left mouse button, and drag it to a new location. To use the keyboard, follow these steps:

1. Press **Alt+Spacebar** (or **Alt+–** for a document window in an application) to open the window's Control menu.

2. Press **M** to choose the Move command. The pointer changes to a four-headed arrow.

3. Use the arrow keys to move the window to a new location.

4. When the window is located where you want it, press **Enter**. To cancel the operation and return the window to its original location, press **Esc**.

# Closing a Window

When you're finished working with a window you should close it. This can help speed up Windows, conserve memory, and keep your desktop from becoming cluttered.

To close a window with the mouse:

1. Click the **Control-menu** icon to display the Control menu.

2. Click the **Close** command to close the window.

 **TIP**  **Quickie Close**  To quickly close a window with the mouse, click the **Close** (X) button or double-click the **Control-menu** icon.

If you'd rather use the keyboard, select the window you want to close and press **Alt+F4**.

In this lesson, you learned how to use windows. In the next lesson, you'll learn how to use the Windows Help sytem.

# Using Windows Help

*In this lesson, you learn how to get help, use Help's shortcut buttons, and use the What's This? feature.*

## Getting Help in Windows

Windows offers several ways to get online help, instant on-screen help for menu commands or other tools. Online help is information that appears in its own window whenever you request it. The Help feature is organized like a reference book with three tabs: Contents, Index, and Find. The Contents and Index features show you step by step how to use commands and functions and how to perform operations in Windows applications and accessories. The Find feature enables you to search for specific words and phrases in a Help topic. Whether you use the keyboard or the mouse to access Help, help information is always at your fingertips. If you do not know or cannot remember how to perform some task, you can let the Windows Help system to tell you how.

**TIP** **Consistent Help Systems** You should take the time now to master the Windows Help system because the Help systems in all Microsoft Office products are very similar.

To get help on common tasks, follow these steps:

1. Click the **Start** button. The Start menu appears.
2. Choose **Help** from the Start menu. The Help Topics: Windows Help window appears, showing a list of Help topics.
3. Click the **Contents** tab to browse through the Help topics listed in the Help window; or click the **Index** tab to search for a specific Help topic; or click the **Find** tab to search for specific words or phrases in a Help topic.

**TIP**  **Fast Help**  You can press **F1** at any time to access the Help system from within a program.

**New and Improved Help**  The Help systems in Windows 3.1 and Windows 95 are organized differently. Whereas Windows 3.1 is divided into the categories Contents, Search, and Glossary, Windows 95 is divided into the categories Contents, Index, and Find. In addition, you no longer have to scroll through the Help window to find a topic because the list of Help topics is short: they all fit on one small screen.

# Using the Contents Feature

You can get help with common tasks using Help's Contents feature. The Contents feature displays the top level groups of information covered in Help, such as How To and Tips and Tricks. When you open a major group, a list of main topics appears. As you can see in Figure 3.1, both the major groups and the main topics in each group are represented by book icons, and subtopics are represented by page icons (with a question mark). You can simply select a book to see a list of the subtopics.

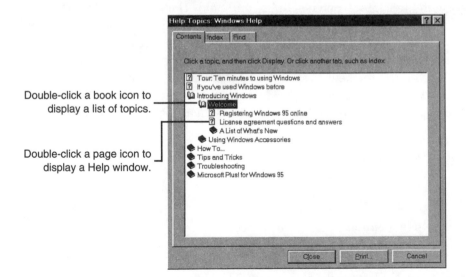

**Figure 3.1**  The Help Topics: Windows Help window.

Follow these steps to use Help's Contents feature.

1. Click the main group that contains the Help topic you want to open. The group's name becomes highlighted.

2. Click the **Open** button to open the group. A list of chapters in that group appears.

3. Click the chapter that contains the Help topic you want to open. The chapter name becomes highlighted.

4. Click the **Open** button to open the chapter. A list of subtopics appears below the open chapter.

5. Click the subtopic you want to display and click the **Display** button that appears. A window appears, displaying the Help information.

6. After you read the explanation, click the **Close** (X) button in the Help window's title bar to close the Help window.

If you want to print the list of Help topics in the Help Topics: Windows Help window, click the **Print** button at the bottom of the window. The Print dialog box appears. Click the **OK** button to print the list of Help topics and subtopics.

## Using the Index Feature

Help's Index feature provides a list of Help topics arranged alphabetically in the Index list box. In Figure 3.2, for example, the "copying" topic appears in the topic text box and is highlighted in the topic list.

In some cases, Windows displays more than one related topic in the topic list, and you can select which topic you need more information on. The Index is especially useful when you cannot find a particular Help topic in Help Contents' list of topics.

To use the Help Index, follow these steps:

1. Click the **Index** tab in the Windows Help window. The Index options are displayed.

2. Type a topic in the text box. This enters the topic for which you want to search and scrolls to the first entry that matches the word you typed. That topic appears highlighted in the topic list.

3. (Optional) Click a subtopic if necessary.

4. Click the **Display** button, and Windows displays the selected Help topic information in a Windows Help window.

5. When you are finished reading the Help information, click the **Close** (X) button to close the Windows Help window.

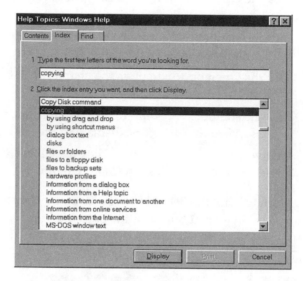

**Figure 3.2** The Index tab in the Windows Help window.

 **TIP** **Topic List** As an alternative to typing something in the text box, you can scroll through the topic list and select the topic you want.

# Using the Find Feature

You can search for specific words and phrases in a Help topic instead of searching for a Help topic by category.

The first time you use the Find tab, you have to help Windows create a list that contains every word from your Help files. A special dialog box will guide you. Then you can search for words and phrases similar to existing words and phrases in a Help topic. The Find feature is especially useful when you cannot find a particular Help topic in Help Contents' or Index's list of topics.

To build a word list (the first time only), follow these steps:

1. Click the **Find** tab in the Windows Help dialog box. The dialog box that appears gives an explanation of the Find feature and gives you these options: Minimize Database Size, Maximize Search Capabilities, and Customize Search Capabilities.

2. Choose **Minimize Database Size** to create a short word list, choose **Maximize Search Capabilities** to create a long word list, or choose **Customize Search Capabilities** to create a shorter word list if you have limited disk space.

3. Click the **Next** button to continue.

4. Click the **Finish** button to create the word list.

After Windows creates the word list, the Find tab contains a text box, a word list, and a topic list.

To search for words or a phrase in a Help topic, follow these steps:

1. Type the word you want to find in the first text box at the top of the dialog box. This enters the word for which you want to search and scrolls to the first entry that matches the word you typed. The word appears highlighted in the word list.

2. (Optional) Click another word in the word list to narrow the search if necessary.

3. Click a topic in the topic list and click the **Display** button. Windows displays the selected Help topic information in a Windows Help window.

4. When you are finished reading the Help information, click the **Close** (X) button to close the Windows Help window.

**TIP**  **Topic List**   Instead of typing something in the text box, you can scroll through the word list and select the word you want from the list. If you want to find words similar to the words in a Help topic, click the **Find Similar** button.

**Accidents Happen**   If you don't want to use the first list that Windows created, don't worry. You can rebuild that list to include more words or to exclude words. Simply click the **Rebuild** button and choose a word list option

**CAUTION**   to re-create the word list.

# Using Help Windows

When you display any Windows Help option, a button bar appears at the top of the Help window; it remains visible as long as you're in Help. This button bar includes three buttons: Help Topics, Back, and Options. Click the **Help Topics** button to return to Help's table of contents. Click the **Back** button to close the current Windows Help window and return to the previous one. Click the **Options** button to display a menu with the following commands:

**Annotate**   Select this command if you want to add notes to the text in the Windows Help window. A dialog box appears, in which you can type and save your text. When you save the annotation, a green paper clip appears to the right of the Help topic to indicate that it has an annotation. Click the paper clip to view the annotation.

**Copy**   Select this command to copy Help text to the Clipboard.

**Print Topic**   Select this command to display the Print dialog box. Then click the **OK** button to print the topic using the current printer settings, or click the **Properties** button to change printer settings.

**Font**   Select this command to change the size of the font displayed in the Windows Help window. When you select this command, another menu appears from which you can select Small, Normal, or Large. A check mark indicates the current size.

**Keep Help on Top**   Select this command if you want the Windows Help window to always be in the foreground of your screen. When you select this command, another menu appears, from which you can select Default, On Top, or Not On Top. A check mark indicates the current selection.

**Use System Colors**   Select this command if you want Windows to use regular system colors for Help windows. When you select this command, a dialog box appears, informing you that you must restart Help for the color change to take effect. Choose **Yes** to close Help; choose **No** to return to the Windows Help window.

Help windows often display shortcut buttons as well. Using shortcut buttons, you can jump to the area of Windows to which the Help information refers. For example, suppose you're reading a Help topic that contains information on how to change the wallpaper on the desktop (see Figure 3.3). You click the shortcut button (the button with an arrow that curves up and to the left) to jump to the Control Panel's Properties for Display dialog box from within Help. There you can make the necessary changes and get on with your work.

To use a shortcut button, simply click it. You're immediately taken to that area of Windows.

Shortcut button ——

Click an underlined ——
term for a definition.

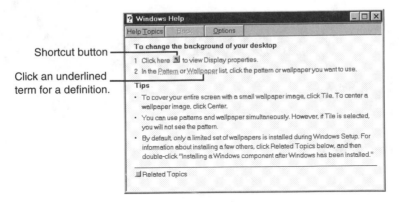

**Figure 3.3**   The shortcut button in the Help window.

# Using the What's This? Feature

The What's This? feature provides a handy way of getting more information about dialog box options. You activate this feature by selecting the question mark (?) icon that appears at the right end of the title bar in most Windows dialog boxes.

The following steps teach you how to use the What's This? feature to display a description of any option in a Windows dialog box.

**1.** Click the **?** icon in the upper-right corner of a Windows dialog box. A large question mark appears next to the mouse pointer.

**2.** Click any option in the dialog box. Windows displays a box containing a short description of the item you selected.

**3.** When you are finished reading the Help information, click anywhere on the screen to close the Help box.

**TIP**   **Quick Description**   If you right-click an option in a dialog box, a shortcut menu appears displaying one menu command: What's This?. Click **What's This?** to view a description of the option.

In this lesson, you learned how to access the Windows Help system. In the next lesson, you'll learn how to shut down Windows.

# Shutting Down Windows

*In this lesson, you learn the various ways you can shut down and restart Windows.*

You can shut down Windows in one of three ways: you can shut down the computer, you can restart the computer, or you can restart the computer in MS-DOS mode. The following sections cover each of these methods.

## Shutting Down the Computer

Before you shut down Windows, you should save any work you have in progress and close any open DOS applications so you won't lose any data. In most Windows applications, you choose File, Save to save a document, and then choose File, Exit to exit the application. If you don't save your data and close open applications, when you shut down, Windows closes each application for you and asks you to confirm saving each file.

To shut down the computer, follow these steps:

1. Click the **Start** button. The Start menu appears.
2. Choose **Shut Down** from the Start menu. The Shut Down Windows dialog box appears (see Figure 4.1), displaying a list of shut down options.
3. Choose the **Shut Down the Computer?** option and click **Yes**. Windows prompts you to turn off your computer.
4. Turn off your computer.

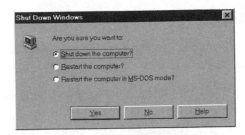

**Figure 4.1**  The Shut Down Windows dialog box.

TIP  **Shutting Down**  If you close all open documents and applications and return to the Windows desktop, you can press **Alt+F4** to shut down the computer.

Because you can work with several documents and applications at one time, you may get carried away and forget to save a document before you shut down. Fear not: Windows protects you from losing your data. For example, if you're working on a WordPad document and try to shut down Windows without saving the document, the dialog box shown in Figure 4.2 appears, prompting you to save your changes.

**Figure 4.2**  WordPad prompts you to save changes before shutting down.

Select **Yes** to save the changes; select **No** to discard any changes you made; select **Cancel** to cancel the shut down command altogether.

**Forget to Save?**  This message is your only warning. If you accidentally respond No to saving changes, the changes you made in the document are lost.

CAUTION

# Restarting the Computer

When you experience system problems, you can restart the computer to clear up any problems you have encountered. To do so, follow these steps:

1.  Click the **Start** button. The Start menu appears.
2.  Choose **Shut Down** from the Start menu. The Shut Down Windows dialog box appears (Figure 4.1), displaying a list of shut down options.
3.  Choose the **Restart the Computer?** option and click **Yes**. Windows restarts your computer. If you're on a network, Windows asks you to log in.

**Restarting the Computer**   Choosing the Restart the Computer? option in Windows' Shut Down Windows dialog box is different from pressing Ctrl+Alt+Delete. If you press Ctrl+Alt+Delete in Windows, the Close Program dialog box appears, in which you can end selected tasks or choose the Shut Down option.

# Restarting the Computer in MS-DOS Mode

You can run most DOS programs from within Windows, but occasionally you may find a program that performs poorly from within Windows. In most cases, you can fine-tune its properties to run correctly, but you might find it simpler to restart the computer in MS-DOS mode and run the program from there. Because Windows does not load when the computer restarts, any conflicts with Windows are eliminated.

Before restarting your computer, make sure you save your work and close any open applications. Then follow these steps:

1.  Click the **Start** button. The Start menu appears.
2.  Choose **Shut Down** from the Start menu. The Shut Down Windows dialog box appears (Figure 4.1), displaying a list of shut down options.
3.  Choose the **Restart the Computer in MS-DOS Mode?** option and choose **Yes**. Your computer is restarted, and the MS-DOS prompt appears on-screen.
4.  To return to Windows, type **EXIT** at the MS-DOS prompt and press **Enter**. The computer restarts.

# Closing All Programs and Logging On As a Different User

If you're on a network, you can log off the computer and let someone else sign in on your machine. This is useful if you have to share a computer with another user. To log off, choose the **Close All Programs and Log On As a Different User** option in the Shut Down Windows dialog box. Choose **Yes**, and then enter your network password.

 **Logoff**  The Logoff feature in Windows 95 is not available in Windows 3.1 unless you're running Windows for Workgroups.

In this lesson, you learned how to shut down Windows. In the next lesson, you'll learn how to start and exit applications.

# Starting and Exiting Applications

*In this lesson, you learn how to start Windows applications, use a document window, and exit Windows applications.*

## Starting Windows Applications

A Windows application is a program designed to take advantage of the graphical user interface (GUI) built into Windows. As you learned in Lesson 1, a GUI provides a common interface between you and your programs that enables you to use the same procedures to execute commands in most compatible applications. That means that you can start (and exit) most Windows applications using the same procedures. If you are using a non-Windows (DOS) application through Windows, you will need to consult that application's manual to learn how to start and exit.

There are several ways to start a Windows application. This lesson discusses four of those ways.

### Using the Programs Menu

To start an application from the Programs menu using the mouse, follow these steps:

1. Click the **Start** button. The Start menu appears.
2. Point to **Programs** in the Start menu. The Programs menu appears.
3. Click the program folder that contains the program icon for the application you want to use. For example, if you want to use WordPad, open the **Accessories** folder to access the WordPad program icon (see Figure 5.1).

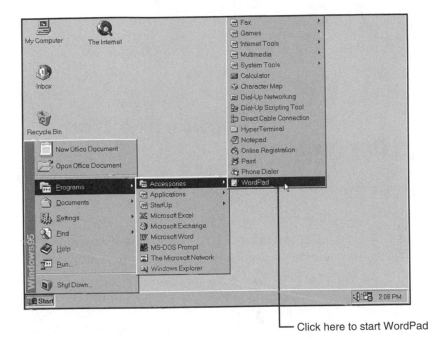

Click here to start WordPad

**Figure 5.1**  Program icons in the Accessories program folder.

4. Click the program icon for the application you want to start, and the application window appears.

To start an application from the Programs menu using the keyboard, follow these steps:

1. Press **Ctrl+Esc** to access the Start menu.
2. Press **P** to select Programs. The Programs menu appears.
3. Use the arrow keys to highlight the program folder that contains the program item for the application you want to use. Press **Enter** to select the folder.
4. Use the arrow keys to highlight the program icon for the application, and then press **Enter** to start the application. The application window appears.

# Starting an Application When You Start Windows

To view the applications in the Startup folder, click the **Start** button, select **Programs**, and select **Startup**.

**27**

**Startup**  The Startup folder functions much the same way the Startup program group does in the Windows 3.1 Program Manager.

# Starting an Application from a Document

There are several ways that you can start an application from a document. You can start an application from the Documents list by following these steps:

1. Click the **Start** button. The Start menu appears.
2. Click **Documents**, and the Documents list appears, displaying the names of the 15 documents you've used most recently.
3. Click the document you want. Windows opens the application in which the document was created and then opens the document.

You can also open a document from the Explorer or My Computer by simply double-clicking on the document. Windows immediately starts the application in which the document was created and opens the document.

# Using the Run Command

You can use the Run command to start applications that you use infrequently and that are not listed in the Programs menu. Or you might start a program with the Run command so you can enter command parameters or options that change the way the application starts. For example, if you start a word processing program using the Run command, you can add a parameter that tells the application to open a specific file automatically upon startup.

**TIP**  **What Are Your Options?**  Check the documentation that comes with your software to find out about the available startup options. You may want to jot down special startup commands you plan to use often.

To use the Run command, follow these steps:

1. Click the **Start** button. The Start menu appears.
2. Choose **Run**, and the Run dialog box appears (see Figure 5.2).
3. Type the required command in the **Open** text box. Figure 5.2 displays the command that opens a setup program on a floppy disk in drive A.

**4.** When the command is complete, click **OK**. (If you decide not to use the Run command, click **Cancel**.)

**TIP** **Can't Remember the Command?** If you don't remember the command that runs the application, click the **Browse** button in the Run dialog box. In the Browse dialog box that appears, choose the files you want to run.

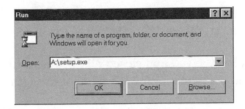

**Figure 5.2** You can start any program with the Run command.

# Working with Document Windows

When you use certain applications with Windows, you will create documents. For example, any letter you write in Word for Windows, or any drawing you create in Windows' Paint program, is contained in a document. These documents are sometimes called files or document files. When you are working on a document, it appears in a window.

When you start an application, the application automatically creates a window for a new document. In most applications, you can create another document window by choosing the File, New command from that application's menu bar. The application creates a new window so you can start a new document, but any other document you might have been working on remains available. (If you're using WordPad, you can open only one document at a time. However, you can have multiple WordPad windows open simultaneously.)

When you are finished with a document, always save your changes by choosing **File**, **Save**; then close the document window by choosing **File**, **Close** or by double-clicking the document window's **Control-menu** icon. This ensures that the document will not be lost or damaged accidentally. When you close a document window, the application remains open. The next section explains how to close the document window(s) and exit the application.

# Exiting Windows Applications

Before you exit an application, be sure to save and close any documents you have worked on in that application (using the commands on the File menu).

 **TIP** **Forget to Save Your Changes?** If you attempt to close a document window or exit an application without saving your changes, Windows will ask you if you want to save before closing. To save any changes, click **Yes**; to exit without saving, click **No**; to remain in the application, click **Cancel**.

Once you have saved and closed all document files, you can exit a Windows application using any of the following four methods.

- To exit an application using its Control-menu icon (the icon in the upper-left corner of the application window), double-click the **Control-menu** icon. If you prefer to use the keyboard, press **Alt+Spacebar** to open the application's Control menu, and press **C** to choose the Close command.

- To exit an application using its Close button, click the **Close** button (the button with an X at the right end of the application's title bar).

- To exit an application using the menus, choose **File**, **Exit**. You can click the menu and command with the mouse, or you can press **Alt+F** to open the File menu and press **X** to select Exit.

- The quickest way to exit is to use the shortcut key: press **Alt+F4**.

 **TIP** **Exit Quickly** You can right-click the application's button on the taskbar to display the shortcut menu. Then choose **Close** to close the application.

 **Exiting Windows Applications** Exiting Windows applications in Windows 95 and Windows 3.1 is handled the same way except that the Control menus look different, and application windows in Windows 3.1 do not have a Close button.

In this lesson, you learned how to start applications, use a document window, and exit applications. In the next lesson, you'll learn how to work with multiple windows.

# Working with Multiple Windows

*In this lesson, you learn how to arrange windows, move between windows in the same application, and move between applications.*

In Windows, you can use more than one application at a time, and in each Windows application, you can work with multiple document windows. As you can imagine, opening multiple applications, each with its own windows, can make your desktop pretty cluttered. That's why it's important that you know how to manipulate and switch between windows. The following sections explain how to do just that.

## Arranging Windows

When you have multiple windows open, some windows are inevitably hidden by others, which makes the screen confusing. You can use the commands on the taskbar's shortcut menu (which you access by right-clicking the taskbar) to arrange windows.

### Cascading Windows

A good way to get control of a confusing desktop is to right-click a blank area of the taskbar and choose the **Cascade** command from the shortcut menu. When you choose this command, Windows lays all the open windows on top of each other so that the title bar of each is visible. Figure 6.1 shows the resulting cas- caded window arrangement. To access any window that's not on top, simply click its title bar.

Each title bar is aligned in a cascading group.

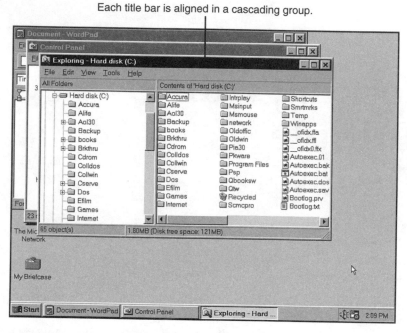

**Figure 6.1** Cascaded windows.

# Tiling Windows

If you need to see all of your open windows at the same time, use the Tile command on the shortcut menu. When you choose this command, Windows resizes and moves each open window so that they appear side by side horizontally or vertically.

Right-click a blank area of the taskbar and choose the **Tile Horizontally** command from the shortcut menu to create an arrangement similar to that shown in Figure 6.2. To arrange the windows in a vertically tiled arrangement (as shown in Figure 6.3), right-click a blank area of the taskbar and choose the **Tile Vertically** command.

If you want to minimize all the windows at once, right-click a blank area of the taskbar and choose **Minimize All Windows**. The open windows disappear from the desktop, but the application buttons remain visible on the taskbar.

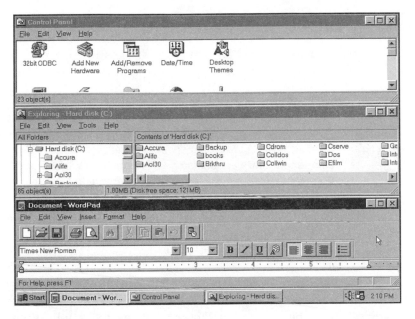

**Figure 6.2** Horizontally tiled windows.

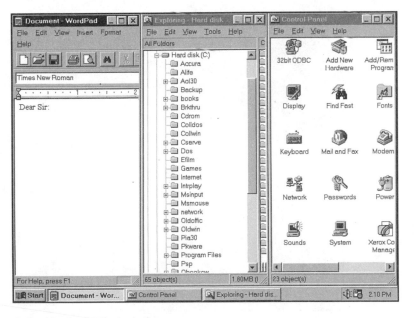

**Figure 6.3** Vertically tiled windows.

# Moving Between Applications

Windows enables you to have multiple applications open at the same time. This section tells you how to move between applications using the taskbar.

**Moving Between Applications**   The Task List in Windows 3.1 has been replaced by the taskbar in Windows 95. In Windows 95, when you press Alt+Tab to switch to a different application, the icons and application names of all open windows appear in one dialog box. In Windows 3.1, you have to cycle through all the open applications until you get to the one you want.

The taskbar is a button bar that appears at the bottom of your screen by default. Each button on the taskbar represents an open window. The taskbar button of the currently active window looks like it's pressed in.

To quickly switch between applications using the taskbar, simply click the button for the application to which you want to switch. Windows immediately takes you to the application. Figure 6.4 shows two applications represented on the taskbar.

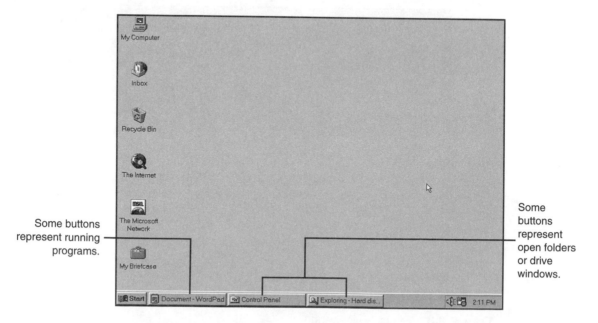

**Figure 6.4**   The taskbar buttons.

**TIP**  **Bypass the Taskbar**  Press and hold the **Alt** key and press the **Tab** key (continue to hold down Alt). A dialog box appears, displaying the icons and application names of all open applications. Each time you press Tab, a new (open) application becomes selected, and a border appears around the selected icon. When the application you want is selected, release the Alt key. Windows switches you to that application. If (while the dialog box is still on-screen) you decide you don't want to switch to that application, press **Esc** and release the Alt key.

# Moving Between Windows in the Same Application

As I said earlier, in addition to working in multiple applications in Windows, you also can open multiple windows within an application. Moving to a new window means you are changing the window that is active. If you are using a mouse, you can move to a window by clicking any part of it. When you do, the title bar becomes highlighted, and you can work in the window.

To move to the next document window using the keyboard, press **Ctrl+F6**; to move to the previous document window, press **Ctrl+Shift+F6**. Figure 6.5 shows Microsoft Word with three open documents. One document, Julie's Letter, is minimized. Minimized windows within applications appear at the bottom of the application window (not in the taskbar).

**TERM**  **Active Window**  The window currently in use. You can tell which window is active because its title bar is highlighted a different color than the others.

**TIP**  **Moving Between Windows**  In Windows 3.1 andWindows 95, you can also use the Window menu to move between windows in the same application.

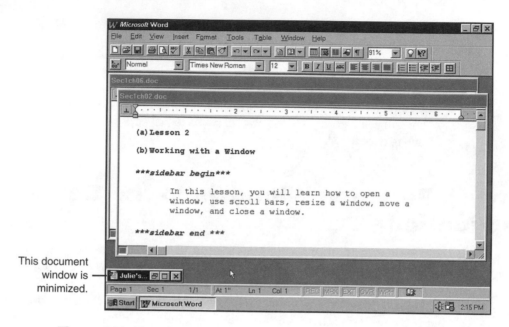

This document window is minimized.

**Figure 6.5**  Three open documents in Microsoft Word.

In this lesson, you learned how to arrange windows, switch between open applications, and switch between windows in the same application. In the next lesson, you'll learn how to use the Windows Explorer to view a disk's contents.

# Viewing Drives, Folders, and Files with Windows Explorer

7

*In this lesson, you learn how to use the Windows Explorer to view a disk's contents.*

## Starting the Windows Explorer

To start the Windows Explorer, follow these steps:

1. Open the **Start** menu and choose **Programs**.
2. From the Programs menu, choose **Windows Explorer**. The Windows Explorer window appears (see Figure 7.1).

**Managing Files** The Windows Explorer in Windows 95 replaces Windows 3.1's File Manager.

## Using the Windows Explorer Window

Figure 7.1 shows the Windows Explorer window. The All Folders window (the left side of the screen) shows all the folders on the selected drive (in this case, drive C).

The left side of the Windows Explorer window contains the folder list, a graphical representation of the folders and subfolders on your system. (The folder list on your screen will probably contain different folders from those shown in Figure 7.1.) In Figure 7.1, you can see that drive C contains a folder named Windows, and the Windows folder has many subfolders, including one named Command.

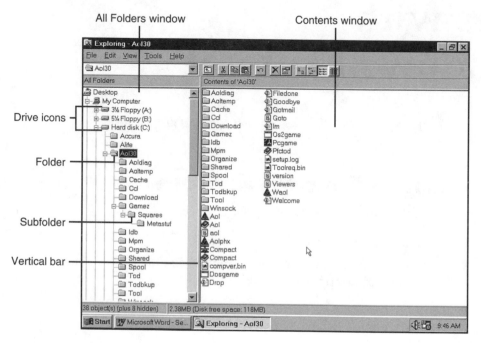

**Figure 7.1** The Windows Explorer window, displaying the All Folders window.

 **Folders and Subfolders** The folder that leads to all other folders (much like the trunk of a tree leads to all branches and leaves) is the main folder. In Figure 7.1 the main folder is C:\. Any folder can have a subfolder. Subfolders are like file folders within file folders; they help you organize your files. In Figure 7.1, Command is a subfolder of Windows.

The right side of the window contains a list of the files in the folder that's currently highlighted in the folder list. Notice that the folder icon next to the Windows folder (the highlighted folder) appears as an open folder. In this figure, the files in the Windows folder are listed in the right half of the Windows Explorer window.

# Selecting Folders

When you select a folder using the folders list, its contents are displayed on the right side of the Explorer window. To select a folder with the mouse, simply click the folder you want. Table 7.1 shows the keys you can use to select a folder with the keyboard.

**Table 7.1**  Keys for Selecting a Folder

| Key | Function |
| --- | --- |
| ↑ | Selects the folder above the selected one. |
| ↓ | Selects the folder below the selected one. |
| ← | Closes the selected folder. |
| → | Opens the selected folder. |
| Home | Selects the first folder in the folder list. |
| End | Selects the last folder in the folder list. |
| First letter of folder name | Selects the first folder that begins with that letter. Press the letter again if necessary, until you select the folder you want. |

# Opening and Closing Folders

In Figure 7.1, the folders list shows the subfolders of the Windows folder. You can close (decrease the detail of) the folders list so that subfolders do not appear, or you can open (increase the detail of) the folders list so it shows all folders. A plus sign (+) next to a folder indicates that there are subfolders to display; a minus sign (–) next to a folder indicates that the folder has been opened and can be closed.

To open or close a folder with the mouse, just double-click the folder icon. To open or close a folder with the keyboard, use the arrow keys to select the folder and press + (plus) to open it or – (minus) to close it.

**It's Only for Show**  Closing and opening affects this display only; it doesn't alter your folders in any way.

CAUTION

# Changing Drives

You can change drives to see the folders and files contained on a different disk. To change drives with the mouse, click the drive icon on the All Folders list. Using the keyboard to change to a floppy drive, press the first number for the drive type (for example, press **3** for a 3.5" floppy drive). Press **H** to change to your hard disk, or use arrow keys to move from any other drive in the tree to your hard drive.

# Changing the Windows Explorer Display

The commands in Windows Explorer's View menu enable you to change how the folders window and the files list window display information. You can control the size of the windows, whether or not the toolbar and status bar are displayed, and how the files in the files list window are displayed.

When you change the Windows Explorer's display settings to suit your needs, Windows remembers those settings. They remain the same every time you start Windows (until you change them again).

## Sizing the Windows

In the Windows Explorer screens you've seen so far, both the folders window and the list of files were shown. You can change the way each is shown by changing the amount of window space allotted to each. For example, you may want to see more files and less white space around the folders list. Follow these steps to change the way the window space is divided between the panes:

1. A vertical gray line appears in the Folders window, representing the divider between the two panes. Point to the gray line, and the mouse pointer changes to a short vertical bar with two arrows.

2. Drag the line to where you want it. The window display changes accordingly (see Figure 7.2).

 **Changing the Display**    You change the size of the window panes in the Windows Explorer the same way you changed them in the Windows 3.1 File Manager window.

The vertical bar has been moved to the left.

Mouse pointer

Notice that the All Folders window now has a horizontal scroll bar.

**Figure 7.2**   The changed window.

# Changing the File List Display

By default, the Windows Explorer shows only the file names and icons for each folder. However, you can change the display to include more information about each file if you want. The View menu provides you with four options you can use to customize the file list display: Large Icons, Small Icons, List, and Details.

The View, List command tells Windows to display only the icons and file names for each folder (as shown in Figure 7.2). This is the default display. Choose **View**, **Details** to have Windows display the following information about each file:

- Size in bytes
- File type (to describe the file—such as Folder, Application, Help, Settings, and so on)
- Last modification day and date

You can also change the size of the icons that Windows displays in the files list window. Choose **View**, **Large Icons** to display large icons with the file names beneath the icons. Choose **View**, **Small Icons** to display small icons with the file names to the right of the icons.

**Changing the Files List**   The View, Large Icons and View, Small Icons commands in Windows 95 are not available in Windows 3.1. The View, List and View, Details commands in Windows 95 replace the View, Partial Details and View, All Files Details commands in Windows 3.1.

 TIP   **Small Icons versus List**   Small Icons and List views both show small icons with the name to the right. The difference is how the files and folders are arranged. In List view, they're arranged in columns. In Small Icons view, they're arranged in rows.

## Controlling the Order of the Display

As you can see in Figure 7.2, the files in the folder are listed in alphabetical order by file name. If you prefer, you can have Windows arrange the icons differently, by using one of the following methods:

* Choose **View**, **Arrange Icons**, **By Type** to arrange files alphabetically by their file type.

* Choose **View**, **Arrange Icons**, **By Size** to arrange files from smallest to largest.

* Choose **View**, **Arrange Icons**, **By Date** to arrange files alphabetically by date from newest to oldest.

**Controlling the Order of the Display**   The View, Arrange Icons command in Windows 95 replaces the View, Sort command in Windows 3.1.

## Displaying the Toolbar

You can display the Windows Explorer toolbar at the top of the Windows Explorer window (as shown in Figure 7.3) by choosing **View**, **Toolbar**. Then you can click on the buttons on the toolbar instead of choosing menu commands. Table 7.2 shows the buttons on the Windows Explorer toolbar.

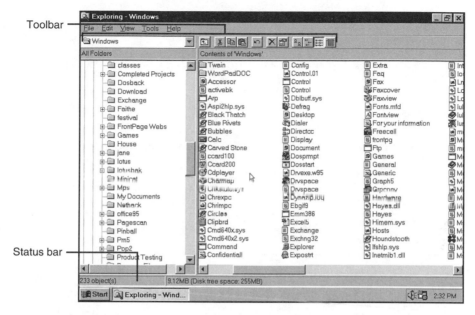

Toolbar

Status bar

**Figure 7.3** The toolbar and status bar are displayed.

**Table 7.2** Windows Explorer Toolbar Buttons

| Button | Name | Description |
|--------|------|-------------|
| | Up One Level | Displays the folder up one level from the folder currently displayed in the Folder text box. |
| | Cut | Cuts the selected file or folder and places it on the Clipboard. |
| | Copy | Copies the selected file or folder to the Clipboard. |
| | Paste | Pastes the contents of the Clipboard to the location selected in the list. |
| | Undo | Undoes the last file or folder operation. |
| | Delete | Deletes the selected file or folder. |

*continues*

**43**

**Table 7.2** Continued

| Button | Name | Description |
|--------|------|-------------|
| | Properties | Displays the properties of the selected file or folder. |
| | Large Icons | Displays large icons in the contents window. |
| | Small Icons | Displays small icons in the contents window. |
| | List | Displays a list of files and folders with names and icons. |
| | Details | Displays a detailed list of files and folders. |

## Displaying the Status Bar

Initially, Windows displays the status bar at the bottom of the Windows Explorer window (see Figure 7.3). If you want to hide the status bar, open the **View** menu and select **Status Bar** (to deactivate it). To redisplay it, repeat the previous command sequence.

# Closing the Windows Explorer

If you're not going to use the Windows Explorer again right away, you should close it instead of minimizing it in order to conserve system resources. To close the Windows Explorer, click the **Close** (X) button or double-click the **Control-menu** icon.

In this lesson, you learned how to use the Windows Explorer to examine the contents of a disk. In the next lesson, you'll learn how to create and delete files and folders.

# Creating and Deleting Files and Folders

8

*In this lesson, you learn how to create and delete files and folders.*

## Creating a File or Folder

Some files and folders are created automatically when you install a program. For example, when you install Word for Windows, the installation program creates a folder on your hard drive and places the Word for Windows files in that folder. However, you can also create files and folders yourself.

There are several reasons you may want to create a folder. Many application installation programs create a folder when you install the application on your computer. If one of your application installation programs does not, you will want to create a folder for that application.

A more common reason to create a folder is to store document files. For example, you may want to create a folder to store documents you create with WordPad so the document files won't be scattered among the more than one hundred Windows program files in the Windows folder. Having a separate folder for WordPad documents makes it much easier to find and manipulate the documents you create.

**My Documents**   Microsoft Office automatically creates a folder called My Documents in your Windows directory; by default, that's where it stores your files from Office programs.

# Creating a Folder with Windows Explorer

To create a folder using the Windows Explorer, follow these steps:

1. Open the **Start** menu, choose **Programs**, and choose **Windows Explorer**. The Windows Explorer window appears.

2. Highlight the folder in the folders window under which you want to create the new folder. (The folder you create will be a subfolder of the folder you highlight.) If you don't want the new folder to be a subfolder of another folder, highlight the **(C:)** folder.

3. Select **File**, **New Folder**. A folder icon named New Folder appears at the bottom of the files list.

4. Type the new folder name using up to 255 characters (including spaces) in the text box that appears next to the new folder icon. The name you type replaces the words **New Folder** as you type.

5. Press **Enter**, and Windows renames the new folder.

**Creating and Deleting Folders**   The File, New Folder command in Windows 95 replaces the File, Create Directory command in Windows 3.1. You use the same process to delete a folder in Windows 95 (see "Deleting a File or Folder") that you did to delete a directory in Windows 3.1.

# Creating a Folder with My Computer

To create a folder with My Computer, follow these steps:

1. In My Computer, open the icon or folder in which you want to create a folder.

2. Select **File**, **New**. Windows creates a new folder icon.

3. Type a new name for the folder and press **Enter**.

# Deleting a File or Folder

There will come a time when you need to delete a file or folder. For example, you may have created a file or folder by mistake, or you may want to remove the files or folder for an application you no longer use, or you may need to make more room on your hard drive.

**Better Safe Than Sorry**   Before you delete anything, it is a good idea to make a backup copy of any files or folders you might need later. See Lesson 13 for directions on how to copy files and folders.

To delete a file or folder, follow these steps:

**1.** In the My Computer window or the Windows Explorer folders list, select the file or folder you want to delete. Be aware that when you delete a folder, Windows deletes all files in that folder.

**2.** Choose **File**, **Delete** or press the **Delete** key. The Confirm Folder Delete dialog box appears, indicating what will be deleted and asking you to confirm the deletion.

**3.** Look through the Confirm Folder Delete dialog box carefully to make certain you are deleting what you intended to delete.

**4.** Select **Yes** to delete everything listed in the dialog box.

**Deleting a File or Folder**   The File, Delete commands in Windows 95 and Windows 3.1 are similar. In Windows 95, however, you see only the Confirm Delete dialog box; in Windows 3.1, you see the Delete dialog box and then the Confirm Delete dialog box. Also, Windows 95 deletes the files from the Windows Explorer or the My Computer window and moves them to the Recycle Bin. If you needed to, you could restore any files from the Recycle Bin.

**I Didn't Mean to Do That!**   If you delete a folder or file by mistake, immediately choose **Edit**, **Undo Delete** to restore the deleted folder(s) and file(s).

**47**

# Working with the Recycle Bin

The files you delete in Windows are stored temporarily in the Recycle Bin. You can retrieve files from the Recycle Bin if you decide you need them again, or you can purge the deleted files when you're sure you no longer need them. By purging deleted files, you make more room on your disk.

To retrieve files you've deleted, follow these steps:

1. Double-click the **Recycle Bin** icon. The Recycle Bin window appears.
2. Click the file you want to retrieve. To select multiple files, hold down **Ctrl** and click each one.
3. Select **File**, **Restore**. Windows restores the files to their original locations.

Follow these steps to purge deleted files in the Recycle Bin:

1. Select **File**, **Empty Recycle Bin**. A confirmation dialog box appears.
2. Choose **Yes** to delete all the files.
3. Click the **Close** button to close the Recycle Bin window.

 **TIP** **Purge Files Individually**   To delete only one file from the Recycle Bin, select the file, open the **File** menu, choose **Delete**, and click **Yes**. Windows purges only that file.

 **Recycle Bin**   The Recycle Bin is a new feature in Windows 95; it is not available in Windows 3.1.

In this lesson, you learned how to create and delete files and folders. In the next lesson, you'll learn how to move and copy files and folders.

# Moving and Copying Files and Folders

*In this lesson, you learn how to select multiple files and folders and how to copy and move them.*

## Selecting Multiple Files or Folders

To really speed up operations, you will want to select multiple files or folders and then execute commands that affect the entire group. For example, you may want to select several files to copy to a disk. Copying them all at once is much faster than copying each file individually. The following sections explain how you can select multiple files and folders.

## Selecting Multiple Contiguous Files or Folders

It is easy to select multiple files or folders that are displayed *contiguously* in Windows Explorer's files list window or My Computer.

 **Contiguous Files** When the files that you want to select are listed next to each other in the Windows Explorer—without any files in-between them that you don't want—they are contiguous.

Follow these steps to select contiguous files or folders with the mouse:

**1.** Click the first file or folder that you want to select. When you click it, it becomes highlighted.

**2.** Hold down the **Shift** key and click the last file or folder that you want to select. All the items between (and including) the first and last selections are highlighted. Figure 9.1 shows a selection of contiguous files.

**Figure 9.1**   Selected contiguous files are highlighted.

Follow these steps to select contiguous files or folders with the keyboard:

**1.** Use the arrow keys to move the highlight to the first file or folder that you want to select. (Press **Tab** to move the highlight bar between the folders window and the files list window.)

**2.** Hold down the **Shift** key and use the arrow keys to extend the highlight to the last file or folder you want to select.

To deselect a contiguous group of files or folders, select a file or folder outside the selected items.

# Selecting Noncontiguous Files or Folders

Often, the files or folders you want to select are *noncontiguous*: they are separated by several files that you do not want. To select such noncontiguous files or folders, you use the Ctrl key.

To select items with the mouse, hold down the **Ctrl** key and click the files or folders you want. Each item you click becomes highlighted and remains highlighted until you release the Ctrl key. Figure 9.2 shows a selection of multiple noncontiguous files. To deselect items with the mouse, click any file or folder.

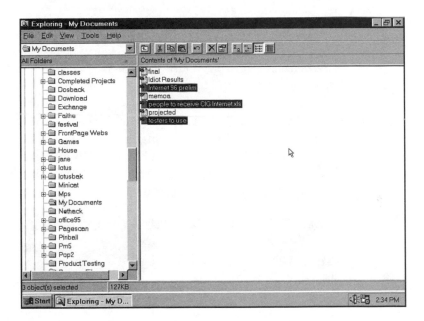

**Figure 9.2** Selecting multiple noncontiguous files.

TIP **Narrowing the Selection** If you want to select or deselect files with related names, choose the **Tools, Find, Files or Folders** command. Enter the characters you want to find in the **Named** text box and choose **(C:)** from the **Look In** drop-down list. Then click **Find Now**. When Windows displays the files you want to select or deselect, choose **Edit, Select, All** from the menu bar of the Find dialog box to select all the files in the Search Results window. Then deselect any listed files that you don't want selected. (Lesson 10 explains in more detail how to use the Find command.)

**Selecting Files or Folders**  You select files or folders in Windows 95 the same way you select files and directories in Windows 3.1.

# Moving or Copying Files or Folders

To move or copy files or folders through the Windows Explorer or My Computer, you *drag and drop*—that is, you select the items you want from your source folder, "drag" them to the destination folder, and "drop" them there. You'll learn the details of using this technique later in this section.

TIP  **Move versus Copy**  When you *move* the file or folder, it no longer exists in its original location—only in the new location. When you *copy* a file or folder, the original file or folder remains in its original location, and a copy of the file or folder is placed in a second location.

Before you move or copy, make sure the source file or folder is visible so you can highlight the file(s) you're going to drag. Also, make sure that the destination drive or folder is visible. In Figure 9.3, the source folder (My Documents), the source file (the memoa file), and the destination folder (the empty WordPadDOC folder) are all visible.

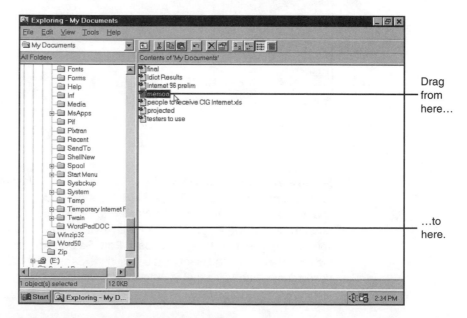

**Figure 9.3**  The selected file can be moved or copied.

# Copying Files and Folders

With the mouse, use this procedure to copy:

**1.** Select the files or folders to copy.

**2.** Press the **Ctrl** key and drag the files or folders to the destination drive or folder.

**3.** Release the mouse button and the Ctrl key.

With the keyboard, use this procedure to copy:

**1.** Select the files or folders to copy.

**2.** Select **Edit**, **Copy**.

**3.** Select the destination drive or folder.

**4.** Select **Edit**, **Paste**. Figure 9.4 shows the result of the copy and paste operations. The WordPad document file has been copied into the WordPadDOC folder.

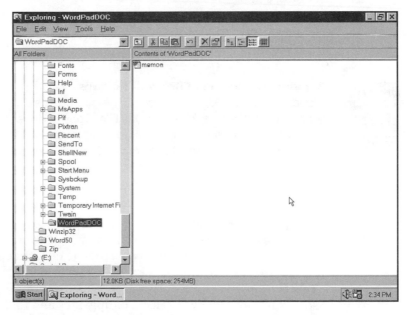

**Figure 9.4**  The completed copy operation.

**TIP**  **The File Is Already There**   If you attempt to copy a file or folder to a location in which a file or folder with the exact same name exists, Windows lets you know with a message that says **This folder already contains a file called "filename". Would you like to replace the existing file with this one?** Click **Yes** to replace the existing file, or click **No** to stop the copy operation.

# Moving Files and Folders

With the mouse, follow these steps to complete a move:

**1.** Select the files or folders to move.

**2.** Drag the files or folders to the destination drive or folder.

**3.** Release the mouse button.

With the keyboard, complete a move using these steps:

**1.** Select the files or folders to move.

**2.** Select **Edit**, **Cut**.

**3.** Select the destination drive or folder.

**4.** Select **Edit**, **Paste**.

**Copying and Moving Files and Folders**   Copying and moving files and folders in Windows 95 and Windows 3.1 is similar. The Edit, Copy and Edit, Cut commands in Windows 95 replace the File, Copy and File, Move commands in Windows 3.1. Also, the Copy and Move confirmation dialog boxes you saw in Windows 3.1 do not appear in Windows 95, which makes it quicker to copy and move files and folders.

**TIP**  **Wrong Move or Copy?**   If you move or copy the wrong files or folders, you can choose **Edit**, **Undo Copy** in the Windows Explorer menu bar or click the **Undo** button on the Windows Explorer toolbar to undo the operation.

In this lesson, you learned how to select multiple files and folders and how to copy and move files and folders. In the next lesson, you'll learn how to rename and find files and folders.

# Renaming and Finding Files and Folders

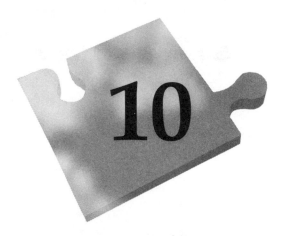

*In this lesson, you learn how to rename and find files and folders.*

## Renaming Files or Folders

To rename your files, follow these steps:

**1.** In the Windows Explorer or My Computer window, select the file or folder you want to rename.

**2.** Choose **File**, **Rename**. A box appears around the file or folder name, and the name is highlighted.

**3.** Type the new name for the file or folder. As you type, the new name replaces the old name.

**4.** Press **Enter** when you finish typing.

**CAUTION**

**It Worked Yesterday**   Never rename program files. Many applications will not work if their files have been renamed.

**Renaming Files or Folders**   The File, Rename commands in Windows 95 and Windows 3.1 are similar. However, you type the new name next to the icon in Windows 95, whereas in Windows 3.1, you type the new name into the Rename dialog box.

# Searching for a File

As you create more files, the capability to find a specific file becomes more critical. You can search for either a single file or a group of files with similar names using the Tools, Find command. To search for a group of files, use the asterisk wild card (*) with a partial file name to narrow the search. You can also perform a partial name search without wild cards, search by last modification date, save complex searches, and do a full text search. Table 10.1 shows some search examples and their potential results.

**Wild Cards**  When you're not sure of the file name you want to find, you can use the asterisk wild card (*) to replace multiple characters in the file name or the question mark wild card (?) to replace one character in the file name.

**Table 10.1**  Search Examples and Their Results

| Characters Entered for Search | Sample Search Results |
| --- | --- |
| mem?.doc | mem1.doc, mem2.doc, memo.doc |
| mem1.doc | mem1.doc |
| mem*.doc | mem1.doc, mem2.doc, mem10.doc, memos.doc |
| c*.exe | calc.exe, calendar.exe |
| *.exe | calc.exe, calendar.exe, notepad.exe |
| c*.* | calc.exe, calendar.exe, class.doc |

To search for a file, follow these steps:

1. Click the **Start** button, select **Find**, and select **Files or Folders**. The Find dialog box appears.

2. In the **Named** text box, enter the characters you want to find, using wild cards to identify unknown characters (see Figure 10.1).

3. If you want to search the entire drive, choose **C:** in the **Look In** text box (if it's not already there) and make sure the **Include Subfolders** check box is selected.

   If you want to search only the main folder, make sure the **Include Subfolders** check box is not selected.

If you want to search a specific folder, click the **Browse** button and select a folder from the folders list.

**4.** If you want to search for a file according to its last modification date, select the **Date Modified** tab and select the date options you want.

**5.** If you want to search for a certain type of file, select the **Advanced** tab and choose a file type in the **Of Type** drop-down list box.

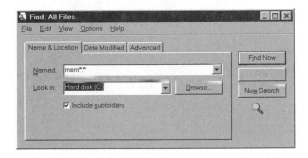

**Figure 10.1**  A completed Find dialog box.

**6.** When you finish setting options, select the **Find Now** button to begin the search. The search results window appears under the Find dialog box, showing the files that were found (see Figure 10.2).

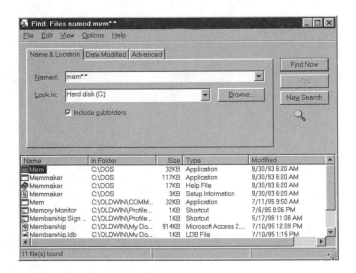

**Figure 10.2**  The search results appear below the Find settings.

**Searching for a File**   The Find command in Windows 95 replaces the File, Search command in Windows 3.1.

In this lesson, you learned how to rename a file or folder and search for a file or folder. In the next lesson, you'll learn how to set up for Windows printing.

# Getting Ready to Print

*In this lesson, you learn to check printer installation and add a printer.*

## Checking the Printer Installation

When you installed Windows, Setup configured any printers connected to your computer and created the links to those printers automatically. Before you attempt to print, however, you need to make sure the settings are correct.

To check the print setup from Windows, go to the Printers folder by choosing **Start**, **Settings**, **Printers**. The Printers folder appears (see Figure 11.1).

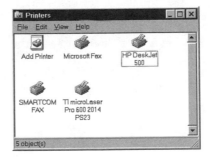

**Figure 11.1**   The Printers folder. You may have different printers.

 **TIP**   **Easy Access to the Printers Folder**   You can access the Printers folder from three other places in Windows: the My Computer window, the bottom of the folders list in the Windows Explorer, and the Control Panel Printers icon.

From the Printers folder, you can select the installed printer you want to check and open the Properties sheet to check the settings. To do so, right-click the printer icon in the Printers window to open the shortcut menu, and then choose **Properties** to display the Properties sheet. Figure 11.2 shows the Properties sheet for the HP DeskJet 500 printer.

**Figure 11.2**  The Properties sheet for the HP DeskJet 500 printer.

You can choose from the following tabs in the Properties sheet to check the settings.

- The *General* options include the printer name, comments, separator page, and print test page.
- The *Details* tab displays the details about your installed printer. On it, you see the port connection to which your printer is attached (Print to the following port). This port is usually LPT1 (for parallel printers) or COM1 (for serial printers).

**Printer Port**  The connection on your computer to which your printer's cable is attached. If the port description indicates **Not Present**, Windows doesn't detect that port on your computer. Check your printer manual to see whether your printer uses the parallel or serial port.

- The Paper options enable you to enter information about the paper size and paper source and to set the orientation to either Portrait (in which the short side of the paper is at the top) or Landscape (in which the long side of the paper is at the top).

- The Graphics options enable you to enter information about resolution in dots per inch (the more dots the finer the resolution), dithering (none, coarse, fine, line art, error diffusion), and intensity (from darkest to lightest). If you have a PostScript printer, your options will be different.

- The Fonts options list the installed printer fonts and enable you to install and remove printer fonts.

- The Device options enable you to change the print quality and printer memory. Check your printer manual if you are not sure of the amount of memory in your printer.

 **Checking the Printer Installation**  The Printers folder in Windows 95 replaces the Printers feature in the Control Panel of Windows 3.1.

You may have other tabs too, depending on the printer model. For example, PostScript printers will have a PostScript tab.

Once you have all the options set the way you want them, click the **OK** button in the Properties sheet to return to the Printers folder.

# Setting a Default Printer

The default printer is the printer that the computer assumes is connected to your computer unless you select another printer. The default printer is the first one that appears in the Printers folder list. Windows automatically sets up a default printer when you install Windows. Almost all Windows applications print using the Printers folder and the default printer defined through it. To set up a default printer, follow these steps:

1. From the Printers folder, double-click the icon that represents the printer you want to set as the default. The print queue window opens.

2. In the print queue, choose the **Printer**, **Set as Default** command to specify the default printer.

> **TIP**  **Quick Method**  Right-click a printer icon and choose **Set As Default** from the shortcut menu.

## Checking Your Equipment

In addition to making sure Windows is ready for printing, you'll want to check your equipment. Be sure to double-check the following things:

- Is the cable between the computer and the printer securely attached on each end?
- Is the printer turned on?
- Is the printer ready for the computer's transmission with the On Line light on?
- Is paper loaded in the printer?

# Adding a Printer

The Add Printer wizard in the Printers folder lets you add new printers to the list of installed printers available in the Printers folder. This wizard simplifies the process of adding a printer.

To add a new printer, follow these steps:

1. In the Printers window, double-click the **Add Printer** icon. The Add Printer Wizard dialog box appears.
2. Click the **Next** button.
3. Choose **Local Printer** (or **Network Printer** if you are using a networked printer) and click the **Next** button.
4. Select a printer from the **Manufacturers** list box. The wizard displays a list of printer models in the Models list box.
5. Select a printer model.
6. Click **OK**, and then follow the prompts in each wizard dialog box to install the new printer.

**CAUTION**  **What Disk?**  When you install new features to your Windows environment, have your installation diskettes close at hand. In the example above, Windows will probably ask you to insert one of the disks containing the printer drivers before it can carry out your instructions.

**Adding a Printer** You can add a printer with the Add Printer Wizard in Windows 95 instead of choosing the Add button in the Printer dialog box in Windows 3.1.

In this lesson, you learned how to check your printer's installation and add a printer. In the next lesson, you will learn how to manage print jobs in Windows.

# Printing with the Printers Folder

*In this lesson, you learn to manage jobs you send to any printer.*

## Printing from a Windows Application

To print from any Windows application, choose **File**, **Print**. A Print dialog box appears, asking you to specify a number of options. The options available depend on the application. When you click OK in this dialog box, the application hands off the font and file information to the Printers folder. This enables you to continue working in your application while your job is printing. The Printers folder acts as the "middleman" between your printer and the application from which you are printing.

**Print Jobs**   Windows creates a print job (or simply a job) when you choose the Print command from the application you are working in.

**Printers Folder**   Each printer icon in the Printers folder in Windows 95 handles print jobs instead of using a separate Print Manager as in Windows 3.1.

# Checking the Print Queue

When you print a document, the printer usually begins processing the job immediately. But what happens if the printer is working on another job that you (or someone else if you're working on a network printer) sent? In this case, the Printers folder acts as a print queue and holds the job until the printer is ready for it.

 **Print Queue**  A holding area for jobs waiting to be printed. If you were to list the contents of the queue, the jobs would appear in the order they were sent to the Printer.

Figure 12.1 shows a document in the print queue. As you can see, the print queue window displays the document name, status, owner, progress (pages), and started at (time and date). Notice also that the printer's status shows that it is printing. This indicates the document was just sent to the queue and is beginning to print.

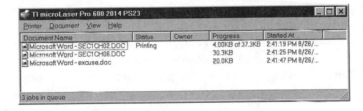

**Figure 12.1**  The print queue window.

To display the print quene, follow these steps:

1. Click the **Start** button and choose **Settings**. The Settings menu appears.
2. Choose **Printers**, and the Printers folder appears.
3. Double-click the printer icon for the printer to which you are printing. The print queue window appears with a list of queued documents. If no documents are waiting to print, there won't be any jobs listed below the column headings.

 **TIP**  **Display the Print Queue Quickly**  Double-click the printer icon that appears on the taskbar immediately after printing a document.

# Controlling the Print Job

You can control print jobs once they're in the queue. This includes changing the order in which the jobs print, pausing and resuming the print job, and deleting a job before it prints.

## Reordering Jobs in the Queue

To change the order of a job in the queue, simply drag the job entry to a new position in the list.

**CAUTION**

**First Come, First Served**   You can't reorder or place a job before the job that is currently printing.

## Pausing and Resuming the Print Queue

You may want to pause the queue and then resume printing later. For example, the paper in the printer may be misaligned. Pausing the print queue will give you time to correct the problem.

To pause the print queue, choose **Printer**, **Pause Printing** or press **Alt+P** and then **A** while in the print queue window. To resume printing, choose **Printer**, **Pause Printing** again from the print queue menu bar or press **Alt+P** and then **A**.

**CAUTION**

**Printer Stalled**   Your printer may stall while it's processing your print job. If it does, Windows displays the word stalled in the printer status line. Press **Alt+P** and then **A** to start printing again. This gets the printer going again, but chances are that a problem such as the printer being out of paper or ink caused the printer to stall. If so, the queue will stall again, and you'll have to refer to your printer manual or contact a technical person to help you.

## Deleting a Print Job

Sometimes, you'll send a document to be printed and then change your mind. For example, you may think of other text to add to the document or realize you forgot to spell-check your work. In such a case, deleting the print job is easy. Follow these steps:

1. Click the **Start** button and choose **Settings**. The Settings menu appears.
2. Choose **Printers**, and the Printers folder appears.

**3.** Double-click the printer icon for the printer to which you are printing. The print queue window appears.

**4.** Select the job you want to delete.

**5.** Choose **Document, Cancel Printing**.

TIP    **Clear the Queue!**   To delete all the files in the print queue, choose **Printer, Purge Print Jobs** from the print queue menu bar or click the **Close** (X) button in the upper-right corner of the window.

In this lesson, you learned how to control print jobs. In the next lesson, you learn how to change the desktop and regional settings.

# Controlling the Appearance of Windows

*In this lesson, you learn to control specific aspects of the Control Panel, such as on-screen colors, the appearance of your desktop, and the locale and units settings.*

## Changing Your Desktop

The Control Panel is a folder available through the Settings menu that enables you to control various aspects of Windows (see Figure 13.1).

**Figure 13.1**   The Windows 95 Control Panel.

**My Icons Look Different!** You may not have all of these icons in your Control Panel; some of them do not appear on all computers. For instance, the Desktop Themes icon is present only if you have installed Microsoft Plus!, an add-on pack for Windows.

The Display Properties sheet lets you control many things about your desktop. To access this dialog box, follow these steps:

1. Choose **Start, Settings, Control Panel**. The Control Panel appears (see Figure 13.1).
2. Double-click the **Display** icon. The Display Properties dialog box appears.

**Display Settings** The Display icon in the Windows 95 Control Panel replaces the Color and Desktop icons in the Windows 3.1 Control Panel.

The Display Properties sheet contains several tabs that control different sets of options. The following sections explain how to use these tabs.

## Changing the Desktop Background

You can change a number of visual and performance elements of your desktop through the Control Panel. To change the desktop background, follow these steps:

1. Open the Display Properties sheet (as described earlier in the lesson).
2. If necessary, click the **Background** tab. The Pattern and Wallpaper options appear in the window (see Figure 13.2).
3. Select the options you want, based on these descriptions:

    **Pattern** Select the pattern to be displayed on the desktop. You can choose from a number of simple two-color patterns; check out the sample screen displayed at the top of the dialog box to see an example.

    **Wallpaper** More elaborate than the Pattern selection, the Wallpaper option enables you to display .BMP files on your desktop. Windows comes with some very attractive wallpapers. The wallpaper you select is displayed in the sample screen at the top of the dialog box.

**Display**   Select the type of display you want for the wallpaper. Choose **Tile** to repeat a graphic as many times as necessary to cover the whole desktop. Choose **Center** to display the graphic once in the middle of the desktop; extra space around the wallpaper is filled with the desktop color.

4. When you're satisfied with the settings, click **OK**.

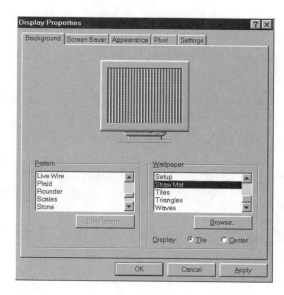

**Figure 13.2**   Straw Mat is selected in the wallpaper options.

# Setting a Screen Saver

Screen savers were originally designed to protect your screen from "burning in" an image that was displayed there too long. Even though today's monitors are advanced enough to eliminate this problem, screen savers are still fun to use. If you select a screen saver, Windows automatically blanks the screen and runs a pattern across it anytime your computer is inactive for a specified length of time. To return to the screen you left and continue working, press a key or move the mouse.

To select a screen saver, follow these steps:

1. Open the Display Properties sheet (as described earlier in this lesson).
2. Click the **Screen Saver** tab.

3. Open the **Screen Saver** drop-down list box and click a screen saver. The sample screen at the top of the page shows the current selection.

4. In the **Wait** text box, enter the number of minutes you want to delay the screen saver.

5. Click **OK**.

# Changing Appearance Settings

With the Control Panel, you can change the appearance of your desktop by setting the colors of many components in Windows. The capability to control the color of certain Windows elements can help you learn to use the program faster: You're able to look for a particular color and shape, instead of just a shape. Or you can adjust the colors displayed on your color monitor just for a change of pace.

Follow these steps to change the Windows screen colors from the Control Panel:

1. Open the Display Properties sheet (as described earlier in the lesson).

2. Click the **Appearance** tab. The color scheme options appear in the window.

3. Click the **Scheme** drop-down arrow, and the predefined scheme options appear.

4. Use the arrow keys to scroll through the scheme options. The display above the Scheme text box illustrates the current selection. Select the scheme you want to use.

5. Click **OK** or press **Enter** to make your choice. Figure 13.3 shows the Slate color scheme selected in the Appearance page.

After you become more comfortable with Windows, go into the Appearance page and create your own color scheme. You can assign different colors to the various Windows elements (title bar, buttons, menus, and so on). To do so, click the element in the sample area that you want to change, and then choose a color from the **Color** drop-down list. To save your creation as a Windows scheme, click the **Save As** button, enter a name for the color scheme, and click **OK**.

**Color Scheme**   A color scheme is a set of predefined or customized colors that applies a different color to a different part of the screen. Color schemes make each Windows element easy to identify.

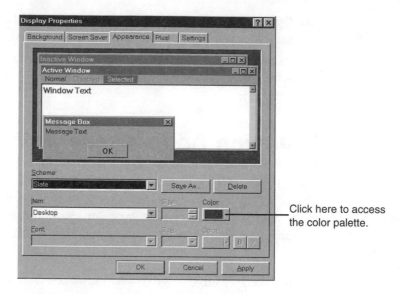

Click here to access
the color palette.

**Figure 13.3**   The Slate scheme as selected on the Appearance page.

# Changing Regional Settings

Most readers will use Windows in the United States. However, if you work in an international setting, you may want to make some changes in the Regional Settings Properties sheet. You can configure Windows to use settings familiar to your region, nationality, and number system. For example, if a United States firm creates letters or documents to be sent abroad to Spain, regional settings would benefit everyone because they would ensure that all numeric and other settings are indigenous to Spain.

Follow these steps to control the regional settings:

1. Select **Start**, **Settings**, **Control Panel**. The Control Panel window opens.
2. Double-click the **Regional Settings** icon. The Regional Settings Properties sheet appears (see Figure 13.4).
3. Make changes on any of the following pages:

    **Regional Settings**   Windows has a number of standard locale settings on how units are displayed, page setup defaults, and so on. Use the Locale option on the Regional Settings page to choose the locale setting you want to use.

**Number** Use the Number options to change the way Windows displays numbers.

**Currency** Use the Currency options to change the way Windows displays positive and negative currency values.

**Time** Use the Time options to change the way Windows displays time values.

**Date** Use the Date options to change the way Windows displays long and short dates.

**Regional Settings** The Regional Settings icon in the Windows 95 Control Panel replaces the International Settings icon in the Windows 3.1 Control Panel.

**4.** Click **OK**, and the changes are made.

**Figure 13.4** The Regional Settings Properties sheet.

In this lesson, you learned to change the desktop and change regional settings from the Control Panel. In the next lesson, you'll learn how to run DOS applications.

# Word

# Getting Started with Word

*In this lesson, you learn how to start and exit Word, identify the parts of the Word screen, and the basics of entering text.*

## Starting Word for Windows

You start Word from the Windows Start menu. Follow these steps:

1. Open the Start menu by clicking the **Start** button.
2. On the Start menu, click **Programs**.
3. On the next menu, click **Microsoft Word**.

Another way to start Word is to open the Start menu and click **New Office Document**. Or, if the Office Shortcut Bar is displayed along the right edge of your screen, click the **New Office Document** button. Either way, the New dialog box appears. In this dialog box, click the **General** tab (if necessary), and then double-click the **Blank Document** icon.

**Can't Find Microsoft Word on the Menu?** You must install Word (or Office) on your system before you can use it. Refer to section 7 for installation instructions.

CAUTION

## Understanding the Word Screen

When you start Word, you see a blank document ready for you to enter text. Before you begin, however, you need to know about the various parts of the screen (see Figure 1.1). You'll use these screen elements, described in Table 1.1, as you work on your documents.

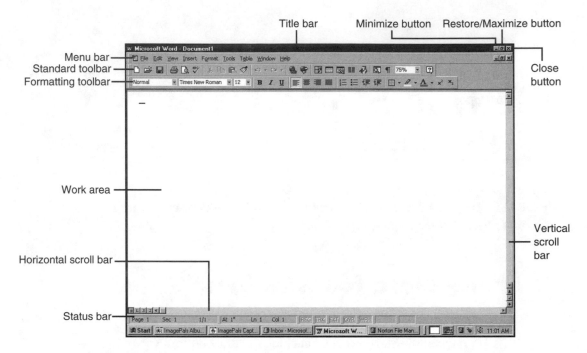

**Figure 1.1**  Word's opening screen is a blank document.

**Table 1.1**  Parts of the Word Screen

| Screen Element | Function |
| --- | --- |
| Work area | Your document displays here for text entry and editing. Figure 1.1 shows a blank document. |
| Title bar | The program name, user name, and the name of the current document display here. At the right end of the title bar are buttons to minimize, restore, and close the program. |
| Menu bar | Menu headings on this bar let you access Word's menu commands. |
| Toolbars | The small pictures, or *buttons,* on the toolbars let you select commonly needed commands by clicking the mouse. |
| Status bar | Word displays information about the document and the state of the keyboard lock keys on the status bar. |
| Scroll bars | You click on the scroll bars to move around in your document. |

| Screen Element | Function |
|---|---|
| Minimize button | Click this button to temporarily hide Word (to shrink it to an icon on the taskbar). You can then click the Microsoft Word button on the taskbar at the bottom of your screen to redisplay Word. |
| Close button | Click this button to close Word. |
| Restore/Maximize button | Click this button to enlarge Word to full-screen or to shrink Word to a partial-screen window. |

# Using Menus and Toolbars

As you use Word, you will issue commands to tell Word what actions you want done. You can carry out most Word commands using either the menus or the toolbars. The method you use depends on your personal preference.

To select a menu command:

**1.** Open a menu by clicking the menu title on the menu bar. You can also open a menu by holding down the **Alt** key and pressing the underlined letter in the menu title. For example, press **Alt+F** (hold down **Alt** and press **F**) to open the File menu.

**2.** With the menu open, click the desired command or press the underlined letter of the command name.

Throughout this book, I use a shorthand method of specifying menu commands. For example, if I say click **File**, **Open**, it means to open the File menu and select the Open command.

**Change Your Mind?**   If you change your mind about a menu command, press the **Esc** key twice or click anywhere outside the menu to close the menu without making a selection.

**CAUTION**

Figure 1.2 shows the open File menu. Word uses several elements on its menus to provide you with additional information. Table 1.2 explains these elements.

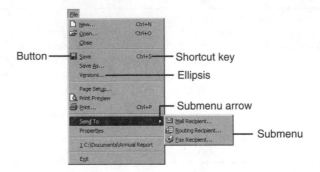

**Figure 1.2** The File menu with the Send To submenu displayed.

**Table 1.2** Parts of a Menu

| Menu Element | Function |
| --- | --- |
| Button | If the menu command has a corresponding toolbar button, the button is displayed next to the menu command. |
| Ellipsis (…) | Indicates that the menu command leads to a dialog box. |
| Submenu arrow | Indicates that the menu command leads to another menu (called a submenu). |
| Shortcut key | Identifies the keys you can use to select the menu command using the keyboard. |

You can use shortcut keys to select some commands without using the menus at all. Shortcuts keys are listed on the menu next to the corresponding command. In Figure 1.2, for example, you can see that the shortcut key for the Open command is Ctrl+O. This means that pressing Ctrl+O (press and hold the **Ctrl** key, press the **O** key, and then release both keys) has the same effect as clicking **File**, **Open**.

To use the toolbars, simply use your mouse to click the desired button. The buttons have pictures on them to help you identify each button's function. You can jog your memory by resting the mouse cursor on a button for a few seconds without clicking. Word will display a ScreenTip next to the button identifying its function.

CAUTION

**What's This?**   Press **Shift+F1** to activate What's This? help. Then click any element on the Word screen to view information about it.

# Working in Dialog Boxes

Many of Word's commands result in a dialog box. Word uses dialog boxes to obtain additional information required to carry out a command. Each dialog box is different, but they all use the same basic elements.

In a dialog box, press the **Tab** key to move from item to item; press **Shift+Tab** to move backwards. You can click an item or press **Alt** plus the underlined letter to select an item. When the dialog box selections are complete, press **Enter** or click the **OK** button to accept your entries and carry out the command. Click the **Cancel** button or press **Esc** to close the dialog box without carrying out the command.

# Entering Text and Moving Around

Word displays a blinking vertical line in the work area. This is the *cursor* or *insertion point*, and it identifies the location in the document where text will be inserted and where certain editing actions will occur. To enter text, simply type it on the keyboard. You should not press Enter at the end of a line—Word will automatically wrap the text to a new line when you reach the right margin. Press Enter only when you want to start a new paragraph.

If you make a mistake, there are a couple of ways you can delete it:

- Press the **Backspace** key to erase characters to the left of the cursor.
- Press the **Delete** key to erase characters to the right of the cursor.

You can move the cursor around to add and edit text in different document locations. Table 1.3 describes the basic cursor movements.

**Table 1.3**  Moving the Cursor

| *To Move the Cursor...* | *Do This...* |
| --- | --- |
| To any visible location | Click in the location |
| One character right or left | Press the right or left arrow key |
| One line up or down | Press the up or down arrow key |
| To the start or end of the line | Press the **Home** or **End** key |
| To the start or end of the document | Hold the **Ctrl** key and press **Home** or **End** |

You'll learn more about moving around Word in Lesson 3.

# Quitting the Program

When you are finished working with Word, you have several options for exiting the program. All of these methods have the same result:

- Click **File**, **Exit**.
- Press **Alt+F4**.
- Click the **Close** (X) button at the right end of the title bar.

If you are saving the document for the first time, Word prompts you to save it before exiting. For now, you can just select **No**. You'll learn about saving documents in Lesson 4.

In this lesson, you learned how to start and exit Word, how to use menus and toolbars, and you learned about the basics of entering and editing text. The next lesson shows you how to create a new Word document.

# Creating a New Document

*In this lesson, you learn how to create a new Word document and about the relationship between documents and templates. You also learn how to use wizards.*

## Understanding Document Templates

To work effectively with Word, you must understand that every Word document is based on a *template*. As the name suggests, a template is a model for a document.

**Document Template**   A model for a new document that may contain text and/or formatting.

Some templates contain no text, giving you a blank document with some basic formatting specifications in which you are responsible for entering all of the text. Other templates contain text and/or detailed formatting specifications. For example, if you write a lot of business letters, you could use a template that contains the date, your return address, and a closing salutation. When you create a new document based on that template, all of those elements will automatically be in the document—all you need to do is add the other parts. If a template contains formatting, all documents based on that template will have a uniform appearance (for example, the same font and margins).

Word comes with a variety of predefined templates that are ready for you to use. These templates cover a range of common document needs, such as fax forms, memos, business letters, and Web pages. You can also create your own templates. In this lesson, you will learn how to use Word's predefined templates. Lesson 15 shows you how to create your own templates.

# Starting a New Document

Many of the documents you create will be based on the Normal template, which creates a blank document. As you learned in Lesson 1, when you start Word it automatically opens a blank document for you to work with. If Word is already running, you can create a blank document by clicking the **New** button on the toolbar.

To start a document based on another non-blank template, follow these steps:

**1.** Click **File**, **New**. The New dialog box appears (see Figure 2.1).

**2.** The tabs along the top of the dialog box list the different template categories. Click the tab corresponding to the category of document you want to create.

**3.** Click the icon that corresponds to the template you want. If a preview of the template's appearance is available, it will appear in the Preview area.

**4.** Click **OK**. Word creates the document and displays it, ready for editing.

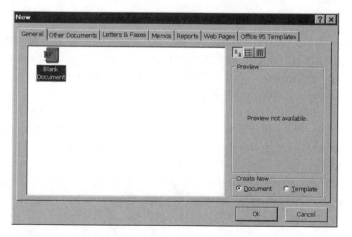

**Figure 2.1** The New dialog box.

When you create a document based on a template, the template's text and formatting will be displayed in the new document. There's nothing special about document text that came from a template—you can edit it just like any other text. You can also edit the actual templates, as you'll learn in Lesson 15.

**TIP** **Word on the Web: Web Templates** Select the **Web Pages** tab in the New dialog box for templates that are useful for Web document.

Some templates contain *placeholder* text that you must replace. For example, the résumé template contains a dummy name and biography that you must delete and replace with your own information. The document might display text such as **[Click here and type your name]**. Simply follow the instructions displayed in brackets.

**No Templates?** If you can't find any templates, they probably were not installed with Word. You can reinstall Word, choose the **Custom Setup** installation option, and specify which templates you want installed.

**CAUTION**

# Using Wizards

Some of Word's templates are a special kind of template called a *wizard*. Whereas a standard template is a static combination of text and formatting, a wizard is an active tool that asks you questions about the document you want to create, and then uses your answers to create the new document. When you're starting a new document, you can recognize a wizard in the New dialog box by its title and the small "magic wand" in its icon.

Each wizard is unique, but they all follow the same basic procedures. There are a number of steps in a wizard; each step asks you for certain information about the document you want to create. Figure 2.2 shows an example; this is a step in the Fax Wizard.

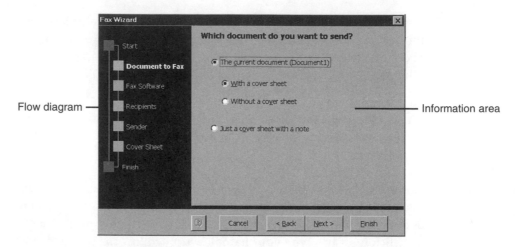

Flow diagram ——                                        —— Information area

**Figure 2.2**  The Fax Wizard dialog box.

Table 2.1 describes the different components of the wizard dialog box.

**Table 2.1**  The Parts of a Wizard Dialog Box

| Wizard Component | Function |
| --- | --- |
| Title bar | Shows the name of the wizard that is running. |
| Flow diagram | Graphically represents the wizard steps, with the current step highlighted. Click any step to go directly to it. |
| Information area | Requests document information from you. |
| Cancel button | Cancels the wizard without creating a new document. |
| Back button | Moves to the previous wizard step. |
| Next Button | Moves to the next wizard step. |
| Finish button | Ends the wizard and creates the new document based on the information you have entered so far. |
| Help button | Click to display Help information about using the wizard. |

To create a new document using a wizard, follow these steps:

1. Click **File**, **New** to open the New dialog box (refer to Figure 2.1).
2. Click the tab corresponding to the category of document you are creating. (Not all tabs contain wizards, however.)

**3.** Click the icon of the wizard you want to use and click **OK**.

**4.** In the wizard dialog box, enter the information Word needs, based on how you want the document created. Then click **Next**.

**5.** Repeat step 4 for each of the wizard steps. If needed, click **Back** one or more times to return to an earlier step to make changes in the information.

**6.** At the last wizard step, click **Finish** to close the wizard and create the new document.

 TIP  **Know Your Templates**  Spend some time becoming familiar with Word's various predefined templates; they can save you a lot of time.

In this lesson, you learned about document templates and how to create a new document. You also learned how to use wizards. The next lesson teaches you how to perform basic editing tasks in Word.

# Basic Editing Tasks

*In this lesson, you learn how to enter text, move around a document, and perform other basic editing tasks.*

## Entering Text

When you start a new Word document based on the Normal template, you see a blank work area that contains only two items:

- **Blinking vertical line**   This is the cursor, or insertion point, which marks the location where text you type appears in the document and where certain editing actions occur.
- **Horizontal line**   This marks the end of the document.

In a new empty document, these two markers are at the same location. To enter text, simply type it using the keyboard. As you type, the text appears, and the insertion point moves to the right. If the line of text reaches the right edge of the screen, Word automatically starts a new line; this is called *word wrapping*. Do not press Enter unless you want to start a new paragraph. If you enter more lines than will fit on the screen, Word scrolls previously entered text upward to keep the cursor in view. Figure 3.1 shows word wrap as well as the end of document marker and cursor.

**TIP**   **Leave It to Word Wrap**   Press Enter only when you want to start a new paragraph.

Press Enter here
to start a new
paragraph.

When the text
reached here…

…word wrap started
a new line here.

End of document
marker

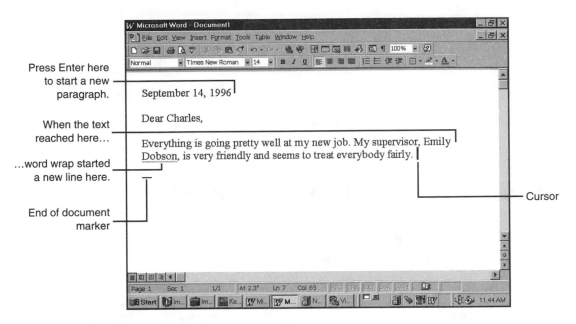

Cursor

**Figure 3.1** Using Enter and word wrap.

# Paragraphs in Word

The idea of paragraphs is important in Word because certain types of formatting apply to individual paragraphs. In Word, you end one paragraph and start a new one by pressing **Enter**. Word inserts a new, blank line and positions the cursor at the beginning of it.

 On your screen, the result may look the same as if word wrap had started the new line, but the difference is that Word has inserted a *paragraph mark*. These marks are normally invisible, but you can display them by clicking the **Show/ Hide ¶** button on the Standard toolbar. Click the button again to hide the marks. This tool is very useful when you need to see exactly where the paragraphs begin and end in your document.

**TIP** **Other Marks?** When you display paragraph marks, Word also displays dots for spaces and arrows for tabs.

To combine two paragraphs into a single paragraph, follow these steps:

1. Move the cursor to the beginning of the first line of the second paragraph.
2. Press **Backspace** to delete the paragraph mark.

# Moving Around the Document

As you work on a document, you will often have to move the cursor to view or work on other parts of the text. Most of the time you'll use the keyboard to do that, as explained in Table 3.1.

**Table 3.1**  Moving the Cursor with the Keyboard

| *To Move...* | *Perform This Action...* |
| --- | --- |
| Left or right one character | Press ← or → |
| Left or right one word | Press **Ctrl+←** or **Ctrl+→** |
| Up or down one line | Press ↑ or ↓ |
| Up or down one paragraph | Press **Ctrl+↑** or **Ctrl+↓** |
| To the start or end of a line | Press **Home** or **End** |
| Up or down one screen | Press **Page Up** or **Page Down** |
| To the top or bottom of the current screen | Press **Ctrl+Page Up** or **Ctrl+Page Down** |
| To the start or end of the document | Press **Ctrl+Home** or **Ctrl+End** |

You can also navigate with the mouse. If the desired cursor location is in view on the screen, simply click the location. If the desired location is not in view, you must scroll to bring it into view and then click the location. Table 3.2 describes how to scroll with the mouse.

**Table 3.2**  Scrolling with the Mouse

| To Scroll... | Do This... |
| --- | --- |
| Up or down one line | Click the up or down arrow on the vertical scroll bar. |
| Up or down one screen | Click the vertical scroll bar between the box and the up or down arrow. |
| Up or down any amount | Drag the scroll box up or down. |
| Up or down one page | Click the Previous Page or Next Page button on the vertical scroll bar. |

Note that scrolling with the mouse does not move the cursor; the cursor remains in its original location while the screen displays another part of the document. You must click the new location to move the cursor there.

 **TIP**  **Quick Go To**  Press **Shift+F5** one or more times to move the cursor to locations in the document that you edited most recently.

# Selecting Text

Many tasks you'll perform in Word will require that you first select the text you want to modify. For example, to underline a sentence, you must select the sentence first and then click the **Underline** button. Selected text appears on the screen in reverse video, as shown in Figure 3.2, which has the phrase **Dear Ms. Kennedy:** selected.

You can select text with either the mouse or the keyboard. With the mouse, you can use the selection bar, an unmarked column in the left document margin. When the mouse pointer moves from the document to the selection bar, it changes from an I-beam to an arrow pointing up and to the right. Table 3.3 lists the methods you can use to select text.

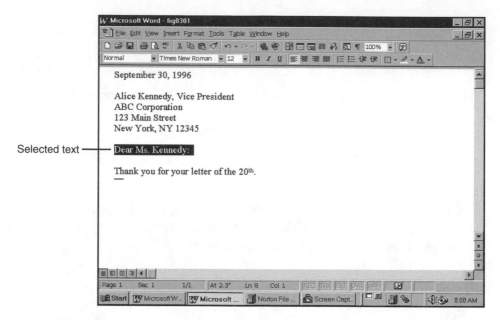

Selected text ———

**Figure 3.2** Selected text appears in reverse video.

**Table 3.3** Methods of Selecting Text

| *To Select Text...* | *Perform This Action with the Mouse...* |
| --- | --- |
| Any amount | Point at the start of the text, press and hold the left mouse button, and drag the highlight over the text. |
| One word | Double-click anywhere on the word. |
| One sentence | Press and hold Ctrl and click anywhere in the sentence. |
| One line | Click the selection bar next to the line. |
| Multiple lines | Drag in the selection bar next to the lines. |
| One paragraph | Double-click the selection bar next to the paragraph. |
| Entire document | Press and hold Ctrl and click anywhere in the selection bar. |
| Any amount | Move the insertion point to the start of the text, press and hold Shift, and move the insertion point to the end of the desired text using the movement keys described in Table 3.1. |
| Entire document | Press Ctrl+A. |

To cancel a selection, click anywhere on the screen or use the keyboard to move the insertion point.

**TIP**   **Fast Select**   Double-click a word to select it quickly. Hold **Ctrl** and double-click to select an entire sentence.

When you are selecting text by dragging with the mouse, Word's default is to automatically select entire words. If you need to select partial words you can turn this option off (or back on) as described here:

**1.** Click **Tools**, **Options** to open the Options dialog box.

**2.** Click the **Edit** tab.

**3.** Click the **When Selecting**, **Automatically Select Entire Word** check box to turn it on or off.

**4.** Click **OK**.

# Deleting, Copying, and Pasting Text

You have already learned how to use the Delete and Backspace keys to delete single characters. In addition, you can delete larger amounts of text, and you can move or copy text from one document location to another.

To delete a block of text, first select the text. Then do one of these things:

- To simply delete the text, press **Delete** or **Backspace**.
- To delete the text and replace it with new text, type the new text.

To move or copy text, start by selecting the text. Then follow these steps:

**1.** To copy the text, click **Edit**, **Copy**; or click the **Copy** button on the Standard toolbar; or press **Ctrl+C**.

To move the text, click **Edit**, **Cut**; or click the **Cut** button on the Standard toolbar; or press **Ctrl+X**.

**2.** Move the cursor to the location where you want the text moved or copied.

**3.** Click **Edit**, **Paste**; or click the **Paste** button on the Standard toolbar; or press **Ctrl+V**.

You can also use the mouse to move and copy text. This technique, called drag-and-drop, is most convenient for small amounts of text and when both the "from" and "to" locations are visible on-screen. Here's how you drag-and-drop:

1. Select the text.

2. Point at the text with the mouse. The mouse pointer changes from an I-beam to an arrow.

3. To copy the text, press and hold **Ctrl**. To move the text, do not press any key.

4. Drag to the new location. As you drag, a vertical dotted line indicates the text's new location.

5. Release the mouse button and, if you are copying, the Ctrl key.

**CAUTION**

**Make a Mistake?**   You can recover from most editing actions (such as deleting text) by clicking **Edit**, **Undo** or by pressing **Ctrl+Z**.

In this lesson, you learned how to enter text, move around the document, and perform other basic editing tasks. In the next lesson, you'll learn how to save and retrieve documents.

# Saving and Opening Documents

*In this lesson, you learn how to name your document, save it to disk, and enter summary information. You also learn how to open a document you saved earlier.*

## Saving a New Document

When you create a new document in Word, it is stored temporarily in your computer's memory under the default name Document*n*, where *n* is a number that increases by 1 for each new unnamed document. Word only only "remembers" the document until you quit the program or turn off the computer. To save a document permanently so you can retrieve it later, you must assign a name and save it to disk. These steps show you how to do just that.

1. Click **File**, **Save** or click the **Save** button on the Standard toolbar. The Save As dialog box appears (see Figure 4.1).

2. In the **File Name** text box, enter the name you want to assign to the document file. The name can be up to 256 characters long and should be descriptive of the document's contents.

3. If you want to save the document in a different folder or drive, click the **Save In** drop-down arrow and select a different folder and/or drive.

4. Click **Save**. The document is saved to disk, and the name you assigned appears in the title bar.

Save In list box

File Name text box

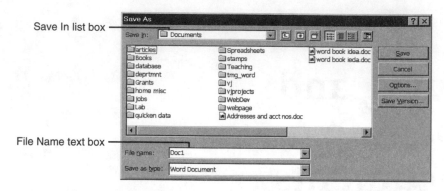

**Figure 4.1**   The Save As dialog box.

> **TIP   Word on the Web**   Documents you make publicly available on your Web site must be saved in hypertext markup language (HTML) format. Word provides a separate command for saving in this format: **File, Save as HTML**.

# Saving a Document As You Work

After naming and saving a document, you still need to save it periodically as you work to minimize data loss in the event of a power failure or other system problem. After you name a document, you can easily save the current version:

- Click **File**, **Save**.
- Click the **Save** button on the Standard toolbar.
- Press **Ctrl+S**.

Word automatically saves the document with its current name, and no dialog boxes appear.

> **TIP   Don't Forget!**   Save your document regularly as you work on it. If you don't, you may lose your work if there is a power outage or other problem.

# Changing a Document's Name

After you name a document, you may need to change its name. For example, you might want to keep an old version of a document under its original name and then save a revised version under a new name. To change a document name, follow these steps:

1. Click **File**, **Save As**. The Save As dialog box appears, showing the current document name in the File Name text box.
2. In the **File Name** box, change the file name to the new name.
3. (Optional) Select a different folder in the **Save In** list box to save the document in a different folder.
4. Click **Save**, and Word saves the document under the new name.

# Using Document Properties

Every Word document has a set of properties that provide information about the document. Some properties contain summary information that you enter, while others contain information that is automatically generated by Word. To enter or view a document's properties, follow these steps:

1. Click **File**, **Properties** to open the Properties dialog box.
2. Click the **Summary** tab, and you'll see the options shown in Figure 4.2.
3. Enter or edit any summary information you want. These are the summary information properties you will use most often:

> **Title**   Enter the title of the document. This is not the same as the document's file name.
>
> **Subject**   Enter a phrase that describes the subject of the document.
>
> **Author**   Word automatically fills this field with the user name you entered when you installed the program. You can change it if necessary.
>
> **Company**   Your company name. This may be automatically entered for you based on your Windows installation.
>
> **Category**   Enter a word or phrase that describes the type of document.
>
> **Keywords**   Enter one or more words related to the document contents.
>
> **Comments**   Enter any additional information you want saved with the document.

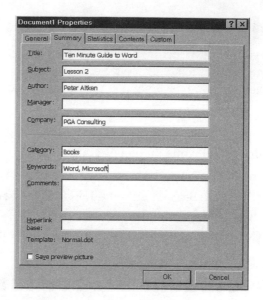

**Figure 4.2** Entering document summary information.

**4.** Click **OK**. Word saves the document properties along with the document.

Word automatically generates useful statistics about each document, such as the number of words it contains and the date and time the document was created. To view a document's statistics, select the **File**, **Properties** command and click the **Statistics** tab.

TIP **Quick Word Count** To get a quick count of the words and other elements in your document, click **Tools**, **Word Count**.

# Opening a Document

You can open any document created with Word for Windows to continue working on it. You can also open documents that were created with other programs, such as WordPerfect.

To open an existing file, click **File**, **Open** or click the **Open** button on the Standard toolbar. The Open dialog box appears (see Figure 4.3).

Look In drop-down list    Up One Level button    Preview button

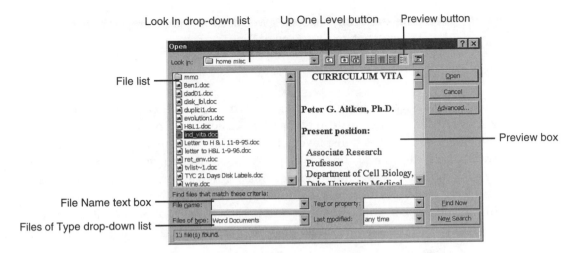

File list

Preview box

File Name text box

Files of Type drop-down list

**Figure 4.3**  The Open dialog box.

The file list shows all of the Word documents and folders in the current folder. Each document is represented by a small page icon that appears next to its name; folders have a file folder icon next to them. The Look In list box shows the name of the current folder. You can take the following actions in the Open dialog box:

- To open a file, click its name in the file list or type its name into the **File Name** list box; then press **Enter** or click the **Open** button. Or you can simply double-click the file name.
- To preview the contents of a file, click the file name, and then click the **Preview** button. Click the **Preview** button again to turn preview off.
- To look for files other than Word documents, click the **Files of Type** drop-down arrow and select the desired document type.
- To move up one folder, click the **Up One Level** button.
- To move down one level to a different folder, double-click the folder name in the file list.
- To move to another folder, click the **Look In** drop-down arrow and select the desired folder.

**Folder**  Windows uses folders to organize files on a disk. Before Windows 95, folders were called subdirectories.

**TIP**  **Word on the Web**   To open a Web document for editing in Word, select **HTML Document** from the **Files of Type** list. Then select the document and click Open.

To quickly open a document you recently worked on, you can use Word's Recently Used File List instead of the Open dialog box. To view this list, open the **File** menu. The list is displayed at the bottom of the menu just above the Exit command. To open a file on the list, press the number corresponding to the file, or click the file name with the mouse. This list displays the document files that you have saved most recently. If you have just installed Word, there will be no files displayed here, of course. If you have saved files and the list still doesn't display them, see the next paragraph.

You can control how many files appear on the Recently Used File List and whether the list appears at all. Click **Tools**, **Options** to open the Options dialog box. Click the **General** tab if necessary. Click the **Recently Used File List** check box to turn it on or off to control the display of the list. To change the number of files displayed in the list, enter a number in the **Entries** text box or click the up/down arrows to change the existing entry. Click **OK** when you're finished.

 **TIP**  **Quick Open**   You can open a Word document (and start Word if it is not already running) by double-clicking the document name or icon in the Windows Explorer or My Computer window.

In this lesson, you learned how to name your document, save it to disk, and enter summary information. You also learned how to open a document you saved earlier. The next lesson shows you how to find and replace text.

# Finding and Replacing Text

*In this lesson, you learn how to find specific text in your document, and how to automatically replace it with new text.*

## Searching for Text

Word can search through your document to find occurrences of specific text. Word's default is to search the entire document; that's what it does unless you select some text before you issue the command. If you select text first, it searches only the selected text.

To search for specific text, select a block of text (if necessary). Then follow these steps:

1. Click **Edit**, **Find** or press **Ctrl+F**. The Find dialog box appears (see Figure 5.1).

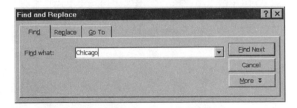

**Figure 5.1**   The Find tab in the Find and Replace dialog box.

2. In the **Find What** text box, enter the text you want to search for. The text you enter is called the *search template*.

3. Click **Find Next**. Word looks through the document for text that matches the search template. If it finds matching text, it highlights it in the document and stops; the Find dialog box remains on-screen.

**4.** Click **Find Next** to continue the search for other instances of the search template. Or, press **Esc** to close the dialog box and return to the document. The found text remains selected.

When Word finishes searching the entire document, it displays one of two messages. It will inform you that the search template cannot be found, or it will let you know the search is complete.

**TIP**   **Repeat Searches**   When you open the Find dialog box, the previous search template (if there was one) will still be displayed in the **Find What** text box. This makes it easy to repeat the previous search.

**TERM**   **Search Template**   The search template is the model for the text you want to find.

# Using Search Options

The default Find operation locates the search template you specify without regard to the case of letters or whether it's a whole word or part of a word. For example, if you enter the search template "the," Word will find "the," "THE," "mother," and so on. You can refine your search by using Word's search options. To do so, click the **More** button in the Find dialog box. The dialog box expands to offer additional options (see Figure 5.2).

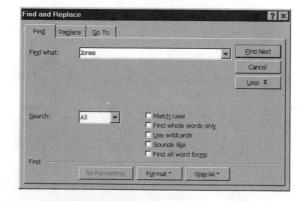

**Figure 5.2**   Setting options for the Find command.

You can choose from the following options:

- **Match Case**   Requires an exact match for upper- and lowercase letters. By selecting this check box, "The" will match only "The" and not "the" or "THE."
- **Find Whole Words Only**   This will match whole words only. If you select this check box, "the" will match only "the"—not "mother," "these," and so on.
- **Use Wildcards**   Permits the use of the * and ? wild cards in the search template. The * wild card stands in for any sequence of 0 or more unknown characters; the ? wild card stands in for any single unknown character. Thus the template "th?n" would match "thin" and "then" but not "thrown" or "thn." And the template "th*n" would match "thin," "thn," "thrown," and so on.
- **Sounds Like**   Finds words that sound similar to the template. If you select this check box, for example, "their" will match "there."
- **Find All Word Forms**   Locates alternate forms of the search template. For example, "sit" will match not only "sit" but also "sat" and "sitting." This check box is not available if you select the Use Wildcards check box.

To control the extent of the search, click the **Search** drop-down arrow and select one of the following options:

- **All**   Searches the entire document.
- **Down**   Searches from the cursor to the end of the document.
- **Up**   Searches from the cursor to the start of the document.

**CAUTION**

**Can't Find It?**   If you can't find text that you're sure is in the document, check the spelling of the search template and make sure unwanted search options are not enabled.

# Finding and Replacing Text

Word's Replace command lets you search for instances of text and replace them with new text. This can be very helpful if, for example, you misspelled the same word multiple times in the same document. To replace text, follow these steps:

1. Click **Edit**, **Replace** or press **Ctrl+H**. The Replace dialog box appears (see Figure 5.3).

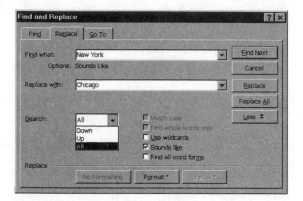

**Figure 5.3**   The Replace tab in the Find and replace dialog box.

**TIP**   **Find or Replace**   You can access the Find dialog box from the Replace dialog box (and vice versa) by clicking the corresponding tab.

2. In the **Find What** text box, enter the text you want to replace.

3. In the **Replace With** text box, enter the replacement text.

4. (Optional) Click the **More** button and specify search options as explained in the previous section.

5. Click **Find Next** to locate and highlight the first instance of the target text.

6. For each occurrence Word finds, respond using one of these buttons:

   - Click **Replace** to replace the highlighted instance of the target text and then locate the next instance of it.

   - Click **Find Next** to leave the highlighted instance of the target text unchanged and to locate the next instance.

   - Click **Replace All** to replace all instances of the target text in the entire document.

**TIP**  **Deleting Text**  To delete the target text, follow the previous steps but leave the Replace With text box empty.

 **Recovery!**  If you make a mistake replacing text, you can recover by clicking **Edit, Undo Replace**.

**CAUTION**

In this lesson, you learned how to search for and replace text in your document. In the next lesson, you will learn about Word's screen display options.

# Screen Display Options

*In this lesson, you learn how to control the Word screen display to suit your working style.*

## Document Display Options

Word offers several ways to display your document. Each of these views is designed to make certain editing tasks easier. The available views include:

- **Normal**    Best for general editing tasks.
- **Page Layout**    Ideal for working with formatting and page layout.
- **Online Layout**    Optimized for viewing on-screen.
- **Outline**    Designed for working with outlines.

The view you use has no effect on the contents of your document or on the way it will look when printed. They affect only the way the document appears on-screen.

## Normal View

Normal view is suitable for most editing tasks; it is the view you will probably use most often. This is Word's default view. All special formatting is visible on-screen, including different font sizes, italic, boldface, and other enhancements. The screen display of your document is essentially identical to how the document will appear when printed. However, Word does not display certain aspects of the page layout, which makes it easier and quicker for you to edit. For example, you do not see headers and footers or multiple columns.

 To select Normal view, click **View**, **Normal** or click the **Normal View** button at the left end of the horizontal scroll bar. Figure 6.1 shows a document in Normal view.

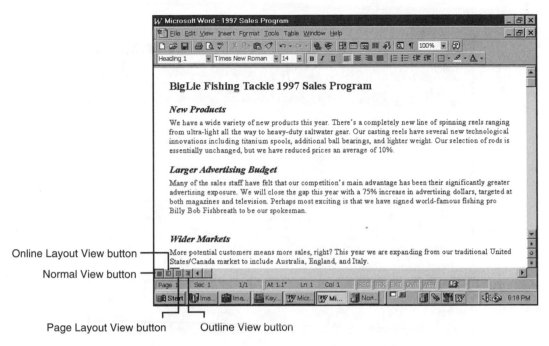

Online Layout View button ——

Normal View button ——

Page Layout View button          Outline View button

**Figure 6.1**   A document displayed in Normal view.

# Page Layout View

Page Layout view displays your document exactly as it will print. Headers, footers, and all other details of the page layout appear on-screen. You can edit in Page Layout view; it's ideal for fine-tuning the details of page composition. Be aware, however, that the additional computer processing required makes display changes relatively slow in Page Layout view, particularly when you have a complex page layout.

**TIP**   **Sneak Preview**   Use Page Layout view to see what your printed document will look like before you actually print. The Print Preview feature (File, Print Preview) is preferred for previewing entire pages.

Click **View**, **Page Layout** (or click the **Page Layout View** button) to switch to Page Layout view. Figure 6.2 shows a sample document in Page Layout view.

Header

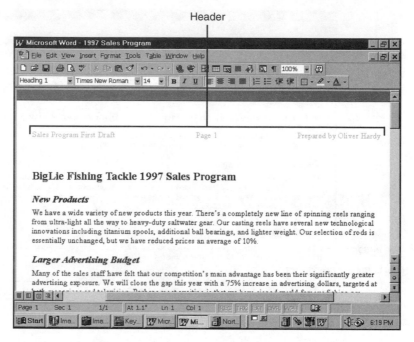

**Figure 6.2**  A document in Page Layout view displays the header.

# Online Layout View

Online Layout view is optimal for reading and editing a document on-screen. Legibility is increased by using larger fonts; displaying shorter lines of text; hiding headers, footers, and similar elements; and basing the layout on the screen as opposed to the printed page. Also, the document map is displayed on the left side of the screen (the document map is covered later in this lesson). The screen display will not match the final printed appearance. Online Layout view is ideal for editing the document text, but is not suited for working with page layout or graphics.

TIP    **Content Editing**  Use Online Layout view when editing the document's contents, not the appearance.

Click **View**, **Online Layout** (or click the **Online Layout View** button) to switch to Online Layout view.

When you're in Online Layout view, the horizontal scroll bar and its View buttons are hidden. You must use the **View** menu commands to switch to a different view. Figure 6.3 shows a document in Online Layout view.

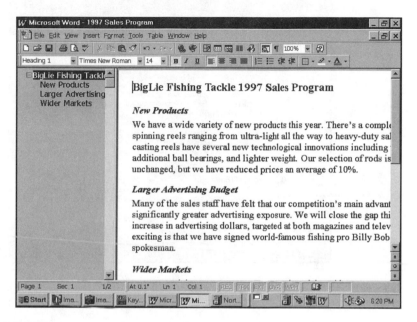

**Figure 6.3** A document displayed in Online Layout view.

# Outline View

Use Outline view to create outlines and to examine the structure of a document. Figure 6.4 shows a document in Outline view. In this view, you can choose to view only your document headings, thus hiding all subordinate text. You can quickly promote, demote, or move document headings along with subordinate text to a new location. For this view to be useful, you need to assign heading styles to the document headings, a technique you'll learn about in Lesson 12.

Click **View**, **Outline** to switch to Outline view, or click the **Outline View** button at the left end of the horizontal scroll bar.

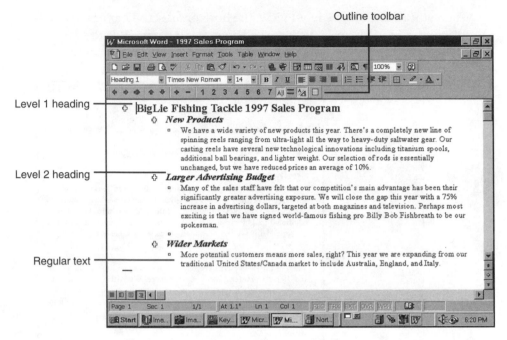

Outline toolbar

Level 1 heading

Level 2 heading

Regular text

**Figure 6.4**  A document displayed in Outline view.

# Draft Font View

Draft Font view is a display option you can apply in both Normal and Outline views. As you can see in Figure 6.5, Draft Font view uses a single generic font for all text; it indicates special formatting by underlining or boldface. Graphics display as empty boxes. Draft Font view provides the fastest editing and screen display, and it is particularly useful when editing the content of documents that contain a lot of fancy formatting and graphics. This view is ideal when you're concentrating on the contents of your document and not on its appearance.

Follow these steps to turn Draft Font view on or off:

1. Click **Tools**, **Options** to open the Options dialog box.

2. If necessary, click the **View** tab to display the View options.

3. Click the **Draft Font** check box to turn it on or off.

4. Click **OK**.

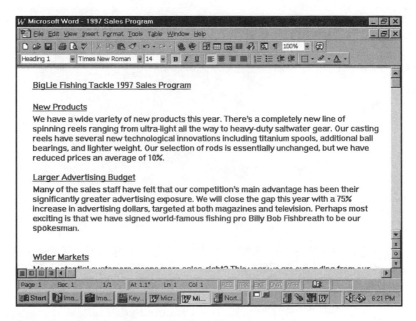

**Figure 6.5** A document displayed in Draft Font view.

# Full Screen View

Full Screen view provides the maximum amount of screen real estate to display your document contents. In Full Screen view, the title bar, menu, toolbars, status bar, and all other Word elements are hidden, and your document occupies the entire screen. You use Full Screen view in combination with other views. Thus you can use Full Screen view in Normal View, Page Layout View, and so on. You can enter and edit text in this view and select from the menus using the usual keyboard commands.

To turn on Full Screen view, click **View**, **Full Screen**. To turn off Full Screen view, select **View**, **Full Screen** again (using the keyboard) or click the **Close Full Screen** box that appears in the lower-right corner of the screen.

# Zooming the Screen

The Zoom command lets you control the size of your document on-screen. You can enlarge it to facilitate reading small fonts, and you can decrease it to view an entire page at one time. Click **View**, **Zoom** to open the Zoom dialog box (see Figure 6.6).

**111**

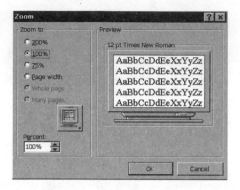

**Figure 6.6**  The Zoom dialog box.

The following options are available in the Zoom dialog box. As you make selections, the Preview area shows you what the selected zoom setting will look like.

- Select **200%**, **100%**, or **75%** to zoom to the indicated magnification. 200% is twice normal size, 75% is three-quarters normal size, and so on.
- Enter a custom magnification percentage of 10–200% in the **Percent** text box.
- Select **Page Width** to scale the display to fit the entire page width on-screen.
- Select **Whole Page** to scale the display to fit the entire page, vertically and horizontally, on-screen.
- Select **Many Pages** to display two or more pages at the same time. Click the **Monitor** button under the Many Pages option, and then drag to specify how many pages to display.

The Whole Page and Many Pages options are available only if you are viewing the document in Page Layout view.

 TIP  **Quick Zoom**  You can quickly change the zoom setting by clicking the **Zoom** drop-down arrow on the Standard toolbar and selecting the desired zoom setting from the list.

# Using the Document Map

The Document Map is a separate pane that displays your document's headings. You do not edit in the Document Map; rather, you use it to quickly move around your document. The Document Map is displayed automatically when you switch to Online Layout view. You can also display it in other views by clicking **View**, **Document Map**. Figure 6.7 shows a document with the map displayed.

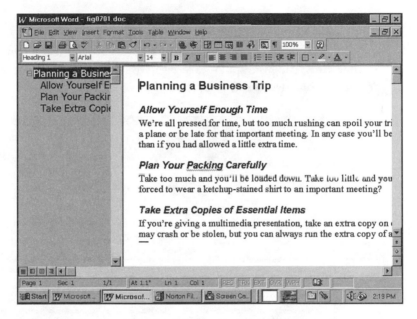

**Figure 6.7**   The Document Map is displayed to the left of the work area.

To use the Document Map, click the desired map heading. The main document window scrolls to that location in the document. You can control the width of the map display by dragging the border between the map and the document to the desired location. Dragging the border to the left edge of the screen has the same effect as turning the Document Map off.

# Splitting the Screen

Word lets you split the work area into two panels, one above the other, so you can view different parts of one document at the same time. Each panel scrolls independently and has its own scroll bars. Figure 6.8 shows a document displayed on a split screen. Editing changes that you make in either panel affect the document. These steps walk you through splitting the screen:

1. Select **Window**, **Split** or press **Ctrl+Alt+S**. Word displays a horizontal split line across the middle of the work area.

2. To accept two equal size panes, click with the left mouse button or press **Enter**. To create different size panes, move the mouse until the split line is in the desired location, and then click or press **Enter**.

When working with a split screen, you move the editing cursor from one pane to the other by clicking with the mouse. To change the pane sizes, point at the split line and drag it to the new location. To remove the split and return to regular view, drag the split line to either the top or the bottom of the work area, or select **Windows**, **Remove Split**.

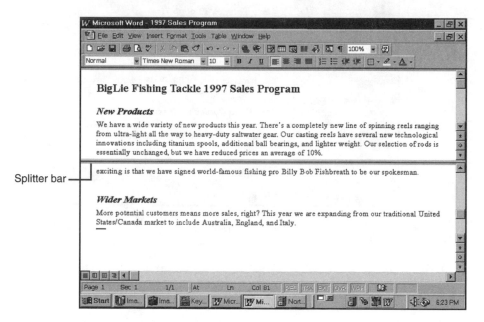

**Figure 6.8** Viewing a document in split screen view.

 **TIP** **Quick Split** You can quickly split the screen by dragging the splitter bar, located just above the up arrow on the vertical toolbar (refer to Figure 6.8).

In this lesson, you learned how to control Word's screen display. In the next lesson, you'll learn how to print and fax your documents.

# Printing, Mailing, and Faxing Your Document

*In this lesson, you learn how to print your document, and how to send a document via e-mail or fax.*

## Printing Using the Default Settings

It's very simple to print using the default settings. This means to print a single copy of the entire document on the default Windows printer. This is all you have to do:

1. Click **File, Print** or click the **Print** button on the Standard toolbar. The Print dialog box appears (see Figure 7.1).
2. Click **OK**, and Word prints the document.

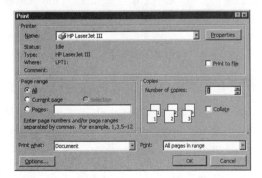

**Figure 7.1** The Print dialog box.

**TIP**  **Another Way to Print**  You can also press **Ctrl+P** to print using the defaults without going to the Print dialog box.

**Printer Not Working?**  Refer to your Microsoft Windows and printer documentation for help. If you're using a network printer, see your network administrator.

CAUTION

# Printing Multiple Copies

With the options in the Print dialog box, you can print more than one copy of a document, and you can specify that the copies be collated. To do either of those, follow these steps:

1. Click **File, Print** or click the **Print** button on the Standard toolbar. The Print dialog box appears.

2. In the **Number of Copies** box (refer to Figure 7.1), enter the desired number of copies. Or click the increment arrows to set the desired value.

3. Click the **Collate** check box to turn that feature on or off.

4. Click **OK**.

**More Than One Printer?**  If you have two or more printers installed, you can select the one to use by clicking the **Name** drop-down arrow at the top of the Print dialog box and selecting the desired printer from the list.

CAUTION

# Printing Part of a Document

Most often you will want to print all of a document. You can, however, print just part of a document, ranging from a single sentence to a range of pages. Follow these steps to print a smaller portion:

1. To print a section of text, select the text. To print a single page, move the cursor to that page.

2. Click **File, Print** or click the **Print** button on the Standard toolbar. The Print dialog box appears.

**3.** In the Page Range area, specify what you want printed:

- Choose **Selection** to print the selected text.

- Choose **Current Page** to print the page containing the cursor.

- **Choose Pages** to print specified pages, and then enter the page numbers in the text box. For example, enter **1–3** to print pages 1 through 3, or enter **2,4** to print pages 2 and 4.

**4.** Click **OK**.

 TIP **Printing Properties** To print a document's properties instead of its text, click the **Print What** drop-down arrow in the Print dialog box and select **Document Properties** from the list.

# Changing Your Print Options

Word offers a number of printing options that you may need to use at times. You can print only the odd-numbered pages or the even-numbered pages. This option is useful to create two-sided output on a standard one-sided printer: print the odd-numbered pages, flip the printed pages over and place them back in the printer's paper tray, and then print the even-numbered pages. You select which pages to print by clicking the **Print** drop-down arrow in the Print dialog box and selecting **Odd Pages** or **Even Pages** from the list. Select **All Pages in Range** to return to printing all pages.

You can set other print options in the Print Options dialog box (shown in Figure 7.2). To display this dialog box, open the Print dialog box as described previously and click the **Options** button.

The following list outlines the options you will use most often.

- **Draft Output** Produces draft output that prints faster, but may lack some graphics and formatting (depending on your specific printer).
- **Reverse Print Order** Prints pages in last-to-first order. This setting produces collated output on printers that have face-up output.
- **Background Printing** Permits you to continue working on the document while printing is in progress. This setting uses additional memory and usually results in slower printing.

**Figure 7.2**  The Print Options dialog box.

- **Update Fields**   Updates the contents of all document fields before printing.
- **Document Properties**   Prints the document's properties in addition to its contents.
- **Comments**   Includes document comments in the printout.

After setting the desired printing options, click **OK** to return to the Print dialog box.

TIP   **Save Paper!**   Use Page Layout view or Print Preview to check the appearance of your document before you print it.

# Faxing a Document

If your system is set up for fax, you can fax a document directly to one or more recipients without having to print a paper copy and feed it into a standard fax machine. This capability saves both time and paper. Follow these steps to fax the current document:

   **1.** Click **File, Send To, Fax Recipient**. Word starts the Fax Wizard.

2. The Fax Wizard takes you through the steps of preparing the fax, choosing a cover page, and selecting recipients. For each step, enter the requested information and click **Next**.

3. After the final step, click **Finish**.

4. If you requested a cover sheet, Word displays it. You can make any additions or changes to the cover sheet at this time.

5. Click the **Send Fax Now** button to send the fax.

**CAUTION**

**No Fax Option?**   If the Fax Recipient option is not available on your Send To submenu, it means that your system has not been set up for faxing.

**TIP**   **Another Way to Fax**   You can also fax a document by selecting Microsoft Fax (or the name of whatever fax program you use) as the destination printer in the Print dialog box and then printing in the usual fashion.

# Mailing a Document

If you have Microsoft Messaging or another e-mail program installed on your system, you can send a document directly to a mail recipient. Here are the steps to take:

1. Click **File**, **Send To**, **Mail Recipient**.

2. Depending on the specifics of your system, Word may ask you to select a profile setting. Generally, the default setting is the one you should select.

3. Next you will see your usual New Message window. The appearance of this window will vary depending on the mail system you are using, but it will be the same mail form that you use for other e-mail messages. Figure 7.3 shows the New Message window used by the Windows Messaging system. The document will already be inserted in the message as an icon. Add text to the message if desired.

4. Fill in the **To...** line of the message with the recipient's address.

5. When the message is complete, click the **Send** button.

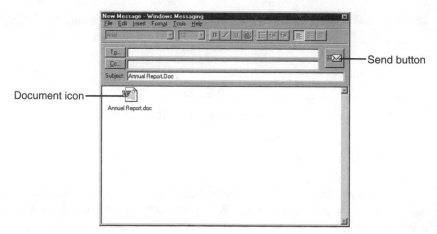

Document icon ─────

Send button ─────

**Figure 7.3**  A new message with the document inserted as an icon.

When the recipient receives your message, he or she will be able to double-click the document icon to open the document in Word for printing, editing, and so on.

In this lesson, you learned how to print your document and how to send it as a fax or as an e-mail message. The next lesson shows you how to use fonts, borders, and shading in your document.

# Fonts, Borders, and Shading

8

*In this lesson, you learn how to use different fonts in your document and how to apply borders and shading.*

## Font Terminology

Word offers you a huge assortment of fonts to use in your documents. Each font has a specific *typeface*, which determines the appearance of the characters. Typefaces are identified by names such as Arial, Courier, and Times New Roman. Each font also has a size, which is specified in *points*. There are 72 points in an inch, so a 36-point font would have its largest characters 1/2 inch tall. Most documents use font sizes in the 8- to 14-point range, but larger and smaller sizes are available for headings and other special needs.

## Selecting a Font

You can change the font of text that already has been typed by first selecting the text. To specify the font for text you are about to type, simply move the cursor to the desired location. Then follow these steps to choose a font for the selected text or the text you're about to type:

1. Click **Format**, **Font** to open the Font dialog box shown in Figure 8.1.
2. The Font text box displays the name of the current font. Scroll through the **Font** list box and select a new font name.

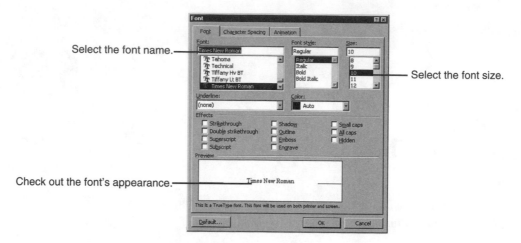

Select the font name.

Select the font size.

Check out the font's appearance.

**Figure 8.1**  The Font dialog box.

**3.** The Size text box displays the current font size. Select a new size from the **Size** list box or type a number in the text box. The Preview box shows the appearance of the selected font.

**4.** Click **OK** to enter your settings.

**TIP**  **Quick Select**  If you want to change the font for a whole document, remember that you can select the entire document by pressing **Ctrl+A**.

You can quickly select a font name and size using the Formatting toolbar. The Font list box and the Font Size list box display the name and size of the current font. You can change the font by clicking the drop-down arrow of either list and making a selection. Note that in the Font list, the fonts you have used recently appear at the top.

**TIP**  **Keyboard Happy?**  From the keyboard, you can access the Font and Font Size lists on the toolbar by pressing **Ctrl+Shift+F** or **Ctrl+Shift+P** (respectively) followed by the down arrow key.

# Using Boldface, Italics, and Underlining

You can apply bold, italics, or underlining to any of Word's fonts. You can also use two or three of these effects in combination. As you can with other formatting, you can apply these effects to existing text by first selecting the text, or you can apply them to text you are about to type.

 The quickest way to assign boldface, italics, or underlining is with the buttons on the Formatting toolbar. Click a button to turn the corresponding attribute on; click it again to turn it off. When the cursor is at a location where one of these attributes is turned on, the corresponding toolbar button appears to be pressed in.

You can also assign font attributes using the Font dialog box. (If you want to use underlining other than the default single underline, you must use this method.) Here's how to use the dialog box:

1. Click **Format**, **Font** to open the Font dialog box.
2. Under Font Style, select **Bold**, **Italic**, or **Bold Italic**. Select **Regular** to return to normal text.
3. Click the **Underline** drop-down arrow and select the desired underline style from the list; or select **None** to remove underlining.
4. Click **OK**.

 **TIP**  **A New Default**  To change the default font used in documents based on the Normal template, open the Font dialog box, select the desired font and attributes, and click the **Default** button.

# Applying Special Font Effects

Word has a number of special font effects that you can use. These include superscript and subscript, strikethrough, and several graphics effects (such as shadow and outline). You can also specify that text be hidden, which means it will not display on-screen or be printed.

To assign special font effects to selected text or text you are about to type, follow these steps:

**123**

**1.** Click **Format, Font** to open the Font dialog box.

**2.** In the Effects area, select the effects you want. To turn on an effect, click to place an X in the check box. To turn off an effect, click to remove the X from the check box. The Preview box shows you what the font will look like with the selected effects.

**3.** When you're satisfied with your settings, click **OK**.

**Where's That Hidden Text?**   To locate hidden text, click **Tools**, **Options**, click the **View** tab, and then select the **Hidden Text** option. Word displays hidden text with a dotted underline. You can also display hidden text by clicking the **Show/Hide ¶** button.

CAUTION

# Displaying Borders

Word's Borders command lets you improve the appearance of your documents by displaying borders around selected text. Figure 8.2 shows examples of the use of borders (and it illustrates shading, covered in the section "Applying Shading" later in this lesson).

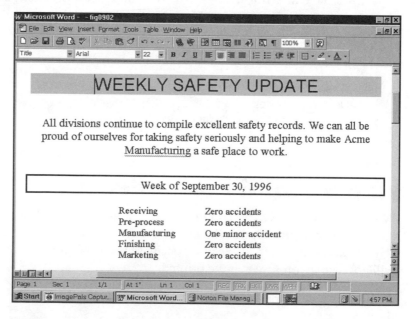

**Figure 8.2**   A document with borders and shading.

You can apply a border to selected text or to individual paragraphs. To put a border around text, select the text. For a paragraph, place the cursor anywhere in the paragraph. The quickest way to apply a border is to use the Border button on the Formatting toolbar. Click the **Border** drop-down arrow to view a palette of available border settings, and then click the desired border diagram. Click the **No Borders** diagram to remove borders.

If you need more control over the appearance of your borders, you must use the Borders and Shading dialog box (see Figure 8.3). To open this dialog box, click **Format**, **Borders and Shading**, and then click the **Borders** tab if necessary.

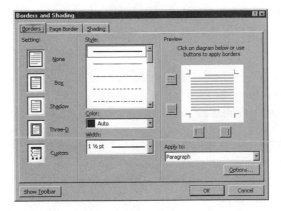

**Figure 8.3**  The Borders tab of the Borders and Shading dialog box.

The steps for creating a border are as follows:

1. Select the general appearance of the borders you want by clicking the corresponding icon in the Setting area (the Custom setting is explained below).

2. In the **Style** list, select the desired line style, color, and width.

3. In the Preview area, click the buttons or click directly on the page diagram to add or remove borders from the four sides of the text.

4. If you selected text before opening the dialog box, use the **Apply To** list to specify whether the border is to be displayed around the selected text or the current paragraph.

5. Click **OK**, and Word puts your settings into effect.

**125**

The normal border settings apply the same line style (solid, dotted, and so on) to all four sides of the border box. To create a custom border that combines different styles, use these steps:

1. Click the **Custom** icon.

2. In the **Style** list, select the line style, color, and width for one side of the border box.

3. In the Preview area, click the button or click directly on the page diagram to specify the side of the border box to which you want to apply the style you selected in step 2.

4. Repeat steps 2 and 3 to specify the style for the other three sides of the border box.

5. Select **OK**.

You can also place borders around entire pages in your document. To do so, click the **Page Border** tab of the Borders and Shading dialog box. This tab looks and operates just as the Borders tab does in terms of specifying the border's appearance. The only difference is specifying where the border will be applied, which is done with the options in the **Apply To** list. You have four choices:

- Whole Document
- This Section
- This Section - First Page Only
- This Section - All Except First Page

You'll learn how to divide a document into sections in Lesson 11.

# Applying Shading

You can use shading to display a background color under text (such as black text on a light gray background). Figure 8.2 shows an example of shading. You can apply shading to selected text or to individual paragraphs. Shading can be made up of a fill color, a pattern color, or a combination of both.

Here's how to apply shading:

1. Select the text to be shaded, or position the cursor anywhere in the paragraph to shade an entire paragraph.

2. Click **Format**, **Borders and Shading** to open the Borders and Shading dialog box. If necessary, click the **Shading** tab (see Figure 8.4).

**3.** To use a fill color, select it from the palette in the Fill area of the dialog box. To use only a pattern color, click the **None** button.

**4.** To use a pattern color, select its style and color from the lists in the Patterns section of the dialog box. To use only a fill color, select the **Clear** style. You can view the appearance of the selected settings in the Preview area of the dialog box.

**5.** If you selected text before opening the dialog box, use the **Apply To** list to specify whether the fill should apply to the selected text or the current paragraph.

**6.** Click **OK**.

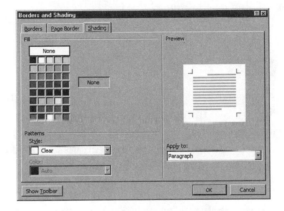

**Figure 8.4**  The Shading tab of the Borders and Shading dialog box.

TIP  **Printing Color?**  Of course, color shading will print in color only if you have a color printer. You need to perform test printouts of pages with shading because how Word displays shading on-screen is often quite different from the final printed results.

In this lesson, you learned how to use fonts, borders, and shading in your documents. In the next lesson, you learn how to control indentation and justification of text, and how to control line breaks.

# Indents and Justification

*In this lesson, you learn how to set the indentation and justification of text in your document, and how to control line breaks.*

## Indentation

The distance between your text and the left and right edges of the page is controlled by two things: the left and right page margins and the text indentation. Margins (which are covered in detail in Lesson 11) are usually changed only for entire documents or large sections of a document. For smaller sections of text, such as individual lines and paragraphs, you will use indentation.

**Indentation**   The distance between a paragraph's text and the margins for the entire document. For example, if the left margin is set at 1" and a particular paragraph has a 1" indentation, that paragraph starts 2" from the edge of the paper.

The easiest way to set indents is by using the Ruler and your mouse. To display the Ruler (or hide it), click **View**, **Ruler**. The numbers on the Ruler indicate the space from the left margin in inches. Figure 9.1 shows the Ruler and identifies the various elements you use to set indents. In addition, the sample text in the figure illustrates the various indent options.

**Rapid Ruler**   Quickly display the Ruler by positioning the mouse pointer at the top edge of the work area for a moment. When you finish using the Ruler, move the mouse pointer away, and the Ruler is automatically hidden again.

First line indent  Other lines indent  Decrease Indent button  Increase Indent button

All lines indent

Right indent

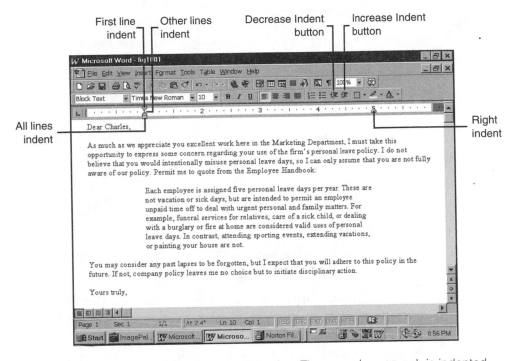

**Figure 9.1** Use the Ruler to set text indentation. The second paragraph is indented one inch from both the right and left margins.

Indentation applies to individual paragraphs. To set indentation for one paragraph, position the cursor anywhere in the paragraph. For more than one paragraph, select those paragraphs. (Otherwise, the new indents will apply only to new paragraphs that you type from the insertion point forward.) Then drag the indent markers on the Ruler to the desired positions. As you drag, a dotted vertical line appears, stretching down through the document to show the new indent's location. Use these guidelines when setting paragraph indentation:

- To change the indent of the first line of a paragraph, drag the **First Line Indent** marker to the desired position.

- To change the indent of all lines of a paragraph except the first one, drag the **Other Lines Indent** marker to the desired position (this is called a *hanging indent*).

- To change the indent of all lines of a paragraph, drag the **All Lines Indent** marker to the desired position.

- To change the indent of the right edge of the paragraph, drag the **Right Indent** marker to the desired position.

You can also quickly increase or decrease the left indent for the current paragraph in 1/2-inch increments by clicking the **Increase Indent** or **Decrease Indent** buttons on the Formatting toolbar. And undoubtedly, the quickest way to indent the first line of a paragraph is to position the cursor at the start of the line and press **Tab**.

**Hanging Indent**   A paragraph in which the first line is indented less than all the other lines.

## Setting Indents with the Paragraphs Dialog Box

Word also gives you the option of setting indents using the Paragraphs dialog box. These steps walk you through that process.

1. Click **Format**, **Paragraph** to open the Paragraph dialog box. Then click the **Indents and Spacing** tab if necessary to display the indents and spacing options (see Figure 9.2).

2. In the Indentation area, click the increment arrows for the **Left** and **Right** text boxes to increase or decrease the indentation settings. To set a first line or a hanging indent, select the indent type in the **Special** drop-down list and enter the indent amount in the **By** text box. The sample page in the dialog box illustrates how the current settings will appear.

3. Click **OK**, and Word applies the new settings to any selected paragraphs or to new text.

**Figure 9.2**   Setting indents in the Paragraph dialog box.

# Setting Text Justification

Justification, sometimes called alignment, refers to the manner in which the left and right ends of lines of text are aligned. Word offers four justification options:

- Left justification aligns the left ends of lines.
- Right justification aligns the right ends of lines.
- Full justification aligns both the left and right ends of lines.
- Center justification centers lines between the left and right margins.

 **Full Justification** Both the left and right edges or paragraphs are aligned. This is accomplished by inserting extra space between words and letters in the text as needed.

Figure 9.3 illustrates the justification options. To change the justification for one or more paragraphs, first select the paragraphs to change. Then click one of the justification buttons on the Formatting toolbar. The toolbar button corresponding to the current paragraph's justification setting appears to be pressed in.

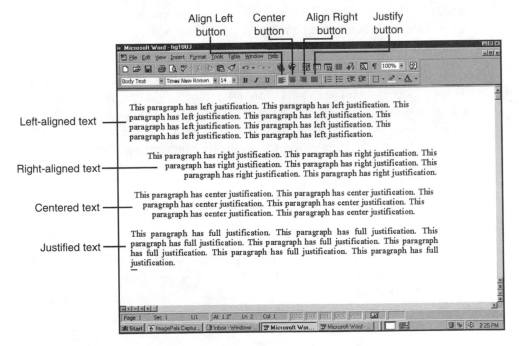

**Figure 9.3** Click these buttons to set text justification.

131

If you prefer to use a dialog box to change justification, select the paragraphs and then use these steps:

1. Click **Format**, **Paragraph** to open the Paragraph dialog box, and click the **Indents and Spacing** tab if necessary.

2. Click the **Alignment** drop-down arrow and select the desired alignment from the list.

3. Select **OK**.

# Controlling Line Breaks

The word wrap feature automatically breaks each line in a paragraph when it reaches the right margin. Word offers a couple of methods for controlling the way lines break. You can prevent a line break from occurring between two specific words to ensure that the words always remain together on the same line. These methods can be particularly useful when you modify indents and justification because this often changes where individual lines break.

Word's default is to break lines as needed at spaces or hyphens. To prevent a line break, you must insert a nonbreaking space or a nonbreaking hyphen instead. To insert a nonbreaking hyphen, press **Ctrl+Shift+- (hyphen)**. To insert a nonbreaking space, press **Ctrl+Shift+Spacebar**.

You can also use an optional hyphen to specify where a word can be broken, if necessary. This is useful with long words that may fall at the end of the line; if word wrap moves the long word to the next line, there will be an unsightly gap at the end of the previous line. An optional hyphen remains hidden unless the word extends past the right margin. Then the hyphen appears, and only the part of the word after the hyphen wraps to the new line. To insert an optional hyphen, press **Ctrl+- (hyphen)**.

Finally, you can insert a line break without starting a new paragraph by pressing **Shift+Enter**.

In this lesson, you learned how to set the indentation and justification of text in your document, and how to control line breaks. The next lesson shows you how to work with tabs and line spacing.

# Tabs and Line Spacing

*In this lesson, you learn how to use and set tab stops, and how to change line spacing.*

## What Are Tabs?

*Tabs* provide a way for you to control the indentation and vertical alignment of text in your document. When you press the **Tab** key, Word inserts a tab in the document and moves the cursor (and any text to the right of it) to the next tab stop. By default, Word has tab stops at 0.5-inch intervals across the width of the page. You can modify the location of tab stops and control the way text aligns at a tab stop.

### Types of Tab Stops

Word offers four types of tab stops, each of which aligns text differently:

- **Left-aligned**   The left edge of text aligns at the tab stop. Word's default tab stops are left-aligned.
- **Right-aligned**   The right edge of text aligns at the tab stop.
- **Center-aligned**   The text is centered at the tab stop.
- **Decimal-aligned**   The decimal point (period) is aligned at the tab stop. You use this type of tab for aligning columns of numbers.

Figure 10.1 illustrates the effects of the four tab alignment options and shows the four markers that appear on the Ruler to indicate the position of tab stops.

Left-aligned tab stop     Center-aligned tab stop     Right-aligned tab stop     Decimal-aligned tab stop

Click here until it shows the marker for the type of tab you want.

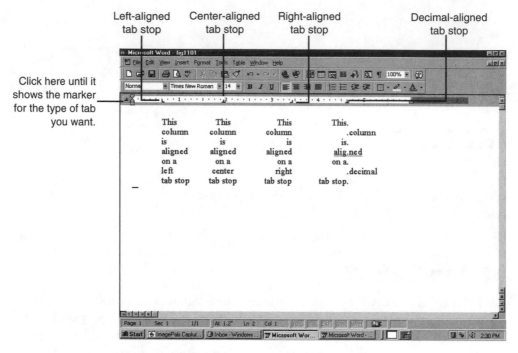

**Figure 10.1** The four tab stop alignment options.

# Changing the Default Tab Stops

Default tab stops affect all paragraphs for which you have not set custom tab stops (covered in the next section). You cannot delete the default tab stops, but you can change the spacing between them. The default tab stop spacing affects the entire document. Here are the steps to follow:

1. Click **Format**, **Tabs** to display the Tabs dialog box, shown in Figure 10.2.

2. In the **Default Tab Stops** box, click the increment arrows to increase or decrease the spacing between default tab stops.

3. Click **OK**.

TIP    **Good-Bye Tab**    To effectively "delete" the default tab stops, set the spacing between them to a value larger than the page width.

**Figure 10.2**   The Tabs dialog box.

# Creating Custom Tab Stops

If the default tab stops are not suited to your needs, you can add custom tab stops. The number, spacing, and type of custom tab stops is totally up to you. Use these steps to set custom tab stops:

**1.** Select the paragraphs that will have custom tabs. If no text is selected, the new tabs will affect the paragraph containing the cursor and new text you type.

**2.** Click the tab symbol at the left end of the Ruler until it displays the marker for the type of tab you want to insert (refer to Figure 10.1).

**3.** Point at the approximate tab stop location on the Ruler, and press and hold the left mouse button. A dashed vertical line extends down through the document to show the tab stop position relative to your text.

**4.** Move the mouse left or right until the tab stop is at the desired location.

**5.** Release the mouse button.

**TIP**   **No Ruler?**   If your Ruler is not displayed, click **View**, **Ruler** or position the mouse pointer near the top edge of the work area for a few seconds.

When you add a custom tab stop, all of the default tab stops to the left are temporarily inactivated. This ensures that the custom tab stop will take precedence. If custom tab stops have been defined for the current paragraph, the custom tabs are displayed on the Ruler; otherwise, the default tab stops are displayed.

# Moving and Deleting Custom Tab Stops

Follow these steps to move a custom tab stop to a new position:

1. Point at the tab stop marker on the Ruler.
2. Press and hold the left mouse button.
3. Drag the tab stop to the new position.
4. Release the mouse button.

To delete a custom tab stop, follow the same steps, but in step 3, drag the tab stop marker off the Ruler. Then release the mouse button.

# Changing Line Spacing

Line spacing controls the amount of vertical space between lines of text. Different spacing is appropriate for different kinds of documents. If you want to print your document on as few pages as possible, use single line spacing to position lines close together. In contrast, a document that will later be edited by hand should be printed with wide line spacing to provide space for the editor to write comments.

Word offers a variety of line spacing options. If you change line spacing, it affects the selected text; if there is no text selected, it affects the current paragraph and text you type at the insertion point.

Follow these steps to change line spacing:

1. Click **Format**, **Paragraph** to open the Paragraph dialog box. If necessary, click the **Indents and Spacing** tab (see Figure 10.3).
2. Click the **Line Spacing** drop-down arrow and select the desired spacing option from the list. The **Single**, **1.5 Lines**, and **Double** settings are self-explanatory. The other settings are:
    - **Exactly**   Space between lines will be exactly the value—in points—that you enter in the **At** text box.
    - **At Least**   Space between lines will be at least the value you enter in the **At** text box; Word will increase the spacing as needed if the line contains large characters.
    - **Multiple**   Changes spacing by the factor you enter in the **At** text box. For example, enter **1.5** to increase spacing by one and a half times, or enter **2** to double the line spacing.

**CAUTION**

**Underline Missing?** If you set line spacing using the Exactly option at the same value as your font size, underline character formatting will display only for the last line of each paragraph.

**3.** To add spacing before the first line or after the last line of the paragraph, enter the desired space (in points), or click the arrows in the **Before** and **After** text boxes.

**4.** Click **OK**.

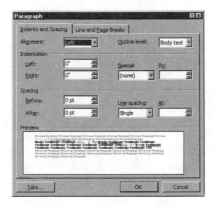

**Figure 10.3** The Paragraph dialog box with the Indents and Spacing options displayed.

In this lesson, you learned how to use and set tab stops, and how to change line spacing. The next lesson shows you how to use margins, pages, and sections.

# Margins, Pages, and Sections

11

*In this lesson, you learn how to use document sections, how to set page margins, how to work with different paper sizes, and how to specify the source of paper used in printing.*

## Using Section Breaks

Word gives you the option of breaking your document into two or more *sections*, each of which can have its own page formatting. You need to use sections only when you want some aspect of page layout, such as page margins (covered later in this lesson) or columns, to apply to only part of the document. The default is for page layout settings such as these to apply to the entire document.

Word offers three types of section breaks. They have the same effect in terms of controlling page layout, but differ as to where the text that comes after the break is placed:

- **Next Page**   The new section begins at the top of the next page. This is useful for section breaks that coincide with major breaks in a document, such as a new chapter starting.
- **Continuous**   The new section begins on the same page as the preceding section. This is useful for a section that has a different number of columns from the preceding one but is still part of the same page. An example would be a newsletter: the title runs across the top of the page in one column, and then after a section break, the body of the newsletter appears below the title in three columns.
- **Odd Page or Even Page**   The new section begins on the next even- or odd-numbered page. This is useful when a section break coincides with a major break (like a chapter) in a document where each chapter must start on an odd page (or an even page).

In Normal view, Word marks the location of section breaks by displaying a double horizontal line with the label **Section Break** followed by the type of break. These markers do not appear in Page Layout view or in printouts.

To insert a section break, follow these steps:

**1.** Click **Insert**, **Break** to open the Break dialog box.

**2.** Select the desired type of section break (as described in the previous list).

**3.** Click **OK**.

A section break mark is just like any character in your document. To delete a section break, place the cursor right before it and press **Delete,** or place the cursor right after it and press **Backspace**. Each section break marker holds the settings for the text that comes before it, so when you delete a section break, text in the section before the break becomes part of the section that was after the break, and it assumes the page layout formatting of that section.

# Inserting Manual Page Breaks

When text reaches the bottom margin of a page, Word automatically starts a new page and continues the text at the top of that page. However, you can manually insert page breaks to start a new page at any desired location. Here's how:

**1.** Click **Insert**, **Break** to open the Break dialog box.

**2.** Select **Page Break**.

**3.** Click **OK**.

 **TIP**  **Quick Breaks**  You can enter a page break by pressing **Ctrl+Enter**. To start a new line without starting a new paragraph, press **Shift+Enter**.

A page break appears in the document as a single horizontal line. Like section break markers, page break markers do not appear in Page Layout view or in printouts. To delete a page break, move the cursor to the line containing the break and press **Delete**.

# Setting Page Margins

The page margins control the amount of white space between your text and the edges of the page. Each page has four margins: left, right, top, and bottom. When you change page margins, the new settings will affect the entire document or, if you have inserted one or more section breaks, the current section.

The easiest way to set page margins is with your mouse and the Ruler. You can work visually instead of thinking in terms of inches or centimeters. To display the Ruler, click **View**, **Ruler** or position the mouse pointer near the top edge of the work area.

You can use the Ruler to change margins only while working in Page Layout view (click **View**, **Page Layout**). In Page Layout view, Word displays both a horizontal ruler at the top of the page and a vertical ruler on the left edge of the page. This permits you to set both the left/right and the top/bottom margins using a Ruler.

On each ruler, the white bar shows the current margin settings, as shown in Figure 11.1. To change the left or right margin, point at the margin marker on the horizontal ruler, at the left or right end of the white bar; the mouse pointer will change to a two-headed arrow. Then drag the margin to the new position. For the top or bottom margin, follow the same procedure using the vertical ruler.

 **Margins**   The margins are the distances between the text and the edges of the page.

Note that the margin symbols—not the small triangular buttons—on the horizontal ruler are the vertical edges of the white margin bar. The small triangular buttons are the indent markers, which you learned about in Lesson 9. If your mouse pointer has changed to a two-headed arrow, you know you have found the margin symbol.

 **TIP**   **Changing Margins**   Margins apply to the entire section, unlike indents (which apply to individual paragraphs). To change the margins for only a portion of a document, insert a section break as described previously in this lesson. You can then specify different margins for each section.

Left margin line

Top margin line

**Figure 11.1** The Ruler displays a white bar showing the current margin settings.

**Can't Change Margins?** Be sure you're in Page Layout view or the rulers won't work for changing margins. (You can, however, drag the indent markers on the ruler in Normal view, as you learned in Lesson 9.)

CAUTION

You can also set the page margins using a dialog box. Use this method when you don't want to use the mouse or need to enter precise margin values. (You also don't have to switch to Page Layout view to do it.) It gives you more control over where in the document the new margins are applied. Here's how:

1. Click **File**, **Page Setup** to open the Page Setup dialog box.

2. If necessary, click the **Margins** tab to display the margins options shown in Figure 11.2.

3. In the **Top**, **Bottom**, **Left**, and **Right** text boxes, enter the desired margin size (in inches) or click the increment arrows to set the desired value. The Preview shows you the effects of your margin settings.

4. If your document will be bound and you want to leave an extra large margin on one side for the binding, enter the desired width in the **Gutter** text box. This extra space will be added to the left margin of every page or, if you select the **Mirror Margins** check box, it will be added to the left

**141**

margin of odd-numbered pages and the right margin of even-numbered pages (which is useful for binding a document that is printed on both sides of the paper).

5. Click the **Apply To** drop-down arrow and select where the new margins will apply from the list. These are your options:

   - **Whole Document** The new margin settings will apply to the entire document.

   - **This Point Forward** Word will insert a continuous section break at the cursor location and apply the new margins to the new section.

   - **This Section** Margins will be applied to the current document section. This option is not available if you have not broken your document into sections.

6. Click **OK**.

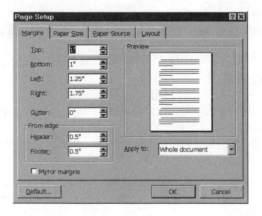

**Figure 11.2** Setting margins in the Page Setup dialog box.

# Controlling Paper Size and Orientation

Word's default is to format documents to fit on standard 8 1/2 × 11-inch letter size paper and to print in portrait orientation, which means the lines of text run parallel to the short edge of the paper. You can specify a different paper size, selecting from several standard paper and envelope sizes or defining a custom paper size. You can also print in landscape orientation, in which the lines of text are parallel to the long edge of the paper.

Follow these steps to specify paper size and orientation:

1. Click **File**, **Page Setup** to open the Page Setup dialog box.
2. If it isn't already on top, click the **Paper Size** tab (see Figure 11.3).
3. Click the **Paper Size** drop-down arrow and select a predefined paper size from the list. Or, enter a custom height and width in the text boxes provided.
4. Select **Portrait** or **Landscape** orientation.
5. Click the **Apply To** drop-down arrow and select the portion of the document to which the new paper setting is to apply:
   - **Whole Document**   The new paper setting will be used for the entire document.
   - **This Point Forward**   Word will insert a continuous section break at the cursor location and apply the new paper settings to the new section.
   - **This Section**   Paper settings will be applied to the current document section. This option is not available if your document has not been broken into sections.
6. Select **OK**.

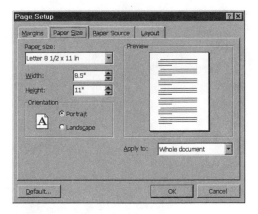

**Figure 11.3**  Setting paper size and orientation.

# Specifying a Paper Source

Some documents require printing on different kinds of paper. For example, with a multipage business letter you may want to print the first page on company letterhead and the other pages on plain paper. Within the limitations of your printer, you can tell Word where it should get the paper for each section of the document. Most laser printers give you two choices: the regular paper tray or manual feed. Advanced printers will have more options, such as two or more paper trays and an envelope feeder.

Use these steps to specify the paper source:

1. Click **File**, **Page Setup** to open the Page Setup dialog box.
2. If it's not on top, click the **Paper Source** tab (see Figure 11.4).
3. In the **First Page** list box, specify the paper source for the first page. The choices available here will depend on your printer model.
4. In the **Other Pages** list box, specify the paper source for the second and subsequent pages.
5. Click the **Apply To** drop-down arrow and select which part of the document the paper source settings are to affect.
6. Select **OK**.

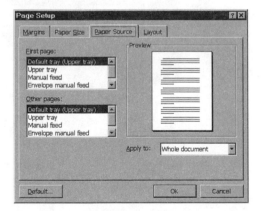

**Figure 11.4** Specifying the paper source.

In this lesson, you learned how to use document sections, how to set page margins, how to work with different paper sizes, and how to specify the source of paper used in printing. In the next lesson, you will learn how to use styles.

# Making the Most of Styles

*In this lesson, you learn how to use styles in your documents.*

## Understanding Styles

Word's styles provide a great deal of power and flexibility when it comes to formatting your document. A *style* is a collection of formatting specifications that has been assigned a name and saved. For example, a given style could specify 14-point Arial font, 1-inch indent, double line spacing, and full justification. After you define a style, you can quickly apply it to any text in your document.

Applying a style is a lot faster than manually applying individual formatting elements, and it has the added advantage of assuring consistency. If you later modify a style definition, all of the text in the document to which that style has been assigned will automatically change to reflect the new style formatting. Word has several predefined styles, and you can create your own.

**TERM**    **What Is a Style?**   A style is a named grouping of paragraph or character formatting that can be reused.

Word has two types of styles:

*Paragraph* styles apply to entire paragraphs and can include all aspects of formatting that affect a paragraph's appearance: font, line spacing, indents, tab stops, borders, and so on. Every paragraph has a style; the default paragraph style is called Normal.

*Character* styles apply to any section of text and can include any formatting that applies to individual characters: font name and size, underlining, boldface, and so on (in other words, any of the formats that you can assign by clicking Format, Font). There is no default character style.

When you apply a character style, the formatting is applied in addition to whatever formatting the text already possesses. For example, if you apply the bold character style to a sentence that is already formatted as italic, the sentence appears in both bold and italic. The uses of styles are covered in this lesson and the next one.

# Assigning a Style to Text

To assign a paragraph style to multiple paragraphs, select the paragraphs. To assign a paragraph style to a single paragraph, place the cursor anywhere in the paragraph. To assign a character style, select the text you want the style to affect. Then follow these steps to apply the desired formatting:

**1.** Click the **Style** drop-down arrow on the Formatting toolbar to see a list of available styles, with each style name displayed in the style's font. Symbols in the list also indicate whether a style is a paragraph or character style, as well as its font size and justification (see Figure 12.1).

**2.** Select the desired style by clicking its name. The style is applied to the specified text.

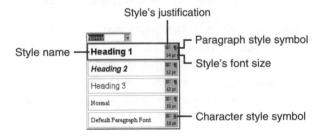

**Figure 12.1**  Select a style from the Style list on the Formatting toolbar.

**TIP**  **Paragraph or Character Style?**  In the Style list, paragraph styles are listed with the paragraph symbol next to them, and character styles are listed with an underlined letter "a" next to them.

To remove a character style from text, select the text and apply the character style **Default Paragraph Font**. This is not really a style; instead it specifies that the formatting defined in the current paragraph style should be used for the text.

# Viewing Style Names

The Style list box displays the name of the style assigned to the text where the insertion point is located. If there is text selected or if the insertion point is in text that has a character style applied, the Style list box displays the character style name. Otherwise, it displays the paragraph style of the current paragraph.

Word can also display the name of the paragraph and character styles assigned to specific text in your document. Follow these steps to see how:

**1.** Press **Shift+F1** or click **Help, What's This?** to activate What's This Help. The mouse cursor displays a question mark.

**2.** Click the text of interest, and Word displays information about the text's assigned style in a balloon (see Figure 12.2).

**3.** Repeat step 2 as needed for other text.

**4.** Press **Esc** when you are done.

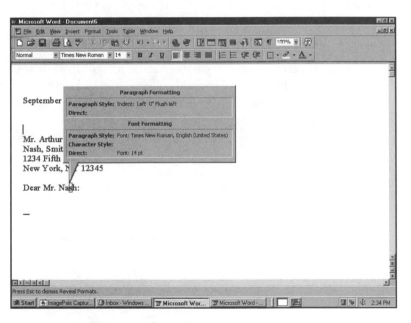

**Figure 12.2**   Displaying text's style information with What's This Help.

# Creating a New Style

You are not limited to using Word's predefined styles. In fact, creating your own styles is an essential part of getting the most out of Word's style capabilities. One way to create a new style is "by example," as described in these steps:

1. Place the insertion point in a paragraph to which you want to apply the new style.

2. Format the paragraph as desired. In other words, apply the formatting you want included in the new style definition.

3. With the insertion point anywhere in the paragraph, click the **Style** list box or press **Ctrl+Shift+S** (both activate the Style list box).

4. Type a name for the new style and press **Enter**.

In step 4, make sure you do not enter the name of an existing style. If you do, that style's formatting will be applied to the paragraph, and the formatting changes you made will be lost. If this happens, you can recover the formatting by clicking **Edit**, **Undo**. Then repeat steps 3 and 4 and give the style a new and unique name.

You can also create a new style by making formatting entries in dialog boxes. You must use this method to create a character style; it is optional for paragraph styles. You can create a new style from scratch, or you can base it on an existing style. If you choose the latter method, the new style will have all of the formatting of the base style plus any additions and changes you make while defining the style. Here are the required steps:

1. Click **Format**, **Style** to open the Style dialog box.

2. Click the **New** button. The New Style dialog box appears (see Figure 12.3).

**Figure 12.3** The New Style dialog box.

3. Click the **Style Type** drop-down arrow and select **Character** or **Paragraph** from the list to indicate the type of style you're creating.

4. Click the **Name** text box and type the name for the new style.

5. If you want to base the new style on an existing style, click the **Based On** drop-down arrow and select the desired base style from the list.

6. If you want the new style to be part of the template that the current document is based on, select the **Add to Template** check box. If this you do not select this check box, the new style will be available only in the current document.

7. (Optional) Select the **Automatically Update** check box if you want Word to add to the style definition all manual formatting changes you make to paragraphs with this style assigned. (This option is available only for paragraph styles.)

8. Click the **Format** button and select **Font** or **Border** to specify the font and/or border of the new style. As you make formatting changes, the Preview box displays an image of what the style will look like, and the Description area provides a description of the style elements.

9. For paragraph styles only, click the **Format** button and select **Paragraph** to set the style's indents and line spacing. Then select **Tabs** to set the new style's tab stops.

10. Click **OK** to return to the Style dialog box.

11. Click **Apply** to assign the new style to the current text or paragraph. Click **Close** to save the new style definition without assigning it to any text.

# Modifying a Style

You can change the formatting associated with any paragraph or character style, whether it is a style you define or one of Word's predefined styles. When you do so, all text in the document that has the style assigned will be modified. Follow these steps to change a style throughout a document:

1. Click **Format**, **Style** to open the Style dialog box (see Figure 12.4).

2. Click the **List** drop-down arrow and select which styles should be displayed in the Styles list:
   - **All Styles**  All styles defined in the current document.
   - **Styles in Use**  Styles assigned to text in the current document.
   - **User Defined Styles**  All user-defined styles in the current document.

3. In the **Styles** list, click the name of the style you want to modify.

4. Click the **Modify** button. The Modify Style dialog box appears; it looks the same as the New Style dialog box (refer to Figure 12.3). Specify the style's new format specifications.

5. Click **OK** to return to the Style dialog box. Then click **Close**.

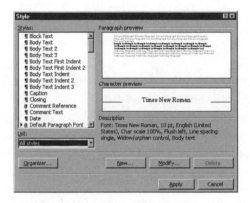

**Figure 12.4**   The Style dialog box.

In this lesson, you learned what styles are, how to apply styles to text, and how to create and modify styles. In the next lesson, you learn how to apply automatic formatting to text.

# Applying Automatic Formatting

*In this lesson, you learn how to use Word's automatic formatting capability.*

## What AutoFormatting Can Do

Automatic formatting is a feature that lets Word analyze the parts of a document, recognize certain elements (such as body text, headings, bulleted lists, and quotations), and then apply appropriate styles to the various text elements to create an attractively formatted document. (You learned about styles in Lesson 12.) You can accept or reject the automatically applied format in part or in whole, and you can later make desired modifications to the document.

In addition to applying styles, automatic formatting removes extra "returns" between paragraphs; automatically formats Internet, network, and e-mail addresses as hyperlinks; applies bold or underline character formatting to text surrounded by asterisks (*) or underscores (_); replaces two hyphens (--) with an em dash (—); and more.

 **TIP** **Word on the Web** If you format Internet and e-mail addresses as hyperlinks, users will be able to access them over the Internet simply by clicking the link in the document.

There are two ways to use automatic formatting: Word can format items as you type them, or you can create an unformatted document and then apply automatic formatting to the entire document.

Is automatic formatting right for you? The only way to find out is to try it yourself. Take a document that's typical of documents you usually work on, save it under a new name (so the original is not changed), and then experiment. You'll soon find out if you like automatic formatting—or if you prefer to format your documents manually.

**TIP**   **Try It Out**   You should give automatic formatting a try. If you like the results, it can save you a lot of time.

# Applying Formatting As You Type

Word can apply a variety of formatting to text as you type it. Some examples include:

- **Tables**   If you type a line of plus signs and hyphens (such as +--+--+) and then press Enter, Word creates a table with one column for each plus sign. Initially, the table will have one row, and the cursor will be positioned in the first cell.

- **Borders**   If you type three or more hyphens, underscores, or equal signs, Word will insert a thin, thick, or double border, respectively.

- **Bulleted Lists**   If you start a paragraph with an asterisk, a lowercase "o," or a hyphen, followed by a space or tab, Word automatically creates a bulleted list.

To set your preferences for which types of formatting are applied as you type, follow these steps:

1. Select **Format**, **AutoFormat** to display the AutoFormat dialog box.
2. Click the **Options** button to open the AutoCorrect dialog box.
3. If necessary, click the **AutoFormat As You Type** tab to see the options shown in Figure 13.1.
4. Select or deselect the check boxes as desired.
5. Click **OK**.

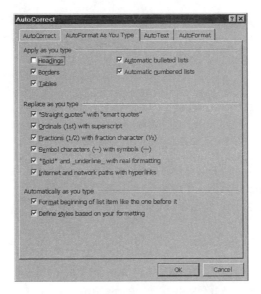

**Figure 13.1** Setting the AutoFormat As You Type options.

Changing options in this dialog box does not affect text that has already been formatted. It affects only text that is typed after the options are changed.

**What Does That Do?** Remember, you can get Help information on any option by clicking the **AutoHelp** button (the question mark) in a dialog box's title bar and then clicking the option in question.

CAUTION

# Applying AutoFormatting to Your Document

Here are the steps required to apply automatic formatting to the entire document after you've typed it:

1. Select **Format, AutoFormat** to open the AutoFormat dialog box.

2. Select **AutoFormat Now** to apply AutoFormatting without reviewing individual changes. Select **AutoFormat and Review Each Change** if you want to be able to accept or reject each format change.

**3.** (Optional) Click the **Document Type** drop-down arrow and select the type of document you are working on from the list.

**4.** Click **OK**.

If you selected **AutoFormat Now** in step 2, Word analyzes your document and applies formatting based on the document contents. You cannot reverse individual formatting changes, but you can undo the entire AutoFormat effect by selecting **Edit, Undo AutoFormat**.

If you selected **AutoFormat and Review Each Change** in step 2, Word formats your document and displays the AutoFormat dialog box shown in Figure 13.2. You can scroll around in your document while this dialog box is displayed to view the changes that Word made. Then click one of the following command buttons to proceed:

- **Accept All**   Accepts all formatting changes.
- **Reject All**   Rejects all formatting changes.
- **Review Changes**   Lets you view each formatting change and accept or reject it (see the next paragraph).
- **Style Gallery**   Displays the Style Gallery, from which you can select an overall "look" for your document. After you select a style, you return to the AutoFormat dialog box.

**Figure 13.2**   The AutoFormat dialog box.

If you decide to review changes, the Review AutoFormat Changes dialog box appears (see Figure 13.3). You use the commands in this dialog box to examine the format changes one at a time, accepting or rejecting each one. Font changes are not reviewed, but all other formatting changes are. While you are working in this dialog box, Word displays the document with marks indicating the changes made. Table 13.1 lists the types of changes you can make and the marks Word displays in your document.

**Table 13.1**   Marks Displayed to Indicate AutoFormat Changes

| Change Made | Mark Displayed |
| --- | --- |
| New style applied to the paragraph | Blue paragraph mark |
| Paragraph mark deleted | Red paragraph mark |
| Text or spaces deleted | Strikethrough |
| Characters added | Underline |
| Text or formatting changed | Vertical bar in left margin |

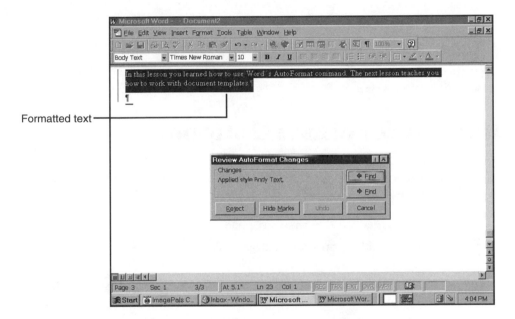

**Figure 13.3**   The Review AutoFormat Changes dialog box.

Word searches for the AutoFormatting changes that were made and highlights each one in the document. Use the command buttons in the dialog box to tell Word what to do with each AutoFormatting change:

← **Find** tells Word to locate and highlight the previous change.

→ **Find** tells Word to locate and highlight the next change.

**Reject** tells Word to undo the highlighted formatting change.

**Hide Marks** tells Word to hide the indicator marks in the document to make it easier to evaluate its appearance. Click **Show Marks** to redisplay the marks.

**Undo** tells Word to reinstate the previous rejected change.

**Cancel** returns you to the AutoFormat dialog box.

Note that you do not need to take any action to accept a change. If you do not explicitly reject a change, Word automatically accepts it.

CAUTION

**Oops!** To be sure you can recover from unwanted AutoFormat changes, first save your document under a different name.

# Setting AutoFormat Options

The AutoFormat feature has a number of settings that control which document elements it will modify. You can change these options to suit your preferences, as you'll learn in these steps:

1. Select **Format**, **AutoFormat** to open the AutoCorrect dialog box.
2. Click the **AutoFormat** tab to display the AutoFormat options (see Figure 13.4).
3. Select or deselect the various AutoFormat check boxes as desired. Use **AutoHelp** as needed to get information on individual options. (Click the question mark in the dialog box's title bar, and then click the element you need help with.)
4. When you're finished making changes, click **OK**.

Changes you make to AutoFormat options will not affect a previously formatted document, but they will apply to future uses of the AutoFormat command.

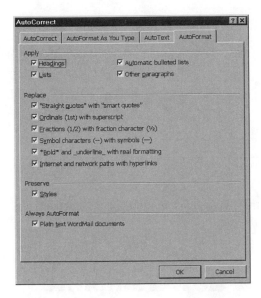

**Figure 13.4** Setting AutoFormat options.

In this lesson, you learned how to use Word's AutoFormat command. The next lesson teaches you how to work with document templates.

# Working with Templates

14

*In this lesson, you learn how to create new document templates and how to modify existing templates.*

## Creating a New Template

You learned in Lesson 4 that every Word document is based on a template, and that Word comes with a variety of predefined templates. You can also create your own templates or modify existing templates to suit your individual needs.

You can create a new template based on an existing template, and the new template will contain all the elements of the base template plus any text or formatting you add. To create a new template from scratch, base it on the Blank Document template. Here are the steps to follow:

1. Select **File**, **New** to open the New dialog box (see Figure 14.1).
2. Click the **Template** option button (in the lower-right corner).
3. If you want the new template based on an existing template, select that template icon in the dialog box. Otherwise, select the **Blank Document** icon.
4. Click **OK**. A blank document-editing screen appears with a default name, such as TEMPLATE1.
5. Enter the boilerplate text and other items that you want to include in the new template, and then apply formatting to the text as desired. You should also create any styles that you want in the template.

**TERM**     **Boilerplate**    This is text that you want to appear in every document based on the new template.

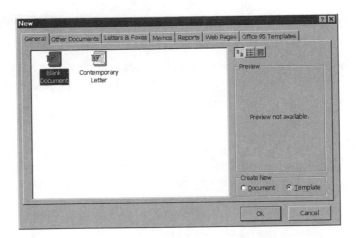

**Figure 14.1** Creating a new template based on the Blank Document template.

**6.** Select **File**, **Save** or click the **Save** button on the Standard toolbar. The Save As dialog box appears.

**7.** If necessary, select the folder you want the new template saved in by double-clicking its name. For example, if it is a template for a letter, you would probably save it in the Letters & Faxes folder.

**8.** In the **File Name** text box, enter a descriptive name for the template, using up to 256 characters. Be sure to use a different name from the template you selected in step 3, or the new template will replace the original one.

**9.** Select **Save**. Word saves the template under the specified name. It is now available for use each time you start a new document.

# Modifying an Existing Template

Suppose you create your own template, but then you find out that you need to change the boilerplate text slightly. You can retrieve any existing template from disk and modify it. Here's how:

**1.** Select **File**, **New** to open the New dialog box.

**2.** Select the tab containing the template you want to modify, and then select the template icon you want to modify.

**3.** Select the **Template** option button.

**4.** Click **OK**.

**5.** Make the desired modifications and additions to the template's text and styles.

**159**

**6.** Select **File, Save** or click the **Save** button on the Standard toolbar, and Word saves the modified template to disk.

When you modify a template, changes you make are not reflected in documents that were created based on the template before it was changed. Only new documents will be affected.

 **TIP**  **Save the Old**  Instead of modifying a template, it's often better to create a new template based on it. This way the original template will still be available should you change your mind or want to use it again.

 **TIP**  **Recycle Old Templates?**  You can use old templates from earlier versions of Word (Word for Windows 95 and Word for Windows 6.0) to create new documents in Word.

# Creating a Template from a Document

Sometimes you will find it useful to create a template based on an existing Word document. Here are the steps to follow:

**1.** Open the document that you want to base the new template on.

**2.** Use Word's editing commands to delete any document text and formatting that you do not want to include in the template.

**3.** Select **File, Save As** to open the Save As dialog box (see Figure 14.2).

**4.** Click the **Save As Type** drop-down arrow and choose **Document Template** from the list. The Save In box automatically changes to indicate the Templates folder.

**5.** If appropriate, double-click the name of the folder in which you want to save the template.

**6.** Type a descriptive name for the template in the **File Name** text box.

**7.** Click **Save**.

In step 5, it's important to select the proper template folder. When you select Document Template in step 4, Word automatically switches to the Templates folder (which is different from where documents are saved). Templates saved in this folder will appear on the General tab in the New dialog box. Because Word organizes templates by category, you may want to place your new template in the appropriate folder because if you don't, you may have trouble finding it later. For example, if you create a template for a memo, save it in the Memos folder so it will appear on the Memos tab in the New dialog box.

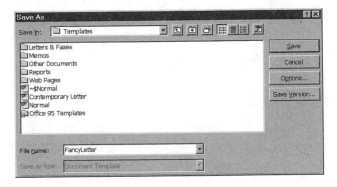

**Figure 14.2** Saving a document template.

# Updating a Document When the Template Changes

If you modify a template, only new documents based on that template will reflect the changes. Existing documents that were based on the old version of the template will not be affected. You can, however, import new styles from a modified template to an existing document. Here's how:

**1.** Open the document.

**2.** Select **Tools, Templates and Add-ins**.

**3.** Select the **Automatically Update Document Styles** check box.

**4.** Select **OK**.

With this check box selected, the document styles will automatically be updated to reflect the styles in its attached template each time the document is loaded. Other elements of a template, such as boilerplate text, will not be affected.

In this lesson, you learned how to create and modify document templates. The next lesson shows you how to use page numbers, headers, and footers in your documents.

# Page Numbers, Headers, and Footers

*In this lesson, you learn how to add page numbers, headers, and footers to your documents.*

## Adding Page Numbers

Many documents—particularly long ones—require that the pages be numbered. Word offers many choices as to the placement and appearance of page numbers. Page numbers are always part of a header or footer. You can place a page number by itself in a header or footer, as covered in this section. You can also include additional information in the header or footer, as covered later in this lesson.

To add page numbers to your document, follow these steps:

1. Select **Insert**, **Page Numbers**. The Page Numbers dialog box appears, as shown in Figure 15.1.

**Figure 15.1**   The Page Numbers dialog box.

2. Click the **Position** drop-down arrow and select the desired position on the page: **Top of Page (Header)** or **Bottom of Page (Footer)**.

3. Click the **Alignment** drop-down arrow and select **Left, Center,** or **Right.** You can also select **Inside** or **Outside** if you're printing two-sided pages and want the page numbers positioned near to (Inside) or away from (Outside) the binding.

4. The default number format consists of Arabic numerals (1, 2, 3, and so on). To select a different format (such as, i, ii, iii), click **Format** and select the desired format.

5. Click **OK**.

When you add a page number using this procedure, Word makes the page number part of the document's header or footer. The next section describes headers and footers.

**TIP** **Can I Print Both Sides?** Two-sided printing is an option on certain printers. Lesson 11 shows you how to set margins for two-sided printing.

**No Page Numbers Command?** When you're in Online Layout view or Outline view, the **Page Numbers** option is not available on the **Insert** menu. In Normal view, you can add page numbers, but you cannot see them.

**CAUTION**

# What Are Headers and Footers?

A *header* or *footer* is text that prints at the top (header) or bottom (footer) of every page of a document. Headers and footers can show the page number; they are also useful for displaying chapter titles, authors' names, and similar information. Word offers several header/footer options, including the following:

- The same header/footer on every page of the document.
- One header/footer on the first page of the document and a different header/footer on all other pages.

- One header/footer on odd-numbered pages and a different header/footer on even-numbered pages.
- If your document is divided into sections, you can have a different header/footer for each section.

**Headers and Footers**   Text that is displayed at the top (header) or bottom (footer) of every page.

# Adding or Editing a Header or Footer

To add a header or footer to your document, or to edit an existing header or footer, follow these steps:

1. If your document is divided into sections, move the cursor to any location in the section where you want the header or footer placed.

2. Select **View**, **Header and Footer**. Word switches to Page Layout view and displays the current page's header enclosed in a nonprinting dashed line (see Figure 15.2). Regular document text is dimmed, and the Header and Footer toolbar is displayed. On the toolbar, click the **Switch Between Header and Footer** button to switch between the current page's header and footer.

3. Enter the header or footer text and formatting using the normal Word editing techniques. Use the **Alignment** buttons on the Formatting toolbar to control the placement of items in the header/footer.

4. Use the other toolbar buttons, which are described in Table 15.1, however you want to in order to customize your header/footer.

5. When finished, click the **Close** button on the Header and Footer toolbar to return to the document.

**TIP**   **Good-Bye, Header!**   To delete the contents of a header or footer, follow the previous steps for editing the header or footer. Select all of the text in the header or footer and press **Delete**.

**Table 15.1** Header and Footer Toolbar Buttons

| Button | Description |
|---|---|
| Insert AutoText ▾ | Inserts an AutoText entry |
| | Inserts a page number code |
| | Inserts the total number of pages |
| | Formats the page number |
| | Inserts a date code |
| | Inserts a time code |
| | Opens the Page Setup dialog box so you can set margins (Lesson 11) |
| | Shows or hides document text |
| | Makes the header/footer the same as the previous one |
| | Switches between header and footer |
| | Shows the previous header or footer |
| | Shows the next header or footer |
| Close | Closes the Header and Footer toolbar and returns to the document |

A page number        Header box

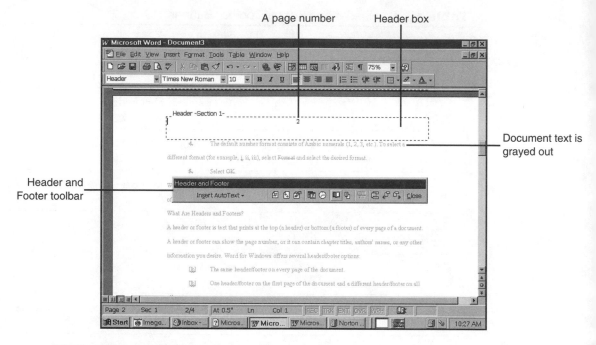

Document text is grayed out

Header and Footer toolbar

**Figure 15.2** The Header and Footer toolbar.

# Creating Different Headers and Footers for Different Pages

Word's default is to display the same header/footer on all the pages in a section or document. One way to have different headers/footers in different parts of the document is to break the document into two or more sections, as explained in Lesson 11. Then you can use the techniques described earlier in the lesson to add a different header/footer to each section.

In addition to using sections, you have the following options:

- One header/footer on the first page with a different header/footer on all other pages.
- One header/footer on odd-numbered pages with another header/footer on even-numbered pages.

To activate one or both of these options:

1. Select **View**, **Header and Footer**.

2. Click the **Page Setup** button on the Header and Footer toolbar. Word displays the Layout tab of the Page Setup dialog box (see Figure 15.3).

3. Select the **Different Odd and Even** check box and/or the **Different First Page** check box.

4. Click **OK** to close the Page Setup dialog box.

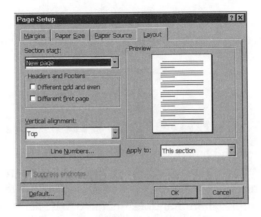

**Figure 15.3**   Setting header/footer options in the Page Setup dialog box.

After selecting one of these header/footer options, you use the techniques described earlier in this lesson (in the section "Adding or Editing a Header or Footer") to add and edit the header/footer text. For example, say you specified Different Odd and Even. If the cursor is on an even-numbered page and you select the View, Headers and Footers command, Word displays the header/footer text that will display on even-numbered pages so you can edit it. If you click the Show Next button on the Header/Footer toolbar, Word moves to the header/footer for odd-numbered pages.

In this lesson, you learned to add page numbers, headers, and footers to a document. In the next lesson, you will learn how to create numbered and bulleted lists.

# Numbered and Bulleted Lists

*In this lesson, you learn how to add numbered and bulleted lists to your documents.*

## Why Use Numbered and Bulleted Lists?

Numbered and bulleted lists are useful formatting tools for setting off lists of information in a document—you've seen plenty of both in this book! Word can automatically create both types of lists. Use bulleted lists for items that consist of related information that does not have to be listed in any particular order. Use numbered lists for items that must fall in a specific order. When you create a numbered or bulleted list, each paragraph is considered a separate list item and receives its own number or bullet.

## Creating a Numbered or Bulleted List

You can create a list from existing text or create the list as you type. To create a numbered or bulleted list from existing text, follow these steps:

1. Select the paragraphs you want in the list.
2. Select **Format**, **Bullets and Numbering** to open the Bullets and Numbering dialog box.
3. Depending on the type of list you want, click the **Bulleted** tab or the **Numbered** tab. Figure 16.1 shows the Numbered tab options, and Figure 16.2 shows the Bulleted tab options.
4. Click the bullet or number style you want.
5. Click **OK**.

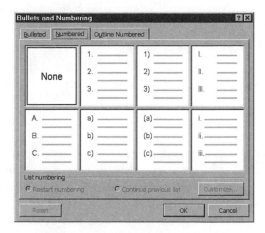

**Figure 16.1** Numbered list style options in the Numbered tab.

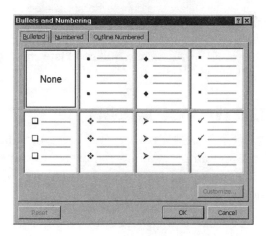

**Figure 16.2** Bulleted list style options in the Bulleted tab.

Follow these steps to create a numbered or bulleted list as you type:

1. Move the insertion point to the location for the list, and then press **Enter**, if necessary, to start a new paragraph.

2. Select **Format, Bullets and Numbering** to open the Bullets and Numbering dialog box.

3. Depending on the type of list you want, click the **Bulleted** tab or the **Numbered** tab.

4. Click the bullet or number style you want.

5. Click **OK**.

6. Type the list elements, pressing **Enter** at the end of each paragraph. Word automatically places a bullet or number in front of each new paragraph.

7. At the end of the last paragraph, press **Enter** twice.

 **TIP**  **Quick Lists**   Quickly create a numbered or bulleted list in the default list style by clicking the **Numbering** or **Bullets** button on the Formatting toolbar before typing or after selecting the list text.

**TIP**   **Automatic Lists**   If the corresponding AutoFormat options are on, Word automatically starts a numbered or bulleted list anytime you start a paragraph with a number and period or an asterisk followed by a space or tab. To turn these options on or off, select **Format**, **AutoFormat**, **Options** and click the **Lists** and the **Automatic Bulleted Lists** check boxes to turn them on or off.

# Using Multilevel Lists

A multilevel list contains two or more levels of bullets or numbering within a single list. For example, a numbered list could contain a lettered list under each numbered item, or each level could be numbered separately, as in an outline. Here's how to create a multilevel list:

1. Select **Format**, **Bullets and Numbering** to open the Bullets and Numbering dialog box.

2. Click the **Outline Numbered** tab to display the multilevel options, as shown in Figure 16.3.

3. Click the list style you want, and then click **OK**.

4. Start typing the list, pressing **Enter** after each item.

5. (Optional) After pressing **Enter**, press **Tab** to demote the new item one level, or press **Shift+Tab** to promote it one level. If you don't do either, the new item will be at the same level as the previous item.

 6. After typing the last item, press **Enter**, and then click the **Numbering** button on the Formatting toolbar to end the list.

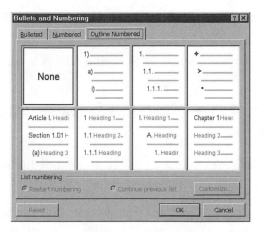

**Figure 16.3** Use the Outline Numbered tab of the Bullets and Numbering dialog box to create a multilevel list.

You can convert regular text or a one-level numbered or bulleted list to a multilevel list. You can also change the style of an existing multilevel list. Here are the steps to follow:

1. Select all the paragraphs you want to include in the new list or whose format you want to modify.

2. Select **Format, Bullets and Numbering**, and then click the **Outline Numbered** tab.

3. Click the desired list style and click **OK**.

4. Move the insertion point to an item in the list whose level you want to change.

5. Click the **Decrease Indent** or the **Increase Indent** button on the Formatting toolbar to change the item's level.

6. Repeat steps 4 and 5 as needed to change other items.

# Removing a Numbered or Bulleted List

Follow these steps to remove bullets or numbers from a list but keep the text and convert it to normal paragraphs:

1. Select the paragraphs from which you want the bullets or numbering removed. This can be the entire list or just part of it. The corresponding

button (Bullets or Numbering) on the Formatting toolbar appears to be pressed in.

2. Click the **Bullets** or **Numbering** button to turn the formatting style off.

# Changing the Format of a Numbered or Bulleted List

You can also change the format of an existing bulleted or numbered list, to change the bullet symbol or the numbering style. Here's how:

1. Select the paragraphs from which you want the bullets or numbering removed. (This can be the entire list or just part of it.)

2. Select **Format, Bullets and Numbering** to open the Bullets and Numbering dialog box.

3. For a bulleted list, click the **Bulleted** tab and select the desired style. Select **None** to remove bullets.

4. For a numbered list, click the **Numbered** tab and select the desired numbering style, or click **None** to remove numbering from the list.

5. Click **OK** to put your changes into effect.

# Adding Items to Numbered and Bulleted Lists

You can add new items to a numbered or bulleted list using the steps here:

1. Move the insertion point to the location in the list where you want the new item.

2. Press **Enter** to start a new paragraph. Word automatically inserts a new bullet or number and renumbers the list items if necessary.

3. Type the new text.

4. (Optional) If it's a multilevel list, click the **Decrease Indent** or the **Increase Indent** button on the Formatting toolbar to change the item's level.

5. Repeat these steps as many times as needed.

This lesson showed you how to create numbered and bulleted lists. The next lesson shows you how to add symbols and other special characters to your document.

# Using Symbols and Special Characters

*In this lesson, you learn how to use symbols and special characters.*

## What Are Symbols and Special Characters?

*Symbols* and *special characters* are not part of the standard character set and, therefore, will not be found on your keyboard. Accented letters (such as é), the Greek letter mu (µ), and the copyright symbol (©) are examples. Even though these characters are not on your keyboard, Word can still insert them in your documents.

## Inserting a Symbol

To insert a symbol in your document, place the insertion point where you want the symbol, and then follow these steps:

1. Select **Insert**, **Symbol** to open the Symbol dialog box (see Figure 17.1). Click the **Symbols** tab if it is not already displayed.

2. Click the **Font** drop-down arrow and select the desired symbol set from the list. Those you will use most often include:

   - **Symbol**  Greek letters, mathematical symbols, arrows, trademark and copyright symbols, and more.
   - **Normal Text**  Letters with accents and other special marks, currency symbols, the paragraph symbol, and more.
   - **WingDings**  Icons for clocks, envelopes, telephones, and so on.

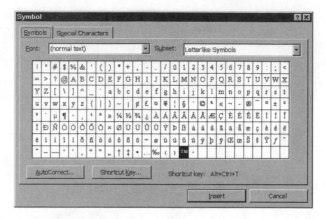

**Figure 17.1** The Symbols dialog box.

**3.** Look through the grid of symbols for the one you want. To see an enlarged view of a symbol, click it.

**4.** To insert a selected symbol, click **Insert**. To insert any symbol (that's not selected), double-click the symbol.

**5.** Click **Close** to close the dialog box after you insert one or more symbols. (Or click the **Cancel** button to close the dialog box without inserting a symbol.)

# Inserting a Special Character

The distinction between "special characters" and "symbols" is not a clear one. In fact, there is some overlap between the two. Symbols include letters with accents and other diacritical marks used in some languages, Greek letters, arrows, and mathematical symbols (such as ±). Special characters include the copyright symbol (©), the ellipsis (…), and typographic symbols such as em spaces (a wider than normal space). You'll see that Word provides many more symbols than it does special characters.

To insert a special character in your document, place the insertion point where you want the character, and then follow these steps:

**1.** Select **Insert**, **Symbol** to open the Symbol dialog box.

**2.** Click the **Special Characters** tab to display the list of available special characters (see Figure 17.2).

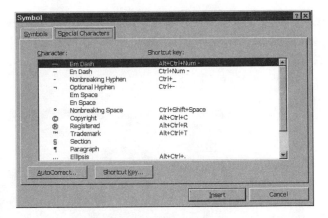

**Figure 17.2** The Special Characters list.

3. Look through the list of special characters for the one you want.

4. To insert a selected character, click **Insert**. To insert any character in the list that's not selected, double-click it.

5. Click the **Close** (X) button to close the dialog box after you insert a character. Or click the **Cancel** button to close the dialog box without inserting a character.

# Assigning Shortcut Keys to Symbols

You may want to assign a shortcut key to any symbol you use frequently. Then you can insert it quickly by pressing that key combination. Most of the special characters already have shortcut keys assigned to them; these key assignments are listed on the Special Characters tab in the Symbol dialog box.

**TIP** **More Shortcuts** You can also use Word's AutoCorrect feature to quickly insert symbols and special characters. See Lesson 13 for more information.

Follow these steps to assign a shortcut key to a symbol:

1. Select **Insert**, **Symbol** and click the **Symbols** tab (refer to Figure 17.1).

2. Click the desired symbol. (If necessary, first select the proper font from the **Font** list.)

**175**

**3.** If the selected symbol already has a shortcut key assigned to it, the key combination appears in the lower-right corner of the dialog box.

**4.** Click the **Shortcut Key** button to display the Customize Keyboard dialog box (see Figure 17.3).

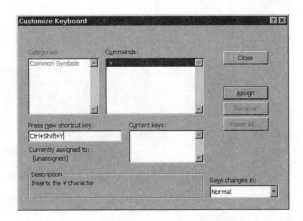

**Figure 17.3**  Assigning a shortcut key to a symbol.

**5.** Press **Alt+N** to move to the **Press New Shortcut Key** text box (or click in that box).

**6.** Press the shortcut key combination you want to assign. Its description appears in the Press New ShortCut Key text box. A list of permitted key combinations follows these steps.

**7.** If the specified key combination is unassigned, Word displays **[unassigned]** under the Press New Shortcut Key text box. If it has already been assigned, Word displays the name of the symbol, macro, or command to which the selected shortcut key is assigned.

**8.** If the shortcut key is unassigned, click **Assign** to assign it to the symbol. If it is already assigned, press **Backspace** to delete the shortcut key display and return to step 6 to try another key combination.

**9.** When you're done, click **Close** to return to the Symbols dialog box, and then click **Close** again to return to your document.

The shortcut keys are really key combinations. You can select from the following key combinations, where *key* is a letter key, number key, function key, or cursor movement key:

Shift+*key*          Alt+Shift+*key*

Ctrl+*key*           Ctrl+Shift+*key*

Alt+*key*            Ctrl+Shift+Alt+*key*

Alt+Ctrl+*key*

# Understanding Special Characters

Some of the special characters that Word offers may seem unfamiliar to you, but they can be quite useful in certain documents. The following are brief descriptions of the less well-known ones:

- **En dash**   A dash that is the same as the standard dash (inserted with the key above the P key on your keyboard). The en dash is properly used in combinations of figures and capital letters, as in "Please refer to part 1–A."

- **Em dash**   Slightly longer than an en dash, the em dash has a variety of purposes, the most common of which is to mark a sudden change of thought. For example, "She said—and no one dared disagree—that the meeting was over."

- **En space**   A space slightly longer than the standard space. This space ( ) is an en space.

- **Em space**   A space slightly longer than the en space. This space (　) is an em space.

- **Non-breaking space**   A space that will not be broken at the end of the line. The words separated by a non-breaking space always stay on the same line.

- **Non-breaking hyphen**   Similar to a non-breaking space. That is to say, two words separated by a non-breaking hyphen will always stay on the same line.

- **Optional hyphen**   A hyphen that will not be displayed unless the word it is in needs to be broken at the end of a line.

In this lesson, you learned how to use symbols and special characters in your Word documents. In the next lesson, you will learn how to proof your document.

# Proofing Your Document

*This lesson shows you how to use Word's spelling and grammar checker, thesaurus, and Print Preview window to proof your document.*

## Using the Spelling Checker

Word's spelling checker lets you verify and correct the spelling of words in your document. Words are checked against a standard dictionary and unknown words are flagged. You can then ignore the word, correct it, or add it to the dictionary.

To check spelling in a portion of a document, select the text to check. Otherwise, Word will check the entire document starting at the location of the cursor. If you want to check starting at the beginning of the document, move the insertion point to the start of the document by pressing **Ctrl+Home**. Then follow these steps:

 1. Select **Tools**, **Spelling and Grammar**, or press **F7**, or click the **Spelling and Grammar** button on the Standard toolbar. The Spelling and Grammar dialog box appears (see Figure 18.1). If you want to check spelling only, deselect the **Check Grammar** check box. The remainder of these steps assume that you are checking spelling only. (If you tell Word to check grammar, it flags suspected grammar errors; how you deal with these is described later in this lesson.)

**2.** When Word locates a word in the document that is not in the dictionary, it displays the word and its surrounding text in the **Not in Dictionary** list box with the word highlighted in red. In Figure 18.1, for example, the word **checcker** is highlighted. Suggested replacements for the word appear in the Suggestions list box (if Word has no suggestions, this box will be empty). For each word that Word stops on, take action in one of these ways:

- To correct the word manually, edit it in the **Not in Dictionary** list box and click **Change**.
- To use one of the suggested replacements, highlight the desired replacement word in the **Suggestions** list box and click **Change**.
- To replace all instances of the word in the document with either the manual corrections you made or the word selected in the Suggestions box, click **Change All**.
- To ignore this instance of the word, click **Ignore**.
- To ignore this and all other instances of the word in the document, click **Ignore All**.
- To add the word to the dictionary, click **Add**.

**3.** Repeat as needed. When the entire document has been checked, Word displays a message to that effect. (Or, you can click **Cancel** at any time to end spell checking early.)

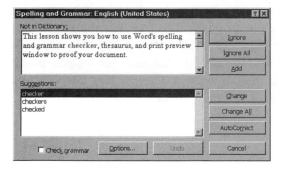

**Figure 18.1** Checking spelling in the Spelling and Grammar dialog box.

**TIP** **Use AutoCorrect** To add a misspelled word and its correction to the AutoCorrect list, select **AutoCorrect** in the Spelling and Grammar dialog box. Future misspellings will then be corrected automatically as you type them.

# Checking Your Grammar

Word can check the grammar of the text in your document, flagging possible problems so you can correct them if needed. Here are the steps required to run the grammar checker:

1.  Select **Tools, Spelling and Grammar**, or press **F7**, or click the **Spelling and Grammar** button on the toolbar. The Spelling and Grammar dialog box appears (refer to Figure 18.1). Make sure the **Check Grammar** check box is selected.

2.  When Word locates a word or phrase with a suspected grammatical error, it displays the word or phrase and its surrounding text in the dialog box with the word highlighted in green and a description of the suspected problem above the text. In Figure 18.2, for example, the word **want** is highlighted and the problem **Subject-Verb Agreement** appears. Suggested fixes, if any, are listed in the Suggestions list box. For each potential mistake that Word stops on, take action in one of these ways:

    *   To manually correct the error, edit the text and click **Change**.
    *   To use one of the suggested replacements, select it in the **Suggestions** list box and click **Change**.
    *   To ignore this instance of the problem, click **Ignore**.
    *   To ignore this instance and all other instances of the problem in the document, click **Ignore All**.

3.  Word will check spelling at the same time it is checking grammar. Deal with spelling errors as explained earlier in this lesson.

4.  Repeat as needed. When the entire document has been checked, Word displays a message to that effect. (Or, you can click **Close** at any time to end grammar checking early.)

CAUTION

**Don't Rely on Word**   Word's grammar checker is a useful tool, but don't rely on it to catch everything. It is no substitute for careful writing and editing.

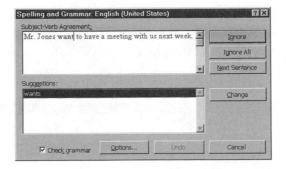

**Figure 18.2** Checking grammar in the Spelling and Grammar dialog box.

# Checking Spelling and Grammar As You Type

In addition to checking your document's spelling and grammar all at once, Word can check text as you type it. Words not found in the dictionary will be underlined with a wavy red line, and suspected grammatical errors will be marked with a wavy green line. You can deal with the errors immediately or whenever you choose. To turn automatic spell/grammar checking on or off:

**1.** Select **Tools**, **Options** to open the Options dialog box.

**2.** If necessary, click the **Spelling and Grammar** tab.

**3.** Select or deselect the **Check Spelling As You Type** and the **Check Grammar As You Type** check boxes.

**4.** Click **OK**.

To deal with a word that has been underlined by automatic spell checking or grammar checking, right-click the word. A pop-up menu appears, containing suggested replacements for the word (if any are found) as well as several commands. Figure 18.3 shows the pop-up menu that appears when you right-click a misspelled word.

For a spelling error, you have the following choices:

- To replace the word with one of the suggestions, click the replacement word.

- To ignore all occurrences of the word in the document, click **Ignore All**.

- To add the word to the dictionary, click **Add**.
- To add the misspelling to the AutoCorrect list, select **AutoCorrect**, and then select the proper replacement spelling.
- To start a regular spelling check, click **Spelling**.

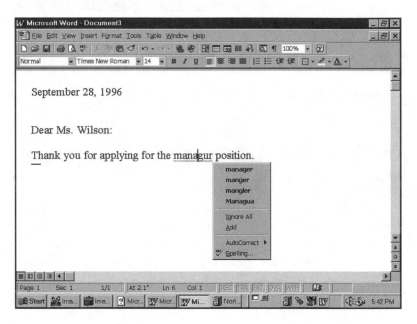

**Figure 18.3** Correcting spelling as you type.

When you right-click a grammatical error, you are offered the following choices:

- Select a suggested replacement to insert it in the document.
- Select **Ignore Sentence** to ignore the possible error.
- Select **Grammar** to start a regular grammar check.

 **TIP** **Hide Spelling/Grammar Marks**  If your document contains words underlined by the automatic spelling or grammar checker and you want to hide the underlines, select **Tools**, **Options**, click the **Spelling and Grammar** tab, and select the **Hide Spelling Errors in This Document** check box or the **Hide Grammatical Errors in This Document** check box. Deselect these check boxes to redisplay the underlines.

# Using the Thesaurus

A thesaurus provides you with synonyms and antonyms for words in your document. Using the thesaurus can help you avoid repetition in your writing (and improve your vocabulary).

 **TERM**    **Synonyms and Antonyms**   Words with the same and opposite meanings, respectively, as a given word.

To use the thesaurus:

1. Place the insertion point on the word of interest in your document.

2. Press **Shift+F7** or select **Tools, Thesaurus**. The Thesaurus dialog box opens (see Figure 18.4). This dialog box has several components:

   - The **Looked Up** list box displays the word of interest.

   - The **Meanings** list box lists alternate meanings for the word. If the word is not found, Word displays an **Alphabetical List** box instead; this list contains a list of words with spellings similar to the selected word.

   - If the thesaurus finds one or more meanings for the word, the dialog box displays the **Replace with Synonym** list showing synonyms for the currently highlighted meaning of the word. If meanings are not found, the dialog box displays a **Replace with Related Word** list.

3. While the Thesaurus dialog box is displayed, take one of these actions:

   - To find synonyms for the highlighted word in the Replace with Synonym list or the Replace with Related Words list (depending on which one is displayed), click **Look Up**.

   - To find synonyms for a word in the Meanings list, select the word and then click **Look Up**.

   - For some words, the thesaurus displays the term **Antonyms** in the **Meanings** list. To display antonyms for the selected word, highlight the term **Antonyms** and then click **Look Up**.

4. To replace the word in the document with the highlighted word in the Replace with Synonym list or the Replace with Related Word list, click **Replace**.

5. To close the thesaurus without making any changes to the document, click **Cancel**.

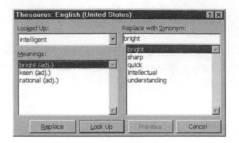

**Figure 18.4**  The Thesaurus dialog box.

**TIP**  **What Does It Mean?**  You can use the thesaurus like a dictionary to find the meaning of any word you are not familiar with.

# Using Print Preview

Word's Print Preview feature lets you view your document on the screen exactly as it will be printed. While Page Layout view also displays your document in its final form, Print Preview offers some additional features that you may find useful. To use Print Preview, select **File, Print Preview** or click the **Print Preview** button on the Standard toolbar. The current page appears in the Preview window (see Figure 18.5).

These guidelines outline your available options in the Preview window:

- Press **Page Up** or **Page Down** or use the vertical scroll bar to view other pages.
- Click the **Multiple Pages** button and drag over the page icons to preview more than one page at once. Click the **One Page** button to preview a single page.
- Click the **Zoom Control** drop-down arrow and select a magnification to preview the document at different magnifications.
- Click the **View Ruler** button to display the Ruler. You can then use the Ruler to set page margins and indents as described in Lessons 9 and 11.
- Click the **Magnifier** button and click in the document to enlarge that part of the document.

- Click the **Shrink to Fit** button to prevent a small amount of text from spilling onto the document's last page. Word will attempt to adjust formatting to reduce the page count by one.

- Click the **Print** button to print the document. Click again to return to the original view.

- Click **Close** or press **Esc** to end Print Preview display.

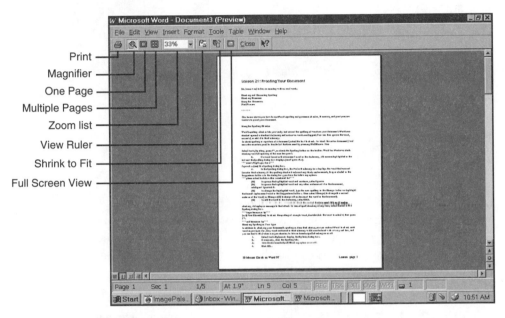

**Figure 18.5** The Print Preview screen.

In this lesson, you learned how to use Word's proofing tools to check your document's spelling and grammar, and how to use the thesaurus and Print Preview. The next lesson shows you how to use tables.

# Working with Tables

19

*In this lesson, you learn how to add tables to your document, and how to edit and format tables.*

## What's a Table?

A *table* lets you organize information in a row and column format. Each entry in a table, called a *cell*, is independent of all other entries. You can have almost any number of rows and columns in a table. You also have a great deal of control over the size and formatting of each cell. A table cell can contain text, graphics, and just about anything that a Word document can contain. The one exception is that a table cannot contain another table.

 **TIP** **On the Table** Use tables for columns of numbers, lists, and anything else that requires a row and column arrangement.

## Inserting a Table

To insert a new empty table at any location within your document, follow these steps:

1. Move the cursor to the document location where you want the table.

2. Select **Table, Insert Table**. The Insert Table dialog box appears (see Figure 19.1).

3. In the **Number of Columns** and **Number of Rows** text boxes, click the arrows or enter the number of rows and columns the table should have. (You can adjust these numbers later.)

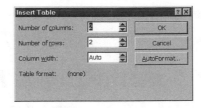

**Figure 19.1** The Insert Table dialog box.

**4.** To apply one of Word's automatic table formats to the table, click the **AutoFormat** button, select the desired format, and click **OK**. (AutoFormat is covered in more detail later in this lesson.)

**5.** In the **Column Width** text box, select the desired width for each column (in inches). Select **Auto** in this box to have the page width evenly divided among the specified number of columns.

**6.** Select **OK**. Word creates a blank table with the cursor in the first cell.

**TIP**  **Quick Tables** To quickly insert a table, click the **Insert Table** button on the Standard toolbar and drag over the desired number of rows and columns.

# Working in a Table

When the cursor is in a table cell, you can enter and edit text as you would in the rest of the document. Text entered in a cell automatically wraps to the next line within the column width. You can move the cursor to any cell by clicking it. You can also navigate in a table using the following special key combinations:

| Press This... | To Move Here... |
| --- | --- |
| Tab | The next cell in a row |
| Shift+Tab | The previous cell in a row |
| Alt+Home | The first cell in the current row |
| Alt+Page Up | The top cell in the current column |
| Alt+End | The last cell in the current row |
| Alt+Page Down | The last cell in the current column |

If the cursor is at the edge of a cell, you can also use the arrow keys to move between cells. To insert a Tab in a table cell, press **Ctrl+Tab**.

# Editing and Formatting a Table

After you create a table and enter some information, you can edit its contents and format its appearance to suit your needs. The following sections explain common editing and formatting tasks you might want to perform.

## Deleting and Inserting Cells, Rows, and Columns

You can clear individual cells in a table, erasingtheir contents and leaving the cells blank. To clear the contents of a cell, simply select the cell and press **Delete**.

 **TIP**   **Fast Select!**   You can select the text in the cell or the entire cell itself. To select an entire cell, click in the left margin of the cell, between the text and the cell border. The mouse pointer changes to an arrow when it's in this area.

You can also remove entire rows and columns. When you do so, columns to the right or rows below move to fill in for the deleted row or column. To completely remove a row or column from the table, follow these steps:

1. Move the cursor to any cell in the row or column to be deleted.
2. Select **Table**, **Delete Cells**. The Delete Cells dialog box appears (see Figure 19.2).
3. Select **Delete Entire Row** or **Delete Entire Column**.
4. Click **OK**, and Word deletes the row or column.

**Recovery**   Remember that you can undo table editing actions with the **Edit**, **Undo** command.

CAUTION

**Figure 19.2** The Delete Cells dialog box.

Follow these steps to insert a single row or column into a table:

1. Move the cursor to a cell to the right of where you want the new column or below where you want the new row.

2. Select **Table, Insert Columns** to insert a new blank column to the left of the selected column. Select **Table, Insert Rows** to insert a new blank row above the selected row.

**CAUTION**

**Changing Commands?** The commands on the Table menu change according to circumstances. For example, if you select a column in a table, the Insert Columns command is displayed, but the Insert Rows command is not.

Use these steps to insert more than one row or column into a table:

1. Select cells that span the number of rows or columns you want to insert. For example, to insert three new rows between rows 2 and 3, select cells in rows 3, 4, and 5 (in any column).

2. Select **Table, Select Row** (if inserting rows) or **Table, Select Column** (if inserting columns).

3. Select **Table, Insert Rows** or **Table, Insert Columns** as appropriate.

**TIP** **Add a Row** To insert a new row at the bottom of the table, move the cursor to the last cell in the table and press **Tab**.

To insert a new column at the right edge of the table, follow these steps:

1. Click just outside the table's right border.

2. Select **Table, Select Column**.

3. Select **Table, Insert Columns**.

# Moving or Copying Columns and Rows

Here's how to copy or move an entire column or row from one location in a table to another:

1. Select the column or row by dragging over the cells, or by clicking in the column or row and selecting **Table**, **Select Row** or **Table**, **Select Column**.

2. To copy, press **Ctrl+C** or click the **Copy** button on the Standard toolbar. To move, press **Ctrl+X** or click the **Cut** button.

3. Move the cursor to the new location for the column or row. (It will be inserted above or to the left of the location of the cursor.)

4. Press **Ctrl+V** or click the **Paste** button on the Standard toolbar.

# Changing Column Width

You can quickly change the width of a column with the mouse.

1. Point at the right border of the column whose width you want to change. The mouse pointer changes to a pair of thin vertical lines with arrowheads pointing left and right.

2. Drag the column border to the desired width.

You can also use a dialog box to change column widths. Follow these steps to learn how:

1. Move the cursor to any cell in the column you want to change.

2. Select **Table**, **Cell Height and Width**. The Cell Height and Width dialog box appears (see Figure 19.3). If necessary, click the **Column** tab to display the column options.

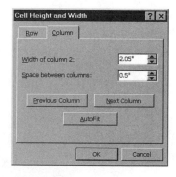

**Figure 19.3** Changing column width.

3.  In the **Width of Column** text box, enter the desired column width, or click the up and down arrows to change the setting. Note that the label identifies which column you are working on by number. To automatically adjust the column width to fit the widest cell entry, click the **Autofit** button.

4.  Change the value in the **Space Between Columns** text box to modify spacing between columns. Changing this setting increases or decreases the amount of space between the text in each cell and the cell's left and right borders.

5.  Click **Next Column** or **Previous Column** to change the settings for other columns in the table.

6.  Click **OK**. The table changes to reflect the new column settings.

# Table Borders

Word's default is to place a single, thin border around each cell in a table. However, you can modify the borders or remove them altogether. The techniques for working with table borders are essentially the same as for adding borders to other text (see Lesson 8). Briefly, here are the steps involved.

1.  Select the table cells whose borders you want to modify.

2.  Select **Format, Borders and Shading** to display the Borders and Shading dialog box. Click the **Borders** tab if necessary (refer to Figure 8.3).

3.  Select the desired border settings, using the Preview box to see how your settings will appear.

4.  Click **OK**.

In a table with no borders, you can display non-printing gridlines on-screen to make it easier to work with the table. Select **Table, Show Gridline** to display gridlines. When you finish working with the table, select **Table, Hide Gridlines** to turn them off.

# Automatic Table Formatting

Word provides a variety ofpredefined table formats. Using these formats makes it easy to apply attractive formatting to any table. These steps show you how to use a predefined table format:

1.  Place the cursor anywhere in the table.

2. Select **Table, Table AutoFormat**. The Table AutoFormat dialog box appears (see Figure 19.4). This is the same dialog box you would see if you selected AutoFormat in the Insert Table dialog box when first creating a table (as covered earlier in this lesson).

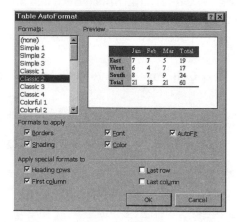

**Figure 19.4**  The Table AutoFormat dialog box.

3. The **Formats** list names the available table formats. As you scroll through the list, the Preview box shows the appearance of the highlighted format.

4. Select and deselect the formatting check boxes as needed until the Preview shows the table appearance you want.

5. When you're satisfied with what you see in the Preview area, click **OK**. Word applies the selected formatting to the table.

In this lesson, you learned how to add tables to your document, and how to edit and format tables. The next lesson shows you how to use columns in your documents.

# Using Columns in Your Document

*In this lesson, you learn how to format your document text in two or more columns per page.*

## Why Use Columns?

Columns are commonly used in newsletters, brochures, and similar documents. The shorter lines of text provided by columns are easier to read, and they provide greater flexibility in formatting a document with graphics, tables, and so on. Word makes it easy to use columns in your documents. Figure 20.1 shows a document formatted with two columns.

The columns you create in Word are *newspaper* style columns, in which the text flows to the bottom of one column and then continues at the top of the next column on the page. For side-by-side paragraphs, such as you would need in a résumé or a script, use Word's table feature, which is covered in Lesson 19.

When you define columns with text selected, the column definition will apply to the selected text. Word will insert section breaks before and after the selection. If you do not select text first, the column definitions will apply to the entire document unless you divided the document into two or more sections, in which case the columns will apply only to the current section. See Lesson 11 for more information about document sections.

Line between columns

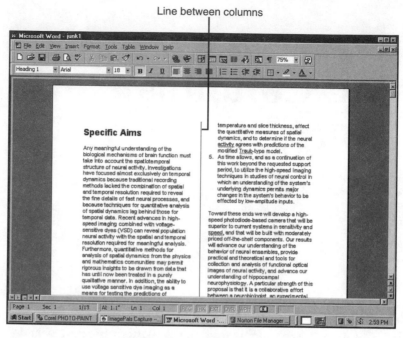

**Figure 20.1**  A document formatted with two columns.

# Creating Columns

Word has four predefined column layouts:

- Two equal width columns
- Three equal width columns
- Two unequal width columns with the wider column on the left
- Two unequal width columns with the wider column on the right

You can apply any of these column formats to an entire document, to one section of a document, to selected text, or from the insertion point onward. Follow these steps to learn how:

**1.** If you want only a part of the document in columns, select the text you want in columns, or move the insertion point to the location where you want columns to begin. Word will insert section breaks before and/or after the text, as appropriate.

**2.** Select **Format**, **Columns** to open the Columns dialog box (see Figure 20.2).

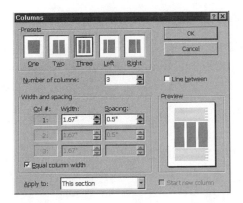

**Figure 20.2**   The Columns dialog box.

**3.** Under Presets, click the column format you want.

**4.** Click the **Apply To** drop-down arrow and specify the extent to which the columns should apply. The following options are available:

- **Whole Document**   This is available only if the document has not been broken into sections.

- **This Section**   Available only if you have broken the document into sections.

- **This Point Forward**   Word will insert a section break at the current cursor location and apply the new column setting to the latter of the two sections.

**5.** Select the **Line Between** check box to display a vertical line between columns (like in a newspaper).

**6.** Click **OK**.

**TIP**   **Quick Columns**   To display selected text, the current section, or the entire document in one to four equal width columns, click the **Columns** button on the Standard toolbar and then drag over the desired number of columns.

**CAUTION**   **No Columns?**   Columns display on-screen only in Page Layout view. In Normal view, Word displays only a single column at a time (although your multiple columns will look fine when printed, even from Normal view). To switch to Page Layout view, select **View**, **Page Layout**.

# Modifying Columns

You can modify existing columns, change the number of columns, change column widths, and change the spacing between columns. Here's how:

1. Move the cursor to the columns you want to modify.

2. Select **Format**, **Columns** to open the Columns dialog box (refer to Figure 20.2). The options in the dialog box will reflect the current settings for the columns you selected.

3. To apply a different predefined column format, click the desired format in the Presets area of the dialog box.

4. To change the width or spacing of a specific column, enter the desired width and spacing values (or click the arrows) in the column's **Width** and **Spacing** text boxes. The Preview box shows you what the settings will look like.

5. When you're satisfied with what you see in the Preview area, click **OK**.

# Turning Columns Off

To convert multiple column text back to normal text (which is really just one column), follow these steps:

1. Select the text that you want to change from multiple columns to a single column.

2. Select **Format**, **Columns** to open the Columns dialog box (refer to Figure 20.2).

3. Under Presets, select the **One** option.

4. Click **OK**.

 **TIP** **A Quicker Way** To quickly convert text in columns back to normal single-column text, select the text, click the **Columns** button on the Standard toolbar, and drag to select a single column.

This lesson showed you how to arrange text in columns. The next lesson shows you how to work with graphics in your document.

# Adding Graphics to Your Document

*In this lesson, you learn how to add graphics to your documents and how to create your own drawings.*

## Adding a Graphic Image

A *graphic image* is a picture that is stored on disk in a graphics file. Word can utilize graphics files created by a variety of applications, including PC Paint-brush, Windows' own Paint program, Lotus 1-2-3, Micrografx Designer, and AutoCAD. Additionally, your Word installation includes a small library of clip art images that you can use in your documents. Figure 21.1 shows a document with a graphic image.

To add a graphic image to a Word document, follow these steps:

1. Move the insertion point to the location for the graphic.
2. Select **Insert**, **Picture**, **From File**. The Insert Picture dialog box appears (see Figure 21.2).
3. If necessary, click the **Look In** drop-down arrow to specify the folder where the graphic file is located.
4. The large box in the center of the dialog box normally lists all graphics files in the specified directory. To have the list restricted to certain types of graphics files, click the **Files of Type** drop-down arrow and select the desired file type from the list.

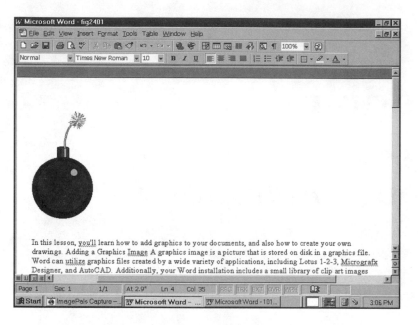

**Figure 21.1**   A document with a graphic.

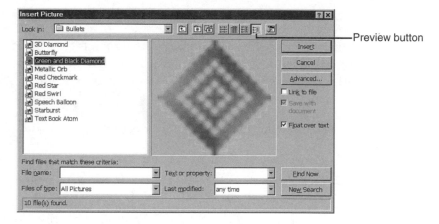

**Figure 21.2**   The Insert Picture dialog box.

**5.** Type the name of the file to insert in the **File Name** text box, or select the file name from the list.

**6.** To preview the picture in the Preview box, click the **Preview** button.

**7.** Choose from the following options:

- Select **Link to File** if you want the graphic in your document updated if the graphics file on disk changes.

- If you selected **Link to File**, you can select **Save with Document** to save a copy of the picture with the document. Although this increases the document's file size, it makes it possible for the picture to be displayed even if the original file is no longer available.

- Select **Float over Text** to enable the picture to be displayed "behind" or "over" text and other objects (otherwise the image will be displayed inline with text).

**8.** Click **OK**, and Word inserts the graphic into your document.

# Adding Clip Art

Clip art is a special category of pictures that consists of generally small, simple images that you use to add visual appeal and interest to your documents. Word comes with an extensive gallery of clip art that you can use freely. Here's how to add a clip art image to a document:

**1.** Move the cursor to the document location where you want the image.

**2.** Select **Insert**, **Picture**, **Clip Art** to open the Microsoft Clip Gallery dialog box (see Figure 21.3).

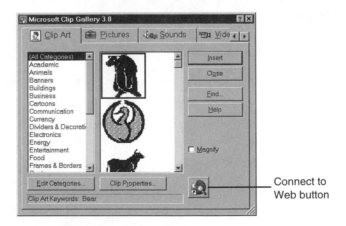

**Figure 21.3** Selecting clip art from the Microsoft Clip Gallery.

3. In the list on the left, select the desired category of images. Or, select **(All Categories)** to view all clip art images.

4. Scroll through the image list until you find the image you want. Then click it to select it.

5. Click **Insert** to add the image to your document.

**TIP**  **Word on the Web**  If you have Internet access, you can click the **Connect to Web** button in the Microsoft Clip Gallery dialog box to connect to Microsoft's Web site to access additional clip art images.

# Displaying Graphics

The screen display of graphics images can slow down screen scrolling. If you're working on the document text in Page Layout or Online Layout view and don't need to see the images, you can speed up screen display by displaying empty rectangles called *placeholders* in place of the images (images are automatically hidden in Normal and Outline view). In addition, if you selected the Link to File option when inserting the graphic file, Word inserts a field code in the document. The screen will display this code instead of the picture when field codes are displayed.

**TERM**  **Field Code**  A code in a document that tells Word to display a certain item, such as a graphic.

Here's how to control the display of graphics:

1. Select **Tools**, **Options** to open the Options dialog box.

2. If necessary, click the **View** tab to display the View options.

3. In the Show section, select or deselect the **Picture Placeholders** and **Field Codes** check boxes as desired.

4. Click **OK**.

The screen display of placeholders or field codes does not affect printing; the actual graphics are always printed in the document.

**TIP**   **Speed It Up!**   When working on a document that contains a lot of graphics, you can speed up screen display and scrolling by displaying placeholders for the graphics.

# Cropping and Resizing a Graphic

Before you can work with a graphic in your document, you must select it. There are two ways to do this:

- Click the graphic.
- Using the keyboard, position the insertion point immediately to the left of the graphic, and then press **Shift+→**.

A selected graphic is surrounded by eight small black squares called *sizing handles*. Figure 21.4 shows sizing handles around a selected clip art image.

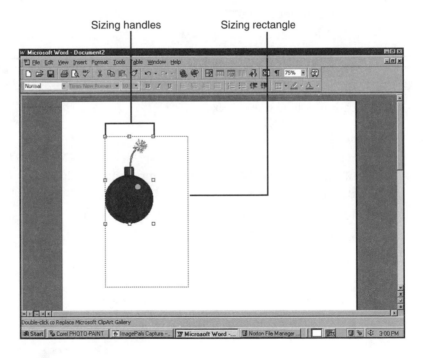

**Figure 21.4**   Resizing a selected graphic.

You can resize a graphic in your document to display the entire picture at a different size. You can also *crop* a graphic to hide portions of the picture that you don't want to display. To resize or crop a graphic, follow these steps:

1. Select the graphic.

2. Point at one of the resizing handles. The mouse pointer changes to a double-headed arrow.

3. Do either or both of the following, depending on how you want to modify the image:

    - To resize the graphic, press the left mouse button and drag the handle until the outline of the graphic reaches the desired size. You can either enlarge or shrink the graphic.

    - To crop the graphic, press and hold **Shift**, and then press the left mouse button and drag a handle toward the center of the graphic.

4. Release the mouse button.

# Deleting, Moving, and Copying Graphics

To delete a graphic, select it and press **Delete**. To move or copy a graphic to a new location, follow these steps:

1. Select the graphic.

2. To copy the graphic, press **Ctrl+C**, or select **Edit**, **Copy**, or click the **Copy** button on the Standard toolbar. To move the graphic, press **Ctrl+X**, or select **Edit**, **Cut**, or click the **Cut** button on the Standard toolbar.

3. Move the cursor to the new location for the graphic.

4. Press **Ctrl+V**, or select **Edit**, **Paste**, or click the **Paste** button on the Standard toolbar.

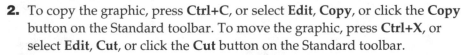
**TIP** **Drag That Image** If the image and its destination are both in view, you can move it by dragging it to the new location. To copy instead of moving, hold down **Ctrl** while dragging.

# Drawing in Your Document

In addition to adding existing graphics to a document, Word lets you create your own drawings. The drawing tools that are available let even the complete non-artist create professional-looking drawings. To draw, you must display the Drawing toolbar. **Select View**, **Toolbars**, **Drawing**. Figure 21.5 shows the Drawing toolbar and identifies the buttons on it.

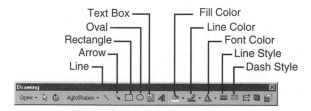

**Figure 21.5** The Drawing toolbar.

The process of drawing consists of the following general actions:

- Adding drawing objects to the document. The available objects include lines, arrows, shapes, and text. Most of Word's drawing objects are called *AutoShapes*.

- Moving drawing objects to new locations and changing their size and proportions.

- Modifying drawing objects. For example, you might change the thickness of a line, the color of text, or the type of arrowhead on an arrow.

The Drawing toolbar displays buttons for the most commonly needed drawing objects: lines, arrows, 3-D shapes, and so on. (You access the less common drawing objects via menus or dialog boxes associated with the Drawing toolbar.) The following list explains the most frequently used drawing procedures.

- To draw an object, click its button on the Drawing toolbar. Or, click the **AutoShapes** button and select the shape from the list. Then draw in the document to insert the object. Hold down **Shift** while drawing to draw an object with a 1:1 aspect ratio (for example, to draw a square or circle instead of a rectangle or ellipse).

- To select an object you have already drawn, click it. The object will display small rectangles called *resizing handles*. Hold down **Shift** and click to select more than one object. Press **Delete** to delete the selected object(s).
- To move a selected object, point at it (but not at a handle) and drag to the new location.
- To change a selected object's size or shape, point at one of its resizing handles and drag to the desired size/shape.
- To change the color of an object's line, click the **Line Color** button on the Drawing toolbar and select the desired color.
- To change the interior color of a solid object, click the **Fill Color** button and select the desired color.
- To change the thickness or style of the lines used for an object, select the object and click the **Line Style** or **Dash Style** button.
- To add a text label, click the **Text Box** button, drag in the document to add the text box, and then type the text. Click outside the text box when you're done.

Word's drawing capabilities go much further than what is described here. You should experiment on your own to discover their full capabilities.

In this lesson, you learned how to add graphics and drawings to your documents. The next lesson teaches you how to work with multiple documents.

# Working with Multiple Documents

*This lesson shows you how to simultaneously edit multiple documents in Word.*

## Multiple Documents?

Being able to work on one document at a time is often all you need, but in some situations the capability to work on multiple documents at once can be very useful. For example, you can refer to one document while working on another, and you can copy and move text between documents. Word lets you have as many documents as you need open simultaneously.

## Starting or Opening a Second Document

While you're working on one document, you can start a new document or open another existing document at any time. Use one of the following methods:

- To create a new document based on the Normal template, click the **New** button on the Standard toolbar.

- To create a document based on another template or one of Word's wizards, select **File**, **New**.

 **TIP** **Opening Multiple Documents at Once**  In the Open dialog box, you can select multiple documents by holding **Shift** and clicking the document names. Then click **Open** to open all of the selected documents.

- To open an existing document, select **File**, **Open** or click the **Open** button on the Standard toolbar.

A new window opens and displays the document you created or opened. Both the newly created and the original documents are in memory and can be edited, printed, and so on. You can continue opening additional documents until all of the files you need to work with are open.

# Switching Between Documents

When you have multiple documents open at one time, only one of them can be *active* at a given moment. The active document is displayed on-screen (although inactive documents may be displayed as well). The title bar of the active document is displayed in a darker color, and if documents are overlapping each other, the active one will be on top. The important thing you need to remember is that the active document is the only one affected by editing commands.

To switch between open documents, follow these steps:

1. Open the **Window** menu. At the bottom is a list of all open documents with a check mark next to the name of the currently active document (see Figure 22.1).

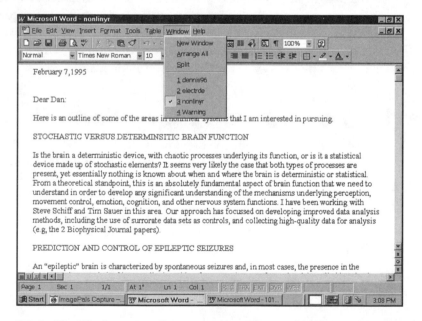

**Figure 22.1** The Window menu lists open documents and indicates the currently active document.

**2.** Select the name of the document you want to make active. (You can click the document name or press the corresponding number key.) The selected document becomes active and appears on-screen.

**3.** (Optional) To cycle to the next open document, press **Ctrl+F6**.

# Controlling Multiple Document View

Word gives you a great deal of flexibility in displaying multiple documents. You can have the active document occupy the entire screen, with other open documents temporarily hidden. You can also have several documents displayed at the same time, each in its own window. A document window can be in one of three states:

- **Maximized**   The window occupies the entire work area, and no other open documents are visible. When the active document is maximized, its title appears in Word's title bar at the top of the screen. Figure 22.2 shows a maximized document.

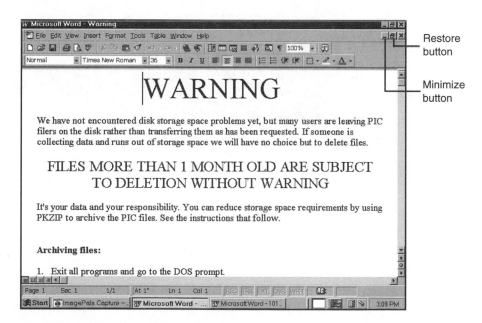

**Figure 22.2**   A maximized document window.

- **Minimized**   The window is reduced to a small icon displayed at the bottom of the Word screen. The document title is displayed on the icon.
- **Restored**   The document window assumes an intermediate size, and the document title is displayed in the title bar of its own window instead of Word's title bar. Figure 22.3 shows both a restored and a minimized document.

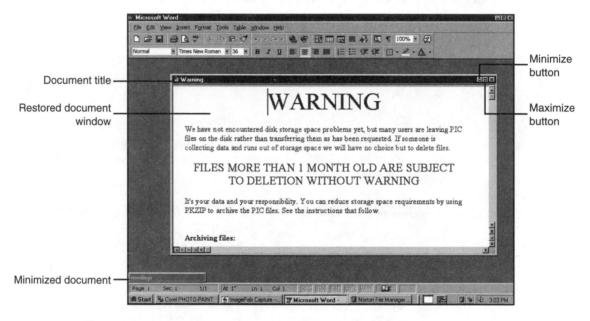

**Figure 22.3**   Restored and minimized document windows.

You can control the display of multiple documents in the following ways:

- To restore or minimize a maximized window, click its **Restore** or **Minimize** button.
- To maximize or minimize a restored window, click its **Maximize** or **Minimize** button.
- To display a minimized window, click its icon. Then either click its **Restore** or **Maximize** button or select from the pop-up menu that appears.

When a document is in the restored state, you can control the size and position of its window. To move the window, click its title bar and drag it to the new position. To change window size, point at a border or corner of the window (the mouse pointer changes to a two-headed arrow), and then click and drag the window to the desired size.

# Viewing All Open Documents

Word has a command that displays all of your open documents. Select **Window**, **Arrange All** to tile all document windows. When you tile your documents, every open document is displayed in a small window, and none of the windows overlap. If you have more than a few documents open, these windows will be quite small and won't be very useful for editing. They are useful, however, for seeing exactly which documents you have open and finding the one you need to work in at the moment. Figure 22.4 shows the result of the Window, Arrange All command with four documents open.

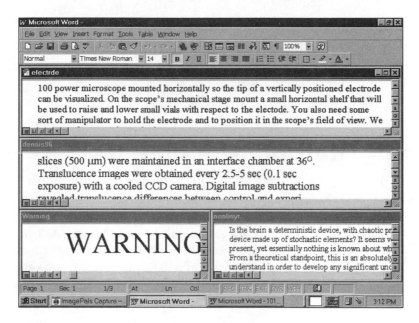

**Figure 22.4** The Arrange All command displays all open documents, each in its own window.

# Moving and Copying Text Between Documents

When you have more than one document open, you can move and copy text and graphics between documents. Follow these procedures to learn how:

**1.** Make the source document active, and then select the text and/or graphic you want to move or copy.

**2.** Press **Ctrl+X**, or select **Edit**, **Cut**, or click the **Cut** button on the Standard toolbar if you want to move the text. Press **Ctrl+C**, or select **Edit**, **Copy**, or click the **Copy** button on the Standard toolbar to copy the text.

**3.** Make the destination document active. Move the insertion point to the location for the text.

**4.** Press **Ctrl+V**, or select **Edit**, **Paste**, or click the **Paste** button on the Standard toolbar.

If both documents are visible, you can copy or move text from one to the other with drag-and-drop, as described here:

**1.** Select the text to be copied or moved.

**2.** Point at the selected text. To move the text, press and hold the left mouse button. To copy the text, press **Ctrl** and the left mouse button.

**3.** Drag to the new location for the text and release the mouse button (and the Ctrl key, if you were copying).

# Saving Multiple Documents

When you're working with multiple documents, you save individual documents with the **File**, **Save** and **File**, **Save As** commands you learned about in Lesson 4. These commands save the active document only. There is no command to save all open documents in one step. If you attempt to close a document that has not been saved, you will be prompted to save it. If you try to quit Word with one or more documents unsaved, you will be prompted one-by-one to save each document.

**TIP** **No Save All** The Save All command that was available in earlier versions of Word is not present in Word 97.

# Closing a Document

You can close an open document when you finish working with it. These steps teach you how to close a document:

**1.** Make the document active.

**2.** Select **File**, **Close** or click the **Close** button at the right end of the document's title bar. (Be sure not to click the Close button in Word's main title bar.)

**3.** If the document contains unsaved changes, Word prompts you to save the document. Click **Yes** to save the file, or click **No**. Either way, Word closes the document.

This lesson showed you how to simultaneously edit multiple documents in Word.

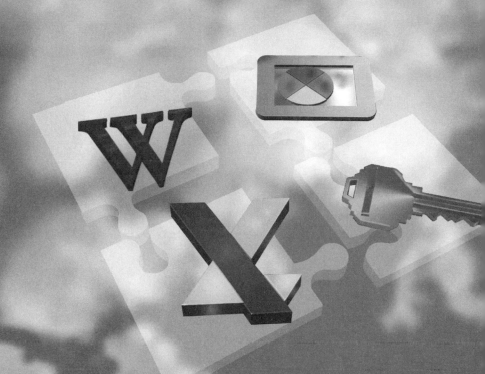

# Excel

# Starting and Exiting Excel

*In this lesson, you learn how to start and end a typical Excel work session.*

## Starting Excel

After you installed Excel (as covered in Lesson 1 of Part 7 of this book), the installation program returned you to the desktop. To start Excel from there, follow these steps:

1. Click the **Start** button, and the Start menu appears.
2. Choose **Programs**, and the Programs menu appears.
3. Choose the **Microsoft Excel** program item to start the program.

The Excel opening screen appears (see Figure 1.1), displaying a blank *workbook* labeled Book1. Excel is now ready for you to begin creating your workbook.

**Workbook**   An Excel file is called a *workbook*. Each workbook consists of three worksheets (although you can add or remove worksheets as needed). Each worksheet consists of columns and rows that intersect to form boxes called *cells* into which you enter text. The tabs at the bottom of the workbook (labeled Sheet1, Sheet2, and so on) let you flip through the worksheets by clicking them with the mouse.

**What's the Office Assistant?**   When you first start Excel, you're greeted by an animated icon called the Office Assistant. He's there to offer help, and he'll pop up from time to time whenever you encounter new features. You'll find information about the Office Assistant in Part 7, Lesson 2. For now, close the Assistant by clicking **Start Using Microsoft Excel**.

Menu bar —
Standard toolbar —
Formatting toolbar —

Worksheet area —

Office Assistant —

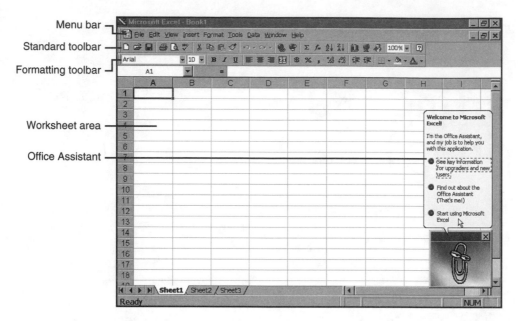

**Figure 1.1** Excel's opening screen displays a blank workbook named Book1.

You can also start Excel by opening an existing workbook. (You can do this only after you've created and saved a workbook, as you'll learn to do in upcoming lessons.) To start Excel and have Excel automatically open a workbook for you, follow these steps:

1. Click the **Start** button, and the Start menu appears.

2. Click **Open Office Document**. Excel displays the Open Office Document dialog box, displaying the contents of the My Documents folder.

3. Because you typically save your workbooks to the My Documents folder, they should be displayed at this point. However, if you don't see your workbook file listed, change to the folder that contains the workbook you want to open.

4. Click the workbook's file name to select it. Then click **Open** to open it and start Excel.

If you installed the Office Shortcut Bar, you can also start Excel by clicking the **Excel** button on the Shortcut Bar.

# A Look at the Excel Screen

You will perform most operations in Excel using commands available through the menu bar at the top of the screen, and the Standard and Formatting toolbars just below the menu bar. In the next two lessons, you'll learn about the operations you can perform using the menu bar and the Standard toolbar.

# Exiting Excel

To exit Excel and return to the Windows desktop, perform either of these two steps:

- Open the **File** menu and select **Exit**.

  or

- Click the **Close** (X) button in the Excel window.

If you changed the workbook in any way without saving the file, Excel displays a prompt asking if you want to save the file before exiting. Select the desired option. See Lesson 6 for help in saving your workbook.

In this lesson, you learned how to start and exit Excel. In the next lesson, you'll learn about the Excel workbook window.

# Examining the Excel Window

*In this lesson, you learn the basics of moving around in the Excel window and in the workbook window.*

## Parts of the Excel Window

As you can see in Figure 2.1, the Excel window contains many common Windows elements, including a menu bar (from which you can select commands), a Status bar (which displays the status of the current activity), and toolbars (which contain buttons and drop-down lists that provide quick access to common commands and features).

**CAUTION**

**Missing Status Bar?** By default, Excel does not display the status bar. To display it, open the **Tools** menu, select **Options**, and click the **View** tab. In the Show area, select **Status Bar** and click **OK**.

In addition, the window contains some elements that are unique to Excel, including:

**Formula bar** When you enter information into a *cell*, anything you type appears in the Formula bar. The cell's location also appears in the Formula bar.

**TERM**

**Cell** Each page in a workbook is a separate worksheet, and each worksheet contains a grid consisting of alphabetized columns and numbered rows. Where a row and column intersect, they form a box called a *cell*. Each cell has an *address* that consists of the column letter and row number (A1, B3, C4, and so on). You enter data and formulas in the cells to create your worksheets. You'll learn more about cells in Lessons 4 and 5.

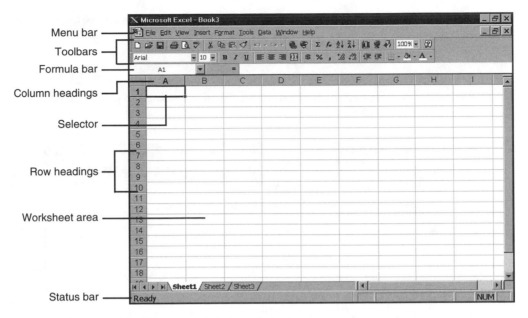

Menu bar
Toolbars
Formula bar
Column headings
Selector
Row headings
Worksheet area
Status bar

**Figure 2.1** Elements of the Excel window.

**Workbook window** Each Excel file is a workbook that consists of one or more worksheets. You can open several files (workbooks) at a time, each in its own window.

**Column headings** The letters across the top of the worksheet, which identify the columns in the worksheet.

**Row headings** The numbers down the side of the worksheet, which identify the rows in the worksheet.

**Selector** The outline that indicates the active cell (the one in which you are working).

# Moving from Worksheet to Worksheet

By default, each workbook starts off with three worksheets. You can add worksheets to or delete worksheets from the workbook as needed. Because each workbook consists of one or more worksheets, you need a way of moving from worksheet to worksheet easily. Use one of the following methods:

- Press **Ctrl+PgDn** to move to the next worksheet or **Ctrl+PgUp** to move to a previous one.

  or

- Click the tab of the worksheet you want to go to (see Figure 2.2). If the tab is not shown, use the tab scroll buttons to bring the tab into view, and then click the tab.

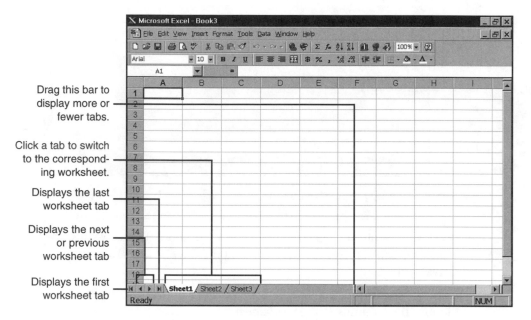

Drag this bar to display more or fewer tabs.

Click a tab to switch to the corresponding worksheet.

Displays the last worksheet tab

Displays the next or previous worksheet tab

Displays the first worksheet tab

**Figure 2.2**   You can move from worksheet to worksheet with tabs.

## Moving Within a Worksheet

Once the worksheet you want to work on is displayed, you'll need some way of moving to the various cells within the worksheet. Keep in mind that the part of the worksheet displayed on-screen is only a small part of the actual worksheet. To move around the worksheet with your keyboard, use the keys listed in Table 2.1.

**Table 2.1** Moving Around a Worksheet with the Keyboard

| Press This... | To Move... |
|---|---|
| ↑ ↓ ← → | One cell in the direction of the arrow. |
| Ctrl+↑ or Ctrl+↓ | To the top or bottom of a data region (the area of a worksheet that contains data). |
| Ctrl+← or Ctrl+→ | To the leftmost or rightmost cell in a data region. |
| PgUp | Up one screen. |
| PgDn | Down one screen. |
| Home | Leftmost cell in a row. |
| Ctrl+Home | Upper-left corner of a worksheet. |
| Ctrl+End | Lower-right corner of the data area. |
| End+↑, End+↓, End+←, End+→ | If the active cell is blank, moves in the direction of the arrow to the *first* cell that contains data. If the active cell contains an entry, moves in the direction of the arrow to the *last* cell that has an entry. |

If you have a mouse, you can use the scroll bars to scroll to the area of the screen that contains the cell you want to work with. Then click the cell to make it the active cell.

Keep in mind that as you scroll, the scroll box moves within the scroll bar to tell you where you are within the file. In addition, the size of the scroll box changes to represent the amount of the total worksheet that is currently visible. If the scroll box is large, you know you're seeing most of the current worksheet in the window. If the scroll box is small, most of the worksheet is currently hidden from view.

**TIP**    **Fast Scrolling**    If you want to scroll to a specific row within a large worksheet, press and hold the **Shift** key while you drag the scroll box. The current row is displayed as you move the scroll box.

**TIP** **Move to a Specific Cell** To move quickly to a specific cell on a worksheet, type the cell's address in the **Name** box at the left end of the Formula bar and press **Enter**. A cell address consists of the column letter and row number that define the location of the cell (for example **C25**). To go to a cell on a specific worksheet, type the worksheet's name, an exclamation point, and the cell address (such as **sheet3!C25**) and press **Enter**.

## Scrolling Through a Worksheet with the IntelliMouse

With Office 97, Microsoft introduces a new mouse called the Microsoft IntelliMouse. If you've installed the IntelliMouse, you can use it to move through a worksheet even more quickly than you can with a conventional mouse. Here's how:

| To... | Do This... |
|---|---|
| Scroll a few rows | Rotate the wheel in the middle of the mouse forward or backward. |
| Scroll faster (pan) | Click and hold the wheel button, and then drag the mouse in the direction in which you want to pan (scroll fast). The further away from the origin mark (the four-headed arrow) you drag the mouse, the faster the panning action. To slow the pan, drag the mouse back toward the origin mark. |
| Pan without holding | To pan without holding the wheel button down, simply click it once and then move the mouse in the direction in which you want to pan. You'll continue to pan when you move the mouse until you turn panning off by clicking the wheel again. |

# Changing the View of Your Worksheet

There are many ways to change how your worksheet appears within the Excel window. Changing the view has no effect on how your worksheets will look when printed, but changing the view and getting a different perspective often helps you see your data more clearly. For example, you can enlarge or reduce the size of its text in order to view more or less of the worksheet at one time. You can also "freeze" row or column headings so you won't lose your place as you scroll through a large worksheet.

# Magnifying and Reducing the Worksheet View

To enlarge or reduce your view of the current worksheet, use the Zoom feature. Simply click the **Zoom** button (on the Standard toolbar) and select the zoom percentage you want to use, such as **25%** or **200%**. You can enlarge a specific area of the worksheet if you'd like by selecting it first, opening the **Zoom** menu, and choosing **Selection**.

If you want, you can display your worksheet so that it takes up the full screen—eliminating toolbars, Formula bar, Status bar, and so on—as shown in Figure 2.3. To do so, open the **View** menu and select **Full Screen**. To return to normal view, click **Close Full Screen**.

> **TIP**    **Fast Zoom**    If you use the IntelliMouse, you can zoom in and out quickly by pressing and holding the **Ctrl** key and moving the wheel forward or backward.

Click here to exit full screen view.

| File Edit View Insert Format Tools Data Window Help | | | | | | | |
|---|---|---|---|---|---|---|---|
| | A | B | C | D | E | F | G | H |

**Holly and Roses Garden Club, Gardendale, Indiana**

|  |  |  |  |  |  |
|---|---|---|---|---|---|
| President: | Barbara Bush | | Vice-President: Julie Bounds | | |
| Secretary: | Marti Luck | | Treasurer:  Jennifer Flynn | | |
| Membership for 1996 | Dues: $20, Life Members: $15 | | | | |

| Number | New for 1996? | Name | Dues | Year Joined |
|---|---|---|---|---|
| 1 | NEW | Mrs. Barbara Adamson | $  20.00 | 1996 |
| 2 | | Mrs. Diana Bond | $  20.00 | 1995 |
| 3 | | Mrs. Julie Bounds | $  20.00 | 1996 |
| 4 | | Mrs. Barbara Bush | | 1975 |
| 5 | NEW | Mrs. Mary Jane Brink | $  20.00 | 1996 |
| 6 | | Mrs. Diana Dogwood | $  15.00 | |
| 7 | | Mrs. Lucy Fan | $  15.00 | |
| 8 | | Mrs. Michele Floyd | $  20.00 | 1994 |
| 9 | | Mrs. Jennifer Flynn | $  20.00 | 1995 |
| 10 | NEW | Mrs. Betty High | $  20.00 | 1996 |
| 11 | | Mrs. Addie Howard | $  20.00 | 1992 |
| 12 | | Mrs. Ashley Kay | | 1987 |
| 13 | | Mrs. Rhoda Kuntz | $  15.00 | 1976 |
| 14 | | Mrs. Verna Latinz | $  20.00 | 1995 |
| 15 | | Mrs. Martha Luck | $  20.00 | 1987 |
| 16 | | Mrs. Anne Powell | $  20.00 | 1990 |
| 17 | | Mrs. Julie Powell | $  20.00 | 1994 |
| 18 | | Ms. Suzanne Punch | $  20.00 | 1994 |

Full Screen [X]
Close Full Screen

**Dues Paid** / State Membership List / Calendar 1996 / S

**Figure 2.3**  View your worksheet in a full window.

# Freezing Column and Row Headings

As you scroll through a large worksheet, it's often helpful to freeze your headings so that you can view them with related data. For example, as you can see in Figure 2.4, you need to be able to view the column and row headings in order to understand the data in the cells.

To freeze row or column headings (or both), follow these steps:

**1.** Click the cell to the right of the row headings and/or below any column headings you want to freeze. This highlights the cell.

**2.** Open the **Window** menu and select **Freeze Panes**.

Play around a little, moving the cursor all around the document. As you do, the row and/or column headings remain locked in their positions. This enables you to view data in other parts of the worksheet without losing track of what that data represents. To unlock headings, open the **Window** menu again and select **Unfreeze Panes**.

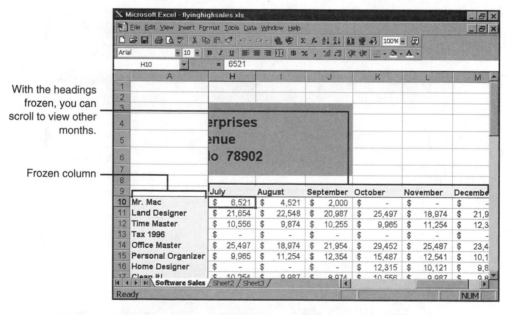

**Figure 2.4** As you scroll, the frozen headings remain in place.

# Splitting Worksheets

Sometimes when you're working with a large worksheet, you find yourself wanting to view two parts of it at one time in order to compare data. To view two parts of a worksheet, you *split* it. Figure 2.5 shows a split worksheet.

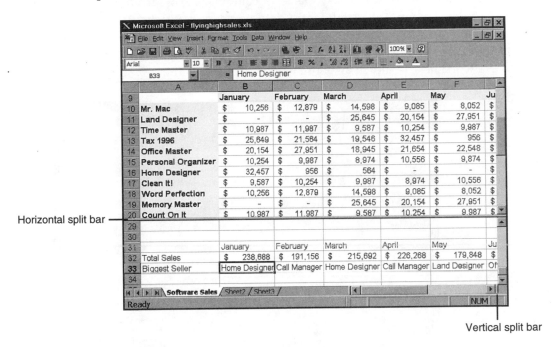

Horizontal split bar

Vertical split bar

**Figure 2.5**   Split a worksheet to view two parts at one time.

Follow these steps to split a worksheet:

**1.** Click either the vertical or the horizontal split bar.

**2.** Drag the split bar into the worksheet window.

**3.** Drop the split bar, and Excel splits the window at that location. When you scroll, the two panes automatically scroll in synch.

To remove the split, drag it back to its original position on the scroll bar.

# Hiding Workbooks, Worksheets, Columns, and Rows

For those times when you're working on high priority or top secret information, you can hide workbooks, worksheets, columns or rows from prying eyes. For example, if you have confidential data stored in one particular worksheet, you can hide that worksheet, yet still be able to view the other worksheets in that workbook. You can also hide particular columns (see Figure 2.6) or rows within a worksheet—or even an entire workbook if you want.

Columns D and E, which contain addresses and phone numbers, are hidden from view.

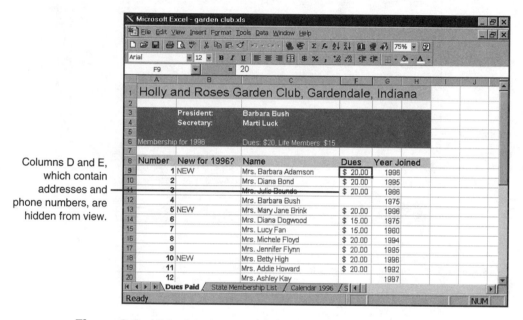

**Figure 2.6**  Hide data to prevent it from being viewed, printed, or changed.

So in addition to hiding data in order to prevent it from appearing on a report, you might hide it to prevent it from accidentally being changed. When data is hidden, it cannot be viewed, printed, or changed. This is *unlike* other changes you might make to the view (such as changing the zoom percentage), which do not affect your worksheet when printed. Hiding data *does* prevent that data from being printed.

Use these methods to hide data:

- To hide a *workbook*, open the **Window** menu and select **Hide**.
- To hide a *worksheet*, click its tab to select it. Then open the **Format** menu, select **Sheet**, and select **Hide**.
- To hide *rows* or *columns*, click a row or column heading to select it. Then open the **Format** menu, select **Row** or **Column**, and select **Hide**.

**TIP**  **Hide More Than One**   To select several worksheets, press and hold **Ctrl** while you click each tab. To select several rows or columns, press and hold **Ctrl** while you click each heading.

Of course, whenever you need to, you can redisplay the hidden data easily. To redisplay hidden data, select the hidden area first. For example, select the rows, columns, or sheets adjacent to the hidden ones. Then repeat the previous steps, selecting **Unhide** from the appropriate menus.

**You Can't Hide It Completely!**   It's easy to undo the command to hide data, so you can't really hide data completely as a means of security. If you give the workbook file to someone else, for example, he or she can easily
**CAUTION**  unhide and view the data you hid.

In this lesson, you learned about the elements of the Excel window and how to move around within workbooks and worksheets. You also learned how to change the view of your worksheet, freeze column and row headings, and hide data. In the next lesson, you will learn how to use Excel's toolbars.

# Using Excel's Toolbars

*In this lesson, you learn how to use Excel's toolbars to save time when you work. You also learn how to arrange them for maximum performance.*

## Using the Toolbars

Unless you tell it otherwise, Excel displays the Standard and Formatting toolbars as shown in Figure 3.1. To select a tool from a toolbar, simply click the tool.

**CAUTION**

**Off Duty**   If a tool appears grayed, it is currently unavailable. Tools become unavailable when they are not applicable to your current activity.

**TERM**

**What Is a Toolbar?**   An Excel toolbar is a collection of tools or icons displayed in a long bar that can be moved and reshaped to make it more convenient for you to use. Each icon represents a common command or task.

Here are some easy ways to learn about the available toolbar buttons:

- To view the name of a button, position the mouse pointer over it. Excel displays a ScreenTip, which displays the name of the button (as shown in Figure 3.1).

- To get help with the command associated with a particular button, press **Shift+F1**. The mouse pointer changes to a question mark. Move the question mark pointer over a button and click it.

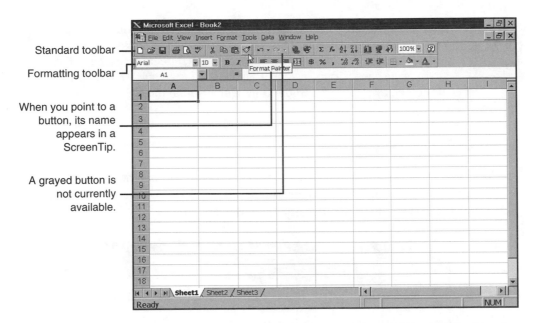

Standard toolbar ⎯

Formatting toolbar ⎯

When you point to a button, its name appears in a ScreenTip.

A grayed button is not currently available.

**Figure 3.1**   The Standard and Formatting toolbars contain buttons for Excel's most commonly used features.

# Turning Toolbars On and Off

By default, Excel initially displays the Standard and Formatting toolbars. If you find that you don't use these toolbars, you can turn one or both of them off to free up some screen space. In addition, you can turn on other toolbars (although some toolbars appear on their own when you perform a related activity).

Follow these steps to turn a toolbar on or off:

1. Open the **View** menu and choose **Toolbars**. A submenu appears.
2. A check mark next to a toolbar's name indicates that the toolbar is currently being displayed. To turn a toolbar on or off (whichever it's not), simply click its name in the list to add or remove the check mark.

**TIP**   **Quick View**   To display a hidden toolbar quickly, right-click on an existing toolbar and select the toolbar you want to display from the shortcut menu.

**229**

**Excel on the Web** Excel for Windows 97 allows you to open Web pages within its window, which you'll learn to do Part 7, Lesson 6. When you're working on the Web, the Web toolbar is displayed. Because the other Excel toolbars are unnecessary in such a situation, you can quickly remove them from the screen by clicking the **Show Only Web Toolbar** button.

# Moving Toolbars

After you have displayed the toolbars you need, you can position them in your work area where they are most convenient. Figure 3.2 shows an Excel screen with three toolbars in various positions on the screen.

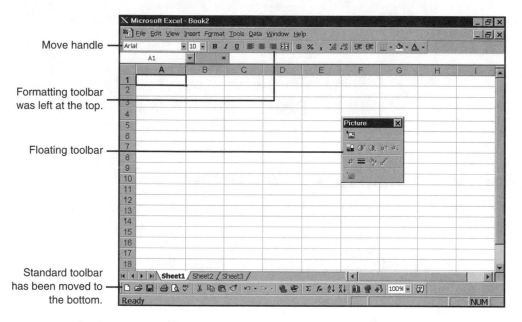

**Figure 3.2** Three toolbars in various positions.

Here's what you do to move a toolbar:

**1.** Click a toolbar's move handle. (If the toolbar is floating in the middle of the window, click its title bar instead.)

**2.** Hold down the mouse button and drag the toolbar to where you want it. You can drag it to a side of the window (to a "dock") or let it "float" anywhere in the window.

Although you can drag a toolbar anywhere, if you drag one that contains a drop-down list (such as the Standard or Formatting toolbar) to the left or right side of the window, the drop-down list buttons disappear. If you move the toolbar back to the top or bottom of the window (or let it float) the drop-down lists reappear.

 **Floating Toolbar**   A floating toolbar acts just like a window. You can drag its title bar to move it or drag a border to size it. If you drag a floating toolbar to the top or bottom of the screen, it turns back into a horizontal toolbar.

 **Quickly Moving a Toolbar**   To quickly move a floating toolbar to the top of the screen, double-click its title bar. To move a docked toolbar into the middle of the window, double-click its move handle.

In Excel for Windows 97, the worksheet's menu bar is treated the same as other toolbars. This means you can move it to the side of a window, or you can float it in the middle if you want. It also means that you can customize the menu bar in a manner similar to toolbars, as discussed in the next section.

# Customizing the Toolbars

If Excel's toolbars provide too few (or too many) options for you, you can create your own toolbars or customize existing toolbars. To customize a toolbar, follow these steps:

1. Right-click on any toolbar and choose **Customize** from the shortcut menu, or open the **Tools** menu and select **Customize**.

2. If the toolbar you want to customize is not currently visible, click the **Toolbars** tab and select it from the list. The toolbar appears.

3. To change the size of the toolbar icons, to turn on or off ScreenTips, or to change the animation of your menus, click the **Options** tab. On the Options tab, select the options you want to apply. For example, to make the toolbar icons larger, click the **Large Icons** option.

4. To add or remove buttons from a toolbar, click the **Commands** tab.

5. To add a button to a toolbar, select its category. (For example, to add the Clear Contents button to a toolbar, select the Edit category.) You can add menus to a toolbar as well; you'll find them listed at the bottom of the

Categories list. Once you've selected the proper category, click the command you want and drag it onto the toolbar, as shown in Figure 3.3.

Drag a button to a toolbar to add it.

**Figure 3.3** To add a button to a toolbar, drag it there.

> **TIP** **Don't Know What an Option Is For?** Simply select the command and then click **Description** to learn what that command does.

**6.** To remove a button from a toolbar, drag it off the toolbar.

**7.** To rearrange the buttons on a toolbar, drag them around within the bar.

**8.** Click the **Close** button when you're finished.

If you decide you don't like the changes that have been made to a toolbar, you can return to its default settings (the way it was before you or someone else changed it). From within the Customize dialog box, click **Toolbars**, highlight the name of the toolbar you want to reset, and then click the **Reset** button.

# Creating Your Own Toolbar

Instead of changing any of the standard Excel toolbars, you can create one of your own and fill it with the tools you use most often. Follow these steps to learn how:

1. Open the **Tools** menu and select **Customize.**
2. Click the **Toolbars** tab.
3. Click the **New** button.
4. Type a name for your new toolbar (such as Jen's Favorites) and click **OK.** Excel creates a new floating toolbar.
5. Click the **Commands** tab, select the proper category for a desired button, and then drag it onto the toolbar.
6. Repeat step 5 to add more buttons to your new toolbar. When you finish, click **Close.**

If you want to delete a custom toolbar, open the **Tools** menu and select **Customize.** In the Toolbars list, click the custom toolbar you want to delete. Then click the **Delete** button in the Customize dialog box.

In this lesson, you learned how to use Excel's toolbars and to customize them for your own unique needs. In the next lesson, you'll learn how to enter different types of data.

# Entering Different Kinds of Data

*In this lesson, you learn how to enter different types of data in an Excel worksheet.*

## The Data Types

To create a worksheet that does something, you must enter data into the cells that make up the worksheet. There are many types of data that you can enter, including:

- Text
- Numbers
- Dates
- Times
- Formulas
- Functions

In this lesson, you'll learn how to enter text, numbers, dates, and times. In Lessons 12, 13, and 14, you'll learn how to enter formulas and functions.

## Entering Text

Text is any combination of letters, numbers, and spaces. By default, text is automatically left-aligned in a cell.

To enter text into a cell:

**1.** Click in the cell in which you want to enter text.

**2.** Type the text. As you type, your text appears in the cell and in the Formula bar, as shown in Figure 4.1.

**3.** Press **Enter**. Your text appears in the cell, left-aligned. (You can also press Tab or an arrow key to enter the text and move to another cell.) And if you've made a mistake and you want to abandon your entry, press **Esc** instead.

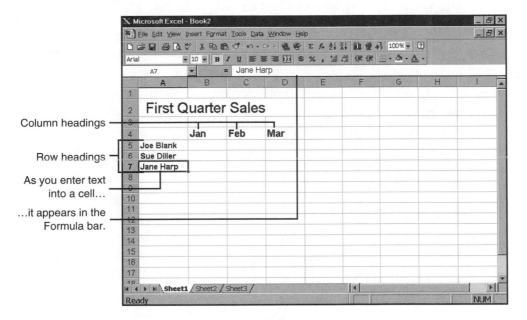

Column headings

Row headings

As you enter text into a cell...

...it appears in the Formula bar.

**Figure 4.1**  Data that you enter also appears in the Formula bar as you type it.

**But It Doesn't Fit!**  To widen a column to display all of its data, move to the column headings bar at the top of the worksheet. Then double-click the *right* border of the column you want to "autofit" to hold your data. See Lesson 18 for **CAUTION**  more help.

**TIP**  **Numbers As Text**  You might want to enter a number that will be treated as text (such as a ZIP code). To do so, precede the entry with a single quotation mark ('), as in **'46220**. The single quotation mark is an alignment prefix that tells Excel to treat the following characters as text and left-align them in the cell.

# Entering Column and Row Headings

Column and row headings identify your data. Column headings appear across the top of the worksheet beneath the title. Row headings are entered on the left side of the worksheet, usually in Column A.

Column headings describe what the numbers in a column represent. Typically, column headings specify time periods such as years, months, days, dates, and so on. Row headings describe what the numbers in each row represent. Typically, row headings specify data categories, such as product names, employee names, or income and expense items in a budget.

When entering column headings, press the **Tab** key to move from one cell to the next instead of pressing **Enter**. When entering row headings, use the **down arrow** key instead.

**TIP**     **Entering Similar Data As Headings**   When you need to enter similar data (such as a series of months or years) as column or row headings, there's a trick for entering them quickly. See the section, "Entering a Series with AutoFill," later in this lesson for help.

# Adding Comments to Cells

You can use cell comments to provide detailed information about data in a worksheet. For example, you can create a comment to help remind you of the purpose behind a particular formula or data that should be updated. Once you create a comment, you can display it at any time.

To add a comment to a cell, do the following:

1. Select the cell to which you want to add a comment.

2. Open the **Insert** menu and choose **Comment** or click the **New Comment** button on the Reviewing toolbar.
3. Type your comment, as shown in Figure 4.2.
4. Click outside the cell. A red triangle appears in the upper-right corner of the cell to show that it contains a comment.

To view comments later, point to any cell that contains a red dot in its upper-right corner. Excel displays the comment.

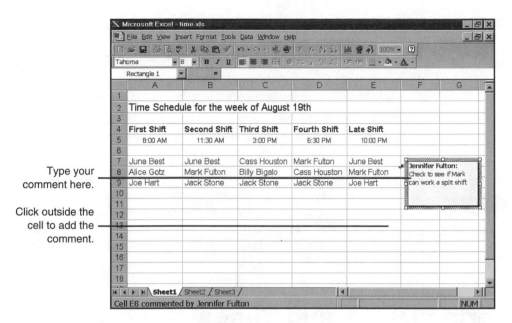

Type your comment here.

Click outside the cell to add the comment.

**Figure 4.2** Adding a cell comment.

To edit a comment, select the cell that contains the note and choose **Insert**, **Edit Comment**. Make your changes, and then click outside the cell to save them. To delete a comment, click the cell, select **Edit**, **Clear**, and then select **Comments**.

# Entering Numbers

Valid numbers can include the numeric characters 0–9 and any of these special characters: + – / . , ( ) $ % . This means that you can include commas, decimal points, dollar signs, percent signs, and parentheses in the values that you enter.

Although you can include punctuation when you type your entries, you may not want to. For example, instead of typing a column of dollar amounts including dollar signs, commas, and decimal points, you can type numbers such as 700 and 81295, and then format the column with currency formatting. Excel then changes your entries to $700.00 and $81,295.00 or to $700 and $81295, depending on the number of decimal points you specify. See Lesson 15 for more information.

To enter a number:

1. Click the cell into which you want to enter a number.
2. Type the number. To enter a negative number, precede it with a minus sign or surround it with parentheses. To enter a fraction, precede it with a 0, as in 0 1/2.
3. Press **Enter**, and the number appears in the cell, right-aligned.

**CAUTION**

**#######**   If you enter a number and it appears in the cell as all pound signs (#######) or in scientific notation (such as 7.78E+06), don't worry—the number is okay. The cell just isn't wide enough to display the entire number. To fix it, move to the column headings at the top of the worksheet and double-click the right border of the column. The column expands to fit the largest entry. See Lesson 18 for more help.

# Entering Dates and Times

You can enter dates and times in a variety of formats. When you enter a date using a format shown in Table 4.1, Excel converts the date into a number that reflects the number of days between January 1, 1900 and that date. Even though you won't see this number (Excel displays your entry as a normal date), the number is used whenever you use this date in a calculation. By the way, the feature that automatically formats your data based on the way you enter it is called AutoFormat.

**Table 4.1**  Valid Formats for Dates and Times

| Format | Example |
| --- | --- |
| M/D | 4/8 |
| M-YY | 4-58 |
| MM/DD/YY | 4/8/58 or 04/08/58 |
| MMM-YY | Jan-92 |
| MMMMMMMM-YY | September-93 |
| MMMMMMMM DD, YYYY | September 3, 1993 |
| DD-MMM-YY | 28-Oct-91 |
| DD-MMM | 6-Sep |

| Format | Example |
|---|---|
| HH:MM | 16:50 |
| HH:MM:SS | 8:22:59 |
| HH:MM AM/PM | 7:45 PM |
| HH:MM:SS AM/PM | 11:45:16 AM |
| MM/DD/YY HH:MM | 11/8/80 4:20 |

Follow these steps to learn how to enter a date or time:

**1.** Click the cell into which you want to enter a date or time.

**2.** Type the date or time in the format in which you want it displayed. You can use hyphens (-) or slashes (/) when typing dates.

**3.** Press **Enter**. As long as Excel recognizes the entry as a date or time, it appears right-aligned in the cell. If Excel doesn't recognize it, it's treated as text and left-aligned.

If you're entering a column of dates, you can specify the date format you want first. Then as you type your dates, Excel will automatically adapt them to fit that format. For example, suppose you like the MMMMMMMMM DD, YYYY format. Instead of typing each date in full, you could select that format for the column and then type 9/3/93, and Excel would change it to display September 3, 1993. To format a column, click the column header to select the column. Then open the **Format** menu and select **Cells**. On the **Numbers** tab, select the date format you want. (See Lesson 5 for more help.)

**CAUTION**

**Not Wide Enough?**  If you enter a long date and it appears in the cell as all number signs (#######), Excel is trying to tell you that the column is not wide enough to display it.

**CAUTION**

**Day or Night?**  Unless you type AM or PM after your time entry, Excel assumes that you are using a 24-hour military clock. Therefore, 8:20 is assumed to be AM, not PM. So if you mean PM, type the entry as 8:20 PM (or 8:20 p if you want to use a shortcut). Note that you must type a space between the time and the AM or PM notation.

# Copying Entries Quickly

You can copy an existing entry into surrounding cells by performing the following steps:

**1.** Click the fill handle of the cell whose contents you want to copy.

**2.** Drag the fill handle down or to the right to copy the data to adjacent cells (see Figure 4.3). A bubble appears to let you know *exactly* what data is being copied to the other cells.

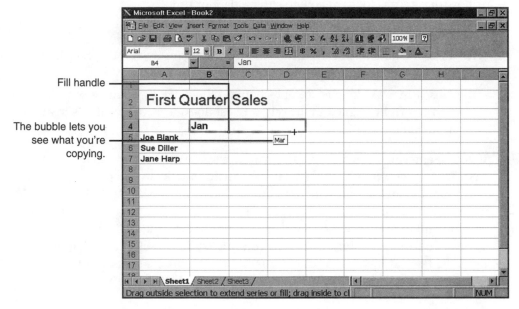

Fill handle

The bubble lets you see what you're copying.

**Figure 4.3**  Drag the fill handle to copy the contents and formatting into neighboring cells.

If you're copying a number, a month, or other item that might be interpreted as a series (such as January, February, and so on), but you *don't* want to create a series—you just want to copy the contents of the cell exactly—press and hold the **Ctrl** key as you drag the fill handle.

**TIP** **Copying Across Worksheets** You can copy the contents of cells from one worksheet to one or more worksheets in the workbook. First select the worksheet(s) you want to copy to by clicking the sheet tabs while holding down the **Ctrl** key. Then select the cells you want to copy (see Lesson 5). Open the **Edit** menu, select **Fill**, and select **Across Worksheets**. Then select **All** (to copy both the cells' contents and their formatting), **Contents**, or **Formats**, and click **OK**.

# Entering a Series with AutoFill

Entering a series (such as January, February, and March or 1994, 1995, 1996, and 1997) is similar to copying a cell's contents. As you drag the fill handle of the original cell, AutoFill does all the work for you, interpreting the first entry and creating a series of entries based on it. For example, if you type Monday in a cell, and then drag the cell's fill handle over some adjacent cells, you'll create the series Monday, Tuesday, Wednesday…. As you drag, the bubble let's you know exactly what you're copying so that you can stop at the appropriate cell to create exactly the series you want.

## Entering a Custom Series

Although AutoFill is good for a brief series of entries, you may encounter situations in which you need more control. Excel can handle several different types of series, as shown in Table 4.2.

**Table 4.2** Data Series

| Series | Initial Entries | Resulting Series |
| --- | --- | --- |
| Linear | 1,2 | 1, 2, 3, 4 |
|  | 100,99 | 100, 99, 98, 97 |
|  | 1,3 | 1, 3, 5, 7 |
| Growth | 10, 20 | 10, 20, 30, 40 |
|  | 10, 50 | 10, 50, 90, 130 |
| Date | Mon, Wed | Mon, Wed, Fri |
|  | Feb, May | Feb, May, Aug |
|  | Qtr1, Qtr3 | Qtr1, Qtr3, Qtr1 |
|  | 1992, 1995 | 1992, 1995, 1998 |

Basically, you make two sample entries for your series in adjacent cells, and Excel uses them to calculate the rest of the series. Here's what you do:

1. Enter the first value in one cell and press **Enter**.

2. Move to the second cell and enter the next value in the series.

3. Select both cells by dragging over them. (See Lesson 6 for more information.) Excel highlights the cells.

4. Drag the fill handle over as many adjacent cells as necessary. Excel computes your series and fills the selected cells with the appropriate values, as shown in Figure 4.4.

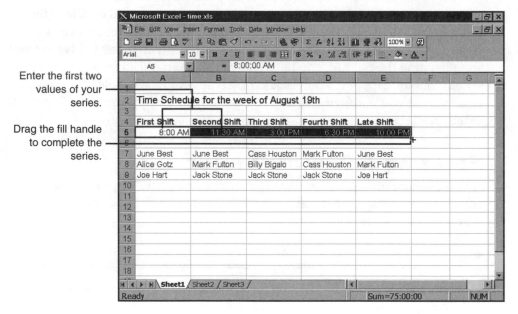

Enter the first two
values of your
series.

Drag the fill handle
to complete the
series.

**Figure 4.4** Drag to create your series.

# Entering the Same Data Over and Over with AutoComplete

When you type the first few letters of an entry, AutoComplete intelligently completes the entry for you based on the entries you've already made in that particular column. AutoComplete works with data entered in columns only, not rows. For example, suppose you want to enter the countries of origin for a series of packages. You type the name of a country once, and the next time you start to type that entry, AutoComplete inserts it for you.

By default, AutoComplete is always turned on, so you don't have to worry about that. However, if it drives you crazy, you can turn it off with the **Tools, Options** command. Click the **Edit** tab and click the **Enable AutoComplete for Cell Values** option to turn it off.

Follow these steps to try out AutoFormat:

1. Type **England** into a cell and press the down arrow key to move to the next cell down. Type **Spain** and press the down arrow key again. Then type **Italy** and press the down arrow key.

2. Type **e** again, and "England" appears in the cell. Press **Enter** to accept the entry. (Likewise, the next time you type **i** or **s**, "Italy" or "Spain" will appear. )

3. To see a list of AutoComplete entries, right-click a cell and select **Pick From List** from the shortcut menu. Excel shows you a PickList of entries (in alphabetical order) that it has automatically created from the words you've typed in the column.

4. Click a word in the PickList to insert it in the selected cell.

In this lesson, you learned how to enter different types of data and how to automate data entry. In the next lesson, you will learn how to edit entries.

# Editing Entries

*In this lesson, you learn how to change data and how to undo those changes if necessary. You also learn how to copy, move, and delete data.*

## Editing Data

After you have entered data into a cell, you may edit it in either the Formula bar or in the cell itself.

To edit an entry in Excel:

1. Click the cell in which you want to edit data.
2. To begin editing, click the Formula bar, press **F2**, or double-click the cell. This puts you in Edit mode; the word **Edit** appears in the status bar.
3. Press ← or → to move the insertion point within the entry. Press the **Backspace** key to delete characters to the left of the insertion point; press the **Delete** key to delete characters to the right. Then type any characters you want to add.

4. Click the **Enter** button on the Formula bar or press **Enter** on the keyboard to accept your changes.

   Or, if you change your mind and you no longer want to edit your entry, click the **Cancel** button or press **Esc**.

## Checking Your Spelling

Excel offers a spell checking feature that rapidly finds and highlights misspellings in a worksheet. To run the spelling checker, follow these steps:

1. Click the **Spelling** button on the Standard toolbar. Excel finds the first misspelled word and displays it at the top of the Spelling dialog box. A suggested correction then appears in the Change To box (see Figure 5.1).

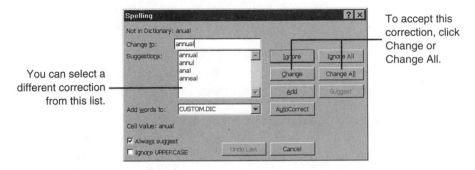

You can select a different correction from this list.

To accept this correction, click Change or Change All.

**Figure 5.1** Correct spelling mistakes with the options in the Spelling dialog box.

2. To accept the suggestion and change the misspelled word, click **Change**. Or, click **Change All** to change all occurrences of the misspelled word.

3. If the suggestion in the Change To box is not correct, you can do any of the following:

   - Select a different suggestion from the Suggestions box, and then click **Change** or **Change All**. (You can display additional words in the Suggestions list by clicking **Suggest**.)
   - Type your own correction in the **Change To** box, and then click **Change** or **Change All**.
   - Click **Ignore** to leave the word unchanged.
   - Click **Ignore All** to leave all occurrences of the word unchanged.
   - Click **Add** to add the word to the dictionary so Excel won't ever flag it as misspelled again.

4. When the spelling checker can't find any more misspelled words, it displays a prompt telling you that the spelling check is complete. Click **OK** to confirm that the spelling checking is finished.

**Choose the Wrong Option?** If you mistakenly select the wrong option, you can click the **Undo Last** button in the Spelling dialog box to undo the last selection you made.

CAUTION

# Using AutoCorrect to Correct Spelling Mistakes

Excel's AutoCorrect feature automatically corrects common typing mistakes as you type. If you type a mistake (such as "teh" instead of "the") and press Enter, Excel enters the corrected text in the cell.

AutoCorrect also corrects two initial capitals. For example, if you type "MAine" and press Enter, Excel will enter "Maine" in the cell. In addition, AutoCorrect capitalizes the first letter of a sentence and the names of days.

You can teach AutoCorrect the errors you normally make, and have it correct them for you as you type. For example, if you always type "breif" instead of "brief," you can add it to the AutoCorrect list. You can also use AutoCorrect to replace an abbreviation, such as ndiv, with the words it represents: Northern Division. Here's how:

1. Open the **Tools** menu and select **AutoCorrect**. The AutoCorrect dialog box appears.
2. Type your error in the **Replace** text box.
3. Type the correction in the **With** text box.
4. Click **Add** to add the entry to the AutoCorrect list.
5. If you want to delete an entry from the AutoCorrect list, select it from the list and click the **Delete** button.

**Too Quick!**  If you want to turn AutoCorrect off because it's "correcting" your entries before you get a chance to stop it, turn off the **Replace Text As You Type** option in the AutoCorrect dialog box.

CAUTION

# Undoing an Action

You can undo almost anything you do while working in Excel, including any change you enter into a cell. To undo a change, click the **Undo** button on the Standard toolbar.

To undo an Undo (reinstate a change), click the **Redo** button in the Standard toolbar.

**Undoing/Redoing More Than One Thing** Normally, when you click the Undo or Redo button, Excel undoes or redoes only the most recent action. To undo (or redo) an action prior to the most recent, click the drop-down arrow on the button and select the action you want from the list. Also new in Excel 97, you can click the **Undo** button multiple times to undo multiple previous actions.

# Selecting Cells

In order to copy, move, or delete the data in several cells at one time, you must select those cells first. Then you can perform the appropriate action.

- To select a single cell, click it.
- To select adjacent cells (a *range*), click the upper-left cell in the group and drag down to the lower-right cell to select additional cells. (If you want more help in selecting ranges of various sizes, see Lesson 9.)
- To select nonadjacent cells, press and hold the **Ctrl** key as you click individual cells.
- To select an entire row or column of cells, click the row or column header. To select adjacent rows or columns, drag over their headers. To select nonadjacent rows or columns, press **Ctrl** and click each header you want to select.

**Range** A selection of adjacent cells.

# Copying Data

When you copy or move data, a copy of that data is placed in a temporary storage area called the *Clipboard*. You can copy data to other sections of your worksheet or to other worksheets or workbooks. When you copy, the original data remains in its place and a copy of it is placed where you indicate.

**What Is the Clipboard?** The Clipboard is an area of memory that is accessible to all Windows programs. The Clipboard is used to copy or move data from place to place within a program or between programs. The techniques that you learn here are the same ones used in all Windows programs.

Follow these steps to copy data:

1. Select the cell(s) that you want to copy.

2. Click the **Copy** button on the Standard toolbar. The contents of the selected cell(s) are copied to the Clipboard.

3. Select the first cell in the area where you would like to place the copy. (To copy the data to another worksheet or workbook, change to that worksheet or workbook first.)

4. Click the **Paste** button. Excel inserts the contents of the Clipboard in the location of the insertion point.

**Watch Out!** When copying or moving data, be careful not to paste the data over existing data (unless, of course, you intend to).

**CAUTION**

You can copy the same data to several places by repeating the Paste command. Data copied to the Clipboard remains there until you copy or cut (move) something else.

## Using Drag-and-Drop

The fastest way to copy something is to drag and drop it. Select the cells you want to copy, hold down the **Ctrl** key, and drag the border of the range you selected (see Figure 5.2). When you release the mouse button, the contents are copied to the new location. (If you forget to hold down the Ctrl key, Excel moves the data instead of copying it.) To insert the data *between* existing cells, press **Ctrl+Shift** as you drag.

To drag a copy to a different sheet, press **Ctrl+Alt** as you drag the selection to the sheet's tab. Excel switches you to that sheet, where you can drop your selection in the appropriate location.

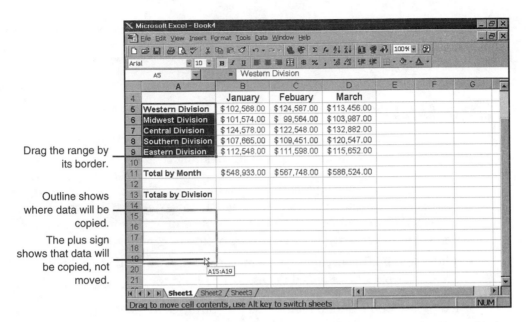

The following labels appear to the left of the figure:

Drag the range by its border.

Outline shows where data will be copied.

The plus sign shows that data will be copied, not moved.

**Figure 5.2**  To copy data, hold down the Ctrl key while dragging the cell selector border.

# Moving Data

Moving data is similar to copying except that the data is removed from its original place and placed in the new location.

To move data, follow these steps:

**1.** Select the cells you want to move.

 **2.** Click the **Cut** button.

**3.** Select the first cell in the area where you would like to place the data. To move the data to another worksheet, change to that worksheet.

**4.** Click **Paste**.

To move data quickly, use the drag-and-drop feature. Select the data to be moved, and then drag the border of the selected cells to its new location. To insert the data between existing cells, press **Shift** while you drag. To move the data to a different worksheet, press the **Alt** key and drag the selection to the worksheet's tab. You're switched to that sheet, where you can drop your selection at the appropriate point.

**TIP** **Shortcut Menu** When cutting, copying, and pasting data, don't forget the shortcut menu. Simply select the cells you want to cut or copy, *right-click*, and choose the appropriate command from the shortcut menu that appears.

# Deleting Data

To delete the data in a cell or cells, you can just select them and press **Delete**. However, Excel offers additional options for deleting cells:

- With the Edit, Clear command, you can delete just the formatting of a cell (or an attached comment), instead of deleting its contents. The formatting of a cell includes the cell's color, border style, numeric format, font size, and so on. You'll learn more about this option in a moment.

- With the Edit, Delete command, you can remove cells and everything in them. This option is covered in Lesson 13.

To use the Clear command to remove the formatting of a cell or a note, follow these steps:

**1.** Select the cells you want to clear.

**2.** Open the **Edit** menu and select **Clear**. The Clear submenu appears.

**3.** Select the desired clear option: **All** (which clears the cells of its contents, formatting, and notes), **Formats**, **Contents**, or **Comments**.

# Finding and Replacing Data

With Excel's Find and Replace features, you can locate certain data and replace it with new data. When you have a label, a value, or formula that is entered incorrectly throughout the worksheet, you can use the Edit, Replace command to search and replace all occurrences of the incorrect information with the correct data.

To find and replace data, follow these steps:

**1.** Open the **Edit** menu and select **Replace**. The Replace dialog box appears, as shown in Figure 5.3.

**2.** Type the text you want to find in the **Find What** text box.

**3.** Click in the **Replace With** text box and type the text you want to use as replacement text.

Type the data you
want to find.

Type its replace-
ment here.

Click here to find the
next occurrence.

Click to replace one
occurrence at a time.

Click to replace all
occurrences at once.

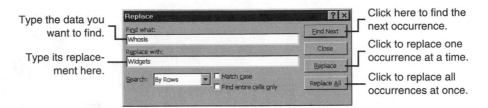

**Figure 5.3**  Finding and replacing data with the Replace dialog box.

**4.** In the **Search** box, choose whether you want to search for your entry by rows or by columns.

**5.** If you want to match the exact case of your entry, click **Match Case**. If you want to locate cells that contain exactly what you entered (and no additional data), click **Find Entire Cells Only**.

**6.** Click **Find Next** to find the first occurrence of your specified text. Then click **Replace** to replace only this occurrence or **Replace All** to replace all occurrences of the data you specified.

In this lesson, you learned how to edit cell data and undo changes. In addition, you learned how to copy, move, and delete data. In the next lesson, you will learn how to work with workbook files.

# Creating and Saving Workbook Files

*In this lesson, you learn how to create new workbooks and save workbook files.*

## Creating a New Workbook

You can create a new *blank* workbook, or you can use a template to create a more complete workbook. A *template* is a predesigned workbook that you can modify to suit your needs. Excel contains templates for creating invoices, expense reports, and other common worksheets.

Here's how you create a new workbook:

1. Pull down the **File** menu and select **New**. The New dialog box appears. As you can see in Figure 6.1, this dialog box contains two tabs: General and Spreadsheet Solutions.

2. To create a blank workbook, click the **General** tab and click the **Workbook** icon.

   To create a workbook from a template, click the **Spreadsheet Solutions** tab. You'll see icons for several common worksheet types. Click the icon for the type of workbook you want to create.

3. Once you've made your selection, click **OK** or press **Enter**. A new workbook opens on-screen with a default name in the title bar. Excel numbers its files sequentially. For example, if you already have Book1 open, the Workbook title bar will read **Book2**.

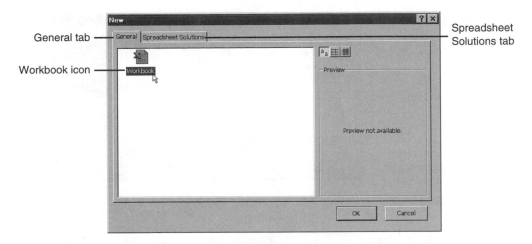

General tab

Workbook icon

Spreadsheet
Solutions tab

**Figure 6.1**  Click the icon for the type of worksheet you want to create.

 **TIP**  **Instant Workbook**  If you want to create a blank workbook (instead of creating one from a template), you can bypass the New dialog box by simply clicking the **New** button on the Standard toolbar. Excel opens a new workbook window without displaying the New dialog box.

 **TIP**  **Fast Start**  When you start Excel, you're normally given a blank worksheet to begin with. However, you can select a template instead. Just click the **Start** button on the Windows taskbar and select **New Office Document**. Excel displays the New Office Document dialog box. Click the **Spreadsheet Solutions** tab, select the type of workbook you want to create, and then click **OK**.

# Saving and Naming a Workbook

Whatever you type into a workbook is stored only in your computer's temporary memory. If you exit Excel, that data will be lost. Therefore, it is important to save your workbook files to a disk regularly.

The first time you save a workbook to a disk, you have to name it. Follow these steps to name your workbook:

 **1.** Open the **File** menu and select **Save,** or click the **Save** button on the Standard toolbar. The Save As dialog box appears (see Figure 6.2).

**253**

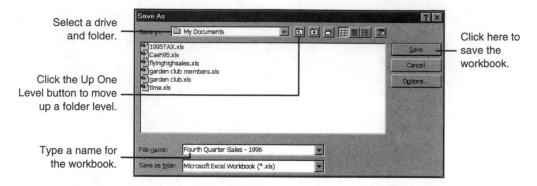

Select a drive and folder.

Click the Up One Level button to move up a folder level.

Type a name for the workbook.

Click here to save the workbook.

**Figure 6.2** The Save As dialog box.

**2.** Type the name you want to give the workbook in the **File Name** text box. You can use up to 218 characters, including any combination of letters, numbers, and spaces (as in **Fourth Quarter Sales - 1996**).

**3.** Normally, Excel saves your workbooks in the My Documents folder. To save the file to a different folder, select it from the **Save In** list. You can move up a folder level by clicking the **Up One Level** button on the Save toolbar at the top of the dialog box. You can change to a different drive by selecting a drive in the Save In box. When you save a file to any of the places listed in the Save In box, here's what happens:

- **Desktop**   Saves the file as an icon on the Windows desktop. Double-click the icon on your desktop to quickly start Excel and open the workbook file at the same time. If you're working on a project in Excel on a daily basis, you might want to have the file icon on the desktop for your convenience.

- **My Computer**   Saves the file to Windows' My Computer folder. Open the My Computer window and double-click the file icon to start Excel and open the workbook file. If you are working in My Computer regularly, it might be convenient to save the file to My Computer. You can also save your file to your hard drive, floppy drive, or CD in My Computer.

- **Network Neighborhood**   Saves the file to Windows' Network Neighborhood. Open Network Neighborhood and double-click the file icon to start Excel and open the workbook file. If you work in Network Neighborhood regularly, it might be convenient to save the file to Network Neighborhood.

**TIP** **Excel on the Web** You can save your worksheet in HTML format and add it to your company's intranet (or Internet) Web site. See Lesson 21 for help.

**4.** Click the **Save** button or press **Enter**.

**TIP** **Default Directory** Normally, files are saved to the My Documents directory. You can change the default to your own private directory if you want. Open the **Tools** menu, select **Options**, and click the **General** tab. Click in the **Default File Location** text box and type a complete path for the drive and directory you want to use (the directory must be an existing one). Click **OK**.

 To save a file you have saved previously (and named), all you do is click the **Save** button. (Or you can press **Ctrl+S** or use the **File, Save** command.) Excel automatically saves the workbook and any changes you entered without displaying the Save As dialog box.

**Excel on the Web** You can save your workbook to an FTP site on the Internet (or a local intranet), provided you have the permission to do so. First, to add the FTP site to the Save As dialog, open the **Save In** list and select **Add/Modify FTP Locations**. In the **Name of FTP Site** text box, enter the site's address, such as **ftp://ftp.microsoft.com**. Select either **Anonymous** or **User** and enter a password if necessary. Click **Add**. Once the site has been added to the Save As dialog box, you can select it from the **Internet Locations (FTP)** folder in the **Save In** list.

# Saving a Workbook Under a New Name

Sometimes you might want to change a workbook but keep a copy of the original workbook, or you may want to create a new workbook by modifying an existing one. You can do this by saving the workbook under another name or in another folder. The following steps show how you do that:

**1.** Open the **File** menu and select **Save As**. You'll see the Save As dialog box, just as if you were saving the workbook for the first time.

**2.** To save the workbook under a new name, type the new file name over the existing name in the **File Name** text box.

3. To save the file on a different drive or in a different folder, select the drive letter or the folder from the **Save In** list.

4. To save the file in a different format (such as Lotus 1-2-3 or Quattro Pro), click the **Save As Type** drop-down arrow and select the desired format.

5. Click the **Save** button or press **Enter**.

 **TIP**    **Backup Files**    You can have Excel create a backup copy of each workbook file you save. That way, if anything happens to the original file, you can use the backup copy. To turn the backup feature on, click the **Options** button in the Save As dialog box, select **Always Create Backup**, and click **OK**. To use the backup file, choose **File**, **Open** to display the Open dialog box, and then select **Backup Files** from the **Files of Type** list. Double-click the backup file in the files and folders list to open the file.

In this lesson, you learned how to create new workbooks and save workbooks. In the next lesson, you'll learn how to open and close workbook files.

# Opening, Finding, and Closing Work-book Files

*In this lesson, you learn how to open and close workbook files.*
*You also learn how to locate misplaced files.*

## Opening an Existing Workbook

If you have closed a workbook and then later you want to use it again, you must reopen it. Follow these steps to open an existing workbook:

**1.** Open the **File** menu and select **Open**, or click the **Open** button on the Standard toolbar. The Open dialog box shown in Figure 7.1 appears.

Select the file you want to open from the list...

...or type the name of the file here.

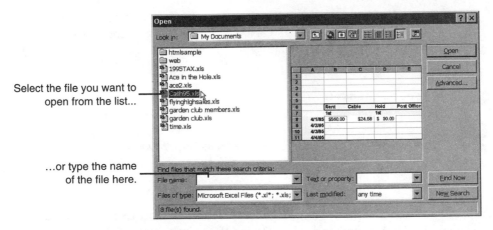

**Figure 7.1** The Open dialog box.

2. If the file is not located in the current folder, open the **Look In** box and select the correct drive and folder.

**Excel on the Web** To open a worksheet on an FTP site to which you have access, select **Internet Locations (FTP)** from the **Look In** box and double-click the FTP site you want to search. Then click the workbook you want to open and click **Open**. To search the Web for a worksheet instead, click the **Search the Web** button at the top of the Open dialog box.

3. Click the file you want to open in the files and folders list. Or, type the name of the file in the **File Name** box. (As you type, Excel highlights the first file name in the list that matches your entry; this is a quick way to move through the list.)

**TIP** **Save Your Favorites** You can save the worksheets you use most often in the Favorites folder by selecting them and clicking the **Look in Favorites** button. Then, whenever you need to, you can open one of those worksheets by clicking the **Look in Favorites** button at the top of the Open dialog box.

4. To see a preview of the workbook before you open it, click the **Preview** button at the top of the dialog box. Excel displays the contents of the workbook in a window to the right of the dialog box.

5. Click **Open** or press **Enter**.

**TIP** **Recently Used Workbooks** If you've recently used the workbook you want to open, you'll find it listed at the bottom of the File menu. Just open the **File** menu and select it from the list.

**Excel on the Web** You can browse the Web for a worksheet with the Search the Web button at the top of the dialog box. But if you know the exact address of the worksheet you want to open—whether it's on the Web or on a local intranet—just type its address (such as **http://www.worldnews.com/facts.xls**) in the **File Name** text box. (You must connect to the Internet before you click Open.)

You can also open a specific workbook when you first start Excel if you want. Just click the **Start** button and select **Open Office Document**. Select the workbook you want to open and click **Open**. Excel starts, with the workbook you selected open and ready to edit.

# Finding a Workbook File

If you forget where you saved a file, Excel can help you. You can use its Find Now option in the Open dialog box. Follow these steps to have Excel hunt for a file for you:

**1.** Open the **File** menu and select **Open**, or click the **Open** button in the Standard toolbar. The Open dialog box appears (see Figure 7.2).

Select the drive or folder to search.

Choose a time period.

Type specific text to look for.

Type the file name to look for.

Click here to search all subfolders.

Click here to begin the search.

Click here to clear all search criteria.

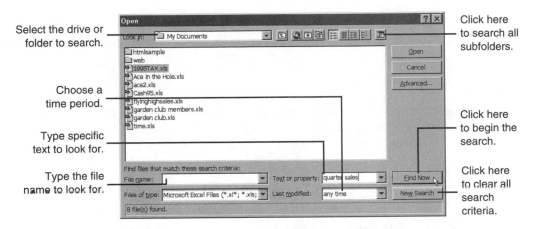

**Figure 7.2** The Search options in the Open dialog box enable you to specify what you want to search for.

**2.** Open the **Look In** box and select the drive or folder you want to search. For example, if you select C:, Excel will search the entire C drive. If you select C: and then select the Excel folder, Excel searches only the EXCEL directory on drive C. You can select My Computer to search all the drives on your computer.

**3.** Narrow your search using any of the following methods:

If you want to search for a particular file, type its name in the **File Name** text box. You can use wild-card characters in place of characters you can't remember. Use an asterisk (*) in place of a group of characters; use a question mark (?) in place of a single character. (For example, if you enter **sales??**, Excel finds all files whose file names begin with the word "sales" followed by two characters, such as SALES01, SALES02, and so on.)

You can search the contents of your workbooks for a particular phrase by typing it in the **Text Or Property** box. For example, type "**brook trout**" to find a workbook that contains the words "brook trout."

To specify a time period for the files you want to search, choose an option from the **Last Modified** box.

To have Excel search all subfolders of the drive you specify, click the **Commands and Settings** button and choose **Search Subfolders** from the pop-up menu that appears.

TIP  **Do Over**   You can clear your search selections by clicking the **New Search** button.

**4.** When you finish entering your search criteria, click the **Find Now** button. Excel finds the files that match the search instructions you entered and displays them in the files and folders list.

**5.** Look through the list, highlight the file you want, and click the **Open** button.

CAUTION  **File Not Found?**   If the file you want is not listed in the files and folders list, you can specify more detailed search criteria by using the Advanced Find feature. Click the **Advanced** button in the Open dialog box. Enter search criteria such as property, condition, or value, and then click the **Find Now** button to search for the file using these additional criteria.

# Moving Among Open Workbooks

Sometimes you may have more than one workbook open at a time. If so, you can switch back and forth as necessary to view or edit their contents. There are several ways to move among open workbooks:

- If part of the desired workbook window is visible, click it.
- Open the **Window** menu and select the name of the workbook to which you want to switch.
- Press **Ctrl+F6** to move from one workbook window to another.

**The Active Window**  If you have more than one workbook open, only the one where the cell selector is located is considered active. The title bar of the active workbook will be darker than the title bars of other open workbooks.

# Closing Workbooks

When you close a workbook, Excel removes its workbook window from the screen. You should close workbooks when you finish working on them to free up your computer's resources so it can respond to your commands more quickly. To close a workbook, follow these steps:

1. If the window you want to close isn't currently active, make it active by selecting the workbook from the list of workbooks at the bottom of the **Window** menu.

2. Click the **Close** (X) button in the upper-right corner of the workbook.

**Close All**  In Excel 97, if you have more than one workbook open, you can close all workbooks at once by holding down the **Shift** key, opening the **File** menu, and selecting **Close All**.

In this lesson, you learned how to open and close workbooks, as well as how to find misplaced workbook files. The next lesson teaches you how to work with the worksheets in a workbook.

# Working with Worksheets

*In this lesson, you learn how to add and delete worksheets with workbooks. You also learn how to copy, move, and rename worksheets.*

## Selecting Worksheets

By default, each workbook consists of three worksheet pages whose names appear on tabs near the bottom of the screen. You can insert new worksheet pages or delete worksheet pages as desired. One advantage to having multiple worksheet pages is to organize your data into logical chunks. Another advantage to having separate worksheets for your data is that you can reorganize the worksheets in a workbook easily.

Before we get into the details of inserting, deleting, and copying worksheets, you should know how to select one or more worksheets. Here's what you need to know:

- To select a single worksheet, click its tab. The tab becomes highlighted to show that the worksheet is selected.

- To select several neighboring worksheets, click the tab of the first worksheet in the group, and then hold down the **Shift** key and click the tab of the last worksheet in the group.

- To select several non-neighboring worksheets, hold down the **Ctrl** key and click each worksheet's tab.

If you select two or more worksheets, they remain selected until you ungroup them. To ungroup worksheets, do one of the following:

- Right-click one of the selected worksheets and choose **Ungroup Sheets**.

- Hold down the **Shift** key and click the active tab.
- Click any tab outside the group.

# Inserting Worksheets

When you create a new workbook, it contains three worksheets. You can easily add additional worksheets to a workbook.

**TIP**  **Start with More**  You can change the number of worksheets Excel places in a new workbook by opening the **Tools** menu, selecting **Options**, clicking the **General** tab, and then changing the number under the **Sheets in New Workbook** option. Click **OK** to save your changes.

Follow these steps to add a worksheet to a workbook:

1. Select the worksheet *before* which you want the new worksheet inserted. For example, if you select Sheet2, the new worksheet (which will be called Sheet4 because the workbook already contains three worksheets) will be inserted before Sheet2.
2. Open the **Insert** menu.
3. Select **Worksheet**. Excel inserts the new worksheet, as shown in Figure 8.1.

**TIP**  **Shortcut Menu**  A faster way to work with worksheets is to right-click the worksheet tab. This brings up a shortcut menu that lets you insert, delete, rename, move, copy, or select all worksheets. When you choose **Insert** from the shortcut menu, Excel displays the Insert dialog box. Click the **Worksheet** icon on the General tab and click **OK** to insert a new worksheet.

# Deleting Worksheets

If you plan to use only one worksheet, you can remove the two other worksheets to free up memory. Here's how you remove a worksheet:

1. Select the worksheet(s) you want to delete.
2. Open the **Edit** menu.
3. Click **Delete Sheet**. A dialog box appears, asking you to confirm the deletion.
4. Click the **OK** button. The worksheets are deleted.

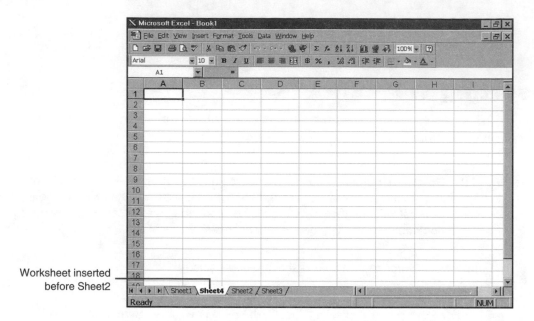

Worksheet inserted
before Sheet2

**Figure 8.1** Excel inserts the new worksheet before the worksheet you selected.

# Moving and Copying Worksheets

You can move or copy worksheets within a workbook or from one workbook to another. Here's how:

**1.** Select the worksheet(s) you want to move or copy. If you want to move or copy worksheets from one workbook to another, be sure to open the target workbook.

**2.** Open the **Edit** menu and choose **Move or Copy Sheet**. The Move or Copy dialog box appears, as shown in Figure 8.2.

**3.** To move the worksheet(s) to a different workbook, select that workbook's name from the **To Book** drop-down list. If you want to move or copy the worksheet(s) to a new workbook, select **(new book)** in the **To Book** drop-down list. Excel creates a new workbook and then copies or moves the worksheet(s) to it.

**4.** In the **Before Sheet** list box, choose the worksheet *before* which you want the selected worksheet(s) to be moved.

To move the selected worksheet(s) to a different workbook, select the workbook from this box.

Turn this option on to copy instead of move.

Choose where to copy or move the worksheet(s).

**Figure 8.2**   The Move or Copy dialog box asks you where you want to copy or move a worksheet.

**5.** To copy the selected worksheet(s) instead of moving them, select **Create a Copy** to put a check mark in the check box.

**6.** Select **OK**. The selected worksheet(s) are copied or moved as specified.

# Moving a Worksheet Within a Workbook by Dragging and Dropping

An easier way to copy or move worksheets within a workbook is to use the drag-and-drop feature. First, select the tab of the worksheet(s) you want to copy or move. Move the mouse pointer over one of the selected tabs, click and hold the mouse button, and drag the tab where you want it moved. To copy the worksheet, hold down the **Ctrl** key while dragging. When you release the mouse button, the worksheet is copied or moved.

# Moving a Worksheet Between Workbooks by Dragging and Dropping

You can also use the drag-and-drop feature to quickly copy or move worksheets between workbooks. First, open the workbooks you want to use for the copy or move. Choose **Window**, **Arrange** and select the **Tiled** option. Click **OK** to arrange the windows so that a small portion of each one appears on-screen. Select the tab of the worksheet(s) you want to copy or move. Move the mouse pointer over one of the selected tabs, click and hold the mouse button, and drag the tab where you want it moved. To copy the worksheet, hold down the **Ctrl** key while dragging. When you release the mouse button, the worksheet is copied or moved.

# Changing Worksheet Tab Names

By default, all worksheets are named "SheetX," where X is a number starting with the number 1. So that you'll have a better idea of the information each sheet contains, you can change the names that appear on the tabs. Here's how you do it:

1.  Double-click the tab of the worksheet you want to rename. The current name is highlighted.

2.  Type a new name for the worksheet and press **Enter**. Excel replaces the default name with the name you typed.

In this lesson, you learned how to insert, delete, move, copy, and rename worksheets. In the next lesson, you'll learn how to work with cell ranges.

# Working with Ranges

*In this lesson, you learn how to select and name cell ranges.*

## What Is a Range?

A *range* is a rectangular group of connected cells. The cells in a range may all be in one column, or one row, or any combination of columns and rows, as long as the range forms a rectangle, as shown in Figure 9.1.

**Figure 9.1** A range is any combination of cells that forms a rectangle.

Learning how to use ranges can save you time. For example, you can select a range and use it to format a group of cells with one step. You can use a range to print only a selected group of cells. You can also use ranges in formulas.

Ranges are referred to by their anchor points (the upper-left corner and the lower-right corner). For example, the ranges shown in Figure 9.1 are B4:G8, A10:G10, and G12.

# Selecting a Range

To select a range using the mouse, follow these steps:

1. To select the same range of cells on more than one worksheet, select the worksheets (see Lesson 8).
2. Move the mouse pointer to the upper-left corner of a range.
3. Click and hold the left mouse button.
4. Drag the mouse to the lower-right corner of the range and release the mouse button. The selected range is highlighted.

There are some techniques that you can use to quickly select a row, a column, an entire worksheet, or several ranges, as shown in Table 9.1.

**Table 9.1**  Selection Techniques

| To Select This... | Do This... |
| --- | --- |
| Several ranges | Select the first range, hold down the **Ctrl** key, and select the next range. Do this for each range you want to select. |
| Row | Click the row heading number at the left edge of the worksheet. You also can press **Shift+Spacebar**. |
| Column | Click the column heading letter at the top edge of the worksheet. You also can press **Ctrl+Spacebar**. |
| Entire worksheet | Click the **Select All** button (the blank rectangle in the upper-left corner of the worksheet, above row 1 and left of column A). You also can press **Ctrl+A**. |
| Range that is out of view | Press **Ctrl+G** (Goto) or click in the **Name** box on the Formula bar, and then type the address of the range you want to select. For example, to select the range R100 to T250, type **R100:T250** and press **Enter**. |

**CAUTION**

**Deselecting a Selection** To remove the range selection, click any cell in the worksheet.

# Naming Cells and Cell Ranges

Up to this point, you have used cell addresses to refer to cells. Although that works, it is often more convenient to name cells with more recognizable names. For example, say you want to determine your net income by subtracting expenses from income (see Lesson 12). You can name the cell that contains your total income **INCOME**, and name the cell that contains your total expenses **EXPENSES**. You can then determine your net income by using the formula:

= INCOME – EXPENSES

Giving the cells memorable names will make the formula more logical and easier to manage. Naming cells and ranges also makes it easier to cut, copy, and move blocks of cells, as explained in Lesson 5.

Follow these steps to name a cell range:

1. Select the range of cells you want to name. Make sure all the cells are on the same worksheet. (You cannot name cells and cell ranges that are located on more than one sheet.)
2. Click in the **Name** box on the left side of the Formula bar (see Figure 9.2).
3. Type a range name using up to 255 characters. Valid names can include letters, numbers, periods, and underlines, but *no* spaces. In addition, a number cannot be used as the first character in the range name.
4. Press **Enter**.
5. To see the list of range names, click the **Name** box's drop-down arrow (on the Formula bar).

Another way to name a range is to select it, open the **Insert** menu, select **Name**, and choose **Define**. This displays the Define Name dialog box shown in Figure 9.3. Type a name in the **Names in Workbook** text box and click **OK**.

Name box ——

Selected range ——

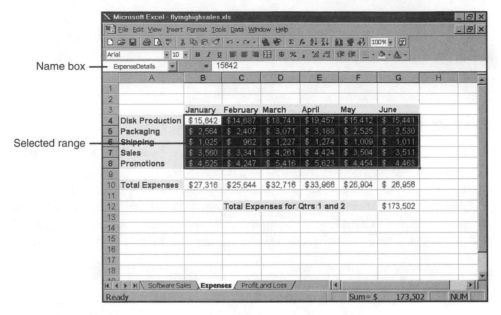

**Figure 9.2**   Type a name in the Name box.

Type a name here. ——

Selected range
appears here. ——

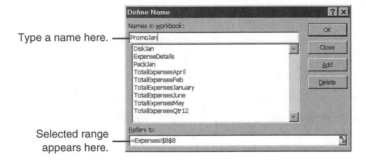

**Figure 9.3**   The Define Name dialog box.

The Define Name dialog box enables you to see what range a range name contains. Click a range name in the Names in Workbook list, and you'll see the cell address(es) assigned to the range name in the Refers To text box. You can edit the range or type a new one.

The dollar signs in the cell addresses indicate absolute cell references, which always refer to the same cell. An absolute cell reference will not be adjusted if changes are made to those cells in the worksheet (see Lesson 13). You don't have to type the dollar signs in the cell address. When you select cells with the mouse, Excel inserts the dollar signs automatically.

This dialog box also lets you delete names. To delete a range name, click a name in the **Names in Workbook** list and click the **Delete** button.

In this lesson, you learned how to select and name ranges. In the next lesson, you will learn how to print your workbook.

# Printing Your Workbook

*In this lesson, you learn how to print a workbook or a portion of one, and how to enhance your printout with headers and footers.*

## Changing the Page Setup

A workbook is a collection of many worksheets, which are like pages in a notebook. You can print the whole notebook at once, or just one or more pages at a time.

Before you print a worksheet, you should make sure that the page is set up correctly for printing. To do this, open the **File** menu and choose **Page Setup**. You'll see the Page Setup dialog box shown in Figure 10.1.

 **TIP** **Right-Click the Workbook's Title Bar** For quick access to commands that affect a workbook, right-click the workbook's title bar. If the workbook is maximized to a full screen (and the title bar is therefore not visible), right-click the Control-menu box to access the shortcut menu. For example, to check the page setup, right-click the title bar or the **Control-menu** box and choose **Page Setup**.

The following list outlines the page setup settings, grouped according to the tab on which they appear.

**Page tab**

**Orientation** Select **Portrait** to print across the short edge of a page; select **Landscape** to print across the long edge of a page. (Landscape makes the page wider than it is tall.)

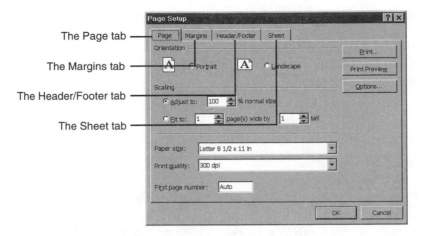

The Page tab ——

The Margins tab ——

The Header/Footer tab ——

The Sheet tab ——

**Figure 10.1**   The Page Setup dialog box.

**Scaling**   You can reduce and enlarge your workbook or force it to fit within a specific page size.

**Paper Size**   This is 8 1/2 by 11 inches by default, but you can choose a different size from the list.

**Print Quality**   You can print your spreadsheet in draft quality to print quickly and save wear and tear on your printer, or you can print in high quality for a final copy. Print quality is measured in dpi (dots per inch); the higher the number, the better the print.

**First Page Number**   You can set the starting page number to something other than 1. The Auto option (default) tells Excel to set the starting page number to 1 if it is the first page in the print job, or to set the first page number at the next sequential number if it is not the first page in the print job.

## Margins tab

**Top**, **Bottom**, **Left**, **Right**   You can adjust the size of the top, bottom, left, and right margins.

**Header, Footer**   You can specify how far you want a Header or Footer printed from the edge of the page. (You use the Header/Footer tab to add a header or footer to your workbook.)

**Center on Page**   You can center your workbook data between the left and right margins (**Horizontally**) and between the top and bottom margins (**Vertically**).

### Header/Footer tab

**Header, Footer**   You can add a header (such as a title) that repeats at the top of each page, or a footer (such as page numbers) that repeats at the bottom of each page.

**Custom Header, Custom Footer**   You can use the Custom Header or Custom Footer button to create headers and footers that insert the time, date, worksheet tab name, and workbook file name.

### Sheet tab

**Print Area**   You can print a portion of a workbook or worksheet by entering the range of cells you want to print. You can type the range, or click the **Collapse Dialog Box** icon at the right of the text box to move the Page Setup dialog box out of the way and drag the mouse pointer over the desired cells. If you do not select a print area, Excel will print either the sheet or the workbook, depending on the options set in the Page tab.

 TIP   **Don't Print That!**   Ordinarily, if there's a portion of your worksheet that you don't want to print, you can avoid it by selecting the area you want to print 'and printing only that selection. However, if the data you want to hide is located *within* the area you want to print, what do you do? In that case, you can hide the columns, rows, or cells to prevent them from being printed. (See Lesson 2 for help.)

**Print Titles**   If you have a row or column of entries that you want repeated as titles on every page, type the range for this row or column, or drag over the cells with the mouse pointer (see Lesson 9).

**Print**   You can tell Excel exactly how to print some aspects of the workbook. For example, you can have the gridlines (the lines that define the cells) printed. You can also have a color spreadsheet printed in black-and-white.

**Page Order**   You can indicate how data in the worksheet should be read and printed: in sections from top to bottom or in sections from left to right. This is the way Excel handles printing the areas outside of the printable area. For example, if some columns to the right don't fit on the first page and some rows don't fit at the bottom of the first page, you can specify which area will print next.

When you finish entering your settings, click the **OK** button.

# Previewing a Print Job

 After you've determined your page setup and print area, you should preview what the printed page will look like before you print. To preview a print job, open the **File** menu and select **Print Preview** or click the **Print Preview** button in the Standard toolbar. Your workbook appears as it will when printed, as shown in Figure 10.2.

**TIP** **Page Setup Print Preview** You can also preview a print job when you are setting up a page or while you are in the Print dialog box. When the Page Setup dialog box is displayed, click the **Print Preview** button. In the Print dialog box, click the **Preview** button.

Mouse pointer allows you to zoom in on a portion of the worksheet.

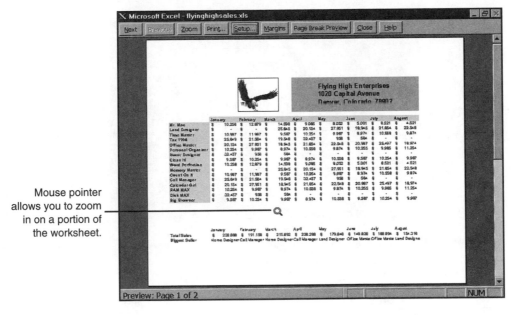

**Figure 10.2** You can preview your workbook before printing it.

**TIP** **A Close-Up View** Zoom in on any area of the preview by clicking it with the mouse pointer (which looks like a magnifying glass). You can also use the **Zoom** button at the top of the Print Preview screen.

# Printing Your Workbook

After setting the page setup and previewing your data, it is time to print. You can print selected data, selected sheets, or the entire workbook.

To print your workbook, follow these steps:

**1.** If you want to print a portion of the worksheet, select the range you want to print (see Lesson 9 for help). If you want to print one or more sheets within the workbook, select the sheet tabs (see Lesson 8). To print the entire workbook, skip this step.

**2.** Open the **File** menu and select **Print** (or press **Ctrl+P**). The Print dialog box appears, as shown in Figure 10.3.

Select the first page to print.

Select the last page to print.

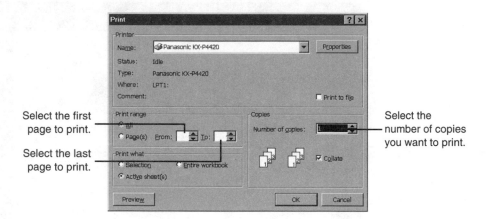

Select the number of copies you want to print.

**Figure 10.3** The Print dialog box.

**CAUTION**

**Too Quick to Print** If you click the Print button instead of using the File, Print command, Excel prints your current worksheet without letting you make any selections.

**3.** Select the options you would like to use:

**Page range** lets you print one or more pages. For example, if the selected print area will take up 15 pages and you want to print only pages 5–10, select **Page(s)**, and then type the numbers of the first and last page you want to print in the **From** and **To** boxes.

**Print what** enables you to print the currently selected cells, the selected worksheets, or the entire workbook.

**Copies** enables you to print more than one copy of the selection, worksheet, or workbook.

**Collate** enables you to print a complete copy of the selection, worksheet, or workbook before the first page of the next copy is printed. This option is available when you print multiple copies.

**4.** Click **OK** or press **Enter**.

While your job is printing, you can continue working in Excel. If the printer is working on another job that you (or someone else, in the case of a network printer) sent, Windows holds the job until the printer is ready for it.

Sometimes you might want to delete a job while it is printing or before it prints. For example, suppose you think of other numbers to add to the worksheet or realize you forgot to format some text; you'll want to fix these things before you print the file. In such a case, deleting the print job is easy. To display the print queue and delete a print job, follow these steps:

**1.** Double-click the **Printer** icon on the Windows taskbar, and the print queue appears, as shown in Figure 10.4.

**2.** Click the job you want to delete.

**3.** Open the **Document** menu and select **Cancel Printing**.

**TIP** **Clear the Queue!** To delete all the files from the print queue, open the **Printer** menu and select **Purge Print Jobs**. This cancels the print jobs, but doesn't delete the files from your computer.

**Upgrade Tip** With Excel 97, you get a newly expanded ability to send your worksheet directly to the people who need it, instead of printing it. Open the **File** menu, select **Send To**, and then select the appropriate option: **Mail Recipient** (to send a workbook via an e-mail message), **Routing Recipient** (to route a workbook over a local network by Microsoft Mail or cc:Mail to several people), or **Exchange Folder** (to post—copy—your workbook to a Microsoft Exchange server).

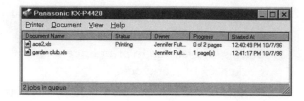

**Figure 10.4** To stop a document from printing, use the print queue.

# Selecting a Print Area

You can tell Excel what part of the worksheet you want to print using the Print Area option. This option lets you single out an area as a separate page and then print that page. If the area is too large to fit on one page, Excel breaks it into multiple pages. If you do not select a print area, Excel prints either the entire worksheet or the entire workbook, depending on the options set in the Print dialog box.

**CAUTION**

**To Include or Not to Include?** When deciding which cells to select for your print area, make sure you do *not* include the title, the subtitle, and the column and row headings in the print area. If you do, Excel may print the labels twice. Instead, print your titles and headings on each page of your printout by following the steps in the upcoming section, "Printing Column and Row Headings."

To select a print area and print your worksheet at the same time, follow these steps:

1. Open the **File** menu and choose **Page Setup**. The Page Setup dialog box appears.
2. Click the **Sheet** tab to display the Sheet options.
3. Click the **Collapse Dialog** icon to the right of the Print Area text box. Excel reduces the Page Setup dialog box in size.
4. Drag over the cells you want to print (see Lesson 9). As you can see in Figure 10.5, a dashed line border surrounds the selected area, and the absolute cell references for those cells appear with dollar signs ($) in the Print Area text box. (If you want to type the range, you don't have to include the $ in the cell references. See Lesson 13 for more information about absolute cell references.)

5. Click the **Collapse Dialog** icon to return to the Page Setup dialog box.

6. Click **Print** in the Page Setup dialog box to display the Print dialog box. Then click **OK** to print your worksheet.

The addresses of the selected cells appear here.

Drag over the desired cells.

Click the Collapse Dialog icon to return to the Page Setup dialog box.

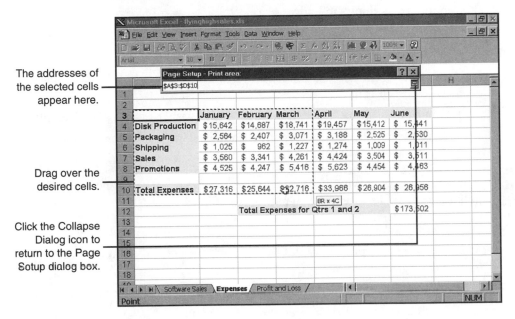

**Figure 10.5**   Selecting a print area.

 **TIP   Set Your Area**   To set the print area without printing, select the cells you want to print later, open the **File** menu, select **Print Area**, and select **Set Print Area**.

 **Remove the Print Area**   To remove the print area, open the **File** menu, select **Print Area**, and select **Clear Print Area**.

**CAUTION**

# Adjusting Page Breaks

When you print a workbook, Excel determines the page breaks based on the paper size and margins and the selected print area. To make the pages look better and break things in logical places, you may want to override the automatic page breaks with your own breaks. However, before you add page breaks, try these options:

- Adjust the widths of individual columns to make the best use of space (see Lesson 18).
- Consider printing the workbook sideways (using Landscape orientation).
- Change the left, right, top, and bottom margins to smaller values.

If after trying these options you still want to insert page breaks, Excel 97 offers you an option of previewing exactly where the page breaks appear and then adjusting them. Follow these steps:

**1.** Open the **View** menu and select **Page Break Preview**.

**2.** If a message appears, click **OK**. Your worksheet is displayed with page breaks, as shown in Figure 10.6.

**3.** To move a page break, drag the dashed line to the desired location.

To delete a page break, drag it off the screen.

To insert a page break, move to the first cell in the column to the *right* of where you want the page break inserted, or move to the row *below* where you want the break inserted. For example, to insert a page break between columns G and H, move to cell H1. To insert a page break between rows 24 and 25, move to cell A25. Then open the **Insert** menu and select **Page Break**. A dashed line appears to the left of the selected column or above the selected row.

**4.** To exit Page Break Preview and return to your normal worksheet view, open the **View** menu and select **Normal**.

Drag a page
break to move it.

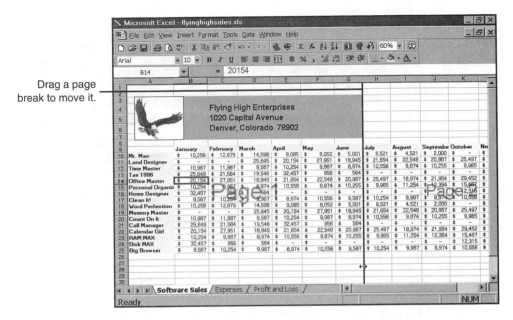

**Figure 10.6** Check your page breaks before printing.

# Printing Column and Row Headings

Excel provides a way for you to select labels and titles that are located on the top edge and left side of a large worksheet, and print them on every page of the printout. This option is useful when a worksheet is too wide to print on a single page. If you don't use this option, the extra columns or rows will be printed on subsequent pages without any descriptive labels.

Follow these steps to print column and/or row headings on every page:

**1.** Open the **File** menu and choose **Page Setup**. The Page Setup dialog box appears.

**2.** Click the **Sheet** tab to display the Sheet options.

**3.** To repeat column labels and a worksheet title, click the **Collapse Dialog** icon to the right of the Rows to Repeat at Top text box. Excel reduces the Page Setup dialog box in size.

**4.** Drag over the rows you want to print on every page, as shown in Figure 10.7. A dashed line border surrounds the selected area, and absolute cell references with dollar signs ($) appear in the Rows to Repeat at Top text box.

Click here to return to the Page Setup dialog box. ⌐

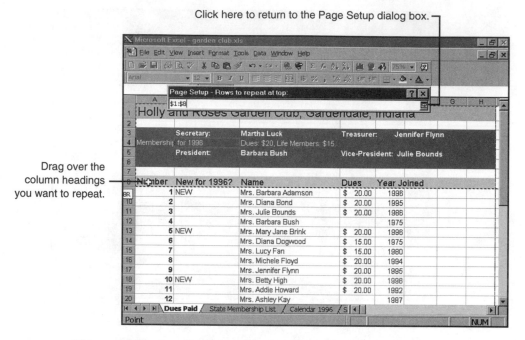

Drag over the
column headings
you want to repeat.

**Figure 10.7**  Specifying headings you want to print on every page.

**5.** Click the **Collapse Dialog** icon to return to the Page Setup dialog box.

**6.** To repeat row labels that appear on the left of the worksheet, click the **Collapse Dialog** icon to the right of the Columns to Repeat at Left text box. Again, Excel reduces the Page Setup dialog box.

**7.** Select the row labels you want to repeat.

**8.** Click the **Collapse Dialog** icon to return once again to the Page Setup dialog box.

**9.** To print your worksheet, click **Print** to display the Print dialog box. Then click **OK**.

**CAUTION**

**Select Your Print Area Carefully**  If you select rows or columns to repeat, and those rows or columns are part of your print area, the selected rows or columns will print twice. To fix this, select your print area again, leaving out the rows or columns you're repeating. See "Selecting a Print Area" earlier in this lesson for help.

# Adding Headers and Footers

Excel lets you add headers and footers to print information at the top and bottom of every page of the printout. The information can include any text, as well as page numbers, the current date and time, the workbook file name, and the worksheet tab name.

You can choose the headers and footers suggested by Excel, or you can include any other text you want. You can also use special commands to control the appearance of the header or footer. For example, you can apply bold, italic, or underline to the header or footer text. You can also left-align, center, or right-align the text (see Lesson 18).

To add headers and footers, follow these steps:

1. Open the **View** menu and choose **Header and Footer**, or click the **Header and Footer** tab in the Page Setup dialog box. The Page Setup dialog box appears (see Figure 10.8).

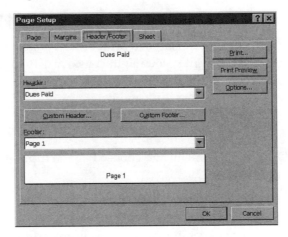

**Figure 10.8**  Adding headers and footers with Header/Footer options.

2. To select a header, click the **Header** drop-down arrow. Excel displays a list of suggested header information. Scroll through the list and click a header you want. The sample header appears at the top of the Header/Footer tab.

**TIP** **Don't See One You Like?** If none of the suggested headers or footers suits you, click the **Custom Header** or **Custom Footer** button and enter your exact specifications.

**3.** To select a footer, click the **Footer** drop-down arrow. Excel displays a list of suggested footer information. Scroll through the list and click a footer you want. The sample footer appears at the bottom of the Header/Footer tab.

**4.** Click **OK** to close the Page Setup dialog box and return to your worksheet. Or click the **Print** button to display the Print dialog box, and click **OK** to print your worksheet.

**Don't Want Any Headers or Footers?** To remove the header and/or footer, choose **None** in the Header and/or Footer suggestions lists.

CAUTION

# Scaling a Worksheet to Fit on a Page

If your worksheet is too large to print on one page even after you change the orientation and margins, you might consider using the Fit To option. This option shrinks the worksheet to make it fit on the specified number of pages. You can specify the document's width and height.

Follow these steps to scale a worksheet to fit on a page:

**1.** Open the **File** menu and choose **Page Setup**. The Page Setup dialog box appears.

**2.** Click the **Page** tab to display the Page options.

**3.** In the **Fit to XX Page(s) Wide By** and the **XX Tall** text boxes, enter the number of pages in which you want Excel to fit your data.

**4.** Click **OK** to close the Page Setup dialog box and return to your worksheet. Or click the **Print** button in the Page Setup dialog box to display the Print dialog box, and then click **OK** to print your worksheet.

In this lesson, you learned how to print a worksheet. In the next lesson, you will learn how to add and remove cells, rows, and columns.

# Inserting and Removing Cells, Rows, and Columns

11

*In this lesson, you learn how to rearrange your worksheet by adding and removing cells, rows, and columns.*

## Inserting Cells

Sometimes, you will need to insert information into a worksheet, right in the middle of existing data. With the Insert command, you can insert one or more cells, or entire rows or columns.

**CAUTION**

**Shifting Cells** Inserting cells in the middle of existing data will cause the data in existing cells to shift down a row or over a column. If your worksheet contains formulas that rely on the contents of the shifting cells, this could throw off the calculations (see Lessons 12 and 13). Be sure to check all formulas that might be affected.

To insert a single cell or a group of cells, follow these steps:

**1.** Select the cell(s) where you want the new cell(s) inserted. Excel will insert the same number of cells as you select.

**2.** Open the **Insert** menu and choose **Cells**. The Insert dialog box shown in Figure 11.1 appears.

**3.** Select **Shift Cells Right** or **Shift Cells Down**.

**Figure 11.1**  The Insert dialog box.

    **4.** Click **OK**. Excel inserts the cell(s) and shifts the data in the other cells in the specified direction.

**TIP**  **Drag Insert**  A quick way to insert cells is to hold down the Shift key and then drag the fill handle (the little box in the lower-right corner of the selected cell or cells—see Figure 11.2). Drag the fill handle up, down, left, or right to set the position of the new cells.

# Merging Cells

In Excel 97, you can merge the data in one cell with other cells to form a big cell that is easier to work with. Merging cells is especially handy when creating a decorative title for the top of your worksheet (see Figure 11.2 for an example). Within a single merged cell, you can quickly change the font, point size, color, and border style of your title. (See Lessons 15, 16, and 17 to learn more about formatting cells.)

To create a title with merged cells, follow these steps:

    **1.** Type your title in the upper-left cell of the range you want to use for your heading. If you have a multiline title, like the one in Figure 11.2, press **Alt+Enter** to insert each new line.

    **2.** Select the range in which you want to place your title.

    **3.** Open the **Format** menu and select **Cells**. The Format Cells dialog box appears.

    **4.** Click the **Alignment** tab.

    **5.** Click **Merge Cells**. You may also want to make adjustments to the text within the merged cells. For example, you may want to select **Center** in the **Vertical** drop-down list to center the text vertically within the cell.

A single cell —

Fill handle —

Select this option. —

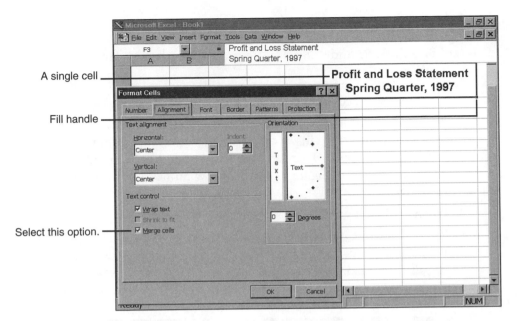

**Figure 11.2**   Merge cells to form a single cell.

**6.** Click **OK** when you're done. The selected cells are merged into a single cell, which you can format as needed.

 You can merge selected cells and center the data in the leftmost cell by clicking the **Merge and Center** button on the Formatting toolbar.

# Removing Cells

In Lesson 5, you learned how to clear the contents and formatting of selected cells. That merely removed what was inside the cells. But sometimes you will want to eliminate the cells completely. When you do, Excel removes the cells and adjusts the data in surrounding cells to fill the gap.

If you want to remove the cells completely, perform the following steps:

**1.** Select the range of cells you want to remove.

**2.** Open the **Edit** menu and choose **Delete**. The Delete dialog box appears.

**3.** Select the desired Delete option: **Shift Cells Left** or **Shift Cells Up**.

**4.** Click **OK**.

# Inserting Rows and Columns

Inserting entire rows and columns in your worksheet is easy. Here's what you do:

1. **To insert a single row or column,** select the cell to the *left* of which you want to insert a column, or *above* which you want to insert a row.

   **To insert multiple columns or rows,** select the number of columns or rows you want to insert. To insert columns, drag over the column letters at the top of the worksheet. To insert rows, drag over the row numbers. For example, select three column letters or row numbers to insert three rows or columns.

2. Open the **Insert** menu.

3. Select **Rows** or **Columns**. Excel inserts the row(s) or column(s) and shifts the adjacent rows down or the adjacent columns right. The inserted rows or columns contain the same formatting as the cells you selected in step 1. Figure 11.3 simulates a worksheet before and after two rows were inserted.

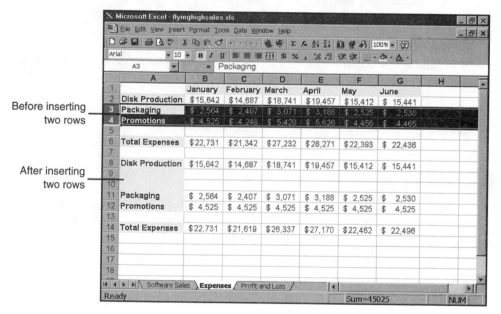

**Figure 11.3** Inserting two rows in a worksheet.

**TIP** **Shortcut Insert** To quickly insert rows or columns, select one or more rows or columns. Then right-click one of them and choose **Insert** from the shortcut menu.

# Removing Rows and Columns

Deleting rows and columns is similar to deleting cells. When you delete a row, the rows below the deleted row move up to fill the space. When you delete a column, the columns to the right shift left.

Follow these steps to delete a row or column:

1. Click the row number or column letter of the row or column you want to delete. You can select more than one row or column by dragging over the row numbers or column letters.

2. Open the **Edit** menu and choose **Delete**. Excel deletes the row(s) or column(s) and renumbers the remaining rows and columns sequentially. All cell references in formulas and names in formulas are updated appropriately, unless they are absolute ($) values (see Lesson 13).

In this lesson, you learned how to insert and delete cells, rows, and columns. In the next lesson, you will learn how to use formulas.

# Performing Calculations with Formulas

*In this lesson, you learn how to use formulas to calculate results in your worksheets.*

## What Is a Formula?

Worksheets use formulas to perform calculations on the data you enter. With formulas, you can perform addition, subtraction, multiplication, and division using the values contained in various cells.

Formulas typically consist of one or more cell addresses and/or values and a mathematical operator, such as + (addition), – (subtraction), * (multiplication), or / (division). For example, if you want to determine the average of the three values contained in cells A1, B1, and C1, you would type the following formula in the cell where you want the result to appear:

=(A1+B1+C1)/3

**Start Right**   Every formula must begin with an equal sign (=).

CAUTION

Figure 12.1 shows several formulas in action. Study the formulas and their results. Table 12.1 lists the mathematical operators you can use to create formulas.

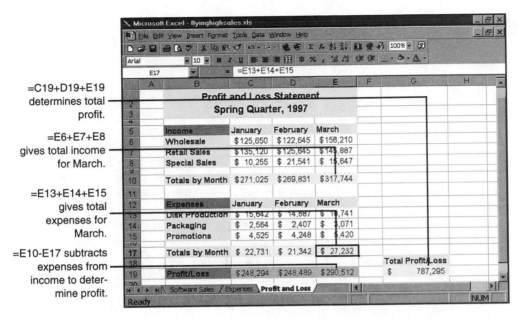

=C19+D19+E19
determines total
profit.

=E6+E7+E8
gives total income
for March.

=E13+E14+E15
gives total
expenses for
March.

=E10-E17 subtracts
expenses from
income to deter-
mine profit.

**Figure 12.1** Type a formula in the cell where you want the resulting value to appear.

**Table 12.1** Excel's Mathematical Operators

| Operator | Performs | Sample Formula | Result |
|---|---|---|---|
| ^ | Exponentiation | =A1^3 | Enters the result of raising the value in cell A1 to the third power. |
| + | Addition | =A1+A2 | Enters the total of the values in cells A1 and A2. |
| − | Subtraction | =A1−A2 | Subtracts the value in cell A2 from the value in cell A1. |
| * | Multiplication | =A2*3 | Multiplies the value in cell A2 by 3. |
| / | Division | =A1/50 | Divides the value in cell A1 by 50. |
| | Combination | =(A1+A2+A3)/3 | Determines the average of the values in cells A1 through A3. |

# Order of Operations

Excel performs the operations within a formula in the following order:

1st      Exponential and equations within parentheses

2nd     Multiplication and division

3rd      Addition and subtraction

For example, given the formula =C2+B8*4+D10, Excel computes the value of B8*4, then adds that to C2, and then adds D10. Keep this order of operations in mind when you are creating equations because it determines the result.

If you don't take this order into consideration, you could run into problems when entering your formulas. For example, if you want to determine the average of the values in cells A1, B1, and C1, and you enter =A1+B1+C1/3, you'll get the wrong answer. The value in C1 will be divided by 3, and that result will be added to A1+B1. To determine the total of A1 through C1 first, you must enclose that group of values in parentheses, as in =(A1+B1+C1)/3.

# Entering Formulas

You can enter formulas in either of two ways: by typing the formula or by selecting cell references. To type a formula, perform the following steps:

**1.** Select the cell in which you want the formula's calculation to appear.

**2.** Type the equal sign (=).

**3.** Type the formula. The formula appears in the Formula bar.

 **4.** Press **Enter** or click the **Enter** button (the check mark), and Excel calculates the result.

  **Unwanted Formula**   If you start to enter a formula and then decide you don't want to use it, you can skip entering the formula by pressing **Esc** or clicking the **Cancel** button.

**CAUTION**

**TIP**   **Name That Cell**   If you plan to use a particular cell in several formulas, you can give it a name, such as "Income." Then you can use the name in the formula, as in =Income+$12.50. To name a cell, use the **Insert**, **Name**, **Define** command.

To enter a formula by selecting cell references, take the following steps:

1. Select the cell in which you want the formula's result to appear.
2. Type the equal sign (=).
3. Click the cell whose address you want to appear first in the formula. The cell address appears in the Formula bar.

**Upgrade Tip** You can refer to a cell in a different worksheet by switching to that sheet and clicking the cell. To refer to a cell in a different workbook, open the workbook and click the cell. In Excel 97, you can even refer to a workbook located on the Internet or an intranet, if you want.

4. Type a mathematical operator after the value to indicate the next operation you want to perform. The operator appears in the Formula bar.
5. Continue clicking cells and typing operators until the formula is complete.
6. Press **Enter** to accept the formula or **Esc** to cancel the operation.

**Error!** If ERR appears in a cell, make sure that you did not commit one of these common errors: try to divide by zero, use a blank cell as a divisor, refer to a blank cell, delete a cell used in a formula, or include a reference to the cell in which the answer appears.

**Natural Language Formulas** Excel 97 now lets you refer to row and column headings (labels) when entering a formula. For example, if you had a worksheet with the row headings "Revenues," "Expenses," and "Profit," and you had column headings for each month, you could enter a formula such as =Jan Profit+Feb Profit or =Revenues–Expenses.

# Calculating Results Without Entering a Formula

You can view the sum of a range of cells simply by selecting the cells and looking at the status bar, as shown in Figure 12.2. You can also view the average, minimum, maximum, and the count of a range of cells. To do so, right-click the status bar and select the option you want from the shortcut menu that appears.

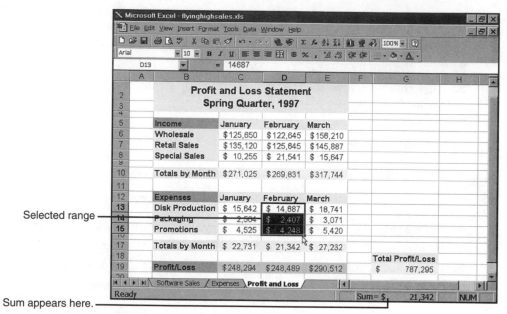

**Figure 12.2** View a sum without entering a formula.

**Where's the Status Bar?** If the status bar is not visible on your screen, you can display it by opening the **View** menu and clicking **Status Bar**.

CAUTION

# Displaying Formulas

Normally, Excel does not display the actual formula in a cell. Instead, it displays the result of the calculation. You can view the formula by selecting the cell and looking in the Formula bar. However, if you're trying to review the formulas in a large worksheet, it might be easier if you could see them all at once (or print them). If you want to view formulas in a worksheet, follow these steps:

**1.** Open the **Tools** menu and choose **Options**.

**2.** Click the **View** tab.

**3.** In the Window Options area, click to select the **Formulas** check box.

**4.** Click **OK**.

TIP **Display Formulas Quickly** You can use a keyboard shortcut to toggle between viewing formulas and viewing values. To do so, hold down the **Ctrl** key and press **'** (the accent key to the left of the 1 key; it has the tilde (~) on it). When you no longer want to view the formulas, press **Ctrl+'** again.

# Editing Formulas

Editing a formula is the same as editing any entry in Excel. Here's how you do it:

**1.** Select the cell that contains the formula you want to edit.

**2.** Click in the Formula bar or press **F2** to enter Edit mode.

TIP **Quick In-Cell Editing** To quickly edit the contents of a cell, double-click the cell. The insertion point appears inside the cell, and you can make any necessary changes.

**3.** Press the left arrow key (←) or right arrow key (→) to move the insertion point. Then use the **Backspace** key to delete characters to the left, or use the **Delete** key to delete characters to the right. Type any additional characters.

**4.** When you finish editing the data, click the **Enter** button on the Formula bar or press **Enter** to accept your changes.

Another way to edit a formula is to click the **Edit Formula** button on the Formula bar. When you do, the Formula bar expands to provide you with help. Make your changes to the formula and then click **OK**.

In this lesson, you learned how to enter and edit formulas. In the next lesson, you will learn how to copy formulas, when to use relative and absolute cell addresses, and how to change Excel's settings for calculating formulas in the worksheet.

# Copying Formulas and Recalculating

*In this lesson, you learn how to copy formulas, use relative and absolute cell references, and change calculation settings.*

## Copying Formulas

When you copy a formula, the formula is adjusted to fit the location of the cell to which it is copied. For example, if you copy the formula =C2+C3 from cell C4 to cell D4, the formula is adjusted for column D: it becomes =D2+D3. This allows you to copy similar formulas (such as the totals for a range of sales items) into a range of cells.

You can copy formulas using the Copy and Paste buttons (see Lesson 5), but there's a faster way.

1. Click the cell that contains the formula you want to copy.
2. Press **Ctrl** and drag the cell's border to the cell to which you want to copy your formula.
3. Release the mouse button, and Excel copies the formula to the new location.

If you want to copy a formula to a neighboring range of cells, follow these steps:

1. Click the cell that contains the formula you want to copy.
2. Move the mouse pointer over the fill handle.
3. Drag the fill handle across the cells into which you want to copy the formula.

**TIP**

**Fast Copy**   If you want to enter the same formula into a range of cells, select the range first. Then type the formula for the first cell in the range and press **Ctrl+Enter**.

**Get an Error?**   If you get an error after copying a formula, verify the cell references in the copied formula. See the next section, "Using Relative and Absolute Cell Addresses," for more details.

**CAUTION**

# Using Relative and Absolute Cell Addresses

When you copy a formula from one place in the worksheet to another, Excel adjusts the cell references in the formulas relative to their new positions in the worksheet. For example, in Figure 13.1, cell B8 contains the formula =B2+B3+B4+B5+B6, which computes the total expenses for January. If you copy that formula to cell C8 (to determine the total expenses for February), Excel automatically changes the formula to =C2+C3+C4+C5+C6. This is how relative cell addresses work.

Cell references are adjusted for column C.

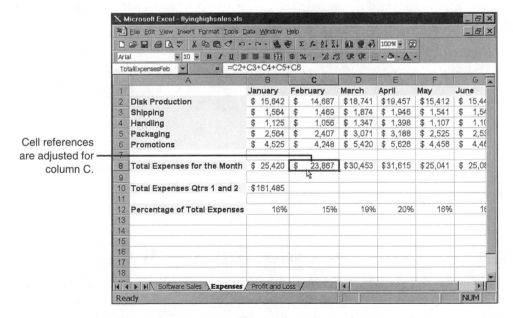

**Figure 13.1**   Excel adjusts cell references when you copy formulas to different cells.

Sometimes you may not want the cell references to be adjusted when you copy formulas. That's when absolute cell references become important.

**Absolute versus Relative**   An *absolute reference* is a cell reference in a formula that does not change when copied to a new location. A *relative reference* is a cell reference in a formula that is adjusted when the formula is copied.

In the example shown in Figure 13.1, the formulas in cells B12, C12, D12, E12, F12, and G12 contain an absolute reference to cell B10, which holds the total expenses for quarters 1 and 2. (The formulas in B12, C12, D12, E12, F12, and G12 divide the sums from row 8 of each column by the contents of cell B10.) If you didn't use an absolute reference, when you copied the formula from B10 to C10, the cell reference would be incorrect, and you would get an error message.

To make a cell reference in a formula absolute, you add a $ (dollar sign) before the letter and number that make up the cell address. For example, the formula in B12 would read as follows:

=B8/$B$10

You can type the dollar signs yourself, or you can press **F4** after typing the cell address.

Some formulas use mixed references. For example, the column letter might be an absolute reference, and the row number might be a relative reference, as in the formula $A2/2. If you entered this formula in cell C2 and then copied it to cell D10, the result would be the formula $A10/2. The row reference (row number) would be adjusted, but the column reference (the letter A) would not be.

**Mixed References**   A reference that is only partially absolute, such as A$2 or $A2. When a formula that uses a mixed reference is copied to another cell, part of the cell reference (the relative part) is adjusted.

# Changing the Calculation Setting

Excel recalculates the formulas in a worksheet every time you edit a value in a cell. However, on a large worksheet, you may not want Excel to recalculate until you have entered all of your changes. For example, if you are entering a lot of changes to a worksheet that contains many formulas, you can speed up the response time by changing from automatic to manual recalculation. To change the recalculation setting, take the following steps:

**1.** Open the **Tools** menu and choose **Options**.

**2.** Click the **Calculation** tab to see the options shown in Figure 13.2.

**3.** Select one of the following Calculation options:

> **Automatic**   This is the default setting. It recalculates the entire workbook each time you edit or enter a formula.
>
> **Automatic Except Tables**   This automatically recalculates everything except formulas in a data table.
>
> **Manual**   This option tells Excel to recalculate only when you say so. To recalculate, you press **F9** or choose the **Tools**, **Options**, **Calculation** command and click the **Calc Now** button. When this option is selected, you can turn the **Recalculate Before Save** option off or on.

**4.** Click **OK**.

Calculation options ———

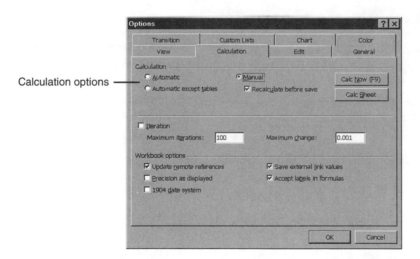

**Figure 13.2**   Change your calculation setting in the Options dialog box.

In this lesson, you learned how to copy formulas. You also learned when to use relative and absolute cell addresses and how to change calculation settings. In the next lesson, you will learn how to use Excel's Function Wizard to insert another type of formula, called a *function*.

# Performing Calculations with Functions

*In this lesson, you learn how to perform calculations with functions and how to use Excel's Function Wizard to quickly insert functions in cells.*

## What Are Functions?

Functions are complex ready-made formulas that perform a series of operations on a specified range of values. For example, to determine the sum of a series of numbers in cells A1 through H1, you can enter the function =SUM(A1:H1) instead of entering =A1+B1+C1 and so on. Functions can use range references (such as B1:B3), range names (such as SALES), and/or numerical values (such as 585.86).

Every function consists of the following three elements:

- The = sign indicates that what follows is a function (formula).
- The function name, such as SUM, indicates which operation will be performed.
- The argument, such as (A1:H1), indicates the cell addresses of the values that the function will act on. The argument is often a range of cells, but it can be much more complex.

You can enter functions either by typing them in cells or by using the Function Wizard, as you'll see later in this lesson.

Table 14.1 shows Excel's most common functions that you'll use most in your worksheets.

**Table 14.1** Excel's Most Common Functions

| Function | Example | Description |
|---|---|---|
| AVERAGE | =AVERAGE(B4:B9) | Calculates the mean or average of a group of numbers. |
| COUNT | =COUNT(A3:A7) | Counts the numeric values in a range. For example, if a range contains some cells with text and other cells with numbers, you can count how many numbers are in that range. |
| COUNTA | =COUNTA(B4:B10) | Counts all cells in a range that are not blank. For example, if a range contains some cells with text and other cells with numbers, you can count how many cells in that range contain text. |
| IF | =IF(A3>=100,A3*2,A2*2) | Allows you to place a condition on a formula. In this example, if A3 is greater than or equal to 100, the formula A3*2 is used. If A3 is less than 100, the formula A2*2 is used instead. |
| MAX | =MAX(B4:B10) | Returns the maximum value in a range of cells. |
| MIN | =MIN(B4:B10) | Returns the minimum value in a range of cells. |
| PMT | =PMT(rate,nper,pv) | Calculates the periodic payment on a loan when you enter the interest rate, number of periods, and principal as arguments. Example: =PMT(.0825/12,360,180000) for 30-year loan at 8.25% for $180,000. |
| PMT | =PMT(rate,nper,,fv) | Calculates the deposit needed each period to reach some future value. Example: =PMT(.07/12,60,,10000) calculates the deposit needed to accumulate $10,000 at an annual rate of 7%, making monthly payments for 5 years (60 months). |
| SUM | =SUM(A1:A10) | Calculates the total in a range of cells. |
| SUMIF | =SUMIF(rg,criteria,sumrg) | Calculates the total of the range *rg* for each corresponding cell in *sumrg* that matches the specified criteria. For example, =SUMIF (A2:A4,>100,B2:B4) adds the cells in the range A2:A4 whose corresponding cell in column B is greater than 100. |

**Excel on the Web** A new function, =HYPERLINK(), is used to create links to Web sites right in your worksheet. For example, =HYPERLINK(http://www.microsoft.com,"Visit Microsoft") will display the words "Visit Microsoft" in a cell. When the user clicks the cell, he or she is connected to the Microsoft home page. You can also use this feature to link to worksheets on your company's intranet.

**Enter Text Right** When entering text into a formula, be sure to surround it with quotation marks, as in "Seattle."

CAUTION

# Using AutoSum

Because SUM is one of the most commonly used functions, Excel provides a fast way to enter it—you simply click the AutoSum button in the Standard toolbar. Based on the currently selected cell, AutoSum guesses which cells you want summed. If AutoSum selects an incorrect range of cells, you can edit the selection.

To use AutoSum, follow these steps:

**1.** Select the cell in which you want the sum inserted. Try to choose a cell at the end of a row or column of data; doing so will help AutoSum guess which cells you want added together.

Σ

**2.** Click the **AutoSum** button in the Standard toolbar. AutoSum inserts =SUM and the range address of the cells to the left of or above the selected cell (see Figure 14.1).

**3.** If the range Excel selected is incorrect, drag over the range you want to use, or click in the Formula bar and edit the formula.

**4.** Click the **Enter** button in the Formula bar or press **Enter**. Excel calculates the total for the selected range.

TIP **Quickie AutoSum** To quickly insert the sum function, select the cell in which you want the sum inserted and double-click the **AutoSum** tool on the Standard toolbar. When you double-click the AutoSum button instead of single-clicking, you bypass the step where Excel displays the SUM formula and its arguments in the cell. Instead, you see the total in the cell and the SUM formula in the Formula bar. The problem with using this method is that you're not given a chance to "second-guess" the range of cells AutoSum decides to add.

The SUM function appears in the selected cell and in the Formula bar.

AutoSum selects a range of cells above or to the left of the selected cell.

The selected range becomes the function's argument.

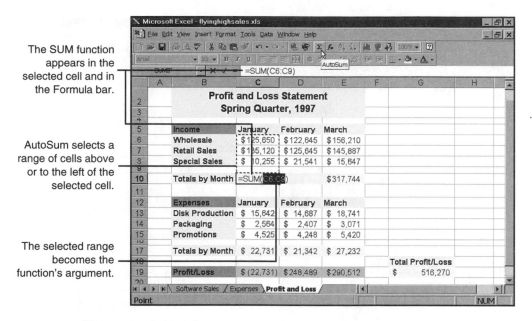

**Figure 14.1** AutoSum inserts the SUM function and selects the cells it plans to total.

# Using AutoCalculate

When you wanted to quickly check a total in earlier versions of Excel, did you ever use a calculator or enter temporary formulas on a worksheet? If you did, you might find Excel's AutoCalculate feature very handy. AutoCalculate lets you quickly check a total or an average, count entries or numbers, and find the maximum or minimum number in a range.

Here's how AutoCalculate works. To check a total, select the range you want to sum. Excel automatically displays the answer in the AutoCalculate area (as shown in Figure 14.2). If you want to perform a different function on a range of numbers, select the range and right-click in the AutoCalculate area to display the shortcut menu. Then choose a function from the menu. For example, choose Count to count the numeric values in the range. The answer appears in the AutoCalculate area.

**Where's My Status Bar?** If the status bar is not displayed, open the **View** menu and click **Status Bar** to turn it on.

CAUTION

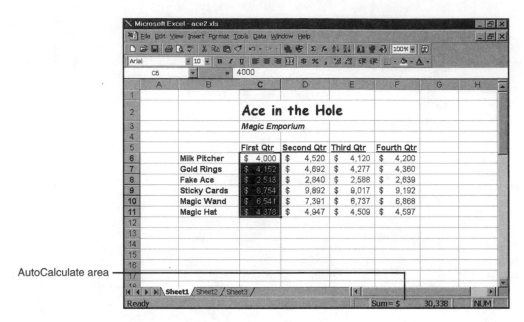

**Figure 14.2** AutoCalculate lets you quickly view a sum.

# Using the Function Wizard

Although you can type a function directly into a cell just as you can type formulas, you may find it easier to use the Function Wizard. The Function Wizard leads you through the process of inserting a function. The following steps walk you through using the Function Wizard:

1. Select the cell in which you want to insert the function. (You can insert a function by itself or as part of a formula.)

2. Type = or click the **Edit Formula** button on the Formula bar. The Formula Palette appears, as shown in Figure 14.3.

3. Select the function you want to insert from the **Functions** list by clicking the **Functions** button (see Figure 14.3). If you don't see your function listed, select **More Functions** at the bottom of the list.

**What's This Function?** If you don't know a lot about a particular function and you'd like to know more, click the **Help** button in the Formula Palette. When the Office Assistant appears, click **Help with the Feature**. Then click **Help on Selected Function**.

**304**

Functions list ——

Edit Formula button ——

Formula Palette ——

Collapse Dialog
button ——

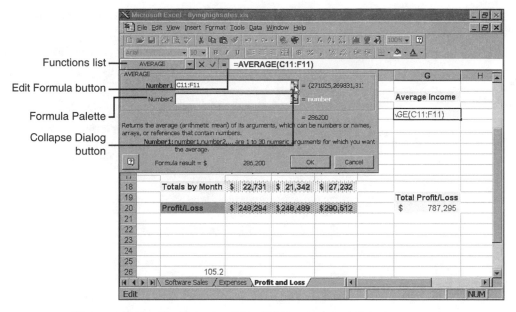

**Figure 14.3** The Function Wizard helps you enter functions.

**4.** Enter the arguments for the formula. If you want to select a range of cells as an argument, click the **Collapse Dialog** button shown in Figure 14.3.

**5.** After selecting a range, click the **Collapse Dialog** button again to return to the Formula Palette.

**6.** Click **OK**. Excel inserts the function and argument in the selected cell and displays the result.

 To edit a function, click the **Edit Formula** button. The Formula Palette appears. Change the arguments as needed and click **OK**.

In this lesson, you learned the basics of dealing with functions, and you learned how to use Excel's Function Wizard to quickly enter functions. You also learned how to quickly total a series of numbers with the AutoSum tool and how to check the sum of numbers with AutoCalculate. In the next lesson, you will learn how to format values in your worksheet.

# Changing How Numbers Look

*In this lesson, you learn how to customize the appearance of numbers in your worksheet.*

## Formatting Values

Numeric values are usually more than just numbers. They represent a dollar value, a date, a percent, or some other value. Excel offers a wide range of number formats, which are listed in Table 15.1.

**Table 15.1**  Excel's Number Formats

| Number Format | Examples | Description |
|---|---|---|
| General | 10.6<br>$456,908.00 | Excel displays your value as you enter it. In other words, this format displays currency or percent signs only if you enter them yourself. |
| Number | 3400.50<br>(−120.39) | The default Number format has two decimal places. Negative numbers appear in red and in parentheses, preceded by a minus sign. |
| Currency | $3,400.50<br>($3,400.50) | The default Currency format has two decimal places and a dollar sign. Negative numbers appear in red and in parentheses. |
| Accounting | $  3,400.00<br>$     978.21 | Use this format to align dollar signs and decimal points in a column. The default Accounting format has two decimal places and a dollar sign. |
| Date | 11/7 | The default Date format is the month and day separated by a slash; however, you can select from numerous other formats. |

| Number Format | Examples | Description |
|---|---|---|
| Time | 10:00 | The default Time format is the hour and minutes separated by a colon; however, you can opt to display seconds, AM, or PM. |
| Percentage | 99.50% | The default Percentage format has two decimal places. Excel multiplies the value in a cell by 100 and displays the result with a percent sign. |
| Fraction | 1/2 | The default Fraction format is up to one digit on either side of the slash. Use this format to display the number of digits you want on either side of the slash and the fraction type (such as halves, quarters, eighths, and so on). |
| Scientific | 3.40E+03 | The default Scientific format has two decimal places. Use this format to display numbers in scientific notation. |
| Text | 135RV90 | Use Text format to display both text and numbers in a cell as text. Excel displays the entry exactly as you type it. |
| Special | 02110 | This format is specifically designed to display ZIP codes, phone numbers, and Social Security numbers correctly, so that you don't have to enter any special characters, such as hyphens. |
| Custom | 00.0% | Use Custom format to create your own number format. You can use any of the format codes in the Type list and then make changes to those codes. The # symbol represents a number placeholder, and 0 represents a zero placeholder. |

After deciding on a suitable numeric format, follow these steps:

1. Select the cell or range that contains the values you want to format.
2. Open the **Format** menu and select **Cells**. The Format Cells dialog box appears, as shown in Figure 15.1.
3. Click the **Number** tab.
4. In the **Category** list, select the numeric format category you want to use. The sample box displays the default format for that category.
5. Make changes to the format as needed.

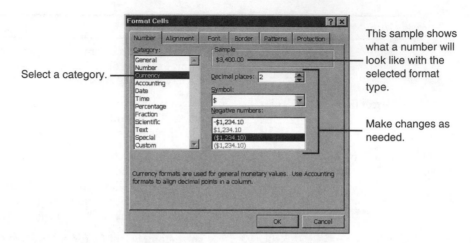

Select a category.

This sample shows
what a number will
look like with the
selected format
type.

Make changes as
needed.

**Figure 15.1** The Format Cells dialog box with the Number tab displayed.

6. Click **OK** or press **Enter**. Excel reformats the selected cells based on your selections.

**CAUTION**

**Removing Formatting** If you want to remove a number format from a cell (and return it to General format), select the cells whose formatting you want to remove, open the **Edit** menu, select **Clear**, then select **Formats**.

# Using the Style Buttons to Format Numbers

The Formatting toolbar (just below the Standard toolbar) contains several buttons for selecting a number format, including the following:

| Button | Name | Example/Description |
|--------|------|---------------------|
| **$** | Currency Style | $1200.90 |
| **%** | Percent Style | 20.90% |

| Button | Name | Example/Description |
|--------|------|---------------------|
|  | Comma Style | 1,200.90 |
|  | Increase Decimal | Adds one decimal place |
| | Decrease Decimal | Deletes one decimal place |

To use one of these buttons, select the cell you want to format and then click the desired button. You can also change the Number format of a cell by using the shortcut menu. Select the cell, right-click to display the shortcut menu, and choose **Format Cells**.

**CAUTION**

**That's Not the Date I Entered!** If you enter a date in a cell that is formatted with the Number format, the date will appear as a number. With the Number format, Excel converts the date to a value that represents the number of days between January 1, 1900 and that date. For example, 01/01/1900 equals 1, and 12/31/1900 equals 366 (1900 was a leap year). To fix your problem, change the cell's formatting from Number format to Date format and select a date type.

**97**

**Upgrade Tip** If you want to highlight cells that meet certain conditions, such as all values that are larger than 1,000, use conditional formatting. See Lesson 16 for more information.

# Creating Your Own Custom Format

If you need to enter special numbers, such as account numbers, you may want to create your own number format and use it to format your account numbers. For example, suppose your account numbers look like this:

10-20190-109

You could create a format like this:

##-#####-###

Then when you enter the number, 9089212098, for example, Excel formats it for you, adding the hyphens where needed:

90-89212-098

**Mixed Metaphors**   Unfortunately, you can't create a format for a value that includes both text and numbers combined.

CAUTION

To create your own format, follow these steps:

1. Open the **Format** menu and select **Cells**.
2. Click the **Number** tab.
3. In the **Category** list, select **Custom**.
4. Type your custom format in the **Type** box and click **OK**.

When entering your format, use the following codes:

| | |
|---|---|
| # | Displays the number (unless it's an insignificant zero) |
| 0 | Adds zeros where needed to fill out the number |
| ? | Adds spaces where needed to align decimal points |

Table 15.2 shows some sample formats.

**Table 15.2**   Sample Custom Formats

| Value Entered | Custom Format | Value Displayed in Cell |
|---|---|---|
| 3124.789 | ####.## | 3124.79 |
| 120.5 | ###.#00 | 120.500 |
| .6345 | 0.## | 0.63 |
| 21456.25 | ##,###.00 | 21,456.25 |
| 120.54 | $##,###.#0 | $120.54 |

You can enter formats for how you want positive and negative numbers displayed, along with zero values and text. Simply separate the formats with a semicolon (;) like this:

##.#0;[MAGENTA] –##.#0;[GREEN] 0.00;@

In this example format, positive numbers entered into the cell are displayed with two decimal places (a zero is added to fill two decimal places if needed). Negative numbers are displayed with a preceding minus sign (–) in magenta. Zero values are displayed as 0.00 in green. Text is permitted in these cells, as indicated by the final format (@). If you do not include the text format, any text you type into the cell simply will not be displayed at all. If you want to add a particular word or words in front of all text entered into a cell, include the word(s) in double quotation marks, as in "Acct. Code:"@.

In this lesson, you learned how to format numbers and create custom formats. In the next lesson, you will learn how to format text.

# Giving Your
# Text a New Look

*In this lesson, you learn how to change the appearance of the text in the cells.*

## How You Can Make Text Look Different

When you type text or numbers, Excel automatically formats it in the Arial font, which doesn't look very fancy. You can change the following text attributes to improve the appearance of your text or set it apart from other text:

**Font**   A typeface—for example, Arial, Courier, or Times New Roman.

**Font Style**   For example, Bold, Italic, Underline, or Strikethrough.

**CAUTION**

**Text Underline versus Cell Border**   You can add underlining to important information in one of two ways. With the underline format explained in this lesson, a line (or lines, depending on which underline format you choose) is placed under the cell's contents. This is different from adding a line to the bottom of a cell's border, which is explained in the next lesson.

**Size**   For example, 10-point, 12-point, or 20-point. (The higher the point size, the bigger the text is. There are approximately 72 points in an inch.)

**Color**   For example, Red, Magenta, or Cyan.

**Alignment**   For example, centered, left aligned, or right aligned within the cell.

**What's a Font?**  A font is a set of characters that have the same typeface, which means they are of a single design (such as Times New Roman). When you select a font, Excel also allows you to change the font's size; add optional *attributes* to the font, such as bold or italic; underline the text; change its color; and add special effects such as strikethrough, superscript, subscript, and small caps.

Figure 16.1 shows a worksheet after some attributes have been changed for selected text.

This text is centered across columns and set in 16-point bold type.

Underline is applied to column headings.

Row headings are set in italics.

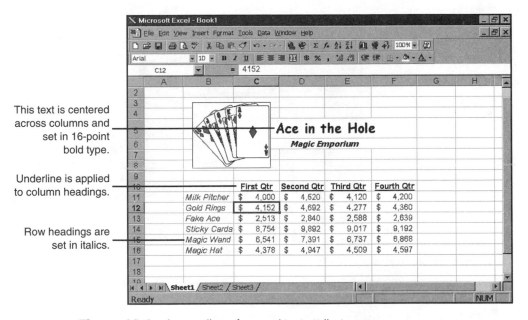

**Figure 16.1**  A sampling of several text attributes.

# Using the Format Cells Dialog Box

You can change the look of your text by using the Format Cells dialog box. Just follow these steps:

**1.** Select the cell or range that contains the text you want to format.

**2.** Open the **Format** menu and choose **Cells**, or press **Ctrl+1**. (You can also right-click the selected cells and choose **Format Cells** from the shortcut menu.)

3. Click the **Font** tab. The Font options jump to the front, as shown in Figure 16.2.

4. Select the options you want.

5. Click **OK** or press **Enter**.

Excel uses a default font to style your text as you type it. To change the default font, enter your font preferences in the Font tab and click the **Normal Font** option. When you click the **OK** button, Excel makes your preferences the default font.

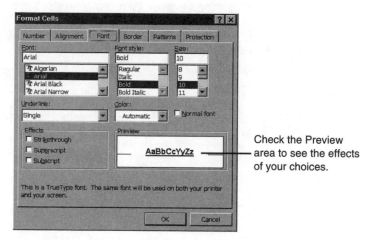

Check the Preview area to see the effects of your choices.

**Figure 16.2** The Format Cells dialog box with the Font tab up front.

**TIP**　**Font Shortcuts**　You can apply certain attributes quickly by using keyboard shortcuts. First select the cell(s), and then press **Ctrl+B** for bold, **Ctrl+I** for Italic, **Ctrl+U** for Single Underline (Accounting style), or **Ctrl+5** for Strikethrough.

# Changing Text Attributes with Toolbar Buttons

A faster way to enter font changes is to use the Formatting toolbar shown in Figure 16.3.

Select a font
size here.    Bold   Italic   Underline

Select a
font here.

Apply a
text color.

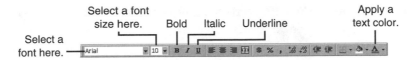

**Figure 16.3** Use the Formatting toolbar to quickly make font changes.

To use a tool to change text attributes, follow these steps:

1. Select the cell or range that contains the text whose look you want to change.

2. To change the font or font size, pull down the appropriate drop-down list and click the font or size you want. You can also type the point size in the **Font Size** box.

3. To add an attribute (such as bold or underlining), click the desired button. When selected, a button looks like it has been pressed in. You can add more than one attribute to text, making it bold and italic, for example.

**TIP**   **Change Before You Type**   You can activate the attributes you want *before* you type text. For example, if you want a title in Bold 12-point Desdemona type, select the cells for which you want to change the attributes, and then set the attributes before you start typing. Unlike in a word processor where you must turn attributes on and off, in Excel, selecting formats for cells in advance of typing your data has no effect on the unselected cells; data in unselected cells will be the default Arial 10-point type.

# Aligning Text in Cells

When you enter data into an Excel worksheet, that data is aligned automatically. Text is aligned on the left, and numbers are aligned on the right. Both text and numbers are initially set at the bottom of the cells. However, you can change both the vertical and the horizontal alignment of data in your cells.

Follow these steps to change the alignment:

1. Select the cell or range you want to align. If you want to center a title or other text over a range of cells, select the entire range of blank cells in which you want the text centered, including the cell that contains the text you want to center.

**2.** Pull down the **Format** menu and select **Cells,** or press **Ctrl+1**. The Format Cells dialog box appears.

**3.** Click the **Alignment** tab. The alignment options appear in front (see Figure 16.4).

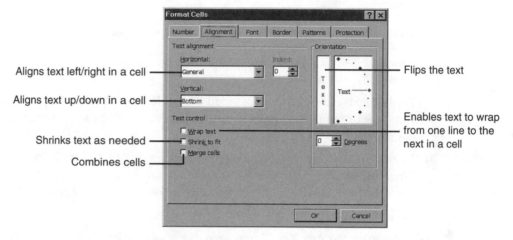

Aligns text left/right in a cell

Aligns text up/down in a cell

Shrinks text as needed

Combines cells

Flips the text

Enables text to wrap from one line to the next in a cell

**Figure 16.4** The Alignmentß options.

**4.** Choose from the following options and option groups to set the alignment:

**Horizontal** lets you specify a left/right alignment in the cell(s). (The Center Across selection centers a title or other text within a range of cells.)

**Vertical** lets you specify how you want the text aligned in relation to the top and bottom of the cell(s).

**Orientation** lets you flip the text sideways or print it from top to bottom (instead of left to right). This option is new to Excel 97.

**Wrap Text** tells Excel to wrap long lines of text within a cell without changing the width of cell. (Normally, Excel displays all text in a cell on one line.)

**Shrink to Fit** shrinks the text to fit within the cell's current width. If the cell's width is adjusted, the text increases or decreases in size accordingly.

**Merge Cells** combines several cells into a single cell. All data is overlaid, except for the cell in the upper-left corner of the selected cells.

**5.** Click **OK** or press **Enter**.

**TIP** **Alignment Buttons** A quick way to align text and numbers is to use the alignment buttons in the Formatting toolbar. The following buttons allow you to align the text:

 Align Left           Align Right

 Center           Merge and Center

New to Excel 97 is the capability to indent your text within a cell. If you're typing a paragraph worth of information into a single cell, you can indent that paragraph by selecting left alignment from the **Horizontal** list box in the Format Cells dialog box (as explained earlier). After selecting left alignment, set the amount of indent you want with the **Indent** spin box.

In addition, you can add an indent quickly by clicking the following buttons on the Formatting toolbar:

 Decrease Indent          Removes an indent or creates a negative indent.

 Increase Indent          Adds an indent.

In this lesson, you learned how to customize your text formatting to achieve the look you want. In the next lesson, you will learn how to add borders and shading to your worksheet.

# Adding Cell Borders and Shading

*In this lesson, you learn how to add pizzazz to your worksheets by adding borders and shading.*

## Adding Borders to Cells

As you work with your worksheet on-screen, you'll notice that each cell is identified by gridlines that surround the cell. Normally, these gridlines do not print; and even if you choose to print them, they may appear washed out. To have more well-defined lines appear on the printout (or on-screen, for that matter), you can add borders to selected cells or entire cell ranges. A border can appear on all four sides of a cell or only on selected sides, whichever you prefer.

**CAUTION** **The Gridlines Don't Print?**  In Excel 97, as in Excel 95, the gridlines do not print by default. But if you want to try printing your worksheet with gridlines first just to see what it looks like, open the **File** menu, select **Page Setup**, click the **Sheet** tab, select **Gridlines**, and click **OK**.

To add borders to a cell or range, perform the following steps:

1. Select the cell(s) around which you want a border to appear.
2. Open the **Format** menu and choose **Cells**. The Format Cells dialog box appears.
3. Click the **Border** tab to see the Border options shown in Figure 17.1.

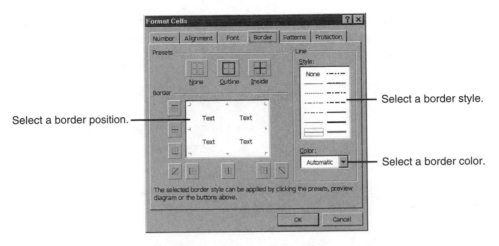

**Figure 17.1** Choose border options from the Format Cells dialog box.

**4.** Select the desired position, style (thickness), and color for the border. You can click inside the Border box itself, or you can click a preset border pattern button to add your border.

**5.** Click **OK** or press **Enter**.

**TIP** **Hiding Gridlines** When adding borders to a worksheet, you might need to hide the gridlines to get a better idea of how the borders will look when printed. Open the **Tools** menu, select **Options**, click the **View** tab, and select **Gridlines** to remove the check mark from the check box. Of course, selecting this option has no effect on whether or not the gridlines actually print, only on whether or not they are displayed on-screen.

To add borders quickly, select the cells around which you want the border to appear, and then click the **Borders** drop-down arrow in the Formatting toolbar. Click the desired border. If you click the **Borders** button itself (instead of the arrow), Excel automatically adds the border line you last chose to the selected cells.

# Adding Shading to Cells

For a simple but dramatic effect, you can add shading to your worksheets. With shading, you can add a color or gray shading to a cell. You can add colors at full strength or partial strength to create the exact effect you want. To lessen the

**319**

strength of the cell color you select, you add your shading with a pattern, such as a diagonal. Figure 17.2 illustrates some of the effects you can create with shading.

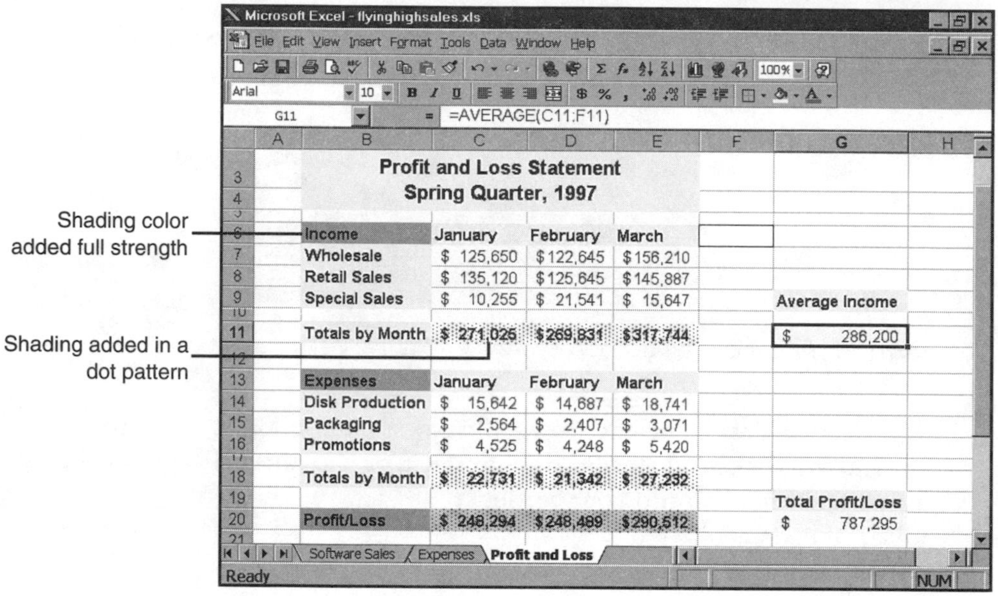

Shading color added full strength

Shading added in a dot pattern

**Figure 17.2** A worksheet with added shading.

Follow these steps to add shading to a cell or range. As you make your selections, keep in mind that if you plan to print your worksheet with a black-and-white printer, your pretty colors may not be different enough to create the effect you want. Select colors that contrast well in value (intensity), and use the Print Preview command (as explained in Lesson 10) to view your results in black-and-white before you print.

1. Select the cell(s) you want to shade.
2. Open the **Format** menu and choose **Cells**.
3. Click the **Patterns** tab. Excel displays the shading options (see Figure 17.3).
4. Click the **Pattern** drop-down arrow, and you will see a grid that contains all the colors from the color palette, as well as patterns. Select the shading color and pattern you want to use. The Color options let you choose a color for the overall shading. The Pattern options let you select a black-and-white or colored pattern that lies on top of the overall shading. A preview of the result appears in the Sample box.

**5.** When you like the results you see, click **OK** or press **Enter**.

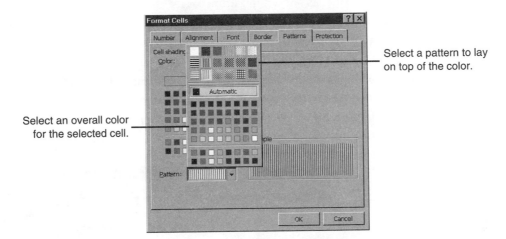

Select a pattern to lay on top of the color.

Select an overall color for the selected cell.

**Figure 17.3** Selecting a shading and a pattern.

A quick way to add cell shading (without a pattern) is to select the cells you want to shade, click the **Fill Color** drop-down arrow, and click the color you want to use.

**TIP** **Quick Color** To add the color shown in the bucket of the Fill Color button, simply click the button itself—do not bother to click the arrow to the right of the button.

If the shading is too dark, consider using the Font Color button (just to the right of the Fill Color button) to select a lighter color for the text.

# Using AutoFormat

Excel offers the AutoFormat feature, which takes some of the pain out of formatting. AutoFormat provides you with 16 predesigned table formats that you can apply to a worksheet.

To use predesigned formats, perform the following steps:

**1.** Select the worksheet(s) and cell(s) that contain the data you want to format.

2. Open the **Format** menu and choose **AutoFormat**. The AutoFormat dialog box appears, as shown in Figure 17.4.

3. In the **Table Format** list, choose the predesigned format you want to use. When you select a format, Excel shows you what it will look like in the Sample area.

4. To exclude certain elements from AutoFormat, click the **Options** button and choose the formats you want to turn off.

5. Click **OK**, and Excel formats your table to make it look like the one in the preview area.

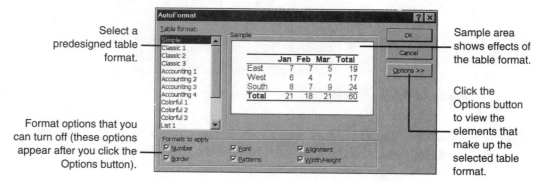

Select a predesigned table format.

Format options that you can turn off (these options appear after you click the Options button).

Sample area shows effects of the table format.

Click the Options button to view the elements that make up the selected table format.

**Figure 17.4**  Use the AutoFormat dialog box to select a prefab format.

**Deformatting an AutoFormat**  If you don't like what AutoFormat did to your worksheet, select the table, open the **Format** menu, and choose **AutoFormat**. From the **Table Format** list, choose **None** to remove the AutoFormat.

# Copying Formats with Format Painter

Excel gives you two ways to copy and paste formatting:

- You can use the Edit, Copy command and then the Edit Paste Special command and select Formats from the Paste options in the Paste Special dialog box.

- You can use the Format Painter button in the Standard toolbar.

The Format Painter lets you quickly copy and paste formats that you have already used in a workbook. Because the Format Painter button is faster, I'll give you the steps you need to paint formats.

1. Select the cell(s) that contain the formatting you want to copy and paste.
2. Click the **Format Painter** button on the Standard toolbar. Excel copies the formatting. The mouse pointer changes into a paintbrush with a plus sign next to it.
3. Click and drag over the cells to which you want to apply the copied formatting.
4. Release the mouse button, and Excel copies the formatting and applies it to the selected cells.

**TIP** **Faster Painter** To paint several areas at one time, double-click the **Format Painter** button. Then drag over the first section you want to paint. The cursor remains as a paintbrush, meaning that you can continue to drag over other cells to paint them too. When you're through, press **Esc** to return to a normal cursor.

# Applying Conditional Formatting

If you want to highlight particular values in your worksheet, you can use conditional formatting. For example, if you want to highlight all sales figures under a particular mark, you could apply a conditional red shading.

To apply conditional formatting, follow these steps:

1. Select the cells you want to format.
2. Open the **Format** menu and select **Conditional Formatting**. The Conditional Formatting dialog box appears, as shown in Figure 17.5.

**Figure 17.5** Apply formats conditionally to highlight certain values.

**3.** To apply a format based on the value found in a selected cell, choose **Cell Value Is** from the **Condition 1** list.

To apply a format based on the value found in a cell outside the selected range, select **Formula Is** from the **Condition 1** list.

**4.** Enter the value or formula you want to use as the *condition* that determines when Excel can apply the formatting you select. If you choose to use a formula, be sure to include the beginning equal (=) sign.

**CAUTION**

**Using a Formula** If you choose Formula Is in step 3, the formula you enter must result in a true or false value (so use the IF statement). For example, if you wanted to format some cells based on whether or not a corresponding value in column A is less than 20% of projected sales (cell D12), you could use this formula:

=IF(A1<20%*$D$12,TRUE,FALSE)

**5.** Click the **Format** button and select the format you want to apply when the condition is true. Click **OK** to return to the Conditional Formatting dialog box.

**6.** (Optional) If you want to add more than one condition, click **Add**. Then repeat steps 3 and 4 to add the condition.

**7.** When you finish adding conditions, click **OK**.

You can copy the conditional formatting from one cell to other cells using the Format Painter button. Simply click the cell whose formatting you want to copy and click the **Format Painter** button. Then drag over the cells to which you want to copy the formatting.

In this lesson, you learned some ways to enhance the appearance of your worksheets. In the next lesson, you will learn how to change the sizes of rows and columns.

# Changing Column Width and Row Height

*In this lesson, you learn how to adjust the column width and row height to make the best use of the worksheet space. You can set these manually or let Excel make the adjustments for you with its AutoFit feature.*

## Adjusting Column Width and Row Height with a Mouse

You can adjust the width of a column or the height of a row by using a dialog box or by dragging with the mouse.

**Why Bother?**   You might not want to bother adjusting the row height because it's automatically adjusted as you change font size. However, if a column's width is not as large as its data, that data may not be displayed and may appear as **########**. In such a case, you must adjust the width of the column in order for the data to be displayed at all.

Here's how you adjust the row height or column width with the mouse:

1. To change the row height or column width for a single row or column, skip to step 2. To change the height or width of two or more rows for columns, select them first by dragging over the row or column headings.

2. Position the mouse pointer over one of the row heading or column heading borders as shown in Figure 18.1. (Use the right border of the column heading to adjust column width; use the bottom border of the row heading to adjust the row height.)

Dragging the right
border of column A —
changes its width.

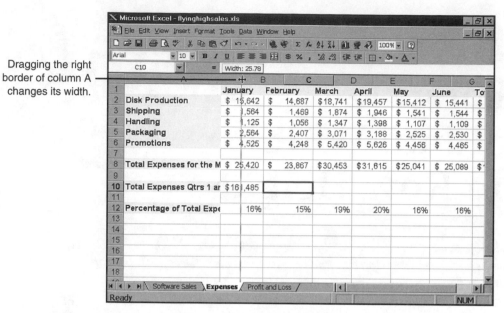

**Figure 18.1** The mouse pointer changes to a double-headed arrow when you move it over a border in the row or column heading.

**3.** Drag the border to the size you need it.

**4.** Release the mouse button, and Excel adjusts the row height or column width.

 **TIP** **AutoFit Cells** To quickly make a column as wide as its widest entry using Excel's AutoFit feature, double-click the right border of the column heading. To make a row as tall as its tallest entry, double-click the bottom border of the row heading. To change more than one column or row at a time, drag over the desired row or column headings, and then double-click the bottommost or rightmost heading border.

# Using the Format Menu for Precise Control

You can change a row or column's size by dragging the border of a row or column. However, you cannot control the size as precisely as you can by providing specific sizes with the Format, Row Height and Format, Column Width commands.

These steps show you how to use the Format menu to change the column width:

1. Select the column(s) whose width you want to change. To change the width of a single column, select any cell in that column.

2. Open the **Format** menu, select **Column**, and select **Width**. The Column Width dialog box appears (see Figure 18.2).

3. Type the number of characters you would like as the width. The default width is 8.43.

4. Click **OK** or press **Enter** to put your changes into effect.

**Figure 18.2**  Changing the column width.

By default, Excel makes a row a bit taller than the tallest text in the row. For example, if the tallest text is 10 points tall, Excel makes the row itself 12.75 points tall. You can use the Format menu to change the row height manually:

1. Select the row(s) whose height you want to change. (To change the height of a single row, select any cell in that row.)

2. Open the **Format** menu, select **Row**, and select **Height**. The Row Height dialog box shown in Figure 18.3 appears.

3. Type the desired height (in points).

4. Click **OK** or press **Enter** to implement the change in your worksheet.

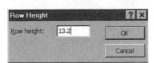

**Figure 18.3**  Changing the row height.

In this lesson, you learned how to change the row height and column width. In the next lesson, you will learn how to create charts.

# Creating Charts

**19**

*In this lesson, you learn to create charts to represent your workbook data as a picture.*

## Chart Types

With Excel, you can create various types of charts. Some common chart types are shown in Figure 19.1. The chart type you choose depends on your data and on how you want to present that data. These are the major chart types and their purposes:

**Pie**   Use this chart to show the relationship among parts of a whole.

**Bar**   Use this chart to compare values at a given point in time.

**Column**   Similar to the Bar chart; use this chart to emphasize the difference between items.

**Line**   Use this chart to emphasize trends and the change of values over time.

**Scatter**   Similar to a Line chart; use this chart to emphasize the difference between two sets of values.

**Area**   Similar to the Line chart; use this chart to emphasize the amount of change in values over time.

Most of these basic chart types also come in three-dimensional varieties. In addition to looking more professional than the standard flat charts, 3-D charts can often help your audience distinguish between different sets of data.

**TERM**   **Embedded Charts**   A chart that is placed on the same worksheet that contains the data used to create the chart. A chart can also be placed on a chart sheet in the workbook so that the worksheet and chart are separate. Embedded charts are useful for showing the actual data and its graphic representation side-by-side.

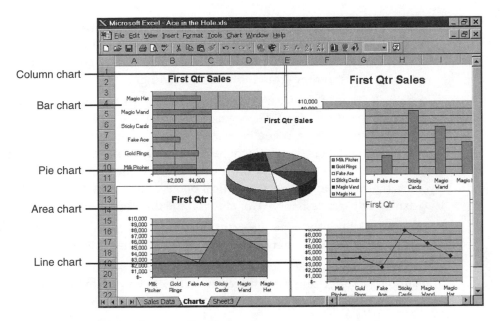

Column chart
Bar chart
Pie chart
Area chart
Line chart

**Figure 19.1** Common Excel chart types.

**Upgrade Tip** Excel 97 includes many new chart types, so have fun when selecting the one you want to use.

# Charting Terminology

Before you start creating charts, familiarize yourself with the following terminology:

**Data Series** The bars, pie wedges, lines, or other elements that represent plotted values in a chart. For example, a chart might show a set of similar bars that reflects a series of values for the same item. The bars in the series would all have the same pattern. If you have more than one pattern of bars, each pattern would represent a separate data series. For instance, charting the sales for Territory 1 versus Territory 2 would require two data series—one for each territory. Often, data series correspond to rows of data in your worksheet.

**Categories** Categories reflect the number of elements in a series. You might have two data series to compare the sales of two different territories and four categories to compare these sales over four quarters. Some charts have only one category, and others have several. Categories normally correspond to the columns that you have in your chart data, and the category labels coming from the column headings.

**Axis**   One side of a chart. A two-dimensional chart has an x-axis (horizontal) and a y-axis (vertical). The x-axis contains all the data series and categories in the chart. If you have more than one category, the x-axis often contains labels that define what each category represents. The y-axis reflects the values of the bars, lines, or plot points. In a three-dimensional chart, the z-axis represents the vertical plane, and the x-axis (distance) and y-axis (width) represent the two sides on the floor of the chart.

**Legend**   Defines the separate series of a chart. For example, the legend for a pie chart will show what each piece of the pie represents.

**Gridlines**   Emphasize the y-axis or x-axis scale of the data series. For example, major gridlines for the y-axis will help you follow a point from the x- or y-axis to identify a data point's exact value.

# Creating a Chart

You can create charts as part of a worksheet (an embedded chart) or as a chart on a separate worksheet. If you create an embedded chart, it will print side-by-side with your worksheet data. If you create a chart on a separate worksheet, you can print it independently. Both types of charts are linked to the worksheet data that they represent, so when you change the data, the chart is automatically updated.

The Chart Wizard button in the Standard toolbar allows you to quickly create a chart. To use the Chart Wizard, follow these steps:

1. Select the data you want to chart. If you typed names or other labels (such as Qtr 1, Qtr 2, and so on) and you want them included in the chart, make sure you select them.

2. Click the **Chart Wizard** button on the Standard toolbar.

3. The Chart Wizard Step 1 of 4 dialog box appears, as shown in Figure 19.2. Select a **Chart Type** and select a **Chart Sub-Type** (a variation on the selected chart type). Click **Next>**.

4. Next you're asked if the selected range is correct. You can correct the range by typing a new range or by clicking the **Collapse Dialog** button (located at the right end of the Data Range text box) and selecting the range you want to use.

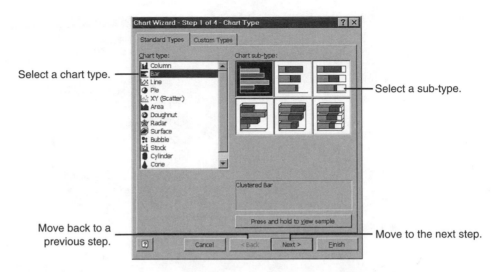

Select a chart type.

Select a sub-type.

Move back to a previous step.

Move to the next step.

**Figure 19.2**  Chart Wizard asks you to choose the chart type you want.

**5.** By default, Excel assumes that your different data series are stored in rows. You can change this to columns if necessary by clicking the **Series in Columns** option. When you're through, click **Next>**.

**6.** Click the various tabs to change options for your chart (see Figure 19.3). For example, you can delete the legend by clicking the **Legend** tab and deselecting **Show Legend**. You can add a chart title on the Titles tab. Add data labels (labels which display the actual value being represented by each bar, line, and so on) by clicking the **Data Labels** tab. When you finish making changes, click **Next>**.

**7.** Finally, you're asked if you want to embed the chart (as an object) in the current worksheet, or if you want to create a new worksheet for it. Make your selection and click the **Finish** button. Your completed chart appears.

**TIP**  **Moving and Resizing a Chart**  To move an embedded chart, click anywhere in the chart area and drag it to the new location. To change the size of a chart, select the chart, and then drag one of its *handles* (the black squares that border the chart). Drag a corner handle to change the height and width, or drag a side handle to change only the width. (Note that you can't really resize a chart that is on a sheet by itself.)

**TIP**  **Create a Chart Fast!**  To create a chart quickly, select the data you want to use and press **F11**. Excel creates a column chart (the default chart type) on its own sheet. You can switch to that sheet, select the chart, and customize it.

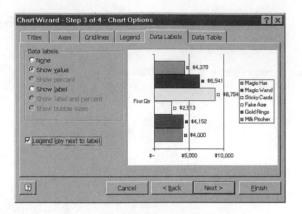

**Figure 19.3** Select from various chart appearance options.

# Customizing Your Chart with the Chart Toolbar

You can use the Chart toolbar to change how your chart looks. If the Chart toolbar is not displayed, you can turn it on by opening the **View** menu, selecting **Toolbars**, and then selecting **Chart**.

Table 19.1 shows each button on the Chart toolbar and explains its purpose.

**Table 19.1** Buttons on the Chart Toolbar

| Button | Name | Use |
|---|---|---|
|  | Chart Objects | Click here to select the part of the chart you want to change. Optionally, you can simply click the part you want to select it. |
|  | Format Object | Click here to change the formatting of the object whose name appears in the Chart Objects text box. |
|  | Chart Type | Click the arrow to change the chart type, from bar to line, for example. If you click the button itself, the displayed chart type will be applied. |

| Button | Name | Use |
|---|---|---|
| | Legend | Click this to display or hide the legend. |
| | Data Table | Click here to add a data table, a grid which displays the data from which the chart was created. |
| | By Row | Click here if your data series are stored in rows. |
| | By Column | Click here if your data series are stored in columns. |
| | Angle Text Downward | Click here to angle text in selected area downward. |
| | Angle Text Upward | Click here to angle text in selected area upward. |

# Saving Charts

The charts you create are part of the current workbook. To save a chart, simply save the workbook that contains the chart. For more details, refer to Lesson 6, "Creating and Saving Workbook Files."

# Printing a Chart

If a chart is an embedded chart, it will print when you print the worksheet that contains the chart. If you want to print just the embedded chart, click it to select it, and then open the **File** menu and select **Print**. Make sure that the **Selected Chart** option is turned on. Then click **OK** to print the chart.

If you created a chart on a separate worksheet, you can print the chart separately by printing only that worksheet. For more information about printing, refer to Lesson 10, "Printing Your Workbook."

In this lesson, you learned about the different chart types and how to create them. You also learned how to save and print charts. In the next lesson, you will learn how to create a database in Excel.

# Working with a Database

*In this lesson, you learn about database basics and how to create your own database.*

## Database Basics

A *database* is a tool used for storing, organizing, and retrieving information. For example, if you want to save the names and addresses of all the people on your holiday card list, you can create a database and then save the following information for each person: first name, last name, street number, and so on. Each piece of information is entered into a separate *field* (cell) in the list. All of the fields for one person in the list make a *record*.

In Excel, a cell is a field, and a row of field entries makes a record. The column headings in the list are called *field names* in the database. Figure 20.1 shows a database and its component parts.

**Database or Data List?** Excel has simplified the database operations by treating the database as a simple *list* of data. You enter the database information just like you would enter data into a worksheet. When you select a command from the Data menu, Excel recognizes the list as a database.

You must observe the following rules when you enter information into your database:

- **Field Names** You must enter field names in the first row of the database. For example, you might type **First Name** for the column that will hold first names, and you might type **Last Name** for the column that will hold last names. Do *not* skip a row between the field names row and the first record.

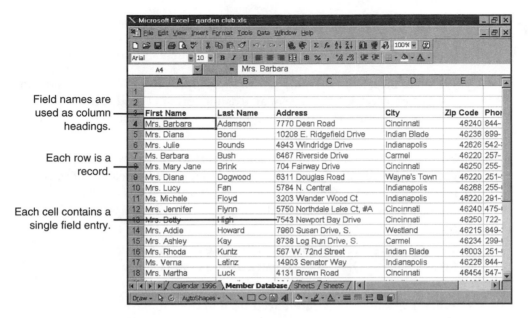

Field names are used as column headings.

Each row is a record.

Each cell contains a single field entry.

**Figure 20.1**   The parts of a database.

- **Records**   Each record must be in a separate row, and there cannot be any empty rows between records.

- **Same Stuff**   The cells in a given column must contain information of the same type. For example, if you have a ZIP code column, all cells in that column must contain a ZIP code, and not some other kind of data. A cell can be left blank if a particular column does not apply to that record.

- **Calculations**   You can create a *calculated field*, which uses information from another field of the same record and produces a result. For example, if you have a column called "Sales Amount," you could use a formula to create the values in a column called "Sales Commission." (To do so, enter a formula, as explained in Lesson 12.)

**TIP**   **Record Numbering**   You might want to add a column that numbers the records. The record number is likely to be the only thing about the record that won't be repeated in another record, and having a unique field could come in handy in advanced databases. Also, if the records are sorted incorrectly, you can use the numbered column to restore the records to their original order.

# Planning a Database

Before you create your database, you should ask yourself these questions:

- **What are the fields that make up an individual record?** If you are creating the database to take the place of an existing form (a Rolodex card, information sheet, or address list), use that form to determine which fields you need.

- **Which types of data might you want to sort by?** If you want to sort by last name, make sure that last name is stored in its own field, and not combined with the first name in a single field. If you want to sort by city, phone number, or ZIP code, make sure that each of these is stored in its own field.

- **Which types of data might you want to search for?** If you want to search for all contacts who work in a particular sales area, make sure you place sales areas in their own field.

- **What is the most often referenced field in the database?** (This field should be placed in the first column.)

- **What is the longest entry in each column?** Use this information to set the column widths. (Or you can make your entries and then use Format Column AutoFit Selection to have Excel adjust the column widths.)

# Creating a Database

To create a database, you don't have to use any special commands. All you do is enter data into the cells as you would enter data on any worksheet. However, as you enter data, you must follow these guidelines:

- You must enter field names in the top row of the database. Enter the first record just below this field names row.

- Type field entries into each cell in a single row to create a record. (You can leave a field blank, but you may run into problems later when you sort the database—that is, if you sort the database by that particular field.)

- Do *not* leave an empty row between the field names and the records or between any records.

- If you want to enter street numbers with the street names at the beginning of the field (such as 155 State Street), start the entry with an apostrophe so that Excel interprets the entry as text instead of as a value. However, note that if you want to enter, for example, One Washington Square Suite 600, you don't need the apostrophe because it begins with text.

- Keep the records on one worksheet. You cannot have a database that spans several worksheets.

**Forget Someone?** To add records to a database, either add the rows above the last row in the database (see Lesson 11, "Inserting and Removing Cells, Rows, and Columns") or select the **Data**, **Form** command and enter the additional records using the data form.

CAUTION

# Using Data Forms to Add, Edit, or Delete Records

Data forms are like index cards: there is one data form for each record in the database, as shown in Figure 20.2. You may find it easier to flip through these data form "cards" and edit entries than to edit them as worksheet data. To edit your database using a data form, perform the following steps:

**1.** Open the **Data** menu and select **Form**. You will see a data form that contains the first record in the database (see Figure 20.2.)

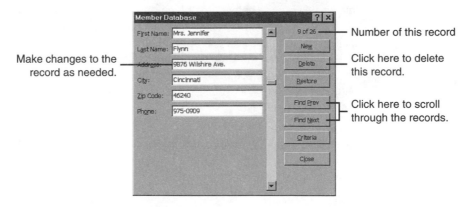

**Figure 20.2** The data form.

**2.** The number of the current record appears in the upper-right corner of the form. Flip to the form you want to edit by using the scroll bar, pressing the up or down arrow key, or clicking **Find Prev** or **Find Next**.

**3.** To edit an entry in a record, tab to the text box that contains the entry and type your correction.

**4.** To delete the current record, click **Delete**.

**5.** Repeat steps 2–4 to change as many records as needed.

**6.** Click the **Close** button when you're done using the data form.

**CAUTION**

**Come Back!**   You can restore field data to what it was before you changed it—provided you haven't changed to a different record. To do so, click the **Restore** button. After you move on to a different record, you'll just have to retype the field data.

You can also use the data form to add records to the database, as described here:

**1.** Open the **Data** menu and choose **Form** to display the data form.

**2.** Click the **New** button.

**3.** Type an entry into each of the text boxes.

**4.** Repeat steps 2 and 3 to add additional records.

**5.** When you finish adding records, click **Close**.

**TIP**   **Template Wizard**   Use the Template Wizard to create a worksheet template into which you can enter some of the data that you later want to save in a database. For example, you could create a sales worksheet and then link it to a client database so you can save information on the items each client purchases. Just open the **Data** menu and select **Template Wizard**. (If you don't see this command, you need to install the Template Wizard add-in.) The Template Wizard walks you step by step through linking cells in the template to fields in a database.

In this lesson, you learned about database basics and how to create a database.

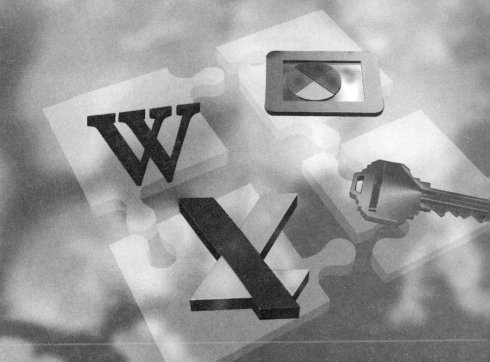

# PowerPoint

# Starting and Exiting PowerPoint

*In this lesson, you learn how to start and exit PowerPoint.*

## Starting PowerPoint

Before you start PowerPoint, you must have PowerPoint installed on your computer (see Lesson 1 in Part 7), and you should have a basic understanding of the Windows 95 or Windows NT operating system. If you need a refresher course in these Windows systems, read Part 1 of this book. Throughout this book, I'll be referring to Windows 95, but keep in mind that in most cases, if you're using Windows NT, the information applies to you, too.

To start PowerPoint, follow these steps:

1. Click the **Start** button.
2. Move your mouse pointer to **Programs**. A menu of programs appears.
3. Move your mouse to **Microsoft PowerPoint** and click (see Figure 1.1). PowerPoint starts and displays the introductory screen shown in Figure 1.2.

The first thing you see when you start PowerPoint is a dialog box in which you choose whether you want to start a new presentation or open an existing one. You'll learn about this dialog box in Lesson 2. For now, click **Cancel** to exit this dialog box.

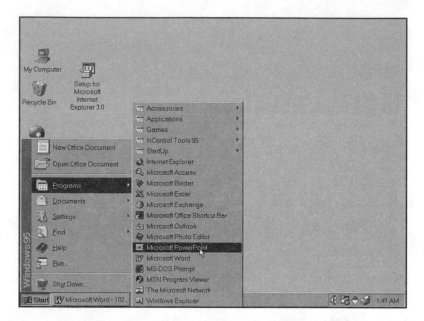

**Figure 1.1** To start PowerPoint, move through the Start button's menu system to Microsoft PowerPoint.

 **TIP** **PowerPoint's Not on the Menu?** You may have specified a different menu when you installed PowerPoint, or you may not have installed PowerPoint yet.

 **CAUTION** **Help! There's a Paper Clip Talking to Me!** No, you haven't lost your mind. That paper clip is one of Microsoft Office's Assistants. Occasionally the little guy gives you a suggestion, and you have to click the appropriate button below his words to move on. The first time you start PowerPoint, he may say something. Clicking the Close (X) button for his window or pressing Esc will enable you to continue with your work. We'll look at the Office Assistants more in Part 7, Lesson 2.

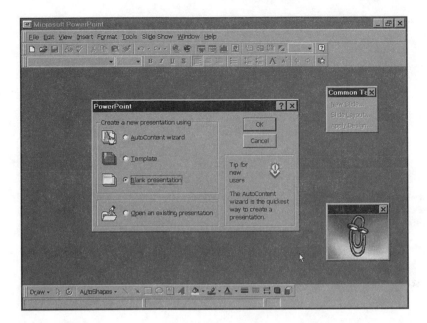

**Figure 1.2**   When you first start PowerPoint, you see an introductory dialog box. (You'll learn about it in Lesson 2.)

# Exiting PowerPoint

When you finish using PowerPoint, you should exit. Don't just turn off your computer! To exit PowerPoint, follow these steps:

**1.** If the PowerPoint dialog box is still on-screen, click the **Cancel** button to close it.

**2.** If this dialog box is not on-screen, do one of the following (see Figure 1.3):

- Click the PowerPoint window's **Close** (X) button.
- Double-click the **Control-menu** icon at the left end of the title bar, or click it once to open the Control menu and then select **Close**.
- Open the **File** menu and select **Exit**.
- Press **Alt+F4**.

**343**

Double-
click here
to close.

Select Exit
from the
File menu.

Click this
Close
button to
close the
PowerPoint
window.

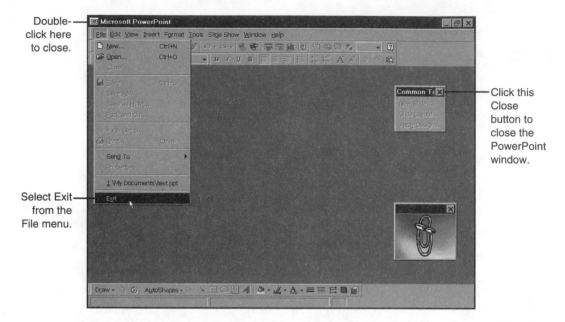

**Figure 1.3**  There are several ways to exit PowerPoint.

**3.** If you're asked if you want to save your changes, select **Yes** if you want to save your changes. (If you choose Yes, see Lesson 5 to learn how to complete the Save As dialog box that appears.) Select **No** if you haven't created anything you want to save yet.

In this lesson, you learned to start and exit PowerPoint. In the next lesson, you'll learn how to create a new presentation.

# Creating a New Presentation

*In this lesson, you learn how to create a presentation in several different ways.*

## Three Choices for Starting a New Presentation

PowerPoint offers you several ways to create a new presentation. Before you begin, decide on the method that's right for you:

- AutoContent Wizard offers the highest degree of help. It walks you through each step of creating the new presentation.

- A template offers a standardized group of slides, all with a similar look and feel, for a particular situation. Each template slide includes dummy text which you can replace with your own text.

- You can choose to start from scratch and create a totally blank presentation, but building the presentation from the ground up is not recommended for beginners.

**Wizards**   Wizards are a special feature that most Microsoft products offer. A wizard displays a series of dialog boxes that ask you design and content questions. You select options and type text. When you are done, the wizard creates something (in this case, a presentation) according to your instructions.

**Template**   A template is a predesigned slide that comes with PowerPoint. When you select a template, PowerPoint applies the color scheme and general layout of the slide to each slide in the presentation.

# A Word About the PowerPoint Dialog Box

If you have just started PowerPoint and the PowerPoint dialog box is displayed, you are ready to start a new presentation (see Figure 2.1). From here, you can choose to create a new presentation using the AutoContent Wizard, a template, or a blank presentation. Just click your choice and click **OK**, and then follow along with the steps in the remainder of this lesson to complete the presentation.

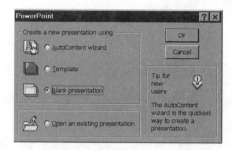

**Figure 2.1**   When you first start PowerPoint, this dialog box greets you. It's one method by which you can create a new presentation.

Unfortunately, this dialog box is available only when you first start the program. Once you close the dialog box, you won't see it again until the next time you start the program. That's why the steps in the remainder of this lesson don't rely on it; instead they show alternative methods for starting a presentation if this dialog box is not available.

# Creating a New Presentation with the AutoContent Wizard

With the AutoContent Wizard, you select the type of presentation you want to create (strategy, sales, training, reporting, conveying bad news, or general), and PowerPoint creates an outline for the presentation.

**TIP**   **Quick Start**   If you click the **AutoContent Wizard** button in the PowerPoint dialog box (shown in Figure 2.1) and then click **OK**, you can skip the first three steps in the following procedure.

Here's how you use the AutoContent Wizard:

1. Open the **File** menu and click **New**. The New Presentation dialog box appears.

2. Click the **Presentations** tab if it's not already on top (see Figure 2.2).

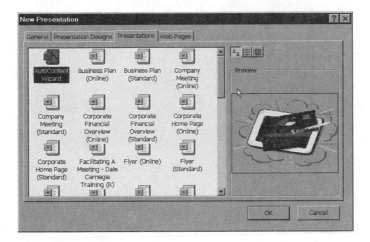

**Figure 2.2** You can start a new presentation from here.

3. Double-click the **AutoContent Wizard** icon. The AutoContent Wizard starts.

**Macro Warning** At step 3, you might get a warning message about macros possibly carrying viruses. Click **Enable Macros** to continue.

**CAUTION**

4. Click the **Next** button to begin.

5. In the dialog box that appears (see Figure 2.3), click the button that best represents the type of presentation you want to create (for example, **Sales/Marketing**).

6. From the list, select a presentation type to further narrow your presentation's purpose (for example, choose **Marketing Plan**). Then click **Next**.

7. Choose the method that best describes how you will give the presentation:

   - **Presentations, Informal Meetings, Handouts** Choose this if you are planning to present the presentation with a live narrator controlling the action.

**347**

- **Internet, Kiosk**  Choose this if you are planning a self-running presentation that does not require a live narrator.

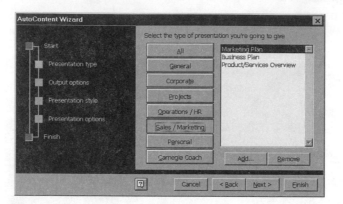

**Figure 2.3**  Answer the AutoContent Wizard's questions and click Next.

**8.** Click **Next** to continue.

**9.** Choose the type of output you need (such as **On-Screen Presentation**) and whether or not you need handouts (click **Yes** or **No**). Then click **Next**.

**10.** Enter the presentation title and your name in the blanks provided. Then click **Next**.

**11.** Click **Finish**. The beginnings of your presentation—with dummy text in place—appear on-screen in Outline view. (You'll learn about Outline view, as well as other views, in Lesson 4.)

**TIP**  **Replacing Dummy Text**  You can start personalizing your presentation right away by replacing the dummy text with your own text. Just select the existing text and type right over it. See Lesson 10 for more information about editing text.

# Creating a New Presentation with a Template

A template is the middle ground between maximum hand-holding (the AutoContent Wizard) and no help at all (Blank Presentation). There are two kinds of templates: Presentation Templates and Presentation Design Templates.

- **Presentation Templates**  These templates offer much of the same help as the AutoContent Wizard—in fact, the AutoContent Wizard bases its presentation types on these. The templates provide a color scheme for slides and a basic outline for slide text. Their names reflect the purpose of the presentation, for example, "Communicating Bad News."

- **Presentation Design Templates**  These templates offer only a color scheme and a "look" for slides; you're on your own to provide the content for each slide.

To start a new presentation using a template, follow these steps:

1. Open the **File** menu and select **New**. PowerPoint opens the New dialog box.

2. If you want to use a presentation template, click the **Presentations** tab. If you want to use a presentation design, click the **Presentation Designs** tab.

3. Click the template you want to use, and a preview of the template appears in the Preview area.

4. After you select the template you want to use, click **OK**. PowerPoint creates the new presentation based on that template.

5. If you have selected a presentation template, you are ready to start editing the slides, just like you did with the AutoContent Wizard. If you have selected a Presentation Design Template, you see the New Slide dialog box (see Figure 2.4). Click the AutoLayout you want to use and click **OK**.

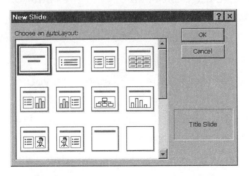

**Figure 2.4**  In the New Slide dialog box, you can choose a predesigned slide layout, or you can choose to design your own.

TIP  **The Next Step?**  To start customizing a Presentation Template, just click on the dummy text and then type new text to replace it. You can work through the whole presentation that way; the upcoming lessons, especially Lesson 10, can help.

To customize a Presentation Design Template, add more slides by clicking the **Insert New Slide** button on the toolbar, and then create your presentation one slide at a time. See Lesson 8 for help.

# Creating a Blank Presentation

Are you sure you want to attempt a blank presentation on your first time out? A blank presentation has no preset color scheme or design, and no dummy text to help you know what to write. To create a blank presentation, follow these steps:

**1.** Open the **File** menu and select **New**.

**2.** Click the **General** tab.

**3.** Double-click the **Blank Presentation** icon. The New Slide dialog box appears (see Figure 2.4).

**4.** Click the **AutoLayout** you want to use and click **OK**.

# What Next?

Now that you have the basic shell of your presentation, you need to modify and customize it. If you're not in a hurry, read the lessons in this part in order so you can learn PowerPoint fully. However, if you are in a hurry, refer to the following lessons:

- To change the view of the presentation so you can work with it more easily, see Lesson 4, "Working with Slides in Different Views."

- To apply a different design template or slide layout, see Lesson 7, "Changing a Presentation's Look."

- To add new slides, see Lesson 8, "Inserting, Deleting, and Copying Slides."

- To rearrange slides, see Lesson 9, "Rearranging Slides in a Presentation."

- To add and edit text, see Lesson 10, "Adding Text to a Slide."

In this lesson, you learned how to create a new presentation. In the next lesson, you'll learn how to control the PowerPoint program with menus and toolbars.

# Getting Around in PowerPoint

3

*In this lesson, you learn how to get around in PowerPoint and enter commands.*

## A Look at PowerPoint's Application Window

If you created a new presentation using the AutoContent Wizard or a template, your screen looks something like the screen shown in Figure 3.1. This screen contains many of the same elements you find in any Windows 95 or Windows NT program: a title bar, window control buttons (Minimize, Maximize, and Close), and a menu bar. For an explanation of these elements, refer to Part 1 of this book.

In addition, you see three toolbars and several windows that are unique to PowerPoint. The following sections explain how to work with these unique items.

**Toolbar**   A toolbar is a collection of buttons that enables you to bypass the menu system. For example, instead of selecting File, Save (opening the File menu and selecting Save), you can click the Save toolbar button to save your work. (You'll learn more about saving in Lesson 5.)

**Turning Off the Office Assistant**   The Office Assistant provides help as you work. If you don't want the Office Assistant on-screen all the time, you can easily make it disappear by clicking the **Close** (X) button in its window. To make it reappear, select **Help, Microsoft PowerPoint Help**. You'll learn more about getting help in Lesson 2 of Part 7.

Standard toolbar
Formatting toolbar

Outlining toolbar

Slide
Miniature
window

Presentation
window

Common
Tasks
window

Office
Assistant
window

Status bar

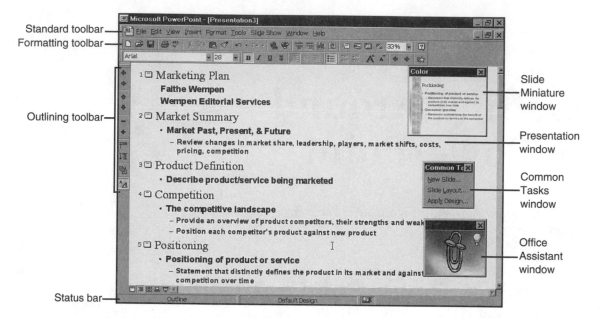

**Figure 3.1**  PowerPoint provides many tools for quickly entering commands.

New to PowerPoint 97 is the Common Tasks window shown in Figure 3.1. This is actually a floating toolbar. (You'll learn about floating toolbars later in this lesson.) You can drag it around on the screen, or you can get rid of it completely by clicking its Close (X) button. You can get it back later by right-clicking any toolbar and selecting **Common Tasks** from the shortcut menu.

# The Presentation Window

In the center of the PowerPoint window is a presentation window. (It's probably maximized, in which case it flows seamlessly into the larger PowerPoint window.) You use this window to create your slides and arrange them into a presentation. At the bottom of the presentation window are several buttons that enable you to change views. Figure 3.1 shows a presentation in Outline view, whereas Figure 3.2 shows the same presentation in Slide view. For details about changing views, see Lesson 4.

**Slide Miniature Window?**  Slide Miniature is a new feature in PowerPoint 97. It enables you to view a small version of a slide even in nongraphical views like the one shown in Figure 3.1. You'll learn more about it in Lesson 4.

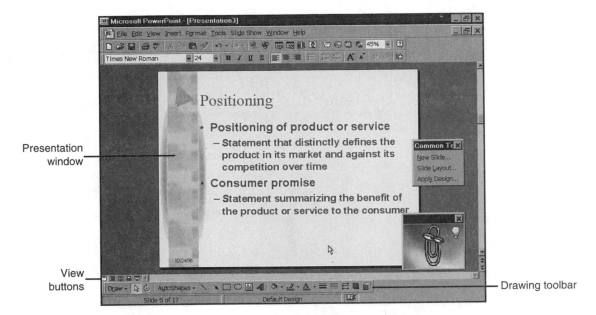

Presentation window

View buttons

Drawing toolbar

**Figure 3.2**  You can change views by clicking a View button.

# Using Shortcut Menus

Although you can enter all commands in PowerPoint using menus, PowerPoint offers a quicker way: context-sensitive shortcut menus like the ones in Windows 95 and Windows NT. To use a shortcut menu, right-click the object you want the command to act on. A shortcut menu pops up (see Figure 3.3), offering commands that pertain to the selected object. Click the desired command.

# Working with Toolbars

PowerPoint displays three toolbars by default: the Standard and Formatting toolbars below the menu bar (see Figure 3.1) and either the Outlining toolbar (on the left) or the Drawing toolbar (on the bottom), depending on the view. To select a button from the toolbar, click the button.

TIP  **PowerPoint on the Web**  There is also a Web toolbar that you can use to browse the World Wide Web through PowerPoint. It isn't turned on by default, but you can activate it by right-clicking on any toolbar and selecting **Web**, as you'll learn later in this lesson.

**353**

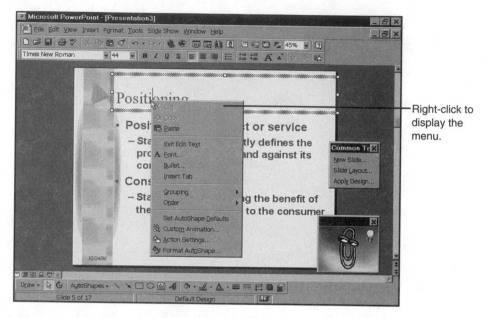

**Figure 3.3**   Display a shortcut menu by right-clicking the object.

# Learning More About Toolbar Buttons

Although I could list and explain all the tools in the Standard toolbar and in all the other toolbars, here are some better ways to learn about the buttons:

- *To see the name of a button,* move the mouse pointer over the button. PowerPoint displays a ScreenTip that provides the name of the button.

- *To learn more about a button,* press **Shift+F1** or select **Help**, **What's This?** and then click the button for which you want more information.

# Turning Toolbars On or Off

If you never use a particular toolbar, you can turn it off to free up some screen space. In addition, you can turn on other toolbars that come with PowerPoint but don't appear automatically. To turn a toolbar on or off, follow these steps:

1. Right-click any toolbar, and a shortcut menu appears (see Figure 3.4). A check mark appears beside each toolbar that is turned on.

2. Click to deselect the displayed toolbar you want to hide, or click to select a hidden toolbar that you want to display. (Remember that check marks appear beside displayed toolbars.)

**Figure 3.4** The shortcut menu for toolbars displays the names of all the toolbars.

When you click a toolbar name on the menu, the menu disappears and that toolbar appears (if it was hidden) or the toolbar disappears (if it was displayed).

## Moving Toolbars

After you have displayed the toolbars you need, you can position them in your work area wherever they are most convenient. Here's how to move a toolbar:

1.  Position the mouse pointer at the far left edge of the toolbar.
2.  Hold down the left mouse button, and drag the toolbar where you want it according to these guidelines:
    *   Drag the toolbar to a toolbar dock. There are four docks: just below the menu bar, on the left and right sides of the application window, and just above the status bar.
    *   Drag the toolbar anywhere else inside the application window to create a floating toolbar (see Figure 3.5).

 **Toolbar Dock** A toolbar dock is a location on the screen where a toolbar can "blend in" and meld with the PowerPoint window, instead of floating in its own separate box. By default, the Standard and Formatting toolbars are docked at the top and the Drawing toolbar is docked at the bottom.

3.  Release the mouse button.

 **What About Drop-Down Lists?** If a toolbar contains a drop-down list, you cannot drag it to the left or right toolbar dock.

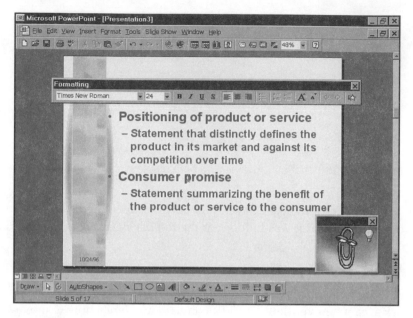

**Figure 3.5**   A floating toolbar.

A floating toolbar acts just like a window. You can drag its title bar to move it or drag a border to size it. If you drag a floating toolbar to a toolbar dock, the toolbar turns back into a normal (nonfloating) toolbar.

 **TIP**   **Customizing a Toolbar**   To customize a toolbar, right-click it and choose **Customize**. You can then drag a toolbar button from one toolbar to another or drag a button off a toolbar (to remove it). To add a button, click the **Commands** tab in the Customize dialog box, and select a feature category from the **Categories** list in the dialog box. Then drag the desired command to any of the toolbars to create a button for it.

In this lesson, you learned about the PowerPoint application and presentation windows, and you learned how to enter commands with shortcut menus and toolbars. In the next lesson, you learn how to work with slides in different views.

# Working with Slides in Different Views

*In this lesson, you learn how to display a presentation in different views, and to edit slides in Outline and Slide views.*

## Changing Views

PowerPoint can display your presentation in different views. Having the option of selecting a view makes it easier to perform certain tasks. For example, Outline view shows the overall organization of the presentation, whereas Slide Sorter view enables you to rearrange the slides. Figure 4.1 shows the available views.

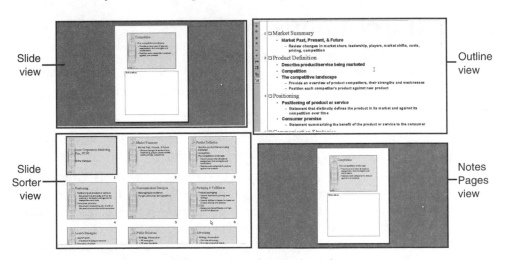

**Figure 4.1** You can change views to make a task easier.

To change views, open the **View** menu and choose the desired view: **Slide**, **Outline**, **Slide Sorter**, or **Notes Pages**. A quicker way to switch views is to click the button for the desired view at the bottom of the presentation window, as shown in Figure 4.2.

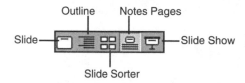

**Figure 4.2**   Use these buttons to change views.

 **Outline to Slide View**   If you're using Outline view, you can quickly display a slide in Slide view by double-clicking the desired slide icon in the outline.

 **What About the Slide Show Button?**   No, I haven't forgotten the Slide Show button. It enables you to view your presentation as a timed slide show. For details, see Lesson 18.

# Moving from Slide to Slide

When you have more than one slide in your presentation, you will need to move from one slide to the next to work with a specific slide. The procedure for selecting a slide depends on which view you are currently using:

- In Outline view, use the scroll bar to display the slide you want to work with. Click the **Slide** icon (the icon to the left of the slide's title) to select the slide, or click anywhere inside the text to edit it.

- In Slide view or Notes Pages view, click the **Previous Slide** or **Next Slide** button just below the vertical scroll bar (as shown in Figure 4.3), or drag the box inside the scroll bar until the desired slide number is displayed, or press **Page Up** or **Page Down**.

- In Slide Sorter view, click the desired slide. A thick border appears around the selected slide.

Drag this box until you reach the desired slide number.

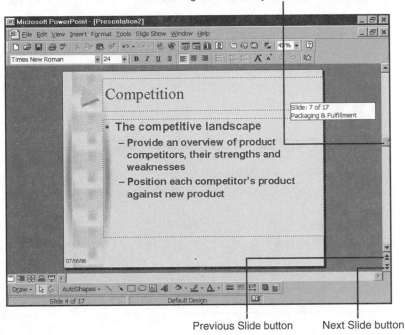

Previous Slide button        Next Slide button

**Figure 4.3**   Use the Previous Slide and Next Slide buttons to move between slides in Slide view or Notes Pages view.

# The Slide Miniature Window

The Slide Miniature window is a new feature in PowerPoint 97 (see Figure 4.4). When it's turned on, it displays the currently selected slide in a small window on top of whatever view you're using. To turn Slide Miniature on or off, select **View, Slide Miniature**.

In Outline view, the Slide Miniature shows a color version of the selected slide. In all other views, it shows an alternate version of the slide. For example, if you are currently displaying the slides on-screen in color, the Slide Miniature window shows them in black-and-white. Conversely, if the slides are displayed in black-and-white, the Slide Miniature window shows them in color.

The Slide Miniature window is especially useful if you are developing a presentation for two different media—for example, an on-screen presentation and a black-and-white set of printouts. Slide Miniature helps you keep an eye on the look of the slides so you do not inadvertently make a change to a color slide, for example, that would make it look unattractive or illegible when printed in black-and-white.

Slide Miniature window

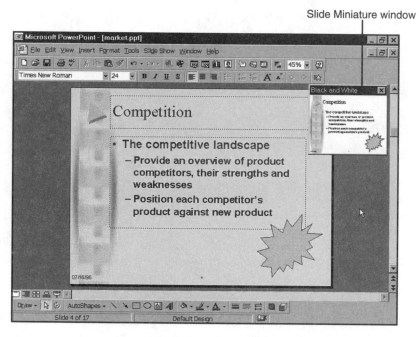

**Figure 4.4**  The Slide Miniature provides a thumbnail sketch of the current slide.

**TIP**  **Color or Black-and-White?**  To toggle between black-and-white and color views on-screen, open the **View** menu and select **Black and White** (if you're currently viewing color) or **Color** (if you're currently viewing black-and-white).

# Editing Slides

If you created a presentation in Lesson 2 using the AutoContent Wizard or a template, you already have several slides, but they may not contain the text you want to use. If you created a blank presentation, you have one slide on the screen that you can edit.

In the following sections, you will learn how to edit text in Outline and Slide views. In later lessons, you will learn how to add and edit text objects, pictures, graphs, organizational charts, and other items.

 **TERM**   **Object**   An object is any item on a slide, including text, graphics, and charts.

# Editing Text in Outline View

Outline view provides the easiest way to edit text (see Figure 4.5). You simply click to move the insertion point where you want it, and then you type in your text. Press the **Del** key to delete characters to the right of the insertion point, or press the **Backspace** key to delete characters to the left.

Position the I-beam pointer where you want the insertion point, and then click.

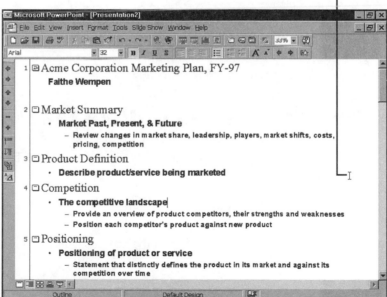

**Figure 4.5**  Switch to Outline view to edit text.

To select text, hold down the left mouse button and drag the mouse over the desired text. You can then press **Del** or **Backspace** to delete the text, or you can drag the text where you want to move it.

**361**

**TIP**   **Auto Word Select**   When you select text, PowerPoint selects whole words. If you want to select individual characters, open the **Tools** menu, select **Options**, click the **Edit** tab, and select **Automatic Word Selection** to turn it off. Click the **OK** button.

# Changing the Text's Outline Level

As you can see from Figure 4.5, your presentation is organized in a multilevel outline format. The slides are at the top level of the outline, and each slide's contents are subordinate under that slide. Some slides have multiple levels of subordination (for example, a bulleted list within a bulleted list).

You can easily change an object's level in Outline view with the Tab key:

- Click the text, and then press the **Tab** key or click the **Demote** button on the Outlining toolbar to demote it one level in the outline.

- Click the text, and then press **Shift+Tab** or click the **Promote** button on the Outlining toolbar to promote it one level in the outline.

In most cases, subordinate items on a slide appear as items in a bulleted list. In Lessons 11 and 12, you will learn how to change the appearance of the bullet, how to change the size and formatting of text for each entry, and how to change how far the text is indented for each level.

## Moving a Line in Outline View

As you work in Outline view you may find that some paragraphs need to be rearranged. One easy way is with the Move Up and Move Down buttons on the Outlining toolbar.

- To move a paragraph up in the outline, select it and click the **Move Up** button.

- To move a paragraph down in the outline, select it and click the **Move Down** button.

**TIP**   **Dragging Paragraphs**   You can quickly change the position or level of a paragraph by dragging it up, down, left, or right. To drag a paragraph, move the mouse pointer to the left side of the paragraph until the pointer turns into a four-headed arrow. Then hold down the left mouse button and drag the paragraph to the desired position.

# Editing in Slide View

Slide view provides an easy way to edit all objects on a slide, including text and graphic objects. As shown in Figure 4.6, you can edit an object by clicking or double-clicking it. For a text object, click the object to select it, and then click where you want the insertion point moved. For a graphic object, double-click it to bring up a set of tools that will help you edit it.

Most text appears on the slide in text boxes. (The only other place text can appear is within a graphic object.) In Lesson 10, you'll learn more about adding text to a slide, including creating your own text boxes on a slide. Then in Lessons 11 and 12 you'll learn how to fine-tune the look of your text for maximum impact.

Editing graphics is a more tricky than editing text. Lessons 13 and 14 discuss placing graphics on slides, and Lessons 15 and 16 cover manipulating graphics.

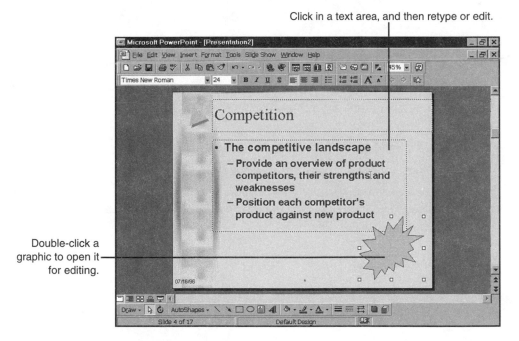

**Figure 4.6**   Slide view enables you to edit both text and graphic objects.

In this lesson, you learned how to change views for a presentation, move from slide to slide, and edit text. In the next lesson, you'll learn how to save, close, and open a presentation.

# Saving, Closing, and Opening Presentations

*In this lesson, you learn how to save a presentation to disk, close a presentation, and open an existing presentation.*

## Saving a Presentation

Soon after creating a presentation, you should save it on disk to protect the work you have already done. To save a presentation for the first time, follow these steps:

1. Select **File**, **Save**, or press **Ctrl+S**, or click the **Save** button on the Standard toolbar. The Save As dialog box appears.

2. In the **File Name** text box, type the name you want to assign to the presentation. Do not type a file extension; PowerPoint automatically adds the extension .PPT (see Figure 5.1).

**Upgrade Tip**   Because PowerPoint 97 is a 32-bit application, you are not limited to the old 8-character file names as you were with PowerPoint versions designed for Windows 3.x. Your file names can be as long as you want (within reason—the limit is 255 characters), and they can include spaces.

3. The Save In box shows which folder the file will be saved in. The default is My Documents. If you want to save to a different drive or folder, see the next section. Otherwise, continue to step 4.

4. Click **Save**.

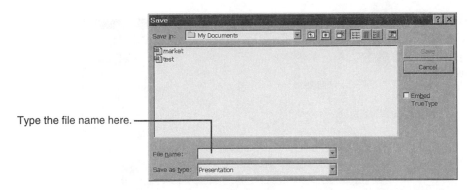

Type the file name here.

**Figure 5.1**   The Save As dialog box.

Once you have named the file and saved it to a disk, you can save any changes you make simply by pressing **Ctrl+S** or clicking the **Save** button on the Standard toolbar. Your data is saved under the file name you already assigned.

To create a copy of a presentation under a different name, select **File, Save As**. The Save As dialog box appears, and you can use it in the same way you did when you originally saved the file.

## Changing the Drive or Folder

The dialog boxes for opening and saving files in Windows 95 are different from the ones in Windows 3.1. The Save As and Open dialog boxes take a bit of getting used to.

To change to a different drive, you must open the Save In or Look In list. (The name changes depending on whether you're saving or opening a file.) Figure 5.2 shows this list in the Open dialog box. From it, choose the drive on which you want to save the file.

Next, you must select the folder where you want to save the file (or open it from). When you select the drive, a list of the folders on that drive appears. Double-click the folder you want to select it.

Table 5.1 explains the buttons and other controls you see in the Save As and Open dialog boxes, as well as in other Windows dialog boxes you may encounter.

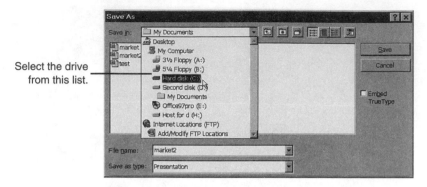

Select the drive
from this list.

**Figure 5.2** Use this list box to choose a different drive.

**Table 5.1** Buttons for Changing Drives and Folders in Dialog Boxes

| Control | Description |
|---------|-------------|
| | Moves to the folder "above" the one shown in the Save In box (that is, the folder in which the current one resides). |
| | Shows the C:\WINDOWS\FAVORITES folder, no matter which folder was displayed before. |
| | Creates a new folder. |
| | Shows the folders and files in the currently displayed folder in a list. |
| | Shows details about each file and folder. |
| | Shows the properties of each file and folder. |
| | Opens a dialog box of settings you can change that affect the dialog box. |
| | (Appears in Open dialog box only.) Switches to Preview view, in which you can see the first slide of a presentation before you open it. |
| | (Appears in Open dialog box only.) Adds a shortcut for the currently displayed folder to the Favorites list. |

# Closing a Presentation

You can close a presentation at any time. If you are working on multiple presentations, it's all right to keep them all open at once, but the more presentations you have open, the slower PowerPoint's response time to your commands will be. So you should close any presentations that you are not working on. (Although this closes the presentation window, it does not exit PowerPoint.) To close a presentation, follow these steps:

**1.** If more than one presentation is open, open the **Window** menu and select the presentation you want to close.

**2.** Choose **File**, **Close**, or press **Ctrl+F4**, or click the **Close** (X) button. If you have not saved the presentation, or if you haven't saved since you made changes, a dialog box appears asking if you want to save.

**3.** To save your changes, click **Yes**. If this is a new presentation, refer to the steps earlier in this lesson for saving a presentation. If you have saved the file previously, the presentation window closes.

# Opening a Presentation

Once you save a presentation to a disk, you can open the presentation and continue working on it at any time. Follow these steps:

**1.** Choose **File**, **Open**, or press **Ctrl+O**, or click the **Open** button on the Standard toolbar. The Open dialog box appears (see Figure 5.3).

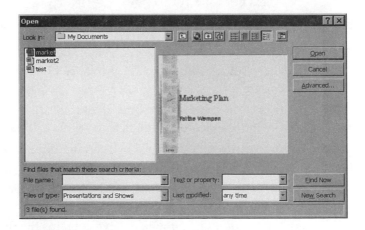

**Figure 5.3** Select the presentation you want to open.

2. If the file isn't in the currently displayed folder, change drives and/or folders (as explained in the section "Changing the Drive or Folder," earlier in this lesson).

3. Double-click the file to open it.

# Finding a Presentation File

If you're having trouble locating your file, PowerPoint can help you look. Follow these steps to find a file:

1. Choose **File**, **Open** if the Open dialog box is not already open.

2. In the **File Name** box at the bottom of the dialog box, type the name of the file you're looking for (refer to Figure 5.3).

 **Wild Cards**   You can use wild cards if you don't know the entire name of a file. The asterisk (*) wild card character stands in for any character or set of characters, and the question mark (?) wild card character stands in for any single character. For example, if you know the file begins with P, you could type **P*.ppt** to find all PowerPoint files that begin with P.

3. (Optional) Enter other search criteria according to these guidelines:
   - If you're looking for a different file type, choose it from the **Files of Type** drop-down list.
   - If you're looking for a file containing certain text, type that text in the **Text or Property** box.
   - If you know when you last modified the file, choose the time interval from the **Last Modified** drop-down list.

4. Click the **Advanced** button. The Advanced Find dialog box appears (see Figure 5.4).

5. In the Look In section at the bottom of the Advanced Find dialog box, narrow the search area as much as possible using these techniques:
   - If you are sure the file is in a certain folder, type that folder's path (such as **C:\WINDOWS**) in the **Look In** box.
   - If you are sure the file is on a certain drive, select that drive from the **Look In** list.
   - If you don't know which drive contains the file, select **My Computer** from the **Look In** list.

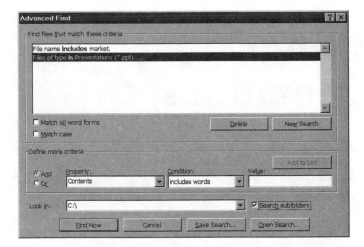

**Figure 5.4**  Use the Advanced Find dialog box to select the folders and drives you want to search.

**6.** Make sure the **Search Subfolders** check box is marked. If it isn't, click it.

**7.** Click the **Find Now** button. The File Open dialog box reappears, displaying the files that match your search criteria.

**8.** Double-click the file you want to open.

**TIP**  **More Search Options**  As you may have noticed in Figure 5.4, there are a lot more complex search options available—too many to cover here. See your PowerPoint documentation for more details.

In this lesson, you learned how to save, close, open, and find presentations. In the next lesson, you will learn how to print a presentation.

# Printing Presentations, Notes, and Handouts

In this lesson, you learn how to select a size and orientation for the slides in your presentation and how to print the slides, notes, and handouts you create.

## Quick Printing—No Options

The quickest way to print is to use all the default settings. You don't get to make any decisions about your output, but you do get your printout without delay. To print a quick copy, use one of these methods:

- Click the **Print** button on the Standard toolbar.
- Choose **File**, **Print** and click **OK**.
- Press **Ctrl+P** and click **OK**.

When you use either of these methods for printing, you get a printout of your entire presentation in whatever view is on-screen. The following list describes what type of printout you can expect from each view.

- **Slide view** The entire presentation prints in Landscape orientation with one slide per page. Each slide fills an entire page.
- **Outline view** The entire outline prints in Portrait orientation.
- **Slide Sorter view** The entire presentation prints in Portrait orientation with six slides per page.
- **Notes Pages view** The entire presentation prints in Portrait orientation with one slide per page. Each slide prints with its notes beneath it.

**Orientation**  The orientation setting tells the printer which edge of the paper should be at the "top" of the printout. If the top is across the wide edge, it's Landscape; if the top is across the narrow edge, it's Portrait.

# Changing the Slide Setup

If you didn't get the printouts you expected from the previous procedure, you can change the output, size, and orientation of the selected presentation in the Slide Setup dialog box. To customize your printouts, follow these steps:

**1.** Choose **File, Page Setup**. The Page Setup dialog box appears on-screen, as shown in Figure 6.1.

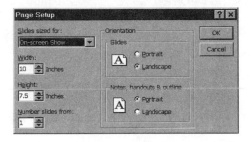

**Figure 6.1**  You can set the position and size of the slides on the page when you print them in Slide view.

**2.** Perform one of the following procedures to set the slide size:

- To use a standard size, select a size from the **Slides Sized For** drop-down list. For example, you can have slides sized for regular 8.5 × 11 paper, 35mm slides, or an on-screen slide show.

- To create a custom size, enter the dimensions in the **Width** and **Height** text boxes.

 **Spin Boxes**  The arrows to the right of the Width and Height text boxes enable you to adjust the settings in those boxes. Click the up arrow to increase the setting by .1 inch, or click the down arrow to decrease it by .1 inch.

3. In the **Number Slides From** text box, type the number with which you want to start numbering slides. (This is usually 1, but you may want to start with a different number if the presentation is a continuation of another.)

4. Under the Slides heading, choose **Portrait** or **Landscape** orientation for your slides.

5. In the Notes, Handouts & Outline section, choose **Portrait** or **Landscape** for those items.

 TIP **Can I Print Notes and Handouts Differently?** If you want your notes printed in portrait orientation and your handouts printed in landscape orientation, choose **Portrait** from the Notes, Handouts & Outline section of the Slide Setup dialog box and print the notes. Then, before you print the handouts, go back to the dialog box and choose **Landscape** from the Notes, Handouts & Outline section.

6. Click **OK**. If you changed the orientation of your slides, you may have to wait a moment while PowerPoint repositions the slides.

# Choosing What and How to Print

If the default print options don't suit you, you can change them. Do you have more than one printer? If so, you can choose which printer to use. For example, you may want to use a color printer for overhead transparencies and a black-and-white printer for your handouts. You can also select options for printing multiple copies and for printing specific slides only.

To set your print options, follow these steps, and then print.

1. Choose **File**, **Print**. The Print dialog box appears, with the name of the currently selected printer in the Name box (see Figure 6.2).

2. If you want to use a printer other than the one that appears, open the **Name** drop-down list and select a different printer.

 TIP **Printer Properties** To make adjustments to your printer's settings, click the **Properties** button in the Print dialog box. The adjustments you can make vary from printer to printer, but you should be able to adjust graphics quality, select paper size, and choose which paper tray to use—among other things.

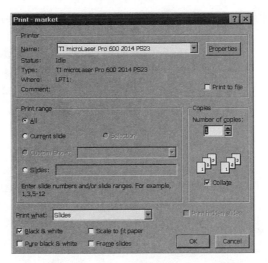

**Figure 6.2** Choose your printing options in the Print dialog box.

**3.** In the Print Range section, choose what to print:
  - Choose **All** to print all the slides in the presentation.
  - Choose **Current Slide** to print only the currently displayed slide.
  - In the **Slides** text box, enter a range of slide numbers—for example, **2–4**—to print multiple consecutive slides.

**4.** Open the **Print What** drop-down list and choose what you want to print. You can print slides, handouts, notes, or outlines.

**5.** If you want more than one copy, enter the number of copies you want in the **Number of Copies** box.

**6.** Select or deselect any of these check boxes in the dialog box as desired:

**Print to File**  Select this option to send the output to a file instead of to your printer.

**Collate**  If you are printing more than one copy, select this check box to collate each printed copy (print in the order 1, 2, 3, 1, 2, 3) instead of printing all the copies of each page at once (in the order 1, 1, 2, 2, 3, 3).

**Black & White**  If you have a black and white printer, select this check box to make the color slides print more crisply. You also can select this check box to force a color printer to produce black-and-white output.

**373**

**Pure Black & White**   This check box is like the preceding one except everything prints in solid black and plain white, with no grey shading. This makes all slides look like line drawings.

**Scale to Fit Paper**   If the slide (or whatever you're printing) is too large to fit on the page, select this check box to decrease the size of the slide to make it fit on the page. Now you won't have to paste two pieces of paper together to see the whole slide.

**Frame Slides**   Select this check box if you want to print a border around each slide.

**Print Hidden Slides**   If you have any hidden slides, you can choose whether or not to print them. If you don't have any hidden slides, this check box will be unavailable. You'll learn about hidden slides in Lesson 9.

 TIP   **Why Would I Print to File?**   If you don't have the printer that you want to use hooked up to your computer, you can print to a file and then take that file to the computer where the printer is. PowerPoint does not have to be installed on the other computer for that computer to print PowerPoint documents.

**7.** Click **OK** to print.

In this lesson, you learned how to print slides, outlines, and notes, and how to set options for your printouts. In the next lesson, you will learn how to change the overall appearance of the slides in a presentation.

# Changing a Presentation's Look

*In this lesson, you learn various ways to give your presentation a professional and consistent look.*

## Giving Your Slides a Professional Look

PowerPoint comes with dozens of professionally designed slides you can use as templates for your own presentations. That is, you can apply one of these predesigned slides to an already existing presentation to give the slides in your presentation a consistent look.

**Template** A template is a predesigned slide that comes with PowerPoint. When you select a template, PowerPoint applies the color scheme and general layout of the slide to each slide in your presentation.

There's another way to make global changes to the entire presentation: you can alter the Slide Master. The Slide Master is not really a slide, but it looks like one. It's a design grid that you make changes on, and these changes affect every slide in the presentation. For example, if you want a graphic to appear on every slide, you can place it on the Slide Master instead of pasting it onto each slide individually. When you apply a template, you are actually applying that template to the Slide Master, which in turn applies the template's formatting to each slide.

**TIP   Changing the Colors on a Single Slide**   If you want to make some slides in the presentation look different from the others, you're in the wrong lesson. Check out Lesson 17 to learn how to apply different color schemes to individual slides.

# Applying a Presentation Design Template

You can apply a different template to your presentation at any time, no matter how you originally create your presentation. To change the template, follow these steps:

 **1.** Click the **Apply Design** button on the Standard toolbar, or choose **Format**, **Apply Design**. The Apply Design dialog box appears (see Figure 7.1).

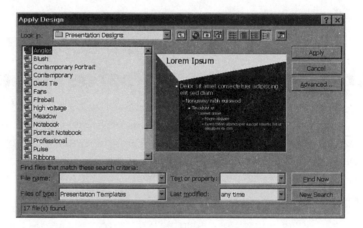

**Figure 7.1**   Choose a different template from the Apply Design dialog box.

**2.** Click a template name in the **Name** list. A sample of the template appears to the right of the list.

**3.** When you find a template you want to use, click **Apply**.

# Using AutoLayouts

While templates enable you to change the color and design of a presentation, AutoLayouts enable you to set the structure of a single slide in a presentation. For example, if you want a graph and a picture on a slide, you can choose an AutoLayout that positions the two items for you.

**TIP** **Individual Slides?** PowerPoint applies AutoLayouts to individual slides, but the template you choose and the Master Layout modifications you make affect the AutoLayouts. This becomes more evident later in this lesson.

To use an AutoLayout, do the following:

**1.** In Slide view, display the slide you want to change.

**2.** Choose **Format, Slide Layout**. The Slide Layout dialog box appears (see Figure 7.2).

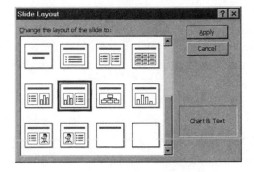

**Figure 7.2** You can change an individual slide's layout with this dialog box.

 **TIP** **Right-Click** A q uick way to display the Slide Layout dialog box is to right-click on the slide in Slide view and select **Slide Layout**.

**3.** Click the desired layout, or use the arrow keys to move the selection border to it.

**4.** Click the **Apply** button, and PowerPoint applies the selected layout to the current slide.

# Editing the Slide Master

Every presentation has a Slide Master that controls the overall appearance and layout of each slide. The Slide Master contains all the formatting information that the template brings to the presentation, such as colors and background patterns, and it also marks where the elements you use from the AutoLayout feature will appear on the slide.

**377**

To make changes to the Slide Master for your presentation, follow these steps:

1. Select **View**, **Master**, **Slide Master**. Your Slide Master appears, as in Figure 7.3.

2. Make any changes to the Slide Master, as you'll learn in upcoming lessons in this book. (Anything you can do to a regular slide, you can do to a Slide Master.)

3. When you're done working with the Slide Master, click the **Close** button (see Figure 7.3) to return to normal view.

The two most important elements on the Slide Master are the Title Area and Object Area for the AutoLayout objects. The Title Area contains the formatting specifications for each slide's title; that is, it tells PowerPoint the type size, style, and color to use for the text in the title of each slide. The Object Area contains the formatting specifications for all remaining text on the slide.

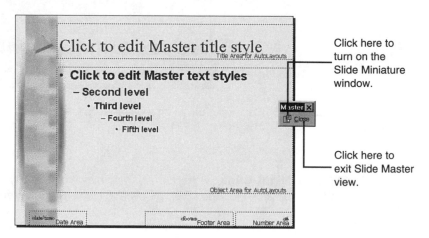

**Figure 7.3** The Slide Master ensures that all slides in a presentation have a consistent look.

**Slide Miniature** As you learned in Lesson 4, Slide Miniature is a new viewing tool in PowerPoint 97. It enables you to see what the slide will look like in another format (for example, in black-and-white if the slide is currently shown in color). Turn back to Lesson 4 for more information.

For most of PowerPoint's templates the Object Area sets up specifications for a bulleted list, including the type of bullet, as well as the type styles, sizes, and indents for each item in the list.

In addition to the Title and Object Areas, the Slide Master can contain information about background colors, borders, page numbers, company logos, clip art objects, and any other elements you want to appear on every slide in the presentation.

The Slide Master is like any slide. In the following lessons, when you learn how to add text, graphics, borders, and other objects to a slide, keep in mind that you can add these objects on individual slides or on the Slide Master. When you add the objects to the Slide Master, they appear on every slide in the presentation.

In this lesson, you learned how to give your presentation a consistent look with templates and AutoLayouts. You also learned how to use the Slide Master to make global changes to your slides. In the next lesson, you will learn how to insert, delete, and copy slides.

# Inserting, Deleting, and Copying Slides

8

*In this lesson, you learn how to insert new slides, delete slides, and copy slides in a presentation.*

## Inserting a Slide

You can insert a slide into a presentation at any time and at any position in the presentation. To insert a slide, follow these steps:

**1.** Select the slide that appears just before the place where you want to insert the new slide. (You can select the slide in any view: Outline, Slides, Slide Sorter, or Notes Pages.)

**2.** Choose **Insert**, **New Slide**, or click the **New Slide** button, or press **Ctrl+M**. In Outline view, PowerPoint inserts a blank slide, into which you can type a title and bulleted list. In all other views, the New Slide dialog box appears (see Figure 8.1).

**3.** In the **Choose an AutoLayout** list, click a slide layout or use the arrow keys to highlight it.

**4.** Click **OK**, and PowerPoint inserts a slide with the specified layout (see Figure 8.2).

**5.** Follow the directions indicated on the slide layout to add text or other objects. In most cases, you click an object to select it and then you type your text.

**TIP** **Cloning a Slide** To create an exact replica of a slide (in any view), select the slide you want to duplicate. Then select **Insert**, **Duplicate Slide**. PowerPoint inserts the new slide after the original slide. You can then move the slide anywhere you want (which you'll learn to do in Lesson 9).

**New Feature!**   The Insert, Duplicate Slide command is new for PowerPoint 97. In previous versions of PowerPoint, you could duplicate a slide only from Outline or Slide Sorter view, and you had to use the Edit, Duplicate command. That command is still available in those views in PowerPoint 97, so you can continue to use it if you are familiar with it.

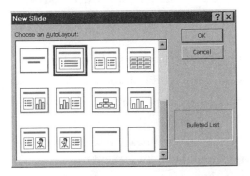

**Figure 8.1**   In the New Slide dialog box, choose a layout for the slide you're inserting.

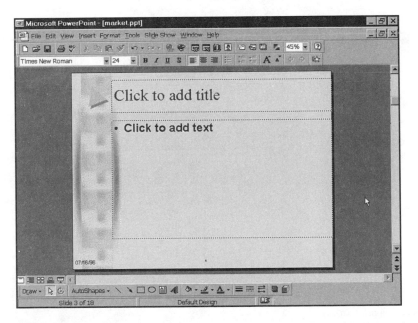

**Figure 8.2**   The new slide contains the blank structure you selected; you supply the content.

# Adding Slides from Another Presentation

If you want to insert some or all of the slides from another presentation into the current presentation, perform these steps:

1. Open the presentation into which you want to insert the slides.
2. Select the slide located before the position where you want to insert the slides.
3. Choose **Insert, Slides from Files**. The Slide Finder dialog box appears.
4. Click the **Browse** button to display the Insert Slides from Files dialog box.
5. Change the drive and/or folder if needed. (Refer to the section "Changing the Drive or Folder" in Lesson 5.)
6. Double-click the name of the presentation that contains the slides you want to insert into the open presentation.
7. Click the **Display** button, and the slides from the presentation appear in the Slide Finder window (see Figure 8.3).

 **TIP** **View the Slides in a Different Way** Click this button if you prefer to see a list of the slide titles instead of three slides at a time. When you click the button, the display changes to a list of titles on the left and a preview window on the right that displays the selected slide.

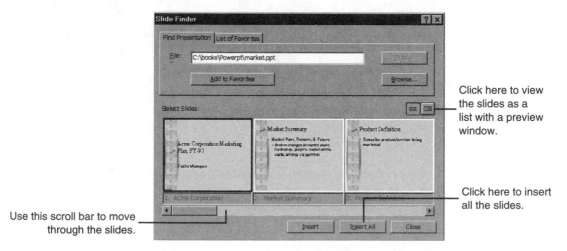

**Figure 8.3** You can select any or all of the slides from the selected presentation to add to the open presentation.

8. Click the slides you want to insert and then click the **Insert** button. If you want to insert all the slides, click the **Insert All** button.

9. When you are finished inserting slides, click the **Close** button. The inserted slides appear right after the slide that you selected in step 2.

 **TIP**   **Make a Favorites List**   If there is a presentation that you regularly use to insert slides from, you can add it to your Favorites List by clicking the **Add to Favorites** button in the Find Slides dialog box. Then the next time you want to insert slides from that presentation, you can click the **List of Favorites** tab in the Find Slides dialog box and select the presentation from the list. You might, for example, have a presentation that contains some standard slides that you include in every presentation for a certain audience.

# Creating Slides from a Document Outline

If you have a word-processing document with outline-style headings in it, PowerPoint can pull the headings from the document and use the headings to create slides with bulleted lists. Follow these steps to create slides from a document outline:

1. Choose **Insert, Slides from Outline**. The Insert Outline dialog box appears.

2. Use the Insert Outline dialog box to locate the document file you want to use. (Refer to "Changing the Drive or Folder" in Lesson 5 if you need help locating the file.)

3. Double-click the name of the document file.

# Selecting Slides

In the following sections, you learn to delete, copy, and move slides. However, before you can do anything with a slide, you have to select the slide. You can select one or more slides, as explained here:

- To select a single slide, click it. (In Slide and Notes Pages views, the currently displayed slide is selected; you don't have to click it.)

- To select two or more neighboring slides in Outline view, click the first slide, press and hold the **Shift** key, and click the last slide in the group.

- To select a rectangular block of neighboring slides in Slide Sorter view, click and drag a "box" around the slides you want to include. All slides that fall into the box you drag become selected (see Figure 8.4).

- To select two or more non-neighboring slides (in Slide Sorter view only), press and hold the **Ctrl** and **Shift** keys and click each slide. You cannot select non-neighboring slides in Outline view.

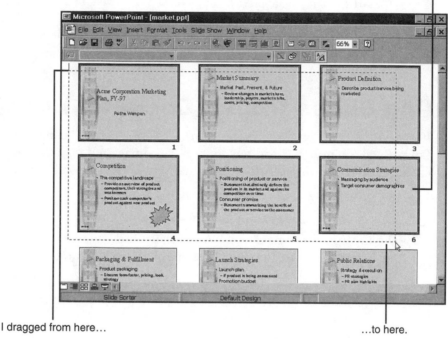

Slides do not have to be completely within the box to be included.

I dragged from here...

...to here.

**Figure 8.4**  You can select a block of slides in Slide Sorter view by dragging a box around them.

# Deleting Slides

You can delete a slide from any view. To delete a slide, perform the following steps:

**1.** Display the slide you want to delete (in Slide or Notes Pages view) or select the slide (in Outline or Slide Sorter view). You can delete multiple slides by displaying or selecting more than one.

**2.** Choose **Edit, Delete Slide**, and the slide disappears.

TIP **Quicker Deleting** In Outline or Slide Sorter view, you can just select the slides you want to delete and press the **Delete** key on the keyboard.

 **Oops!** If you deleted a slide by mistake, you can get it back by selecting **Edit**, **Undo**, or by pressing **Ctrl+Z**, or by clicking the **Undo** button on the Standard toolbar.

CAUTION

# Cutting, Copying, and Pasting Slides

In Lesson 9, you will learn how to rearrange slides in Slide Sorter and Outline views. However, you also can use the cut, copy, and paste features to copy and move slides within the same presentation or into other presentations. To cut (or copy) a slide and paste it in a presentation, perform the following steps:

**1.** Change to Slide Sorter or Outline view.

**2.** Select the slide(s) you want to copy or cut.

**3.** Open the **Edit** menu and select **Cut** or **Copy** to either move or copy the slide(s) to the Windows Clipboard.

TERM **Windows Clipboard** The Windows Clipboard is a temporary holding area for cut or copied items. You can cut or copy items to the Clipboard and then paste them on a slide, or you can cut or copy an entire slide or group of slides.

TIP **Quick Cut or Copy** To bypass the Edit menu, press **Ctrl+C** to copy or **Ctrl+X** to cut, or click the **Cut** or **Copy** button on the Standard toolbar.

**4.** If you want to paste the slide(s) into a different presentation, open that presentation.

**5.** In Slide Sorter view, select the slide after which you want to place the cut or copied slide(s). In Outline view, move the insertion point to the end of the text in the slide after which you want to insert the cut or copied slide(s).

**6.** Choose **Edit**, **Paste** or press **Ctrl+V**. (You can also click the **Paste** button on the Standard toolbar.) PowerPoint inserts the cut or copied slides.

 **TIP** **Drag-and-Drop** Although it's primarily used for moving slides, drag-and-drop also can be used for copying them in Slide Sorter view. You just press and hold **Ctrl** and drag a slide where you want the copy to go. See Lesson 9 for details.

In this lesson, you learned how to insert, delete, cut, copy, and paste slides. In the next lesson, you will learn how to rearrange the slides in your presentation.

# Rearranging Slides in a Presentation

*In this lesson, you learn how to rearrange your slides.*

There will be times when you need to change the sequence of slides in a presentation. PowerPoint has the capability to reorder slides in either Slide Sorter view or Outline view.

## Rearranging Slides in Slide Sorter View

Slide Sorter view shows miniature versions of the slides in your presentation. This enables you to view many of your slides at one time. To rearrange slides in Slide Sorter view, perform the following steps:

 **1.** Switch to Slide Sorter view by selecting **View**, **Slide Sorter** or by clicking the **Slide Sorter** button on the status bar.

**2.** Move the mouse pointer over the slide you want to move.

**3.** Press and hold the left mouse button, and drag to the location in which you want to insert the slide. As you drag, a line appears (as shown in Figure 9.1), showing where you are moving the slide.

**CAUTION**

**Destination Not in View?**   If you have more than six slides in your presentation, you may not be able to see the slide's destination on-screen. Don't worry. Just drag the slide in the direction of the destination, and the display will scroll in that direction.

**TIP**

**Copying a Slide**   You can copy a slide in Slide Sorter view as easily as you can move a slide. Simply hold down the **Ctrl** key when you drag the slide.

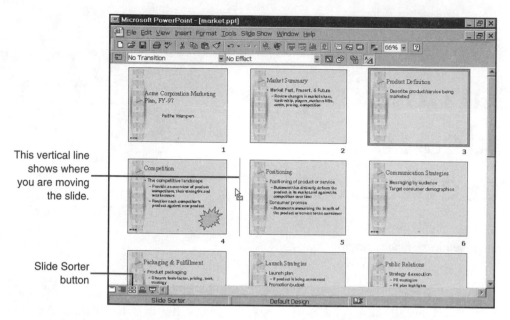

**Figure 9.1** Switch to Slide Sorter view.

This vertical line shows where you are moving the slide.

Slide Sorter button

**4.** When the vertical line is in the location where you want the slide, release the mouse button. PowerPoint places the slide in its new position and shifts the surrounding slides to make room for the new slide.

 TIP **Dragging and Dropping Between Presentations** You can even drag-and-drop slides to copy from one presentation to another. To do so, open both presentations (see Lesson 5 for instructions on how to open presentations). Then choose **Window**, **Arrange All**. The two windows appear side-by-side. Change to Slide Sorter view in each window, and then follow the steps to drag-and-drop slides from one window to the other.

# Rearranging Slides in Outline View

In Outline view, you see the titles and text on each slide. This view gives you a clearer picture of the content and organization of your presentation than the other views, so you may prefer to rearrange your slides in Outline view. Here's how you do it:

 **1.** Switch to Outline view by choosing **View**, **Outline** or by clicking the **Outline** button.

**2.** Click the slide number or the slide icon to the left of the slide you want to move. PowerPoint highlights the contents of the entire slide.

 TIP   **Moving the Contents of a Slide**   If you just want to insert some of the information from a slide into your presentation, you don't have to move the entire slide. You can move only the slide's data—text and graphics—from one slide to another by selecting only what you want to move and dragging it to its new location.

 **3.** Move the mouse pointer over the selected slide icon, press and hold the mouse button, and drag the slide up or down in the outline. Or, select the slide and click the **Move Up** or **Move Down** button on the Outlining toolbar (see Figure 9.2).

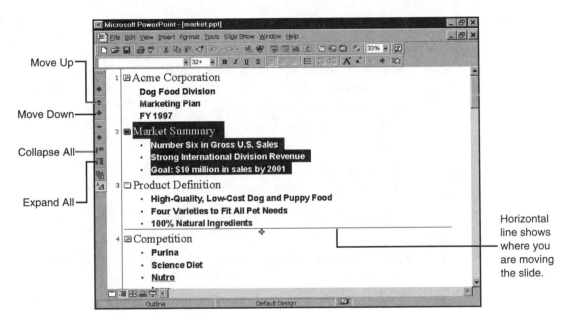

**Figure 9.2**   Drag the selected icon, or click the Move Up or Move Down button.

**4.** When the slide is at the desired new position, release the mouse button. (Be careful not to drop the slide in the middle of another slide. If you do, choose **Edit**, **Undo** and try again.)

**TIP** **Collapsing the Outline** You can collapse the outline to show only the slide titles. This allows you to view more slides at one time and rearrange the slides more easily. To collapse the outline, click the **Collapse All** button on the Outlining toolbar (see Figure 9.2). To restore the outline, click the **Expand All** button.

# Hiding Slides

Before you give a presentation, you should try to anticipate any questions your audience may have and be prepared to answer those questions. You may even want to create slides to support your answers to these questions but keep the slides hidden until you need them. To hide one or more slides, perform the following steps:

1. Display or select the slide(s) you want to hide. (You can hide slides in Slide, Outline, or Slide Sorter view.)

2. Choose the **Slide Show**, **Hide Slide** command. If you are in Slide Sorter view, the hidden slide's number appears in a box with a line through it.

3. To unhide the slide(s), display or select the hidden slide(s) and choose **Slide Show**, **Hide Slide** again.

**TIP** **Right-Click Shortcut** You can right-click a slide and select **Hide** from the shortcut menu that appears to quickly hide a slide.

**TIP** **Printing Hidden Slides?** In Lesson 6, you learned about the Print Hidden Slides check box in the Print dialog box. When printing, select this check box to print the hidden slides.

In this lesson, you learned how to rearrange the slides in a presentation in either Slide Sorter or Outline view, and how to hide slides. In the next lesson, you will learn how to add text to a slide.

# Adding Text to a Slide

*In this lesson, you learn how to add text to a slide and how to change the text alignment and line spacing.*

## Creating a Text Box

As you have learned in previous lessons, you can put text on a slide by typing text in Outline view or by filling in the blanks on an AutoLayout (see Lesson 8). However, these methods both provide fairly generic results. If you want to type additional text on a slide, you must first create a text box.

 **Text Box**   A text box acts as a receptacle for the text. Text boxes often contain bulleted lists, notes, or labels used to point to important parts of illustrations.

To create a text box, perform the following steps:

1. Switch to Slide view or Slide Sorter view. (Refer to Lesson 4 for help with views.) Slide view may give you a clearer view of your work area.
2. If you want the text box to appear on a new slide, insert a slide into the presentation. (Choose **Insert**, **Slide**, as you learned in Lesson 8.)
 3. Click the **Text Box** button on the Drawing toolbar.
4. Position the mouse pointer where you want the upper-left corner of the box to appear.
5. Press and hold the left mouse button and drag to the right until the box is the desired width. (It doesn't matter how far you drag down vertically; the box created will always be the same height—one line.)

**6.** Release the mouse button, and a one-line text box appears (see Figure 10.1).

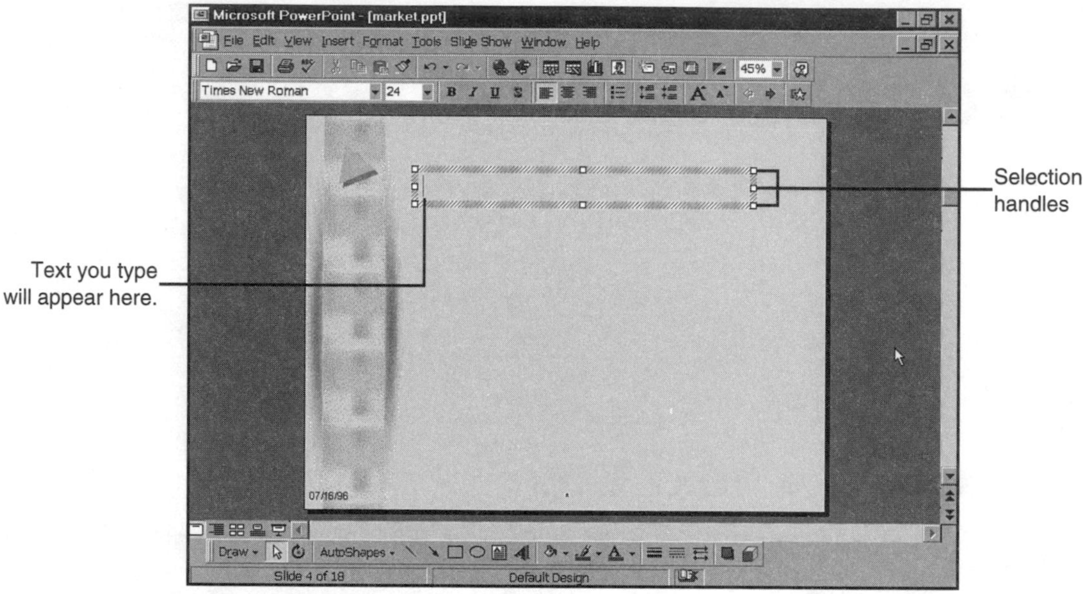

Selection handles

Text you type will appear here.

**Figure 10.1** You can enter text in the text box.

**7.** Type the text that you want to appear in the text box. When you reach the right side of the box, PowerPoint wraps the text to the next line and makes the box one line deeper. To start a new paragraph, press **Enter**.

**8.** When you are done, click anywhere outside the text box to see how the text will appear on the finished slide.

 **TIP** **Framing a Text Box** The border that appears around a text box when you create or select it does not appear on the printed slide. To add a border that does print, see Lesson 16.

# Selecting, Deleting, and Moving a Text Box

If you go back and click anywhere inside the text box, a selection box appears around it. If you click the selection box border, handles appear around the text box, as shown in Figure 10.1. You can drag the box's border to move the box, or you can drag a handle to resize it. PowerPoint automatically wraps the text as needed to fit inside the box.

To delete a text box, select it (so handles appear around it), and then press the **Delete** key.

# Editing Text in a Text Box

To edit text in a text box, first click anywhere inside the text box to select it. Then perform any of the following procedures:

- To select text, drag over the text you want to select. (To select a single word, double-click it. To select an entire paragraph, triple-click.)

 **TIP** **Auto Word Select** When you drag over text, PowerPoint selects whole words. If you want to select individual characters, select the **Tools**, **Options** command, click the **Edit** tab, and deselect the **Automatic Word Selection** check box.

- To delete text, select the text and press the **Delete** key. You can also use the Delete or Backspace keys to delete single characters to the right or left of the insertion point, respectively.
- To insert text, click where you want to insert the text, and then type the text.
- To replace text, select the text you want to replace, and then type the new text. When you start typing, PowerPoint deletes the selected text.

  - To copy and paste text, select the text you want to copy and choose the **Edit**, **Copy** command, or click the **Copy** button on the Standard toolbar, or press **Ctrl+C**. Then move the insertion point to where you want the text pasted (it can even be in a different text box) and choose the **Edit**, **Paste** command, or click the **Paste** button, or press **Ctrl+V**.

 - To cut and paste (move) text, select the text you want to cut and choose the **Edit**, **Cut** command, or click the **Cut** button on the Standard toolbar, or press **Ctrl+X**. Move the insertion point to where you want the text pasted (it can even be in a different text box), and choose the **Edit**, **Paste** command, or click the **Paste** button, or press **Ctrl+V**.

# Changing the Text Alignment and Line Spacing

When you first type text, PowerPoint automatically places it against the left edge of the text box. To change the paragraph alignment, perform the following steps:

1. Click anywhere inside the paragraph you want to realign.
2. Select **Format**, **Alignment**. The Alignment submenu appears.
3. Select **Left**, **Center**, **Right**, or **Justify** to align the paragraph as desired. (See Figure 10.2 for examples.)

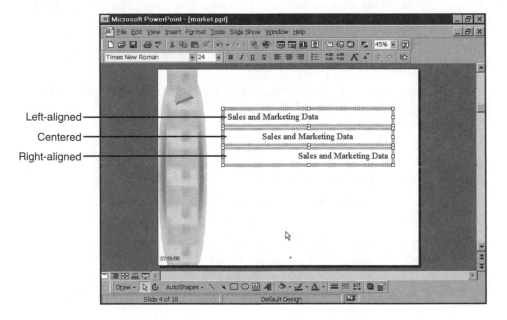

**Figure 10.2** You can align each paragraph in a text box.

 **TIP** **Some Alignment Shortcuts** To quickly set left alignment, press **Ctrl+L** or click the **Left Alignment** button on the Formatting toolbar. To quickly apply right alignment, press **Ctrl+R** or click the **Right Alignment** button. To quickly apply centered alignment, press **Ctrl+C** or click the **Center Alignment** button.

The default setting for line spacing is single-space. To change the line spacing in a paragraph, perform these steps:

**1.** Click inside the paragraph you want to change, or select all the paragraphs you want to change.

**2.** Select **Format, Line Spacing**. The Line Spacing dialog box appears, as shown in Figure 10.3.

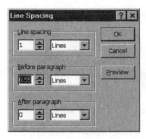

**Figure 10.3** The Line Spacing dialog box.

**3.** Click the arrow buttons to the right of any of the following text boxes to change the line spacing:

**Line Spacing** This setting controls the space between the lines in a paragraph.

**Before Paragraph** This setting controls the space between this paragraph and the paragraph that comes before it.

**After Paragraph** This setting controls the space between this paragraph and the paragraph that comes after it.

 **TIP** **Lines or Points?** The drop-down list box that appears to the right of each setting allows you to set the line spacing in lines or points. A line is the current line height (based on text size). A point is a unit commonly used to measure text. A point is approximately 1/72 of an inch.

**4.** Click **OK**.

# Adding a WordArt Object

PowerPoint comes with an auxiliary program called WordArt that can help you create graphic text effects. To insert a WordArt object into a slide, perform the following steps:

**1.** In Slide view, display the slide on which you want to place the WordArt object.

**2.** Click the **WordArt** button on the Drawing toolbar (at the bottom of the screen). The WordArt Gallery dialog box appears, showing many samples of WordArt types.

**3.** Click the sample that best represents the WordArt type you want, and then click **OK**. The Edit WordArt Text dialog box appears (see Figure 10.4).

**4.** Choose a font and font size from the respective drop-down lists.

**5.** Type the text you want to use in the **Text** box (see Figure 10.4).

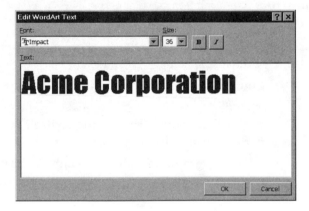

**Figure 10.4**  Enter the text, size, and font to be used.

**6.** Click **OK**, and PowerPoint creates the WordArt text on your slide, as shown in Figure 10.5.

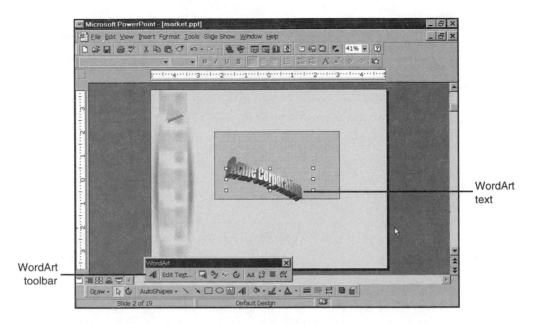

**Figure 10.5** Finished WordArt on a slide, with the WordArt toolbar below it.

After you have created some WordArt, you have access to the WordArt toolbar, also shown in Figure 10.5. You can use it to modify your WordArt. Table 11.1 summarizes the buttons on that toolbar.

**Table 10.1** Buttons on the WordArt Toolbar

| Button | Description |
| --- | --- |
| | Creates a new WordArt object |
| Edit Text... | Edits the text, size, and font of the selected WordArt object |
| | Changes the type of the current WordArt object |
| | Changes the Line and Fill color |
| | Changes the WordArt shape |

*continues*

**Table 10.1**  Continued

| Button | Description |
|---|---|
| | Rotates the WordArt object |
| | Makes all the letters the same height |
| | Changes between vertical and horizontal text orientation |
| | Changes the text alignment |
| | Changes the spacing between letters |

To edit the WordArt object, double-click it to display the WordArt toolbar and text entry box. Enter your changes, and then click outside the WordArt object. You can move the object by dragging its border, or you can resize it by dragging a handle.

In this lesson, you learned how to add text to a slide, change the text alignment and spacing, and add WordArt objects. In the next lesson, you will learn how to use tables, tabs, and indents to create columns and lists.

# Creating Columns and Lists

*In this lesson, you learn how to use tabs to create columns of text and how to use indents to create bulleted lists, numbered lists, and other types of lists.*

## Using Tabs to Create Columns

A presentation often uses tabbed columns to display information. For example, you may use tabs to create a three-column list like the one shown in Figure 11.1.

> In addition to hardware products, we carry a varied line of software:
>
> | **Business** | **Home** | **Education** |
> |---|---|---|
> | WordPerfect | Quicken | Reader Rabbit 2 |
> | Microsoft Word | The New Print Shop | Oregon Trail |
> | PowerPoint | Microsoft Works | BodyWorks |
> | Excel | TurboTax | Where in the World is Carmen Sandiego? |

**Figure 11.1**   You can use tabs to create a multi-column list.

In PowerPoint, you create multiple columns using tab stops. To set the tabs for a multi-column list, perform the following steps:

1. Open the presentation and view the slide you want to work with in Slide View.
2. Create a text box for the text as you learned in Lesson 10.
3. Click anywhere inside the text box for which you want to set the tabs.
4. If you already typed text inside the text box, select the text.

**5.** Select **View**, **Ruler** to display the ruler if it is not displayed.

**6.** Click the tab icon in the upper-left corner of the presentation window until it represents the type of tab you want to set:

Aligns the left end of the line against the tab stop.

Centers the text on the tab stop.

Aligns the right end of the line against the tab stop.

Aligns the tab stop on a period. This is called a decimal tab, and it's useful for aligning a column of numbers that uses decimal points.

**7.** Click in each place on the ruler where you want to set the selected type of tab stop (see Figure 11.2).

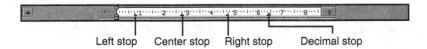

Left stop    Center stop    Right stop    Decimal stop

**Figure 11.2**   The ruler lets you enter and change tab stop settings.

**8.** Repeat steps 5 and 6 to set different types of tab stops in other positions.

**9.** To change the position of an existing tab stop, drag it on the ruler to the desired position. To delete an existing tab stop setting, drag it off the ruler.

**10.** (Optional) To turn off the ruler, select **View**, **Ruler**.

TIP   **Don't Forget the Slide Master**   Throughout this lesson, keep in mind that you can enter your changes on the Slide Master or on individual slides. If you change the Slide Master, the change affects all slides in the presentation. For details on displaying the Slide Master, see Lesson 7.

# Making a Bulleted List

When you enter new slides in Outline view, the default layout is a simple bulleted list. If you've done this (see Lesson 8), you've already created a bulleted list. However, you can also create a bulleted list in a text box that you add to a slide yourself without relying on an AutoLayout. Follow these steps to change some regular text in a text box to a bulleted list:

**1.** Click inside the paragraph you want to transform into a bulleted list, or select one or more paragraphs.

**2.** Select **Format, Bullet**. The Bullet dialog box appears.

 **TIP**  **Quick Bullets** To bypass the Format menu and Bullet dialog box, simply click the **Bullet** button on the Formatting toolbar to insert a bullet, or right-click and select **Bullet** from the shortcut menu. You can click the Bullet button again to remove the bullet.

**3.** Select the **Use a Bullet** check box to enable bullet use.

**4.** Click **OK**. PowerPoint transforms the selected text into a bulleted list. (If you press **Enter** at the end of a bulleted paragraph, the next paragraph starts with a bullet.)

 **TIP** **Moving a Bulleted Item** You can move an item in a bulleted list by clicking the item's bullet and then dragging the bullet up or down in the list.

# Changing the Bullet Character

By default, whenever you click the Bullet button on the Formatting toolbar to insert a bullet, PowerPoint inserts a large dot for the bullet. However, you can change the appearance of the bullet at any time. These steps show you how:

**1.** Select the paragraph(s) in which you want to change the bullet character.

**2.** Select **Format, Bullet**. The Bullet dialog box appears (see Figure 11.3).

**3.** Click the **Bullets From** drop-down arrow and select the character set from which you want to choose a bullet. The dialog box displays the characters in the selected set.

**CAUTION** **Which Character Set?** Each character set is nothing more than a font that's installed on your computer. Some fonts are better suited for bullets than others; open several and examine the characters each one contains. Wingdings is a good choice.

**4.** Click the character you want to use for the bullet, and PowerPoint shows it enlarged so you can see it clearly (as shown in Figure 11.3).

**401**

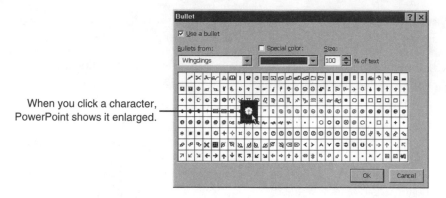

When you click a character, PowerPoint shows it enlarged.

**Figure 11.3**   Choose a different bullet character.

5. To set the size of the bullet, use the up and down arrows to the right of the **Size** text box. Notice that the size of the bullet is not a fixed value—it is relative to the text around it.

6. To select a color for the bullet, click the **Special Color** drop-down arrow and select the color you want.

7. Click **OK**. PowerPoint changes the bullet for all selected paragraphs.

# Using Indents to Create Lists

Indents enable you to move one or more lines of a paragraph in from the left margin. PowerPoint uses indents to create the bulleted lists you encountered in previous lessons. You can use indents in any text object to create a similar list or your own custom list. To indent text, perform the following steps:

1. Select the text box that contains the text you want to indent.

2. If you've already typed text, select the text you want to indent.

3. If the ruler is not visible, select **View**, **Ruler**.

4. Drag one of the following indent markers to set the indents for the paragraph. (These indent markers appear on the ruler, as shown in Figure 11.4.)

    Drag the top marker to indent the first line.

    Drag the bottom marker to indent all subsequent lines.

    Drag the box below the bottom marker to indent all the text.

5. (Optional) To turn the ruler off, select **View**, **Ruler**.

Indent markers—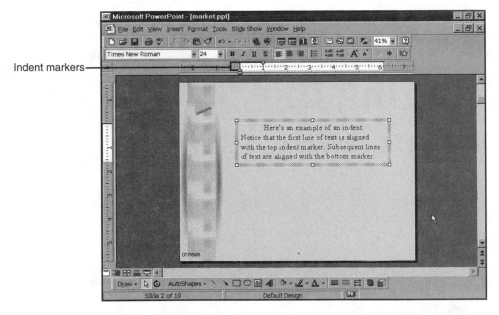

**Figure 11.4** Drag the indent markers to indent your text.

 You can create up to five levels of indents within a single text box. To add an indent level, click the **Demote** button on the Formatting toolbar or press **Tab** when the insertion point is at the beginning of the paragraph. A new set of indent markers appears on the ruler, showing the next level of indents. You can change these new indent settings as explained previously.

After you set your indents, you can create a numbered or bulleted list by performing the following steps:

1. Type a number and a period, or type the character you want to use for the bullet.
2. Press the **Tab** key to move to the second indent mark.
3. Type the text you want to use for this item. As you type, PowerPoint wraps the text to the second indent mark.
4. Repeat steps 1 through 3 for each additional item you add to the list.

In this lesson, you learned how to create columns with tabs, create lists with indents, and change the bullet character for bulleted lists. In the next lesson, you will learn how to change the style, size, and color of text.

# Changing the Look of Your Text

In this lesson, you learn how to change the appearance of text by changing its font, style, size, and color.

## Enhancing Your Text with the Font Dialog Box

You can enhance your text by using the Font dialog box or by using various tools on the Formatting toolbar. Use the Font dialog box if you want to add several enhancements to your text at one time. Use the Formatting toolbar to add one enhancement at a time.

**TERM** **Fonts, Styles, and Effects**   In PowerPoint, a *font* is a family of text that has the same design or typeface (for example, Arial or Courier). A *style* is a standard enhancement, such as bold or italic. An *effect* is a special enhancement, such as shadow or underline.

You can change the font of existing text or of text you are about to type by performing the following steps:

1. To change the font of existing text, select the text first.
2. Choose **Format, Font**. The Font dialog box appears, as shown in Figure 12.1.

 **TIP**   **Right-Click Quick**   You can right-click the text and select **Font** from the shortcut menu instead of performing steps 1 and 2.

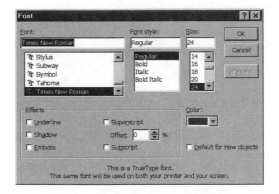

**Figure 12.1**   You can select a font from the Font dialog box.

**3.** In the **Font** list, select the font you want to use.

 **TERM**   **TrueType Fonts**   The "TT" next to some font names identifies those fonts as TrueType fonts. TrueType fonts are *scalable*, which means you can set them at any point size. When you save a presentation, you can choose to embed TrueType fonts so you can display or print the font on any computer, whether or not it has that font installed.

**4.** From the **Font Style** list, select any style you want to apply to the text. (To remove styles from text, select **Regular**.)

**5.** From the **Size** list, select any size in the list, or type a size directly into the box. (With TrueType fonts, you can type any point size, even sizes that do not appear on the list.)

**6.** In the Effects group, select any special effects you want to add to the text, such as **Underline**, **Shadow**, or **Emboss**. You can also choose **Superscript** or **Subscript**, though they are less common.

**7.** To change the color of your text, click the **Color** drop-down arrow and click the desired color. (For more colors, click the **Other Color** option at the bottom of the list and select a color from the dialog box that appears.)

 **TIP**   **Changing the Background Color**   Each presentation has its own color scheme, which includes background and text colors. You'll learn about creating and changing color schemes in Lesson 17.

**8.** Click **OK** to apply the new look to your text. (If you selected text before styling it, the text appears in the new style. If you did not select text, any text you type appears in the new style.)

**CAUTION**

**Title and Object Area Text**   If you change a font on an individual slide, the font change applies to that slide only. To change the font for all the slides in the presentation, you need to change the font on the Slide Master. To change the Slide Master, select **View**, **Master**, **Slide Master**. Select a text area, and then perform the previous steps to change the look of the text on all slides.

# Styling Text with the Formatting Toolbar

As shown in Figure 12.2, the Formatting toolbar contains several tools for changing the font, size, style, and color of text.

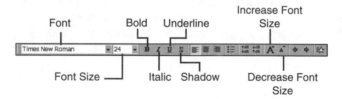

**Figure 12.2**   The Formatting toolbar contains several tools for styling text.

To use the tools, follow these steps:

**1.** To change the look of existing text, select the text.

**2.** To change fonts, open the **Font** drop-down list (see Figure 12.2) and click the desired font.

**3.** To change font size, open the **Font Size** drop-down list (shown in Figure 12.2) and click the desired size, or type a size directly into the box.

**TIP**

**Incrementing the Type Size**   To increase or decrease the text size to the next size up or down, click the **Increase Font Size** or **Decrease Font Size** button on the Formatting toolbar.

**406**

4. To add a style or effect to the text (bold, italic, underline, and/or shadow), click the appropriate button(s):

# Changing Font Color with the Drawing Toolbar

**New Location for Font Color Button**   In earlier versions of PowerPoint, the Font Color button was on the Formatting toolbar instead of the Drawing toolbar.

The Font Color button on the Drawing toolbar (at the bottom of the screen) enables you to change the color of the selected text. The following steps show you how to use the Font Color button:

1. Select the text for which you want to change the color.

2. Click the **Font Color** drop-down arrow on the Drawing toolbar. A menu of options appears (see Figure 12.3).

3. Do one of the following:

   • Click one of the colored blocks to change the font to one of the prechosen colors for the presentation design you're using.

   • Click the **More Font Colors** button to display a Colors dialog box. Then click a color in that box and click **OK**.

Or, click here for more choices.

Click one of these preselected colors to stay within the presentation design's color scheme.

**Figure 12.3**   When you click the arrow next to the Font Colors button, this menu of options appears.

# Copying Text Formats

If your presentation contains text with a format you want to use, you can pick up the format from the existing text and apply it to other text. To copy text formats, perform the following steps:

1. Highlight the text with the format you want to use.

 2. Click the **Format Painter** button on the toolbar. PowerPoint copies the formatting characteristics.

3. Drag across the text to which you want to apply the format. When you release the mouse button, PowerPoint applies the formats.

In this lesson, you learned how to change the appearance of text by changing its font, size, style, and color. You also learned how to copy text formats. In the next lesson, you will learn how to draw objects on a slide.

# Drawing
# Objects on
# a Slide

*In this lesson, you learn how to use PowerPoint's drawing tools
to draw graphic objects on a slide.*

## PowerPoint's Drawing Tools

Although PowerPoint is not a drawing program per se, you can do some simple
drawing with it. For example, you may want to draw a simple logo, or you
might accent your slide with horizontal or vertical lines.

To this end, PowerPoint comes with several drawing tools to help you create
lines and shapes. The Drawing toolbar displays these tools along the bottom of
the presentation window in Slide view and Notes Pages view. There are two
types of tools on the Drawing toolbar: tools for drawing lines and shapes and
tools for manipulating the graphic objects. Here's a look at the drawing ones:

| Tool | Purpose |
|------|---------|
| \ | Draws a straight line |
| ↘ | Draws a straight line with an arrow on the end |
| ▢ | Draws a rectangle |
| ◯ | Draws an ellipse (oval) |

# Drawing a Line or Shape

The general procedure for drawing an object is the same no matter which object you draw:

1. Click the button on the Drawing toolbar for the line or shape you want to draw. For example, to draw a rectangle, click the **Rectangle** button.

2. Position the mouse pointer where you want one end of the line or one corner of the object to be anchored.

3. Press and hold the mouse button, and drag to where you want the opposite end of the line or the opposite corner of the object to appear. Figure 13.1 shows the procedure for drawing a rectangle.

4. Release the mouse button, and the finished line or shape appears.

The outline shows where
the shape will appear.

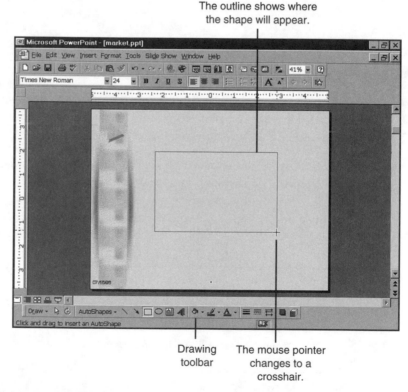

Drawing
toolbar

The mouse pointer
changes to a
crosshair.

**Figure 13.1** The Drawing toolbar contains tools for drawing lines and basic shapes.

> **TIP**  **Squares and Circles**  You can draw a perfect square or circle by holding
> down the **Shift** key as you drag with the **Rectangle** or **Ellipse** tool, respectively.

# Working with AutoShapes

Drawing a complex shape with the rudimentary tools available to you can be
frustrating. That's why PowerPoint comes with several predrawn objects called
*AutoShapes* that you can use. To draw one of these objects, perform the following
steps:

AutoShapes ▾

**1.** Click the **AutoShapes** tool on the Drawing toolbar. A menu of shape types
appears.

**2.** Click the type of shape you want. For example, if you want an arrow,
choose **Block Arrows**. The AutoShapes palette appears for that type of
shape (see Figure 13.2).

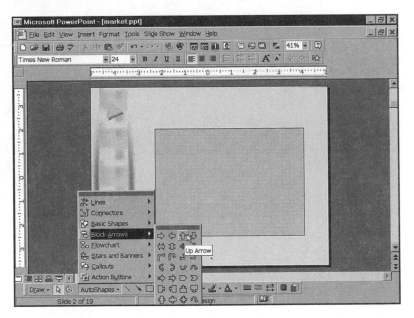

**Figure 13.2**  Select the shape you want from the AutoShapes palette.

**3.** Click the shape you want to draw.

**4.** Move the mouse pointer to where you want a corner or the center of the
shape to be.

**411**

5. (Optional) While drawing the object, hold down one or both of the following keys:

> **Ctrl** to draw the shape out from a center point

> **Shift** to draw a shape that retains the dimensions shown on the AutoShapes palette

6. Hold down the mouse button and drag the mouse to draw the object.

7. Release the mouse button, and the shape appears, as shown in Figure 13.3.

 **TIP** **Changing an Existing Shape** You can change an existing shape into a different shape. Select the shape you want to change, click the **Draw** button on the Drawing toolbar, select **Change AutoShape**, and click the shape you want to use.

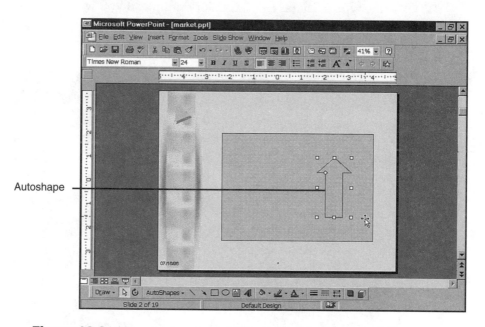

Autoshape

**Figure 13.3** You can draw an AutoShape like this arrow as easily as you can draw any simple rectangle.

# Adding Text to an Object

You can add text to an object you draw. Unlike overlaying a shape with a text box, text typed into a shape stays with the shape when you move it. To insert text into your drawing, follow these steps:

1. Click the object in which you want the text to appear.

2. Type the text. As you type, the text appears in a single line across the object.

3. (Optional) Select **Format**, **Drawing Object**. The Format AutoShape dialog box appears.

4. Click the **Text Box** tab to display the options shown in Figure 13.4.

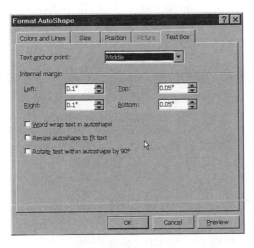

**Figure 13.4** Use the Text Box tab to position your text inside the object.

5. Open the **Text Anchor Point** drop-down list and choose a position for the text in relation to the shape. (Middle is the default.)

6. Set margins for all four sides of the shape (Left, Right, Top, and Bottom) to establish how much white space will be left between the edges of the shape and the text.

7. (Optional) Select any of the following check boxes:

   - **Word Wrap Text in Autoshape** Wraps text to another line if the text is wider than the shape.

   - **Resize Autoshape to Fit Text** Makes the shape larger or smaller so the text fits within the margins you specify in step 5 exactly.

   - **Rotate Text Within Autoshape by 90°** Rotates the text to run the other way (usually vertically) so it will fit better in the shape.

**TIP** **Viewing the Effects of Your Changes** You can drag the title bar of the dialog box to move the dialog box away from the object. Then you can view the effects of your changes by clicking the **Preview** button before you click **OK** to save your changes.

**8.** Click **OK** to save your changes.

You can change the style and alignment of the text in an object in the same way you can change style and alignment in any text box. Refer to Lessons 10, 11, and 12 for details.

# Tips for Working with Objects

Here are some quick tips that can save you some time and reduce frustration as you begin working with objects. You'll learn more about manipulating objects in Lessons 15 and 16.

- If you're going to use the same tool to draw several objects in a row, double-click the tool. The tool stays selected, and you don't have to click it again after you draw each shape.
- To draw an object out from the center instead of from a corner, hold down the **Ctrl** key while dragging.
- To select an object, click it.
- To delete an object, select it and press **Delete**.
- To move an object, select it and drag one of its lines.
- To resize or reshape an object, select it and drag one of its handles.
- To copy an object, hold down the **Ctrl** key while dragging it.

In this lesson, you learned how to use PowerPoint's drawing tools to add drawings to your slides. In the next lesson, you will learn how to add clip art, pictures, sounds, and video clips to your slides.

# Adding Pictures, Sounds, and Video Clips

*In this lesson, you learn how to add PowerPoint clip art, pictures from other graphics programs, sounds, and video clips to a slide.*

## Introducing the Clip Gallery

Microsoft has taken a bold new step in the Office 97 products (of which PowerPoint is one) in handling multiple media such as sounds, videos, and artwork. It's called the Clip Gallery (see Figure 14.1).

Each type of object has its own tab.

List of categories

Previews of objects in the chosen category

Internet icon

**Figure 14.1** The Clip Gallery manages pictures, clip art, videos, and sounds, all in one convenient place.

**Clip Art**   Clip art is a collection of previously created images or pictures that you can place on a slide.

You can open the Clip Gallery in any of these ways:

- Click the **Clip Art** button on the Standard toolbar.
- Select **Insert, Picture, Clip Art**.
- Select **Insert, Movies and Sounds, Sound from Gallery**.
- Select **Insert, Movies and Sounds, Movie from Gallery**.

All of these methods open the Clip Gallery, but a different tab appears on top depending on which method you used. For example, if you use the Insert, Picture, Clip Art command, the Clip Art tab appears on top (as in Figure 14.1).

**TIP**   **PowerPoint on the Web**   Click the **Internet** icon in the corner of the Clip Gallery 3.0 dialog box to connect to Microsoft's Web site and download additional clip art.

# Inserting a Clip on a Slide

Using the Clip Gallery, you can place any of the four types of objects on a slide: clip art, picture, sound, or movie. In the case of the latter two, you then click the object to activate it as necessary during the presentation. For example, you click the sound's icon to make it play. You also can set up sounds and movies to play automatically when a slide displays (which you'll learn to do later in this lesson).

To insert a clip onto a slide, follow these steps:

1. Open the Clip Gallery as described in the previous section.
2. Click the tab for the type of clip you want to insert.
3. Click the category that represents the type of clip you want.
4. Click the clip you want to use.
5. Click the **Insert** button.

**The Clip I Want Isn't on the List!** If you don't see the clip you're looking for, click the **Import Clips** button. Then use the dialog box that appears to locate the clip and import it into the Clip Gallery. From then on, that image will be available on the Clip Gallery tab for its file type.

TIP **PowerPoint on the Web** Artwork, movies, and sounds can really add a lot to a PowerPoint presentation on the Web, but they also add to the size of the file—and consequently, to the time it will take a reader to download it. For this reason, try to be judicious in your use of media on presentations designed for Web use.

# Inserting a Clip from a File

If you have a clip such as a bitmap image, sound file, or movie file stored on disk, you can quickly place it on a slide without using with the Clip Gallery. Just follow these steps:

**1.** Select the slide on which the image should be placed.

**2.** Select **Insert**, **Picture**, **From File**. The Insert Picture dialog box appears (see Figure 14.2).

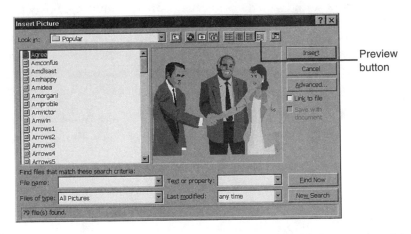

**Figure 14.2** Use the Insert Picture dialog box to place any graphic image on a slide.

3. Select the picture you want to use. You can see a preview of the pictures in the Preview pane to the left of the file list. If the preview does not appear, click the **Preview** button (shown in Figure 14.2) to turn on the preview feature.

4. Click **Insert** to place the image on the slide.

If the picture is too big or too small, you can drag the selection handles (the small squares) around the edge of the image to resize it. (Hold down **Shift** to proportionally resize.) Refer to Lesson 15 for more details about resizing and cropping.

**TIP**  **Movies and Sounds from Files**  You also can insert movies and sounds from files. Just select **Insert**, **Movies and Sounds** and then choose either **Movie from File** or **Sound from File**.

# Choosing When Movies and Sounds Should Play

Slides are static for the most part: they appear, and then they sit there. Movies and sounds, on the other hand, are dynamic: they play at specific times.

When you place a movie or sound on a slide, by default the object does not activate until you click it. For example, a slide may contain a recorded narration that explains a particular graph on the slide, but the narration will not play until the person giving the presentation clicks the sound icon to activate it.

However, you may want some sounds or movies to play automatically at certain times in the presentation. You control this with the following procedure:

1. Click the object (the sound icon or movie image) on the slide.

2. Select **Slide Show**, **Custom Animation**, and the Custom Animation dialog box appears (see Figure 14.3).

3. Choose the **Timing** tab.

4. Click the **Animate** button to indicate that you want the sound or movie to play on the slide.

5. Click the **Automatically** button to indicate you want it to play without user intervention.

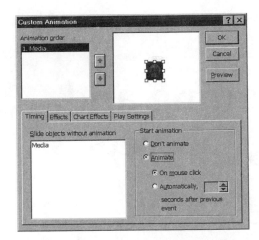

**Figure 14.3** Use this dialog box to set when and how a sound or movie plays.

**6.** In the text box next to the **Automatically** control, enter the number of seconds that PowerPoint should pause after the previous event before playing the object.

 **Previous Event?** If this is the only media clip on this slide, the previous event is the slide itself being displayed. If there is more than one media clip on the slide, you can control the order in which they activate by switching their order in the Animation Order list in the Custom Animation dialog box (see Figure 14.3).

**7.** When you finish setting up your preferences, click **OK**.

 **8.** Switch to Slide Show view to test the slide, making sure you have set up the sound or animation to play when you want it to.

 **TIP** **Continuous Play** You can set a sound or animation to loop continuously by clicking the **Play Settings** tab and selecting the **More Options** button. Select both the **Loop Until Stopped** and **Rewind Movie When Done Playing** check boxes.

In this lesson, you learned how to add clip art images, pictures, sounds, and movies to your slides, and how to control when a movie or sound plays. In the next lesson, you will learn how to reposition and resize objects on a slide.

# Positioning and Sizing Objects

*In this lesson, you will learn how to select, copy, move, rotate, and resize objects on a slide.*

As you may have already discovered, objects are the building blocks you use to create slides in PowerPoint. Objects include the shapes you draw, the graphs you create, the pictures you import, and the text you type. In this lesson and the next one, you will learn how to manipulate objects on your slides to create impressive presentations.

## Selecting Objects

Before you can copy, move, rotate, or resize an object, you must first select the object. Change to Slide view, and use one of these methods to select one or more objects:

- To select a single object, click it. (If you click text, a frame appears around the text; click the frame to select the text object.)

- To select more than one object, hold down the **Shift** key and click each object. Handles appear around the selected objects, as shown in Figure 15.1.

- To deselect selected objects, click anywhere outside the selected objects.

 **TIP** **Using the Selection Tool** The Selection tool on the Drawing toolbar, enables you to quickly select a group of objects. Click the **Selection** tool and use the mouse pointer to drag a selection box around the objects you want to select. When you release the mouse button, PowerPoint selects the objects inside the box.

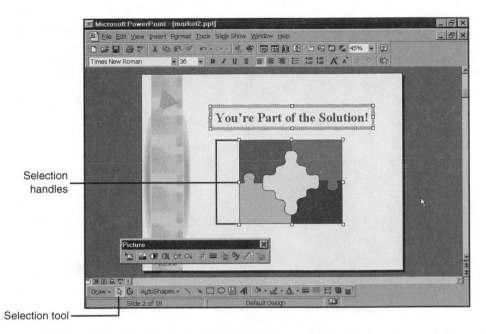

Selection handles

Selection tool

**Figure 15.1** Handles indicate that objects are selected.

# Working with Layers of Objects

As you place objects on-screen, they may start to overlap, making it difficult or impossible to select the objects in the lower layers. To move objects in layers, perform the following steps:

**1.** Click the object you want to move up or down in the stack.

**2.** Click the **Draw** button on the Drawing toolbar to open the Draw menu, and select **Order** (see Figure 15.2).

**3.** Select one of the following options:

**Bring to Front** brings the object to the top of the stack.

**Send to Back** sends the object to the bottom of the stack.

**Bring Forward** brings the object up one layer.

**Send Backward** sends the object back one layer.

**421**

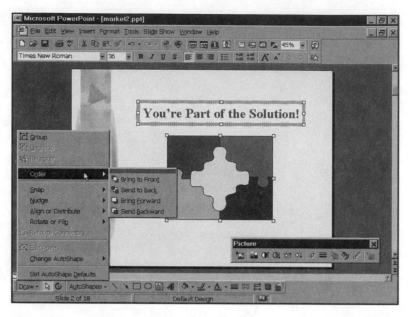

**Figure 15.2**   Use the Draw menu on the Drawing toolbar to change the layer on which a graphic appears on your slide.

# Grouping and Ungrouping Objects

Each object you draw acts as an individual object. However, sometimes you might want two or more objects to act as a group. For example, you may want to make the lines of several objects the same thickness, or you may want to move several objects together.

If you want to treat two or more objects as a group, perform the following steps:

1. Select the objects you want to group. Remember, to select more than one object, hold down the **Ctrl** key and click each one.

2. Click the **Draw** button on the Drawing toolbar to open the Draw menu. Then select **Group**.

3. To ungroup the objects later, select any object in the group and select **Draw, Ungroup**.

# Cutting, Copying, and Pasting Objects

You can cut, copy, and paste objects on a slide to rearrange the objects or to use the objects to create a picture. When you cut an object, PowerPoint removes the object from the slide and places it in a temporary holding area called the Windows Clipboard. When you copy an object, the original object remains on the slide, and PowerPoint places a copy of it on the Clipboard. In either case, you can then paste the object from the Clipboard onto the current slide or another slide.

To cut or copy an object, perform the following steps:

1. Select the object(s) you want to cut (move) or copy.

2. Right-click the selected object and choose **Cut** or **Copy** from the shortcut menu. (Or, select the **Edit**, **Cut** or **Edit**, **Copy** command, or click the **Cut** or **Copy** button on the Standard toolbar.)

3. Display the slide on which you want to place the cut or copied object(s). You can open a different Windows program, to paste it into, if you prefer.

4. Select **Edit**, **Paste** or click the **Paste** button on the Standard toolbar. PowerPoint pastes the object(s) on the slide.

TIP **Keyboard Shortcuts** You can press **Ctrl+X** to cut, **Ctrl+C** to copy, and **Ctrl+V** to paste instead of using the toolbar buttons or the menu.

5. Move the mouse pointer over any of the pasted objects, hold down the mouse button, and drag the objects to where you want them.

6. Release the mouse button.

TIP **Deleting an Object** To remove an object without placing it on the Clipboard, select the object, and then press the **Delete** key or select **Edit**, **Clear**.

TIP **Dragging and Dropping Objects** The quickest way to copy or move objects is to drag-and-drop them. Select the objects you want to move, position the mouse pointer over any of the selected objects, press and hold the mouse button, and drag the objects to where you want them. To copy the objects, hold down the **Ctrl** key while dragging.

# Rotating an Object

The Rotate tools enable you to revolve an object around a center point. To rotate an object to your own specifications, using Free Rotate, do the following:

1. Click the object you want to rotate.

2. Click the **Free Rotate** tool on the Drawing toolbar. The selection handles on the centering line change to circles.

3. Press and hold the mouse button and drag the circular handle until the object is in the position you want (see Figure 15.3).

4. Release the mouse button.

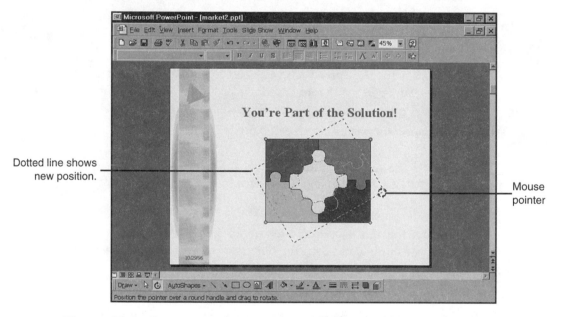

Dotted line shows
new position.

Mouse
pointer

**Figure 15.3** You can drag the circular selection handle to rotate the object.

TIP **Other Rotate Options** The Draw menu (on the Drawing toolbar, shown in Figure 15.2) contains a Rotate/Flip submenu that provides additional options for rotating objects. You can flip an object 90 degrees left or right, or flip the object over an the centering line to create a mirrored image of it.

# Resizing Objects

There may be times when an object you create or import is not the right size for your slide presentation. You can resize the object by performing these steps:

1. Select the object to resize. Selection handles appear.

2. Drag one of the handles (the squares that surround the object) until the object is the desired size:

    • Drag a corner handle to change both the height and width of an object. PowerPoint retains the object's relative dimensions.

    • Drag a side, top, or bottom handle to change the height or width alone.

    • Hold down the **Ctrl** key while dragging to resize from the center of the picture.

3. Release the mouse button, and PowerPoint resizes the object (see Figure 15.4).

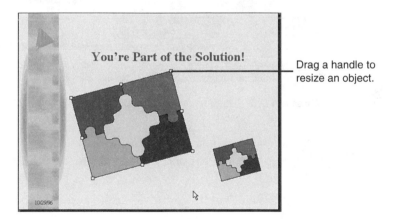

Drag a handle to resize an object.

**Figure 15.4**   Before and after resizing an object.

# Cropping a Picture

Besides resizing a picture, you can crop it. That is, you can trim a side or corner of the picture to remove an element from the picture or to cut off some white space. To crop a picture, perform the following steps:

1. Click the picture you want to crop.

**2.** If the Picture toolbar isn't shown, right-click the picture and select **Show Picture Toolbar** from the menu.

**3.** Click the **Crop** button on the Picture toolbar. The mouse pointer turns into a cropping tool (see Figure 15.5).

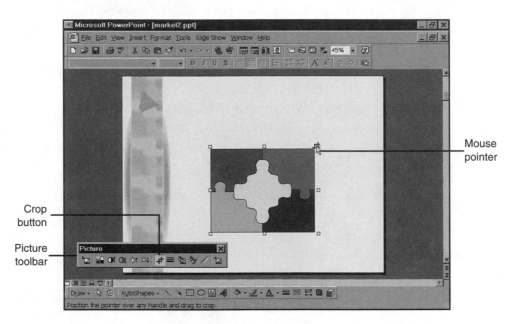

**Figure 15.5**  Use the cropping tool to chop off a section of the picture.

**4.** Move the mouse pointer over one of the handles. (Use a corner handle to crop two sides at once. Use a side, top, or bottom handle to crop only one side.)

**5.** Press and hold the mouse button, and drag the pointer until the crop lines are where you want them.

**6.** Release the mouse button, and the cropped section disappears.

**TIP**  **Uncropping**  You can uncrop a picture immediately after cropping it by selecting **Edit**, **Undo** or by clicking the **Undo** button on the toolbar. You can also uncrop at any time by performing the previous steps and dragging the selected handle in the opposite direction you dragged it for cropping.

In this lesson, you learned how to select, copy, move, rotate, and resize an object on a slide. In the next lesson, you will learn how to change the lines and colors of an object.

# Changing the Look of Objects

*In this lesson, you learn how to add borders, colors, patterns, shadows, and 3-D effects to objects.*

## Changing Line Thickness and Color

In Lesson 13, you learned to draw your own artwork on a slide, and in Lesson 14, you learned to import clip art and other graphics. You can change the appearance of both kinds of artwork by modifying the colors and lines, but the procedures are different depending on whether the art is predrawn (a file you have imported) or whether you drew it with the PowerPoint drawing tools.

**Drawing versus Picture**   In PowerPoint terms, a drawing is artwork that you have created yourself using PowerPoint's drawing tools, while a picture is artwork that you have imported (such as clip art). If you want to change an imported picture's colors, see the section "Changing the Colors of a Picture" later in this lesson.

## Changing a Drawing's Colors and Lines

If the line or shape you draw is not the color you expect it to be, you can change the color. With lines, you have only one color option: change the line. With shapes, you can change the color of both the inside (fill) and the outside border (line).

Follow these steps to change the lines and/or color of any object you've drawn:

1. Right-click the drawn object. A shortcut menu appears.
2. From the shortcut menu, select **Format Drawing Object**, and then click the **Colors and Lines** tab (see Figure 16.1).

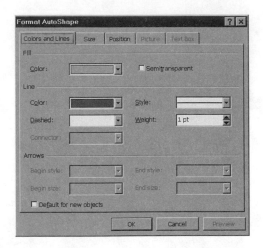

**Figure 16.1**   Change the lines and colors for a drawn object.

**CAUTION**

**Format Drawing Object Is Not on the Menu!**   If you right-click a piece of clip art or another imported graphic instead of one you've drawn yourself, you won't find the Format Drawing Object command. However, you can select **Format Picture** instead and modify the picture's properties as explained in "Changing the Colors of a Picture" later in this lesson.

3. In the Fill section, open the **Color** list and select a different color for the inside of the shape. (This isn't applicable if the drawn object you're formatting is a line.) For more color choices, choose **More Colors** and select from the dialog box that appears.

**TIP**

**Textures and Patterns**   From the **Fill Color** list, you can select **Fill Effects**. This opens a dialog box from which you can choose textures, patterns, and gradients. Some textures are really cool—they look like wood, marble, or granite.

**TERM**

**Semi-Transparent?**   If you want to partially see through a shape to whatever is behind it, click the **Semi-Transparent** check box. For example, if you have a blue shape on a red background and the blue shape is semi-transparent, it appears to be made up equally of red and blue. If you put the same shape on a white background, the shape appears light blue—a mixture of blue and white.

4. In the Line section, open the **Color** drop-down list and choose a line color. For shapes, the Line setting affects the color of the shape's outside border.

5. Choose a line style from the **Style** drop-down list. You can choose thick or thin lines, double lines, and so on.

6. If you want a different thickness, change the number in the **Weight** text box to a higher or lower number. (Measurements are in points. A point is 1/72 of an inch.)

7. If you want the line to be dashed (broken), choose a dash style from the **Dashed** drop-down list.

8. If you want arrows at one or both ends of a line, choose the arrow style from the **Arrows** drop-down list. These controls will be unavailable if you are formatting a shape instead of a line.

9. If you want to draw all objects with these colors and line styles, specify them as the default by clicking the **Default for New Objects** check box.

10. Click **OK**. PowerPoint applies your changes to the shape.

 **TIP**  **Changing the Entire Color Scheme**  If you want to change the entire color scheme for the presentation, don't mess around with individual objects— go straight to Lesson 17 for instructions.

# Changing the Colors of a Picture

When you paste a clip art image or insert a picture on a slide, the picture appears in its original colors. But these colors may clash with the colors in your presentation. To change the colors in a picture, perform the following steps:

1. Click the picture you want to change. A selection box appears around the picture.

2. Do either of the following to open the Recolor Picture dialog box shown in Figure 16.2.

   • If the Picture toolbar is not displayed, right-click the picture and select **Show Picture Toolbar**. Then click the **Recolor Picture** button on that toolbar.

   • Select **Format**, **Colors and Lines**. The Format Picture dialog box appears. Click the **Picture** tab and then the **Recolor** button.

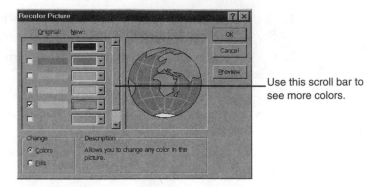

Use this scroll bar to
see more colors.

**Figure 16.2**   Use the Recolor Picture dialog box to change the colors in a picture.

**3.** In the Change area, select **Colors** to change line colors, or select **Fills** to change colors between the lines.

**CAUTION**

**Fills Isn't an Option!**   With some picture types (like the one shown in Figure 16.2), the Fills option will be unavailable. That's okay. Go ahead and select the colors, and the filled-in areas in the picture should change just fine.

**4.** Select a color you want to change in the **Original** list. A check mark appears in the check box next to the color.

**5.** From the **New** drop-down menu to the right of the selected color, choose the color you want.

**TIP**   **Using the Other Option**   At the bottom of each color's drop-down menu is the "Other" option. Select this option if you want to use a color that is not listed on the menu.

**6.** Repeat steps 3 through 5 for each color you want to change.

**7.** If you want to revert to an original color, remove the check mark from beside it.

**8.** Click **OK** to put your changes into effect.

# Drawing a Border Around a Picture

You can frame any object (a picture, a text box, or whatever) by drawing a border around the object. (This is the same as changing the line style and thickness on a drawn object.) To add a border to an object, perform the following steps in Slide view:

1. Select the object you want to frame with a border, such as a text box or clip art object.

2. Choose **Format**, **Colors and Lines**. A dialog box appears that's appropriate for the type of object you selected (for instance, Format Text Box for a text box); the Colors and Lines tab is on top (refer to Figure 16.1).

3. Open the **Color** drop-down list and choose a color for the line.

4. Open the **Style** drop-down list and choose a thickness and style for the line.

5. If you want the line to be dotted or dashed, open the **Dashed** drop-down list and choose a dash style.

6. Click **OK**, and the border appears around the object.

# Adding a Shadow or a 3-D Effect

A shadow gives some depth to an object. Applying a 3-D effect to an object does much the same thing, as you can see in Figure 16.3. The main difference is that a shadow just adds shading behind a two-dimensional object, while a 3-D effect attempts to make the object appear fully three-dimensional. Shadows work with all objects, but 3-D effects work only with drawn artwork.

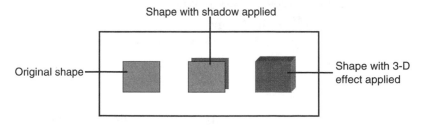

**Figure 16.3** Shadows and 3-D effects can keep your artwork from looking flat and boring.

# Adding a Shadow

To add a shadow to an object, perform these steps:

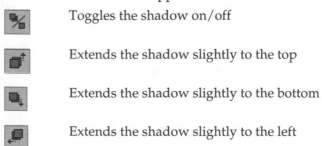

1. Select the object to which you want to add a shadow.
2. Click the **Shadow** tool on the Drawing toolbar. A menu of shadow options appears (see Figure 16.4).

Click here to remove a shadow from an object.

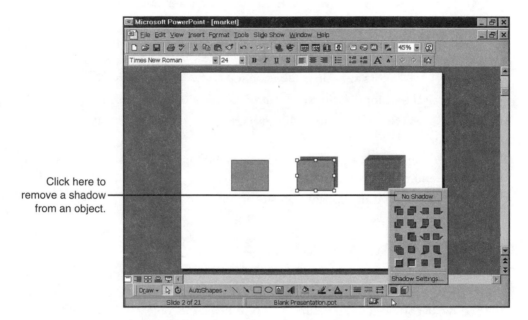

**Figure 16.4**  Click the type of shadow you want to use.

3. Click the type of shadow you want. The shadow is applied to the object.
4. (Optional) To make fine adjustments to the shadow, click the **Shadow** tool again and select **Shadow Settings.** Then select one of the following tools from the Shadow toolbar that appears:

   Toggles the shadow on/off

   Extends the shadow slightly to the top

   Extends the shadow slightly to the bottom

   Extends the shadow slightly to the left

Extends the shadow slightly to the right

 Changes the shadow color

# Adding a 3-D Effect

3-D effects are new for PowerPoint 97. They function like shadows, but they add more of a full three-dimensional look, as you can see in Figure 16.3.  Follow these steps to apply a 3-D effect to an object:

1. Select an object you've drawn with the Drawing toolbar tools (not an imported piece of clip art).

2. Click the **3-D** button on the Drawing toolbar. The 3-D tools appear (see Figure 16.5).

**Figure 16.5**  These 3-D tools enable you to apply a variety of special 3-D effects to a drawn object.

3. Click the 3-D effect that you want.

4. (Optional) Click the **3-D** button again and choose **3-D Settings**. Then select one of the following tools from the 3-D toolbar that appears:

 Toggles between 3-D and regular (2-D)    Adjust depth

 Tilt down    Adjust direction

 Tilt up    Adjust lighting

 Tilt left    Change surface

 Tilt right    Change color

**433**

# Copying the Look of Another Object

If your presentation contains an object that has the frame, fill, and shadow you want to use for another object, you can pick up those design elements and apply them to another object. To do this, perform the following steps:

1. Click the object with the style you want to copy.

 2. Click the **Format Painter** button on the Standard toolbar. PowerPoint copies the style.

3. Click the object to which you want to apply the style. PowerPoint applies the copied style to the new object.

In this lesson, you learned how to use borders, colors, shadows, and 3-D effects to change the look of individual objects on a slide. You also learned how to copy design elements from object to object. In the next lesson, you will learn how to change the background colors and designs that appear on every slide in the presentation.

# Working with Presentation Colors and Backgrounds

*In this lesson, you learn how to change the color scheme and background design of a presentation.*

## Understanding Color Schemes and Backgrounds

*Color schemes* are sets of professionally selected complementary colors that you can use as the primary colors of a presentation. Each color scheme controls the color of the background, lines, text, shadows, fills, and other items on a slide. Using one of these color schemes ensures that your presentation looks appealing and professional.

*Backgrounds* are designs that control the way color appears on a slide. For example, you can select a background that spreads the color out from the upper-left corner to the edges.

You can select a color scheme and background for the Slide Master (which controls all the slides in the presentation), for the current slide, or for all slides in the presentation (thus overriding the Slide Master). Also, you can change individual colors in a color scheme to customize it.

# Selecting a Color Scheme

The basic color scheme of your presentation depends on the active design template. You learned how to change design templates in Lesson 8—select **Format, Apply Design Template**. Design templates include both color schemes and backgrounds.

Within each design template are several variations of one color scheme. All the color schemes in a template use the same basic colors, but each color scheme arranges its colors differently. For example, for on-screen viewing, the color scheme is a dark background and light text; for printing on a color printer, a light background and dark text; and for printing on a one-color printer, a black-and-white color scheme.

You can select a color scheme for one slide or for all the slides in your presentation. To select a color scheme, perform the following steps:

1. If you don't want to change all the slides in the presentation, display or select the slide(s) with the color scheme you want to change.

2. Choose **Format, Slide Color Scheme**. The Color Scheme dialog box appears.

3. Click the **Standard** tab if it's not displayed. The color schemes available for the current design template appear (see Figure 17.1).

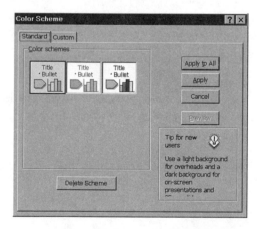

**Figure 17.1** You can choose a standard color scheme from those the current template offers.

**4.** Click one of the color schemes. Then click **Apply** to apply it to the selected slides, or click **Apply All** to apply it to all slides in the presentation.

# Customizing a Color Scheme

Even though each template comes with its own color scheme, you can customize the scheme for a presentation. You can adjust individual colors, or you can radically change them all.

**Be Consistent** Be careful when you change the colors on a single slide. You don't want one slide to clash with the rest of your slides.

**CAUTION**

Follow these steps to customize an existing color scheme:

**1.** If you don't want to change all the slides in the presentation, display or select the slide with the color scheme you want to change.

**2.** Choose **Format**, **Slide Color Scheme**. The Color Scheme dialog box appears.

**3.** Click the **Custom** tab. The dialog box changes, as shown in Figure 17.2.

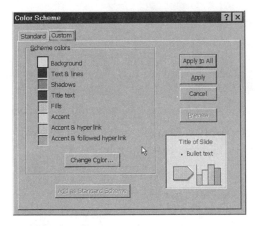

**Figure 17.2** You can change individual colors in a scheme with the Custom tab.

**4.** Click one of the colors (such as **Background**) and click the **Change Color** button. A dialog box appears that enables you to select a new color. For example, the Background Color dialog box is shown in Figure 17.3.

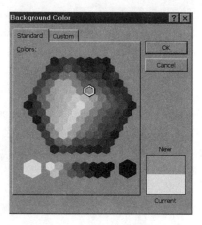

**Figure 17.3**   Each on-screen element has its own dialog box for customizing its color.

**5.** To select a color, click the **Standard** tab, click any color you see, and click **OK**. To create a new color, click the **Custom** tab, use the controls to custom select a color, and click **OK**.

**TIP**   **Custom Controls**   Most beginners use the Standard tab in step 5. There are enough colors shown there to suit most purposes. With the custom controls, you can fine-tune a color's hue, saturation, and luminescence, and you can adjust its red, green, and blue tones numerically.

**6.** Repeat steps 4 and 5 for each color you want to change.

**7.** Click **Apply to All** to apply the new colors to every slide in the presentation, or click **Apply** to apply the colors to the current slide only.

**TIP**   **More Background Controls**   You can change the color of the background using the Format, Slide Color Scheme command. But if you want to change the texture or pattern of the background, or if you want to use a picture as a background, you need to use the Custom Background command discussed later in this lesson.

## Copying a Color Scheme from One Slide to Another

If you want to change the color scheme for an entire presentation, it's best to make the changes to the Slide Master. However, if you want to change several slides, but not all of them, you can make the changes to a single slide and copy that slide's color scheme to the others. Follow these steps to copy a slide's color scheme:

1. Display your presentation in Slide Sorter view.
2. Select the slide containing the color scheme you want to copy.

3. Click the **Format Painter** button on the toolbar.
4. Click the slide to which you want to apply the color scheme.
5. Repeat the process to recolor each slide you want to change.

# Changing the Background Design

An effective background adds a professional look to any presentation. PowerPoint enables you to set the background to any color and to add patterns, textures, and shadings to it.

TIP   **PowerPoint on the Web**   If you are creating a presentation for use on the Web, try to keep the background light-colored, as it will be easier for your readers to view on their monitors. Save dark backgrounds for slides designed to be shown on large screens.

To change the background for your presentation or to modify the existing background, perform the following steps:

1. Display or select the slide with the background you want to change. To change the slide backgrounds in the entire presentation, display the Slide Master.
2. Choose **Format, Background** or right-click the background and select **Background** from the shortcut menu. The Background dialog box appears.
3. Open the **Background Fill** drop-down list (see Figure 17.4).

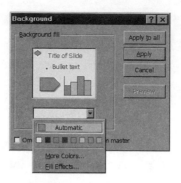

**Figure 17.4**  Choose a color from those shown, or click More Colors or Fill Effects.

**4.** Click one of the following options:

- **Automatic** sets the background to whatever the Slide Master currently shows as the background.

- **A solid color** sets the background to that color.

- **More Colors** opens a Color dialog box similar to the one shown in Figure 17.3, which offers a wide color assortment for you to choose from.

- **Fill Effects** opens a dialog box in which you can choose many special effects such as a gradient fill, textured backgrounds, or pictures used as backgrounds.

**Gradient Fill**  A gradient is where the background starts out one color at the top of the slide and gradually changes to another color. When one of those colors is white (or in some schemes black), it's known as a one-color gradient. When neither color is white (or black), it's a two-color gradient.

**5.** Click **Apply** to apply the background to this slide only, or click **Apply to All** to apply the background to all the slides in the presentation.

In this lesson, you learned how to select and modify a color scheme and how to copy a color scheme from one presentation to another. You also learned how to change the background color and design for a slide or presentation. In the next lesson, you will learn about viewing and enhancing your slide shows.

# Viewing and Enhancing a Slide Show

*In this lesson, you learn how to view a slide show on-screen, make basic movements within a presentation, and create action buttons that let you (or another user) control the action.*

Before you take your presentation "on the road" to show to your intended audience, you should run through it several times on your own computer, checking that all the slides are in the right order.

## Viewing an On-Screen Slide Show

You can preview a slide show at any time to see how the show looks in real life. To view a slide show, perform the following steps:

**1.** Open the presentation you want to view.

 **2.** Click the **Slide Show** button at the bottom of the presentation window. The first slide in the presentation appears full-screen.

**3.** To display the next or previous slide, do one of the following:

- To display the next slide, click the left mouse button, or press the **Page Down** key, or press the right arrow or down arrow key.

- To display the previous slide, click the right mouse button, or press the **Page Up** key, or press the left arrow or up arrow key.

- To quit the slide show, press the **Esc** key.

 TIP **Start the Show!** Clicking the **Slide Show** button is the fastest way to start a slide show. However, you can also start a slide show by selecting **View, Slide Show** or by selecting **Slide Show, View Show**.

# Controlling the Slide Show

While you view a slide show, you can do more than just move from slide to slide. When you move your mouse, notice the triangle in a box at the bottom left corner of the slide show (see Figure 18.1). Click that button, and PowerPoint displays a pop-up menu that contains commands you can use as you actually give the presentation. Those commands are outlined in the following list:

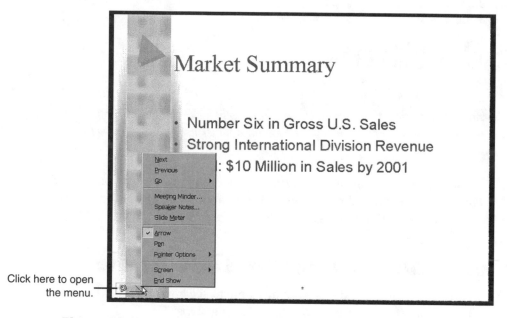

Click here to open the menu.

**Figure 18.1**  You can control the slide show while you present it with this menu.

- The **Next** and **Previous** commands enable you to move from slide to slide. (It's easier to change slides using other methods, though.)

- Choose **Go**, **Slide Navigator** to bring up a dialog box listing every slide in the presentation. You can jump quickly to any slide with it. You can also jump to a slide with a specific title (if you know it) by selecting **Go**, **Title** and choosing the title from the list.

- Click **Meeting Minder** to bring up a window where you can take notes as the meeting associated with your presentation progresses.

- Choose **Speaker Notes** to view your notes for the slide.

- Choose **Slide Meter** to open a dialog box that enables you to control the timing between slides. (More about timing shortly.)

**442**

- **Arrow** and **Pen** are mouse options; Arrow is the default. Your mouse can serve as an arrow to point out parts of the slide, or it can serve as a pen to write comments on the slide or circle key areas as you give your presentation. Keep in mind, however, that it is very difficult to write legibly using an ordinary mouse or trackball.

- **Pointer Options** enables you to choose a color for the pen and indicate whether to display or hide the pointer.

- **Screen** opens a submenu that enables you to pause the show, blank the screen, and erase any pen marks you made on the slide.

- **End Show** takes you back to PowerPoint's slide editing window.

# Setting Slide Show Options

Depending on the type of show you're presenting, you may find it useful to make some fine adjustments to the way the show runs, such as making it run in a window (the default is full-screen) or showing only certain slides. You'll find these controls and more in the Set Up Show dialog box (shown in Figure 18.2). To open it, choose **Slide Show**, **Set Up Show**.

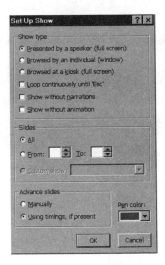

**Figure 18.2**   Use the Set Up Show dialog box to give PowerPoint instructions about how to present your slide show.

In this dialog box, you can:

- Choose which medium the presentation is going to be shown in. Your choices are Presented by a Speaker (Full Screen), Browsed by an Individual (Window), and Browsed at a Kiosk (Full Screen).

- Choose whether to loop the slide show continuously or just show it once. You might want to loop it continuously if it were running unaided at a kiosk at a trade show, for instance.

- Show without narration, if you have created any. (You'll learn about narration later in this lesson.)

- Show without animation, if you have added any.

- Show all the slides or a range of them (which you enter in the From and To boxes).

- Choose a custom show if you have created one. (To create a custom show, such as one that contains a subset of the main show's slides, select **Slide Show**, **Custom Show**.)

- Choose whether to advance slides manually or using timings you set up.

- Choose a pen color.

# Adding Action Buttons to Slides

In the preceding section, you saw how the Set Up Show dialog box enables you to choose between automatic and manual advance. In most cases, you will want to have the slides advance manually because different people read at different speeds. Even if you are creating a presentation for a speaker to give, you will usually want manual advancing because you can't anticipate when the speaker may need extra time to answer a question.

As you saw at the beginning of this lesson, one way to advance or go back in a slide show is to press the **Page Down** key or **Page Up** key on the keyboard. This simple method works fine, except for two things:

- In a kiosk-type setting, you may not want the audience to have access to the computer's keyboard.

- This method simply plods from slide to slide, with no opportunity to jump to special slides or jump to the beginning or end quickly.

A new feature that solves this problem in PowerPoint 97 is the capability of adding action buttons to slides. Action buttons are like controls on an audio CD player: they let you jump to any slide quickly, go back, go forward, or even stop the presentation.

**TIP** **Same Controls on All Slides?** If you want to add the same action buttons to all slides in the presentation, add the action buttons to the Slide Master. To display the Slide Master, select **View**, **Master**, **Slide Master**.

To add an action button to a slide, follow these steps:

1. Display the slide in Slide view.
2. Select **Slide Show**, **Action Buttons**, and then pick a button from the palette that appears next to the command (see Figure 18.3). For instance, if you want to create a button that advances to the next slide, you might choose the button with the arrow pointing to the right.

**Which Button Should I Choose?** Choose any button you like; at this point you are only choosing a picture to show on the button, not any particular function for it. However, you might consider the action that you want the button to perform, and then pick a button picture that matches it well.

**CAUTION**

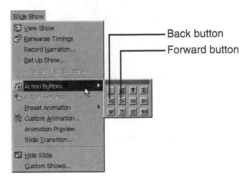

**Figure 18.3** Choose the button you think your reader will most strongly identify with the action you're going to assign to it.

3. Your mouse pointer turns into a crosshair. Drag to draw a box on the slide where you want the button to appear. (You can resize it later if you want, just as you resized graphics in Lesson 15.) PowerPoint draws the button on the slide and opens the Action Settings dialog box (see Figure 18.4).

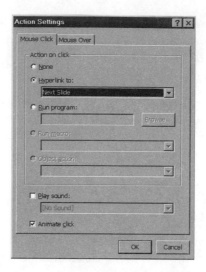

**Figure 18.4**  You can control the way one slide transitions to the next.

**4.** Choose the type of action you want to happen when the user clicks the button. Most of the time you will choose **Hyperlink To**. Your complete list of choices includes:

- **None**
- **Hyperlink To**    This can be a slide, an Internet hyperlink, a document on your computer—just about anything.
- **Run Program**    You can choose to have a program start when the user clicks the button.
- **Run Macro**    If you have recorded a macro, you can have the user run it from the button.
- **Object Action**    If you have embedded (OLE) objects in the presentation, you can have PowerPoint activate one when the button is clicked.

**5.** Open the drop-down list for the type of action you chose and select the exact action (such as **Next Slide**). Or, if you chose **Run Program**, click the **Browse** button and locate the program you want to run.

**6.** (Optional) If you want a sound to play when the user clicks the button, select the **Play Sound** check box and choose a sound from its drop-down list.

**7.** (Optional) If you want it to look animated when the user clicks the button (a nice little extra), leave the **Animate Click** check box marked.

**8.** Click **OK**, and your button appears on the slide.

**9.** View the presentation (as you learned at the beginning of this lesson) to try out the button.

Figure 18.5 shows three buttons added to a slide. Actually, they were added to the Slide Master, so the same buttons appear on each slide in the presentation. This kind of consistency gives the reader a feeling of comfort and control.

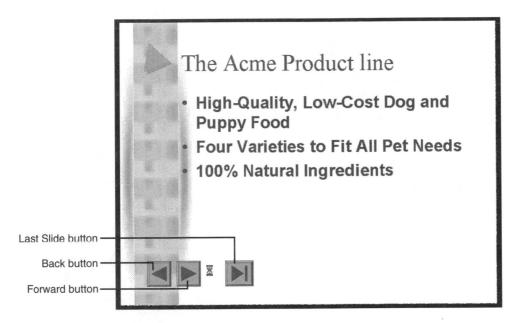

The Acme Product line

- **High-Quality, Low-Cost Dog and Puppy Food**
- **Four Varieties to Fit All Pet Needs**
- **100% Natural Ingredients**

Last Slide button

Back button

Forward button

**Figure 18.5** These control buttons display various slides in the presentation.

**No Controls on Slide 1** When you add action buttons to the Slide Master, they appear on every slide except the first one in the presentation. If you want action buttons on the first slide, you must specifically add them to that slide.

CAUTION

**Don't Group** Each action button must be an independent object on the slide. If you group them together, they won't work properly.

CAUTION

In this lesson, you learned how to display a slide presentation on-screen, move between slides, and create buttons on the slides to control the movement.

# Outlook

# Starting and Exiting Outlook

*In this lesson, you learn to start and exit Outlook.*

## Starting Outlook

You start Outlook from the Windows desktop. After starting the program, you can leave it open on your screen, or you can minimize it. Either way, you can access it at any time during your work day.

To start Microsoft Outlook, follow these steps:

1. From the Windows desktop, click the **Start** button and choose **Programs, Microsoft Outlook**. (If you have customized your Start menu, Outlook may appear within a folder, such as a Microsoft Office folder on the Programs menu.) Or if you have one, you can double-click the shortcut icon on the desktop.

2. If the Choose Profile dialog box appears, click **OK** to accept the default profile and open Microsoft Outlook. Figure 1.1 shows the Outlook screen that appears. (In Windows NT, Outlook cannot detect an existing e-mail provider. The user is prompted to set up the profile. If you need help see your system administrator.)

 **Profile** Information about you and your communications services that is created automatically when you install Outlook. The profile includes your name, user ID, post office, and so on.

3. If the Office Assistant Welcome to Microsoft Outlook box appears, click **OK**.

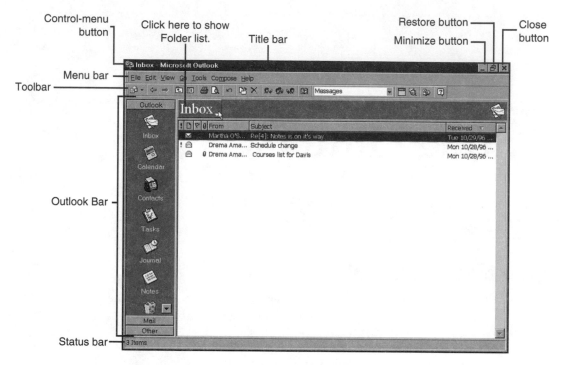

Control-menu button

Click here to show Folder list.

Title bar

Restore button

Minimize button

Close button

Menu bar

Toolbar

Outlook Bar

Status bar

**Figure 1.1**   The Outlook screen includes many icons and items you'll use daily.

# Understanding the Screen

The Outlook screen includes items you can use to navigate and operate the program. If you do not see some of the items listed below on your screen, open the **View** menu and select the command for the appropriate element (such as **Toolbars**, **Status Bar**, **Folder List**, or **Outlook Bar**). A check mark in front of an item means the item is currently showing. Table 1.1 describes the elements you see in the opening screen.

**Table 1.1**   Elements of the Outlook Window

| Element | Description |
| --- | --- |
| Title bar | Includes the name of the application and current folder, plus the Windows Minimize, Maximize, and Close buttons. |
| Control-menu button | Provides such commands as Move, Size, Minimize, and Close, with which you control the Outlook window. |

| Element | Description |
|---|---|
| Minimize button | Reduces the Outlook window to a button on the taskbar; to restore the window to its original size, click the button on the taskbar. |
| Maximize button | Enlarges the Outlook window to cover the Windows desktop. When the window is maximized, the Maximize button changes to a Restore button that you can click to return the window to its previous size. |
| Close (X) button | Closes the Outlook program. |
| Menu bar | Contains menus of commands you can use to perform tasks in the program. |
| Toolbar | Includes icons that serve as shortcuts for common commands, such as creating a new message or printing a message. (See the inside back cover for a description of each tool.) |
| Show Folder list | Displays the current folder. Click this to display a list of Personal Folders you can open. |
| Outlook Bar | Displays icons representing folders: Inbox, Calendar, Contacts, and so on. Click an icon to change to the folder it names. |
| Status bar | Displays information about the contents of the selected folder. |

 TIP  **Finding a Toolbar Button's Purpose**  You can hold the mouse pointer over any toolbar button to view a description of the tool's function.

# Exiting Outlook

When you're finished with Outlook, you can close the program in a couple of different ways. To close Outlook, do one of the following:

- Choose **File, Exit** (to remain connected to the mail program).
- Choose **File, Exit and Log Off** (to disconnect from the mail program).
- Double-click the application's **Control-menu** button.
- Click the application's **Control-menu** button and choose **Close**.
- Press **Alt+F4**.
- Click the **Close** (X) button at the right end of Outlook's title bar.

In this lesson, you learned to start and exit Outlook. In the next lesson, you'll learn about Outlook's tools and controls.

# Using Outlook's Tools

*In this lesson, you learn to change views in Outlook, use the Outlook Bar, and use the Folder List.*

## Using the Outlook Bar

Outlook's components are organized by folder. There is a folder for e-mail, a folder for the calendar, and so on. The Outlook Bar is a tool you can use to quickly change folders in Outlook. The icons in the Outlook Bar represent all of the folders available to you and provide shortcuts to getting to the contents of those folders. Figure 2.1 shows the Outlook Bar.

There are three groups within the Outlook Bar: Outlook, Mail, and Other. Each group contains related folders in which you can work. The Outlook group contains folders for working with different features in Outlook, such as the Inbox, Calendar, Tasks, and so on. The Mail group contains folders for organizing and managing your mail. And the Other group contains folders on your computer for working outside of Outlook. To switch from one group to another, click the **Outlook**, **Mail**, or **Other** button in the Outlook Bar. The Outlook group is displayed by default.

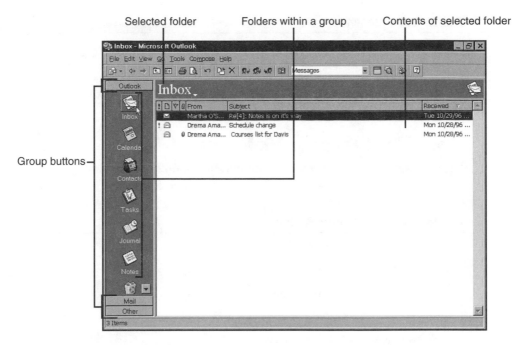

Selected folder      Folders within a group      Contents of selected folder

**Figure 2.1** Use the Outlook Bar to view various items in your work.

# The Outlook Group Folders

The Outlook group's folders in the Outlook Bar enable you to access your work in Outlook. That includes your mail messages, appointments, address list, and so on. Table 2.1 describes each of the folders within the Outlook group.

**Table 2.1** Outlook Group Folders

| Folder | Description |
| --- | --- |
| Inbox | Includes messages you've sent and received via e-mail. |
| Calendar | Contains your appointments, events, scheduled meetings, and so on. |
| Contacts | Lists names and addresses of the people with whom you communicate. |
| Tasks | Includes any tasks you have on your to-do list. |
| Journal | Contains all journal entries, such as phone logs, meeting notes, and so on. |

*continues*

**Table 2.1** Continued

| Folder | Description |
| --- | --- |
| Notes | Lists notes you write yourself or others. |
| Deleted Items | Includes any items you've deleted from other folders. |

# The Mail Group Folders

The Mail group folders provide a method of organizing your incoming and outgoing e-mail messages. Table 2.2 describes each folder in the Mail group.

**Table 2.2** Mail Group Folders

| Folder | Description |
| --- | --- |
| Inbox | Contains all received messages. |
| Sent Items | Stores all messages you've sent. |
| Outbox | Contains messages to be sent. |
| Deleted Items | Holds any deleted mail messages. |

# The Other Group Folders

The Other group contains folders that are on your computer but not within Outlook: My Computer, My Documents, and Favorites. This enables you to access a document or information in any of those areas so that you can attach it to a message, add notes to it, or otherwise use it in Outlook.

For example, with My Computer, you can view the contents of both hard and floppy disks, CD-ROM drives and so on (see Figure 2.2). Double-click a drive in the window to view its folders and files. Double-click a folder to view its contents as well. Then you can attach files to messages or otherwise use the files on your hard drive with the Outlook features.

 **TIP** **Moving On Up** Use the Up One Level toolbar button to return to a folder or drive after you've double-clicked to expand it and view its contents.

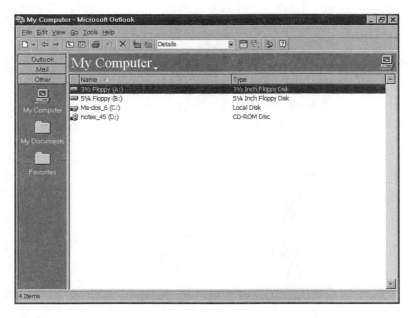

**Figure 2.2**   View your entire system through the My Computer folder in Outlook.

# Using the Folder List

Outlook provides another method of viewing the folders within Outlook and your system: the Folder List. The Folder List displays the folders within any of the three groups (Outlook, Mail, or Other). From the list, you can select the folder you want to view.

To use the Folder List, first select the group you want to view from the Outlook Bar. Then click the **Folder List** button to display the list (see Figure 2.3).

Choose any folder from the list, and its contents appear in the list on the right. If you display another folder in the list on the right, double-click it to display its contents.

Click here to display
the Folder List.

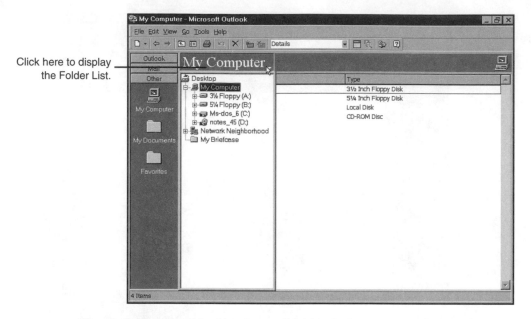

**Figure 2.3**   The Folder List shows all folders in the group you selected.

# Changing Views

In Outlook, views give you different ways to look at the same information in a folder. Each view presents the information in a different format and organization so you can get the most from the program. The following list outlines the view types and provides a brief description of each. A view type determines the basic structure of the view; within each view type, you can change the way you see the information.

**Table view type**   Presents items in a grid of sorts—in rows and columns. Use this view type to view mail messages, tasks, and details about any item.

**Timeline view type**   Displays items as icons arranged in chronological order from left to right on a time scale. Use this to view journal entries and other items in this type of view.

**Day/week/month view type**   Displays items in a calendar view in blocks of time. Use this type for meetings and scheduled tasks.

**Card view type**   Presents items like cards in a card file. Use this to view contacts.

**Icon view type**   Provides graphic icons to represent tasks, notes, calendars, and so on.

 **TIP**   **Looking at the Inbox**   The default view for your Inbox is called Messages with AutoPreview. In it, items appear in columns and rows.

Each folder—Inbox, Calendar, Contacts, and so on—displays its contents in a particular view type, as previously described. Additionally, within each view type, you have a choice of views that further fine-tune the presentation of the information on-screen. You can change a view by clicking the **Current View** drop-down list on the standard toolbar (see Figure 2.4).

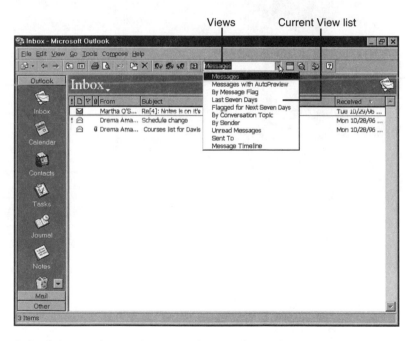

**Figure 2.4**   Select a view to change the format of the information.

As you can see in Figure 2.4, within the Table view type of the Inbox, you can change views so that you can see all messages, messages from the last seven days, messages organized by sender, unread messages only, and so on. Similarly, the Calendar folder—which is arranged in the Day/Week/Month view type by default—enables you to view active appointments, events, recurring appointments, and so on (see Figure 2.5).

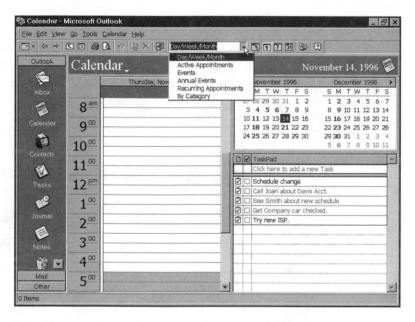

**Figure 2.5** You can choose how to view the contents of the Calendar folder.

As you work your way through the Outlook part of this book, you'll see examples of each view type. When you change folders in Outlook, take a quick look at the available views in the Current View drop-down list.

In this lesson, you learned to change views in Outlook, use the Outlook Bar, and use the Folder List. In the next lesson, you learn to work with incoming mail.

# Working with Incoming Mail

*In this lesson, you learn to read your mail, save an attachment, answer mail, and close a message.*

## Reading Mail

When you log on to Outlook, your Inbox folder appears, and any new messages you've received are waiting for you (see Figure 3.1). As you can see in this figure, the Inbox provides important information about each message. For example, two messages have been labeled as high priority, one is low priority, and one message has an attachment. You'll learn about priorities and attachments in Lesson 7, "Setting Mail Options." In addition, the Status bar at the bottom of the Inbox window indicates how many items the Inbox folder contains and how many of those items are unread.

**TIP**

     **Welcome!**   The first time you log on, you may find a welcome message from Microsoft in your Inbox. After you read the message, you can delete it by selecting it and pressing the **Delete** key.

To open and read your messages, follow these steps:

1. Double-click a mail message to open it. Figure 3.2 shows an open message.
2. To read the next or previous mail message in the Inbox, click the **Previous Item** or the **Next Item** button on the toolbar. Or you can open the **View** menu, choose **Previous** or **Next**, and choose **Item**.

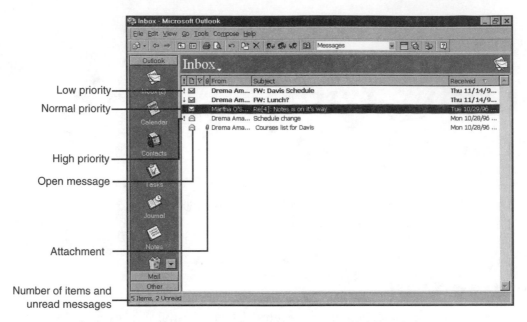

Low priority

Normal priority

High priority

Open message

Attachment

Number of items and
unread messages

**Figure 3.1** Review the sender and subject before opening your mail.

Read previous mail item          Read next mail item

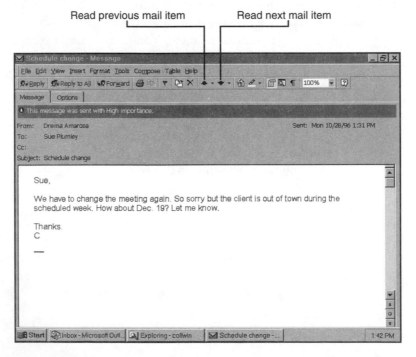

**Figure 3.2** The Message window displays the message and some tools for handling
this message or moving on to another.

**Item**  Outlook uses the word "item" to describe a mail message, an attached file, an appointment or meeting, a task, and so on. "Item" is a generic term in Outlook that describes the currently selected element.

You can mark messages as read or unread by choosing **Edit**, **Mark As Read** or **Edit Mark As Unread**. Outlook automatically marks messages as read when you open them. But you might want to mark messages yourself once in a while (as a reminder, for example). Additionally, you can mark all of the messages in the Inbox as read at one time by choosing **Edit**, **Mark All As Read**. You might want to mark mail messages as read so you don't read them again; you might want to mark important mail as unread so you'll be sure to open it and read it again.

**No Mail?**  If you don't see any new mail in your Inbox, choose **Tools**, **Check for New Mail**, and Outlook will update your mail for you. You can choose **Tools**, **Check for New Mail On** to specify a service other than the default.

# Saving an Attachment

You will often receive messages that have files or other items attached. In the Inbox list of messages, an attachment is represented by a paper clip icon beside the message. You'll want to save any attachments sent to you so you can open, modify, print, or otherwise use the document. Messages can contain multiple attachments.

To save an attachment, follow these steps:

1. Open the message containing an attachment by double-clicking the message. The attachment appears as an icon in the message text (see Figure 3.3).

2. (Optional) You can open the attachment from within the message by double-clicking the icon. The application in which the document was created—Word or Excel, for example—opens and displays the document in the window, ready for you to read. Close the application by choosing **File**, **Exit**.

3. In the message, select the attachment you want to save and choose **File**, **Save Attachments**. The Save Attachment dialog box appears (see Figure 3.4).

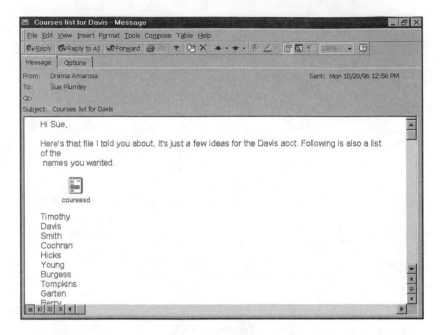

**Figure 3.3**  An icon represents the attached file.

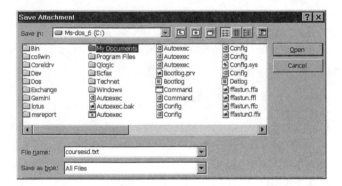

**Figure 3.4**  Save the attachment to a convenient folder.

**4.** Choose the folder in which you want to save the attachment and click
**Save**. (You can change the name of the file if you want.) The dialog box
closes, and you're returned to the Message window. You can open the
attachment at any time from the application in which it was created.

# Answering Mail

You might want to reply to a message after you read it. The Message window enables you to answer a message immediately, or at a later time if you prefer. To reply to any given message, open the message and follow these steps:

**1.** Click the **Reply** button or choose **Compose**, **Reply**. The Reply Message window appears, with the original message in the message text area and the sender of the message already filled in for you (see Figure 3.5).

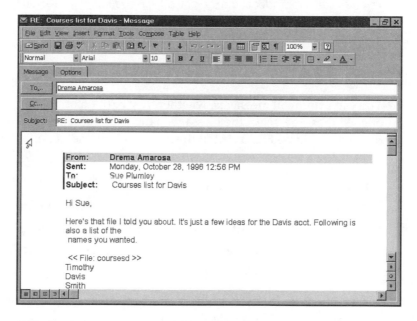

**Figure 3.5** Reply to a message quickly and easily.

**TIP** **Reply to All** If you receive a message that has also been sent to others—as either a message or a "carbon copy" (Cc)—you can click the **Reply to All** button to send your reply to each person who received the message.

**2.** The insertion point is in the message text area, ready for you to enter your reply. Enter the text.

**3.** When you finish your reply, click the **Send** button or choose **File**, **Send**. Outlook sends the message.

You also can send a reply from the Inbox, without opening the message. Suppose, for example, you already read the message and closed it, but now you've decided you want to reply. Select the message in the Inbox list and click the **Reply** button. The Reply Message window appears with the original message in the text area and the sender's name in the To area. Enter your text and send the message as you learned in the previous steps.

 **TIP**  **Reminder**   The next time you open a message; to which you've replied, you'll see a reminder at the top of the Message tab that tells you the date and time you sent your reply.

# Printing Mail

You can print mail messages, whether they're open or not. To print an unopened message, select the message in the message list of the Inbox or other folder and choose **File**, **Print**. If the message is already open, you can follow the steps below:

**1.** Open the message in Outlook.

**2.** Use one of the following methods to tell Outlook to print:

- Click the **Print** button on the toolbar to print using defaults.
- Choose the **File**, **Print** command to view the Print dialog box.
- Press **Ctrl+P**.

**3.** In the Print dialog box, click **OK** to print one copy of the entire message using the printer's default settings.

 **TIP**  **More Print Info**   See Lesson 16, "Printing in Outlook," for detailed information about configuring pages, setting up the printer, and so on.

# Closing a Message

When you finish with a message, you can close it in any of the following ways:

- Choose **File**, **Close**.
- Click the **Control-menu** button and click **Close**.

- Press **Alt+F4**.
- Click the **Close** (X) button in the title bar of the Message window.

In this lesson, you learned to read your mail, save an attachment, answer mail, and close a message. In the next lesson, you will learn to manage your mail messages.

# Managing Mail

4

*In this lesson, you learn to delete and undelete messages, forward messages, and organize messages by saving them to folders.*

## Deleting Mail

You may want to store some important messages, but you'll definitely want to delete much of the mail you receive. Once you've answered a question or responded to a request, you probably won't have need for a reminder of that transaction. You can easily delete messages in Outlook when you're finished with them.

To delete a mail message that is open, do one of the following:

- Choose **Edit, Delete**.
- Press **Ctrl+D**.
-  Click the **Delete** button on the toolbar.

If you have modified the message in any way, a confirmation message appears from the Office Assistant or as a message dialog box. Otherwise, the message is deleted without warning.

If you're in the Inbox and you want to delete one or more messages from the message list, select the single message to delete (or hold down Ctrl and click each message). Then do one of the following:

- Press the **Delete** key.
-  Click the **Delete** button on the toolbar.

# Undeleting Items

If you change your mind and want to get back items you've deleted, you can usually retrieve them from the Deleted Items folder. By default, when you delete an item, it doesn't disappear from your system; it merely moves to the Deleted Items folder. Items stay in the Deleted Items folder until you delete them from that folder—at which point they are unrecoverable.

To retrieve a deleted item from the Deleted Items folder, follow these steps:

1. Click the **Deleted Items** icon in the Outlook Bar to open the folder.

2. Select the items you want to retrieve and drag them to the folder containing the same type of items on the Outlook Bar. Alternatively, you can choose **Edit**, **Move to Folder**, choose the folder to which you want to move the selected items, and click **OK**.

# Emptying the Deleted Items Folder

If you're really sure you want to delete the items in the Deleted Items folder, you can erase them from your system. To delete items in the Deleted Items folder, follow these steps:

1. In the Outlook Bar, choose the **Outlook** group and select the **Deleted Items** folder. All deleted items in that folder appear in the message list, as shown in Figure 4.1.

 2. To permanently delete an item, select it in the Deleted Items folder, and then click the **Delete** tool button or choose **Edit**, **Delete**. (You can choose more than one item by holding down the **Shift** or **Ctrl** key and clicking each one.)

3. Outlook displays a confirmation dialog box asking if you're sure you want to permanently delete the message. Choose **Yes** to delete the selected item.

4. To switch back to the Inbox or another folder, select the folder from either the Outlook Bar or the Folders List.

 **TIP**   **Automatic Permanent Delete**   You can set Outlook to permanently delete the contents of the Deleted Items folder every time you exit the program. To do so, choose **Tools**, **Options** and click the **General** tab. In the General Settings area, select **Empty the Deleted Items Folder Upon Exiting** and click **OK**.

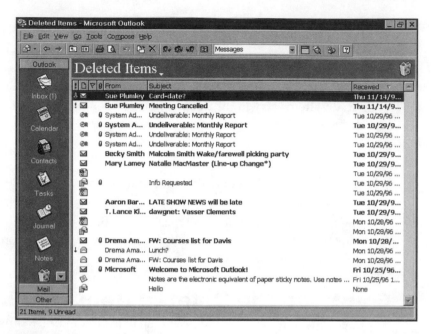

**Figure 4.1** Deleted messages remain in the Deleted Items folder until you permanently delete them.

# Forwarding Mail

Suppose you want to forward mail you receive from a coworker to another person who has an interest in the message. You can forward any message you receive, and you can even add comments to the message if you want.

**Forward Mail** When you forward mail, you send a message you received to another person on the network; you can add your own comments to the forwarded mail, if you want.

You forward an open message or a message selected in the message list in the Inbox in the same way. To forward mail, follow these steps:

1. Select or open the message you want to forward. Then click the **Forward** button or choose **Compose**, **Forward**. The FW Message dialog box appears (see Figure 4.2).

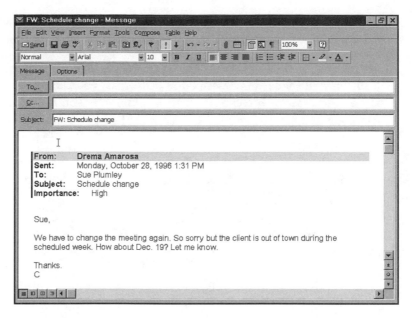

**Figure 4.2**  When you forward a message, the original message appears at the bottom of the message window.

**2.** In the **To** text box, enter the names of the people to whom want to forward the mail. (If you want to choose a person's name from a list, click the **To...** button to display the Select Names dialog box, and then select the person's name.). Lesson 5 explains more about using the Address Book. If you enter multiple names in the To box, separate the names with a semi-colon and a space.

**3.** (Optional) In the **Cc** text box, enter the names of anyone to whom you want to forward *copies* of the message (or click the **Cc...** button and choose the name from the list that appears).

**4.** In the message area of the window, enter any message you want to send with the forwarded text. The text you type will be a different color.

**5.** Click the **Send** button or choose **File**, **Send**.

# Saving Mail to a Folder

Although you'll delete some mail after you read and respond to it, you'll want to save other messages for future reference. You can save a message to any folder you want, but you should use a logical filing system to ensure that you'll be able find each message again later. Outlook offers several methods for organizing your mail.

The easiest method of saving mail to a folder is to move it to one of Outlook's built-in Mail folders (as described in Lesson 2). You can use any of the folders to store your mail, or you can create new folders. Lesson 17, "Maintenance and Management," describes how to create your own folders within Outlook.

To move messages to an existing folder, follow these steps:

**1.** Select one message (by clicking it) or select multiple messages (by **Ctrl**+clicking).

 TIP  **Making Backup Copies**  You can also copy a message to another folder as a backup. To do so, choose **Edit**, **Copy to Folder**.

**2.** Choose **Edit**, **Move to Folder** or click the **Move to Folder** tool button on the toolbar. The Move Items dialog box appears (see Figure 4.3).

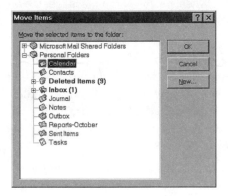

**Figure 4.3**  Choose the folder to which you want to move the selected message(s).

**3.** Select the folder you want to move the item to and click **OK**. Outlook moves the item to the folder for you.

To view the message(s) you've moved, choose the folder from the Outlook Bar or the Folders List. Then click the item you want to view.

In this lesson, you learned to forward messages, delete messages, and organize messages by saving them to folders. In the next lesson, you will learn to work with address books.

# Using the Address Book

*In this lesson, you learn to use Outlook's address book with your e-mail.*

## Using the Postoffice Address List

All of the names within your organization usually appear on the Postoffice Address List created by your system's mail administrator. Anytime you want to send or forward an e-mail, you can select the recipients from that list instead of typing in their names manually. If you're using Windows NT on a network, you may or may not have access to the Postoffice Address List, depending on your permissions and rights. If you have questions, see your network administrator.

**Post Office**   A directory, usually located on the network server, that contains a mailbox for each e-mail user. When someone sends a message, that message is filed in the recipient's mailbox until the recipient receives the mail and copies, moves, or deletes it.

**Postoffice Address List**   A list of everyone who has a mailbox in the post office; it's controlled by the mail administrator.

**Mail Administrator**   The person who manages the e-mail post office. (This person might also be the network administrator, but it doesn't necessarily have to be the same person.)

To use the Postoffice Address List, choose **Tools**, **Address Book** or click the **Address Book** tool button on the toolbar. The Address Book dialog box appears, as shown in Figure 5.1.

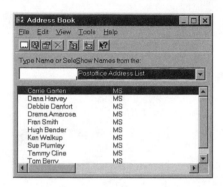

**Figure 5.1** View the Postoffice Address List.

The following list outlines some of the ways in which you might use the Address List:

- To view more details about any entry in the Address Book dialog box, double-click the person's name or click the **Properties** button on the toolbar. The person's Properties dialog box appears, with his or her name, address type, postoffice name, and network type listed on the Address (1) tab. Click **OK** to close this dialog box and return to the Address Book dialog box.

- Click the **Properties** toolbar button and choose the **Address (2)** tab in the person's Properties dialog box to view his or her phone number, office, or department, and any notes or comments that have been added to the description. Click **OK** to close this dialog box and return to the Address Book dialog box.

- To send a message to someone listed in the Address Book, select the name from the Address List and choose **File**, **New Message**. See Lesson 6 for more information.

- If you cannot find a particular name in the list, you can search for it. Choose **Tools**, **Find** or click the **Find** button, and then enter the name for which you're searching in the **Find Name Beginning With** text box. Click **OK** to start the search.

# Using the Personal Address Book

The Personal Address Book contains the names and e-mail addresses of people you contact frequently. You may want to include coworkers from your department, or even people from outside of your office (whom you contact via Internet addresses).

**TIP**   **What Is This?**   You may notice the Outlook Address Book in the list of address books; this book contains entries you create in your Contacts list. For more information about the Contacts list, see Chapter 14.

**CAUTION**   **No Personal Address Book Is Listed?**   If you do not see a Personal Address Book in the Address Book dialog box, you can easily add it to your resources. Close the address book and choose **Tools, Services**. In the Services tab of the dialog box, click the **Add** button, choose **Personal Address Book** from the list, and click **OK**. In the Personal Address Book dialog box, select your preference and click **OK**. Close the Services dialog box and open the address book again; you'll see the Personal Address Book in the list. You may have to exit and restart Outlook.

To add names to the Personal Address Book, follow these steps:

1. Choose **Tools, Address Book** or click the **Address Book** tool button on the toolbar. The Address Book dialog box appears (refer to Figure 5.1).

2. To add name(s) from the Postoffice Address List, select the name(s), and then click the **Add to Personal Address Book** button on the toolbar or choose **File, Add to Personal Address Book**. The name(s) remain on the Postoffice Address List, but Outlook copies them to your Personal Address Book as well.

3. To view your Personal Address Book, select the **Show Names** from the drop-down list and choose **Personal Address Book**. The list changes to display those names you've added to your personal address list, but the dialog box looks the same.

4. To add a completely new address to your Personal Address Book, click the **New Entry** button or choose **File, New Entry**. The New Entry dialog box appears (see Figure 5.2).

**5.** In the **Select the Entry Type** list, choose from the available options. What options you see will depend on the information systems installed to your network; for example, Microsoft Mail, Internet Mail, or some other service may be available. You can add an address entry that corresponds with one of the available information systems.

Additionally, you can choose to add one of the following two items:

**Personal Distribution List**   Use this to create one address entry for a group of recipients. When you send mail to the list name, everyone on the list receives the message. You might use this option for grouping department heads, for example.

**Other Address**   Choose this option to add one new recipient at a time. You can enter a name, e-mail address, and e-mail type for each entry. In addition, you can enter business addresses and phone numbers, and you can add notes and comments to the entry. Use this entry for Internet addresses, for example.

**6.** When you're done working in your Personal Address Book, close the window by choosing **File**, **Close**. You're returned to the Outlook Inbox.

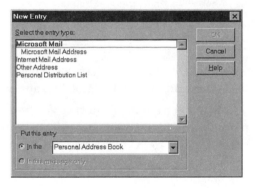

**Figure 5.2**   Choose a source for your new entry.

# Entering an Address in a Message

You can use either address book to choose the names of recipients to whom you want to send new messages, forward messages, or send a reply. Using the address books also makes sending carbon copies and blind carbon copies easy.

**Blind Carbon Copy**   A blind carbon copy (Bcc) of a message is a copy that's sent to someone in secret; the other recipients have no way of knowing that you're sending the message to someone via a blind carbon copy.

To address a message, follow these steps:

1. Choose **Compose**, **New Mail Message** from the Outlook Inbox window.

2. In the Message window, click the **To** button to display the Select Names dialog box.

3. Open the **Show Names from the** drop-down list box and choose either the **Postoffice Address List** or the **Personal Address Book**.

4. From the list that appears on the left, choose the name of the intended recipient and select the **To** button. Outlook copies the name to the Message Recipients list. (You can add multiple names if you want.)

5. (Optional) Select the names of anyone to whom you want to send a carbon copy and click the **Cc** button to transfer those names to the Message Recipients list.

6. (Optional) Select the names of anyone to whom you want to send a blind carbon copy and click the **Bcc** button. Figure 5.3 shows a distribution group listing as the To recipient of a message; in addition, two people are selected to receive blind carbon copies of the same message.

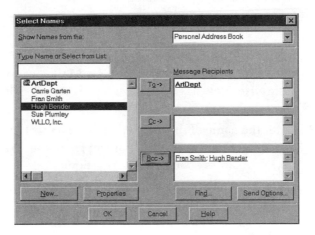

**Figure 5.3** Address messages quickly with the Select Names dialog box.

7. Click **OK** to return to the Message window and complete your message. (For more information about writing messages, see Lesson 6.)

In this lesson, you learned to use the address book with your e-mail. In the next lesson, you will learn to compose a message and format it.

# Creating Mail

6

*In this lesson, you learn to compose a message, format text, check your spelling, and send mail.*

## Composing a Message

You can send a message to anyone for whom you have an address, whether he or she is in your address book or not. And in addition to sending a message to one or more recipients, you can send copies of a message to others on your address list. (See Lesson 5, "Using the Address Book," for information about addressing a message and sending carbon copies.)

To compose a message, follow these steps:

1. In the Outlook Inbox, click the **New Mail Message** button or choose **Compose, New Mail Message**. The Untitled - Message window appears (see Figure 6.1).

2. Enter the name of the recipient in the **To** text box, or click the **To...** button and select the name of the recipient from your Address Book. (See Lesson 5 for information about the Address Book.)

3. Enter the name of anyone to whom you want to send a copy of the message in the **Cc** text box, or click the **Cc...** button and select a name or names from the Address Book.

4. In the **Subject** text box, enter the subject of the message.

5. Click in the text area, and then enter the text of the message. You do not have to press the Enter key at the end of a line; Outlook automatically wraps the text at the end of a line for you. You can use the Delete and Backspace keys to edit the text you enter.

6. When you finish typing the message, you can send the message right away (see "Sending Mail" later in this lesson), or you can check the spelling and formatting as described in the following sections.

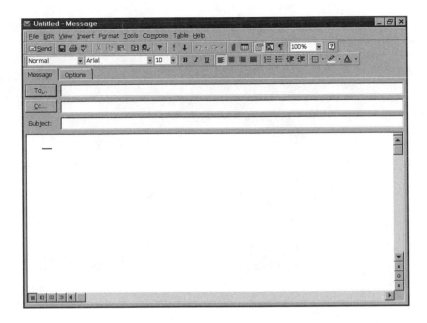

**Figure 6.1** Compose a new message in the Untitled - Message window.

**No Address!** If you try to compose a message to someone without entering an address, Outlook displays the Check Names dialog box, in which it asks you to create an address. You can search for the name among the existing addresses, or you can create a new address for the name in much the same way you would create a new entry in the Address Book (see Lesson 5).

# Formatting Text

You can change the format of the text in your message to make it more attractive, to make it easier to read, or to add emphasis. Any formatting you do transfers to the recipient with the message if the recipient has Outlook; however, if the recipient doesn't have Outlook, formatting may not transfer.

There are two ways to format text. You can format the text after you type it by selecting it and then choosing a font, size, or other attribute; or you can select the font, size, or other attribute and then enter the text.

To format the text in your message, follow these steps:

**1.** If the Formatting toolbar is not showing, choose **View**, **Toolbars**, **Formatting**. Figure 6.2 shows a message with the Formatting Toolbar displayed. Table 6.1 explains the buttons on this toolbar.

**479**

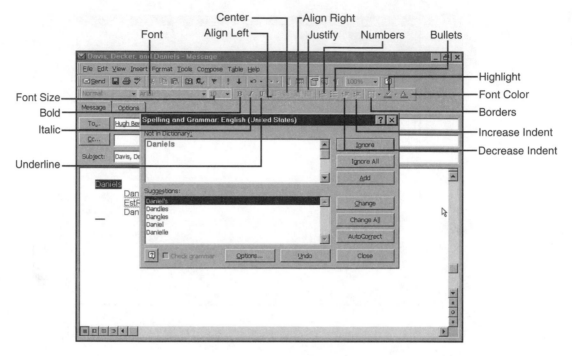

**Figure 6.2** Use the Formatting toolbar to modify your message text.

**2.** To apply a font to the selected or about-to-be-entered text, click the **Font** drop-down arrow on the Formatting toolbar. Scroll through the font list, if necessary, to view all fonts on the system, and then click the font you want to apply to the text.

 **TIP    Quick Format**   You can also format text by choosing **Format**, **Font** and selecting a font, size, style, and so on from the Font dialog box. You also can assign bullets and alignment to text by choosing **Format**, **Paragraph**.

**3.** Assign a size by clicking the **Font Size** drop-down arrow and choosing the size; alternatively, you can enter a size in the **Font Size** text box.

**4.** To choose a color, click the **Font Color** tool button and select a color from the palette box that appears.

**5.** Choose a type style to apply to text by clicking the **Bold**, **Italic**, and/or **Underline** buttons on the Formatting toolbar.

**6.** Choose an alignment by selecting the **Align Left**, **Center**, or **Align Right** button from the Formatting toolbar.

7. Add bullets to a list by clicking the **Bullets** button on the Formatting toolbar.

8. Create text indents or remove indents in half-inch increments by clicking the **Increase Indent** or **Decrease Indent** buttons. (Each time you click the Indent button, the indent changes by half an inch.)

# Checking Spelling

To make a good impression and to maintain your professional image, you should check the spelling in your mail messages before you send them. Outlook includes a spelling checker you can use for that purpose. If you're using Word as your e-mail editor, you'll notice that your grammar is automatically checked as well.

To check the spelling in a message, follow these steps:

1. In the open message, choose **Tools, Spelling and Grammar** or press **F7**. If the spelling checker finds a word whose spelling it questions, it displays the Spelling dialog box (shown in Figure 6.3). If it does not find any misspelled words, a dialog box appears, with a messsage that the spelling and grammar check is complete; click **OK** to close that dialog box.

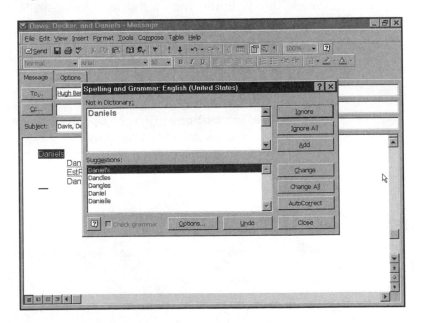

**Figure 6.3**  Check your spelling before sending a message.

**2.** You can do any of the following in response to the word Outlook questions in the Spelling dialog box:

> **Not in Dictionary**   Enter the correct spelling in this text box.
>
> **Suggestions**   Select the correct spelling in this text box, and it automatically appears in the Change To text box.
>
> **Ignore**   Click this button to continue the spelling check without changing this occurrence of the selected word.
>
> **Ignore All**   Click this button to continue the spelling check without changing any occurrence of the word in question throughout this message.
>
> **Change**   Click this button to change this particular occurrence of the word in question to the spelling in the Change To text box.
>
> **Change All**   Click this button to change the word in question to the spelling listed in the Change To text box every time the spelling checker finds the word in this message.
>
> **Add**   Click this button to add the current spelling of the word in question to the dictionary so that Outlook will not question future occurrences of this spelling.
>
> **Undo**   Click this button to reverse the last spelling change you made, thus returning the word to its original spelling.
>
> **Cancel**   Click this button to quit the spelling check.

**3.** When the spelling check is complete, Outlook displays a message box telling you it's done. Click **OK** to close the dialog box.

 TIP   **Set Your Spelling Options**   Click the **Options** button in the Spelling dialog box to set options that tell Outlook to do such things as ignore words with numbers, ignore original message text in forwarded messages or replies, always check spelling before sending, and so on.

# Sending Mail

When you're ready to send your mail message, do one of the following:

- Click the **Send** button.
- Choose **File, Send**.
- Press **Ctrl+Enter**.

**TIP**  **AutoSignature**  Choose **Tools**, **AutoSignature** to have Outlook automatically add a message, quotation, or other text at the end of every message you send. Additionally, after you create an autosignature, you can quickly add it to any message by choosing **Insert**, **AutoSignature**.

 **TIP**  **Using Windows NT 4.0?**  You'll need to check your rights and permissions in relation to sending e-mail within your network. Ask your system administrator for more information.

In this lesson, you learned to compose a message, format text, check your spelling, and send mail. In the next lesson, you'll learn to set mail options and how to tell if the recipient has received your message.

# Setting Mail Options

*In this lesson, you learn to set options for messages and delivery, and for tracking messages.*

## Customizing Options

Outlook provides options that enable you to mark any message with priority status so that the recipient knows you need a quick response, or with a sensitivity rating so your words cannot be changed by anyone after the message is sent. With other available options, you can enable the recipients of your message to vote on an issue by including voting buttons in your message and having the replies sent to a specific location.

You also can set delivery options. For example, you can schedule the delivery of a message for a specified delivery time or date if you don't want to send it right now.

To set message options, open the Untitled - Message window and click the **Options** tab. As you can see in Figure 7.1, the options on this tab are separated into four areas. The next four subsections discuss each of the groups of options in detail.

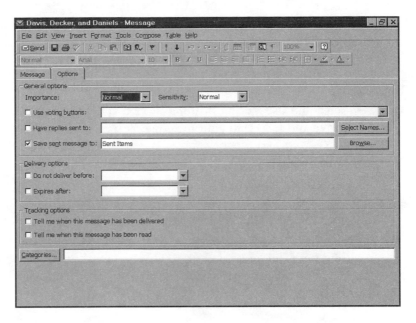

**Figure 7.1** Use the Options tab to govern how your message is sent.

# General Options

In the General Options area, set any of the following options for your message:

- Click the **Importance** drop-down arrow and choose a priority level of **Low**, **Normal**, or **High** from the list. (Alternatively, you could click the **Importance High** or **Importance Low** tool button on the toolbar.) When importance isn't specified, the message is given Normal Importance.

- Click the **Sensitivity** drop-down arrow and choose one of the following options:

  Normal   Use this option to indicate that the message's contents are standard or customary.

  **Personal**   Use this option to suggest that the message's contents are of a personal nature.

  **Private**   Use this option to prevent the message from being modified after you send it.

  **Confidential**   Use this option to denote the message's contents as restricted or private.

**TIP**   **You Can Mark All Messages As Private**   You can mark all of your messages so that no one can tamper with your words by choosing **Tools**, **Options** and clicking the **Sending** tab. In the **Set Sensitivity** box, choose the level you want.

- Select the **Use Voting Buttons** check box to add the default choices (Approve and Reject) to your message. You can also add Yes and No choices or Yes, No, and Maybe choices. If you want to provide other choices, enter your own text in the text box.

- Choose the **Have Replies Sent To** check box and specify in the text box the person to whom you want the replies sent. You can use the **Select Names** button to view the Address Book and choose a name if you want.

- Select the **Save Sent Message To** check box to save your message to the Sent Items folder by default. Or specify another folder to save the message in, using the Browse button and the resulting dialog box if necessary to locate the folder.

## Delivery Options

In addition to message options, you can set certain delivery options, such as scheduling the time of the delivery. In the Delivery Options area of the Options tab (Message window), choose one or both of the following check boxes:

**Do Not Deliver Before**   Check this option to specify a delivery date. Click the down arrow in the text box beside the option to display a calendar on which you can select the day.

**Expires After**   Select this check box to include a day, date, and time of expiration. You can click the down arrow in the text box to display a calendar from which you can choose a date, or you can enter the date and time yourself.

## Tracking Options

You might want to set tracking options so you'll know when the message has been delivered and/or read. Tracking options are like receipts: they notify you that the message arrived safely. You set tracking options from the Options tab of the Untitled - Message window.

Choose one or both of the following Tracking Options: **Tell Me When This Message Has Been Delivered** and **Tell Me When This Message Has Been Read**.

# Categories

Outlook enables you to assign messages to certain categories—such as Business, Goals, Hot Contacts, Phone Calls, and so on. You set the category for a message in the Categories dialog box.

**Categories** Categories offer a way of organizing messages to make them easier to find, sort, print, and manage. For example, to find all of the items in one category, choose **Tools**, **Find Items**. Click the **More Choices** tab, choose **Categories**, and check the category for which you're searching.

To assign a category, follow these steps:

**1.** In the Options tab of the Message window, click the **Categories** button. The Categories dialog box appears (see Figure 7.2).

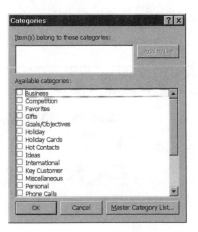

**Figure 7.2** Organize your messages with categories.

**2.** To assign an existing category, select the category or categories that best suit your message from the Available Categories list. To assign a new category, enter a new category in the **Item(s) Belong to These Categories** text box, and then click the **Add to List** button.

**3.** Click **OK** to close the Categories dialog box and return to the Message window.

# Using Message Flags

A message flag enables you to mark a message as important, either as a reminder for yourself or as a signal to the message's recipient. When you send a
message flag, a red flag icon appears in the recipient's message list, and Outlook
adds text at the top of the message telling which type of flag you are sending. In
addition, you can add a due date to the flag, and that date appears at the top of
the message.

The following list outlines the types of flags you can send in Outlook:

| | |
|---|---|
| Call | No Response Necessary |
| Do not Forward | Read |
| Follow Up | Reply |
| For Your Information | Reply to All |
| Forward | Review |

To use a message flag, follow these steps:

**1.** In the Message window, click the **Message Flag** tool or choose **Edit**,
**Message Flag**. The Flag Message dialog box appears (see Figure 7.3).

**Figure 7.3**  Flag a message to show its importance.

**2.** Click the **Flag** drop-down arrow and choose the flag text you want to add
to the message.

**3.** Click the **By** drop-down arrow and select a date from the calendar, or enter
a date manually in the text box.

**4.** Click **OK** to return to the Message window.

**TIP** **View the Message Header**   You can view just the header of a message to allow you more message text room, if you want to hide the Cc, Bcc, and Subject lines. Choose **View**, **Message Header** to show only the To text box and any flag text; select **View**, **Message Header** again to redisplay the Cc, Bcc, and Subject fields.

In this lesson, you learned to set options for messages and delivery, and for tracking messages. In the next lesson, you will learn to attach items to messages.

# Attaching Items to a Message

8

*In this lesson, you learn to attach a file, an object (such as an embedded file), and other items (such as an appointment or task) to a message.*

## Attaching a File

You can attach any type of file to an Outlook message, which makes for a convenient way of sending your files over the network to your coworkers. You might send Word documents, Excel spreadsheets, a PowerPoint presentation, or any other document you create with your Windows applications.

When you send an attached file, it appears as an icon in the message. When the recipient gets the file, he or she can open it within the message or save it for later use. However, the recipient must have the source program that you used to create the file on his or her computer. For instance, if you send a colleague a Microsoft Word file, he must have Microsoft Word in order to view the file he receives.

To attach a file to a message, follow these steps:

1. In the Message window, position the insertion point in the message text, and then choose **Insert**, **File** or click the **Insert File** toolbar button. The Insert File dialog box appears (see Figure 8.1).

2. From the **Look In** drop-down list, choose the drive and folder that contains the file you want to attach.

3. Using the **Files of Type** drop-down list, choose the file type—such as Excel or Word.

4. Select the file you want to attach.

5. Click **OK** to insert the file into the message. Figure 8.2 shows a file inserted as an attachment.

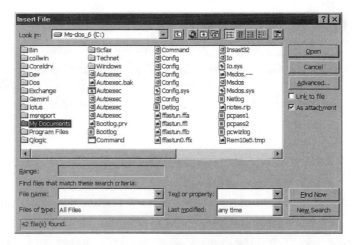

**Figure 8.1**   Select the file you want to attach to a message.

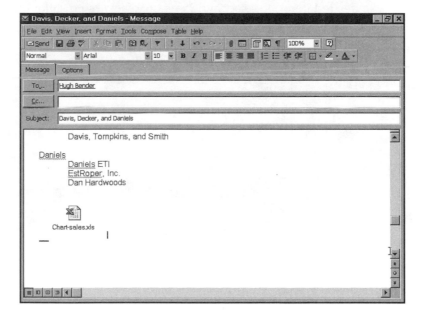

**Figure 8.2**   The recipient can double-click the icon to open the file.

# Attaching Outlook Items

In addition to attaching files from other programs, you can also attach an Outlook item to a message. An Outlook item can be any document saved in one of your personal folders, including a calendar, contacts, journal, notes, tasks, and so on. You can attach an Outlook item in the same manner you attach a file.

Follow these steps to attach an Outlook item:

**1.** In the Message window, choose **Insert**, **Item**. The Insert Item dialog box appears.

**2.** From the **Look In** drop-down list, choose the folder containing the item you want to include in the message.

**3.** Select from the items that appear in the **Items** list (see Figure 8.3). To select multiple adjacent items, hold the **Shift** key and click the first and last desired items; to select multiple nonadjacent items, hold the **Ctrl** key and click the items.

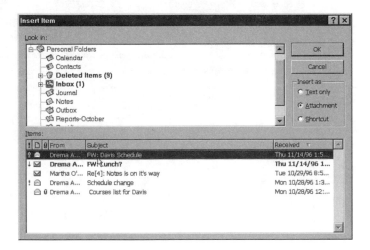

**Figure 8.3**   Select items from any folder in Outlook.

**4.** In the Insert As area, choose from the following option buttons:

> **Text Only**   Inserts the file as text into the message; if your file is not saved as an ASCII or other text-only file, do not use this option.
>
> **Attachment**   Inserts an icon representing the document. The actual file follows the message to the recipient; the recipient saves it as his or her own copy.

> **Shortcut** Inserts a Windows shortcut icon into the text. This option is best used only if the file is stored on a network drive from which the recipient can easily access it through a shortcut.

**CAUTION**

**Text Only Is Only for Text!** If you try to insert a file from Word, Excel, or another application as Text Only, you'll end up with a lot of "garbage" characters in the text. That's because these programs' files contain special formatting codes. The only time you will use Text Only is when you export the data from its native program into a text-only file first.

**5.** Click **OK**, and Outlook inserts the selected items in your message.

**CAUTION**

**It Doesn't Work Without Outlook** If the recipient doesn't have Outlook on his computer, he will not be able to view the attached item. If you know the recipient doesn't have the program, you'll need to cut and paste the data into the message or simply retype it.

# Inserting an Object

Just as you can insert an object—a spreadsheet, chart, drawing, presentation, media clip, clip art, WordArt, and so on—in any Windows application that supports *OLE*, you can also insert an object into an Outlook mail message.

**TERM**

**OLE (Object Linking and Embedding)** A method of exchanging and sharing data between applications; OLE is supported by most Windows applications and all Microsoft programs.

You can insert an existing object into a message, or you can create an object within a message using the source application. For example, you could create an Excel chart within your message using Excel's features through OLE.

When you send a message with an attached object, the object travels with the message to the recipient. As long as the recipient has the application on his computer, he can open the object and view it.

For more information about OLE, see Lesson 5, "Object Linking and Embedding," in Part 7 of this book.

To attach an existing object to a message, follow these steps:

**1.** In the Message window, position the insertion point in the message text and choose **Insert**, **Object**. The Object dialog box appears.

**2.** Click the **Create from File** tab (see Figure 8.4).

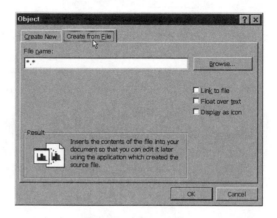

**Figure 8.4**  Insert an object to send with a message.

**3.** In the **File Name** text box, enter the path and the name of the file you want to insert. (You can use the **Browse** button and the resulting dialog box to find the file if you want.)

**4.** Click **OK**. Outlook inserts the object into the message.

After you save and open an object you've received in a message, you can resize the object to suit your needs. First select it, and a frame appears with eight small black boxes (called *handles*) on the corners and along the sides. To resize the object, position the mouse pointer over one of the black handles; the mouse pointer becomes a two-headed arrow. Click and drag the handle to resize the object.

To edit an object, double-click within the frame, and the source application opens from within Outlook. Note that you'll still see your Outlook message and Outlook toolbars; however, you'll also see some Excel tools you can use to edit the object. Figure 8.5 shows an Excel chart object within a message. Notice the Chart toolbar and several chart icons added through OLE for use in editing.

Chart toolbar

Tool buttons added
for Excel chart

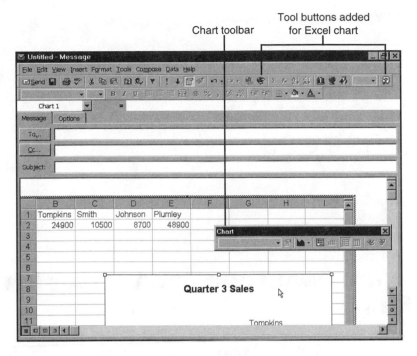

**Figure 8.5**   Edit the object from within your Outlook message.

In this lesson, you learned to attach a file, an object, and other items to a message. In the next lesson, you will learn to organize messages.

# Organizing Messages

*In this lesson, you learn to view sent items, create folders, and move items to a new folder.*

## Viewing Sent Items and Changing Defaults

By default, Outlook saves a copy of all mail messages you send. It keeps these copies in the Sent Items folder, which is part of the Mail group of the Outlook Bar. You can view a list of sent items at any time, and you can open any message in that list to review its contents.

### Viewing Sent Items

To view sent items, follow these steps:

**1.** In the Outlook Bar, choose the **Mail** group.

 **TIP** **Save Time** You can select the Sent Items folder from the Folder List instead of following steps 1–3.

**2.** If necessary, scroll to the Sent Items folder.

**3.** Click the **Sent Items** icon, and Outlook displays a list of the contents of that folder. Figure 9.1 shows the Sent Items list. All messages you send remain in the Sent Items folder until you delete or move them.

**Figure 9.1**  You can open any sent message by double-clicking it.

**4.** (Optional) To view a sent item, double-click it to open it. When you finish with it, click the **Close** (X) button.

# Changing Sent Items Defaults

You can control how Outlook saves copies of your sent messages. To change the default settings for the Sent Items folder, follow these steps:

**1.** Choose **Tools, Options**, and the Options dialog box appears.

**2.** Click the **Sending** tab.

**3.** Choose one or all of the following options (located near the bottom of the dialog box):

> **Save Copies of Messages in "Sent Items" Folder**   When this is checked, Outlook saves copies of all sent messages to the specified folder. (When the check box is empty, no copies of messages are saved automatically.)

> **In Folders Other Than the Inbox, Save Replies with Original Messages**   When this is checked, Outlook saves replies to messages in the same folder in which you store the original message. (When the

check box is empty, it saves replies to the Sent Items folder as long as you've checked the previous check box.)

**Save Forwarded Messages** When this is checked, Outlook saves a copy of each forwarded message you send.

4. Click **OK** to close the dialog box.

**CAUTION**

**Too Much Mail!** If you save all the mail you receive and send, you may accumulate so much mail that you run the risk of running out of disk space. You can and should periodically delete mail from the Sent Items folder by selecting the mail and pressing the **Delete** key; you'll also need to remove the deleted mail from the Deleted Items folder. See Lesson 4, "Managing Mail," for more information. Alternatively, you can create an archive file of the messages you've sent. The archive enables you to save items on disk or elsewhere on the system. See Lesson 19, "Archiving Items," for details.

# Creating Folders

You'll likely want to organize your mail in various folders to make storing items and finding them more efficient. You can create folders within Outlook that make it easier to manage your mail and other items in Outlook.

To create a folder, follow these steps:

1. Choose **File**, **Folder**, **Create Subfolder**. The Create New Folder dialog box appears (see Figure 9.2).

2. In the **Name** text box, enter a name for the folder.

3. Click the **Folder Contains** drop-down arrow, and choose the type of items the folder will store: Mail, Appointments, Contact, Journal, Note, or Task.

4. In the **Make This Folder a Subfolder Of** list, choose the folder in which you want to create the new folder. You can, for example, make the new folder a subfolder of Personal Folders so that it appears in lists with all of the Outlook folders. Or you might want to make it a subfolder of Sent Mail.

5. (Optional) In the **Description** text box, add a comment or brief description of the folder.

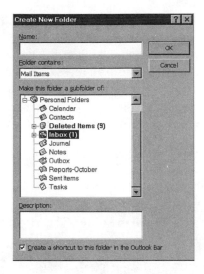

**Figure 9.2**   Create folders to organize your mail and other items.

**6.** (Optional) Click the **Create a Shortcut to This Folder in the Outlook Bar** check box to remove the check mark if you prefer not to see the folder in the Outlook Bar. (By default, the check box is checked so that you will see the new folder in the Outlook Bar.)

**7.** Click **OK** to close the dialog box. The new folder appears on the Outlook Bar and in the Folder List.

**TIP**   **Add Folder Later**   Even if you choose not to add the folder to the Outlook Bar when you create the folder, you can add it later. You simply choose **File**, **Add to Outlook Bar**. In the dialog box that appears, you can select any folder name in Outlook or on the system and add it to the Outlook Bar by selecting it and clicking **OK**.

**CAUTION**   **I Want to Delete a Folder!**   If you added a folder by accident or you change your mind about a folder you've added, you can delete it from Outlook. To delete a folder, select it and then choose **File**, **Folder**, **Delete** *foldername*. You also can rename, move, and/or copy the folder using the commands in the secondary menu that appears when you choose File, Folder.

# Moving Items to Another Folder

You can move items from one folder in Outlook to another; for example, you might create a folder to store all messages pertaining to a specific account or report. You can easily move those messages to the new folder and open them later for reference purposes. You also can forward, reply, copy, delete, and archive any items you move from one folder to another.

To move an item to another folder, follow these steps:

1. From the Inbox or any Outlook folder, open the message you want to move.

2. Choose **File**, **Move to Folder**. The Move Item to dialog box appears (see Figure 9.3).

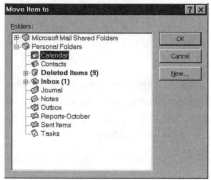

**Figure 9.3**  Choose the folder in which you want to store the message.

3. In the list of folders, select the folder to which you want to move the message.

4. Click **OK**. When you close the message, Outlook stores it in the designated folder.

You can quickly move an unopened message by dragging it from the open folder in which it resides to any folder icon in the Outlook Bar. You can also open the message at any time by opening the folder from the Outlook bar and double-clicking the message. After opening it, you can forward, send, print, or otherwise manipulate the message as you would any other.

In this lesson, you learned to view sent items, create folders, and move items to a folder. In the next lesson, you'll learn to use the Calendar.

# Using the Calendar

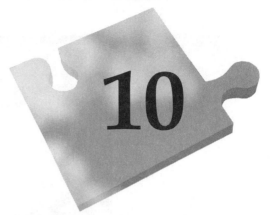

**10**

*In this lesson, you learn to navigate the Calendar, create appointments, and save appointments.*

## Navigating the Calendar

You can use Outlook's Calendar to schedule appointments and create a to-do list, if necessary, to remind you of daily or weekly tasks. You can schedule appointments months in advance, move appointments, cancel appointments, and so on. And the Calendar makes it easy to identify the days on which you have appointments.

To open the Outlook Calendar, click the **Calendar** icon in the Outlook Bar or select the **Calendar** folder from the Folder List. Figure 10.1 shows the Calendar in Outlook.

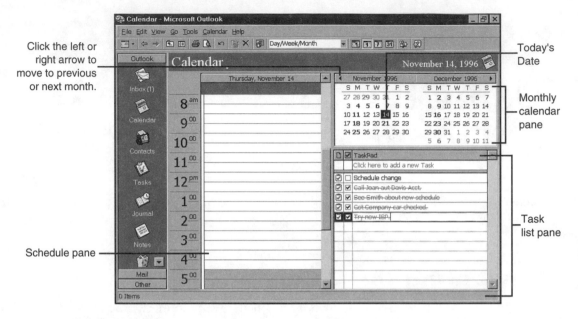

**Figure 10.1**  You can view all appointments and tasks at a glance.

Outlook provides multiple ways for you to move around in the Calendar and view specific dates:

- Scroll through the schedule pane to view the time of the appointment.
- In the monthly calendar pane, click the left and right arrows next to the names of the months to go backward and forward one month at a time.
- In the monthly calendar pane, click a date to display that date in the schedule pane.
- To view a full month in the schedule pane, select the name of the month in the monthly calendar pane.
- To view a week or selected days in the schedule pane, select the days in the monthly calendar pane.
- To add a task to the Task list, click where you see **Click here to add a new Task**.
- Use the scroll bars for the Task list pane to view appointments, if necessary.

**TIP**    **Change the Date Quickly**    To quickly go to today's date or to a specific date without searching through the monthly calendar pane, right-click in the schedule pane and choose either **Go To Today** or **Go To Date**.

# Creating an Appointment

You can create an appointment on any day well past the year 2000 using the Outlook Calendar. When you create an appointment, you can add the subject, location, starting time, category, and even an alarm to remind you ahead of time.

Follow these steps to create an appointment:

**1.** In the monthly calendar pane, select the month and the date for which you want to create an appointment.

**2.** In the schedule pane, double-click next to the time at which the appointment is scheduled to begin. The Untitled - Appointment dialog box appears, with the Appointment tab displayed (see Figure 10.2).

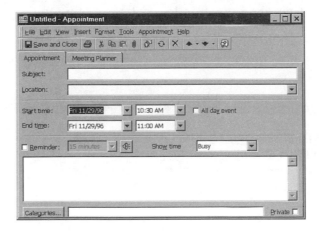

**Figure 10.2**   Enter all the details you need when scheduling an appointment.

**3.** Enter the subject of the appointment in the **Subject** text box (you can use a person's name, a topic, or other information).

**4.** In the **Location** text box, enter the meeting place or other text that will help you identify the meeting when you see it in your calendar.

5. Enter dates and times in the **Start Time** and **End Time** text boxes (or click the drop-down arrows and select the dates and times).

**TIP**   **Autodate It!**   You can use Outlook's Autodate feature: enter a text phrase such as "next Friday" or "noon" in the date and time text boxes, and Outlook figures out the date for you.

6. Select the **Reminder** check box and enter the amount of time before the appointment that you want to be notified. If you want to set an audio alarm, click the alarm bell button and select a specific sound for Outlook to play as your reminder.

7. From the **Show Time As** drop-down list, choose how you want to display the scheduled time on your calendar.

8. In the large text box near the bottom of the Appointment tab, enter any text that you want to include, such as text to identify the appointment, reminders for materials to take, and so on.

9. Click the **Categories** button and assign a category to the appointment.

10. Click the **Save and Close** button to return to the calendar.

The Meeting Planner tab enables you to schedule a meeting with coworkers and enter the meeting on your Calendar. See Lesson 11 for more information.

# Scheduling a Recurring Appointment

Suppose you have an appointment that comes around every week or month, or that otherwise occurs on a regular basis. Instead of scheduling every individual occurrence of the appointment, you can schedule that appointment in your calendar as a recurring appointment.

To schedule a recurring appointment, follow these steps:

1. In the Calendar folder, choose **Calendar, New Recurring Appointment**. The Appointment dialog box appears, and then the Appointment Recurrence dialog box appears (as shown in Figure 10.3).

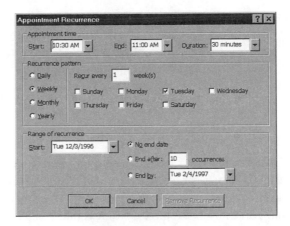

**Figure 10.3**   Schedule a recurring appointment once, and Outlook fills in the appointment for you throughout the Calendar.

**2.** In the Appointment Time area, enter the **Start**, **End**, and **Duration** times for the appointment.

**3.** In the Recurrence Pattern area, indicate the frequency of the appointment: **Daily**, **Weekly**, **Monthly**, or **Yearly**. After you select one of these options, the rest of the Recurrence Pattern area changes.

**4.** Enter the day and month, as well as any other options in the Recurrence Pattern area that are specific to your selection in step 3.

**5.** In the Range of Recurrence area, enter appropriate time limits according to these guidelines:

> **Start**   Choose the date on which the recurring appointments will begin.
>
> **No End Date**   Choose this option if the recurring appointments are not on a limited schedule.
>
> **End After**   Choose this option and enter the number of appointments if there is a specific limit to the recurring appointments.
>
> **End By**   Choose this option and enter an ending date to limit the number of recurring appointments.

**6.** Click **OK** to close the Appointment Recurrence dialog box. The Appointment dialog box appears.

7. Fill in the Appointment dialog box as described previously in this lesson. When you finish, click the **Save and Close** button to return to the Calendar. The recurring appointment appears in your calendar on the specified date and time. A recurring appointment contains a double arrow icon to indicate that it is recurring.

# Planning Events

In the Outlook Calendar, an *event* is any activity that lasts at least 24 hours, such as a trade show or a conference. You can plan an event in the Calendar program to block off larger time slots than you would for normal appointments. In addition, you can schedule recurring events.

To schedule an event, choose **Calendar**, **New Event**. The Event dialog box appears; it looks very much like the New Appointment dialog box. Fill in the **Subject**, **Location**, **Start Time**, and **End Time** text boxes. Make sure the **All Day Event** check box is checked (that's the only difference between an Event and an Appointment). Click the **Save and Close** button to return to the Outlook Calendar. The appointment appears in gray at the beginning of the day for which you scheduled the event.

To schedule a recurring event, choose **Calendar**, **New Recurring Event**. Fill in the Appointment Recurrence dialog box as you learned to in the previous section. When you close the Appointment Recurrence dialog box, the Recurring Event dialog box appears. Fill it in as you would the Event dialog box. Then click the **Save and Close** button.

To edit an event or a recurring event, double-click the event in your calendar. As with a mail message or appointment, Outlook opens the event window so you can change times, dates, or other details of the event.

In this lesson, you learned to navigate the Calendar, create appointments, and save appointments. In the next lesson, you will learn to plan a meeting.

# Planning a Meeting

*In this lesson, you learn to schedule a meeting, enter attendees for a planned meeting, set the meeting date and time, and invite others to the meeting.*

## Scheduling a Meeting

Outlook provides a method by which you can plan the time and date of a meeting, identify the subject and location of the meeting, and invite others to attend the meeting. You use the Calendar folder to plan and schedule meetings.

**Meeting**   In Outlook, a meeting is an appointment to which you invite people and resources.

**Attendees**   The people who will be attending your meeting.

**Resources**   Any equipment you use in your meeting, such as a computer, slide projector, or even the room itself.

To plan a meeting, follow these steps:

**1.** Click the icon for the Calendar folder, and then choose **Calendar, Plan a Meeting**. The Plan a Meeting dialog box appears (see Figure 11.1).

**2.** To enter the names of the attendees, click in the All Attendees list where it says **Type Attendee Name Here**. Enter the name and press **Enter**. Continue adding new names as necessary.

**TIP**   **Invite More People**   You can click the **Invite Others** button to choose names from your Personal Address Book or the Outlook Address Book.

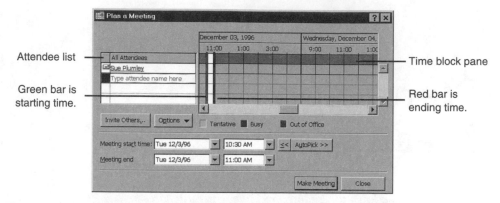

**Figure 11.1**  Choose the date and time of your meeting as well as the attendees.

3. To set a date for the meeting, open the leftmost **Meeting Start Time** drop-down list and select the date from the calendar, or just type the date in the text box. The ending date (in the Meeting End Time drop-down list) automatically shows the same date you set in the Meeting Start Time date box; you can change the End Time date if you want.

4. To set a start time for the meeting, do one of the following:
   - Open the rightmost **Meeting Start Time** drop-down list and select the time.
   - Type a time in the text box.
   - Drag the green bar in the time block pane of the dialog box to set the start time.

5. To set an end time for the meeting, do one of the following:
   - Open the rightmost **Meeting End Time** drop-down list and select the end time.
   - Type a time in the text box.
   - Drag the red bar in the time block pane of the dialog box to change the ending time of the meeting.

6. When you finish planning the meeting, click the **Make Meeting** button. The Meeting window appears (see Figure 11.2), from which you can refine the meeting details, as described in the next section.

# Working Out Meeting Details

After you plan a meeting, Outlook enables you to send invitations, identify the subject of the meeting, and specify the meeting's location. You enter these details in the Meeting dialog box.

When you schedule a meeting (as described in the previous section) you finish by clicking the Make Meeting button in the Plan a Meeting dialog box. When you do that, Outlook displays the Meeting dialog box with the Appointment tab in front (see Figure 11.2).

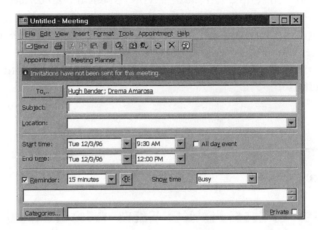

**Figure 11.2** Specify the details about the meeting in the Appointment tab of the Meeting dialog box.

Follow these steps to specify meeting details for a meeting you've already scheduled.

1. If you did not list the attendees in the Plan a Meeting dialog box, either click in the **To** text box and enter the names of the people you want to attend the meeting, or click the **To** button to select the attendees from an address book.

2. In the **Subject** text box, enter a subject for the meeting.

3. In the **Location** text box, enter a location for the meeting.

4. (Optional) You can change the starting and ending dates and/or times in the Appointment tab. You also can choose the Meeting Planner tab to view the meeting in a format similar to that of the Plan a Meeting dialog box;

make any changes to attendees, time, dates, and so on in the Meeting Planner tab.

**5.** (Optional) Select the **Reminder** check box and enter a time for Outlook to sound an alarm to remind you of the meeting.

**6.** (Optional) Enter any special text you want to send the attendees in the text box provided.

**7.** When you're ready to send the invitations to the meeting, click the **Send** button. Close the Meeting window by choosing **File**, **Close**.

When you send an invitation, you're sending an e-mail that requests the presence of the recipient at the meeting. The recipient can reply to your message, save your message, and forward or delete the message, just as he can with any other e-mail message. If you want the recipient to reply, choose **Appointment**, **Request Responses**, and the recipients will be prompted to reply to your invitation.

**An Invitation Mistake** To cancel an invitation after you've sent it, choose Appointment, Cancel Invitation.

CAUTION

# Inviting Others to the Meeting

If you need to add names to your attendees list—either while you're planning the meeting or at some later date—you can use your personal address book and/or the Outlook address book to find the names of the people you want to invite. Additionally, you can choose whether to make the meeting required or optional for each person you invite.

To invite others to the meeting, follow these steps:

**1.** In either the Plan a Meeting dialog box or the Meeting Planner tab of the Meeting dialog box, click the **Invite Others** button. The Select Attendees and Resources dialog box appears, as shown in Figure 11.3.

**2.** Open the **Show Names from The** drop-down list and choose either **Personal Address Book** or **Outlook Address Book**.

**3.** To add a new name to a list, click the **New** button, and then enter the name, e-mail address, phone numbers, and other pertinent information about the name you're adding to the list.

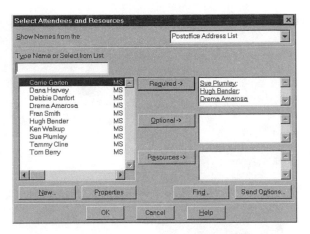

**Figure 11.3**  Use the address books to specify attendees to your meeting.

**4.** Select any name in the list on the left side of the dialog box and click the **Required** or **Optional** button to specify attendance requirements.

TIP  **Reserve Resources**  Click the **New** button to add resources to the list; then notify the person who is in charge of those resources of your meeting.

**5.** Click **OK** to close the dialog box and add any attendees to your list.

# Editing a Meeting

You can edit the details about a meeting, invite additional people, or change the date and time of the meeting at any time by opening the Meeting dialog box.

To open the Meeting dialog box and edit the meeting, follow these steps:

**1.** In the Calendar folder, choose the meeting date in the monthly calendar pane. The date appears in the schedule pane, and the meeting is blocked out for the time period you specified, as shown in Figure 11.4.

**2.** Double-click the meeting block to display the Meeting dialog box. You can edit anything in the Appointment or Meeting Planner tabs.

TIP  **Any Responses?**  Choose the **Show Attendee Status** option in the Meeting Planner tab of the Meeting dialog box to see if the people you invited to the meeting have responded to your invitation.

**511**

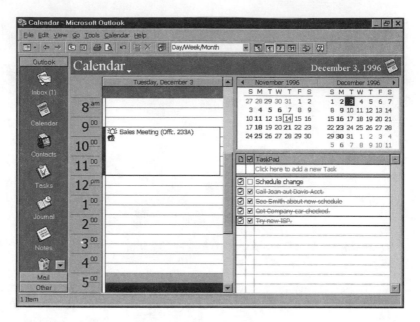

**Figure 11.4**  Select the meeting you want to edit from within the Calendar.

**3.** When you're done, choose **File**, **Close** to close the Meeting dialog box.
If you've made changes to the meeting specifics, you should also send
a message to your attendees to notify them of the change.

In this lesson, you learned to schedule a meeting, enter attendees for a planned
meeting, set the meeting time, and invite others to the meeting. In the next
lesson, you'll learn to create a contacts list.

# Creating a Contacts List

*In this lesson, you learn to create and view a Contacts list, and to send mail to someone on your Contacts list.*

## Creating a New Contact

You use the Contacts folder to create, store, and utilize your Contacts list. You can enter any or all of the following information about each contact:

- Name
- Job title
- Company name
- Address (Street, City, State, ZIP, Country)
- Phone (business, home, business fax, mobile)
- E-mail address
- Web page address
- Comments, notes, or descriptions
- Categories

**Contact**  In Outlook, a contact is any person or company for which you've entered a name, address, phone number, or other information. You can communicate with a contact in Outlook by sending an e-mail message, scheduling a meeting, sending a letter, and so on.

You also can edit the information at any time, add new contacts, or delete contacts from the list. To create a new contact, follow these steps:

1. Click the **Contacts** button or choose the **Contacts** folder. If you haven't used the list before, the folder is empty.

2. Choose **Contacts**, **New Contact**, or simply click the **New Contact** button on the Toolbar. The Contact dialog box appears, with the General tab displayed (see Figure 12.1).

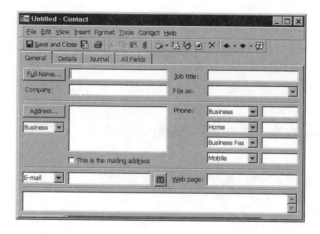

**Figure 12.1**  You can enter as much or as little information about each contact as you need.

3. Click the **Full Name** button to display the Check Full Name dialog box, and then enter the contact's title and full name (including first, middle, and last names) and any suffix you want to include. Alternatively, you can enter the name in the text box.

4. (Optional) Enter the client's company name and job title.

5. In the **File As** drop-down box, enter or select the method by which you want to file your contact's names. You can choose last name first or first name first, or you can enter your own filing system, such as by company or state.

**TIP**  **Keep It Simple**  The default filing method for contacts is last name first, which makes it easy to quickly find the contact when you need it.

6. (Optional) Enter the address in the Address box and choose whether the address is **Business**, **Home**, or **Other**. Alternatively, you can click the

**Address** button to enter the street, city, state, ZIP code, and country in specified areas instead of all within the text block. You can add a second address (say, the Home address) if you want.

**7.** In the Phone drop-down lists, choose the type of phone number—Business, Callback, Car, Home Fax, ISDN, Pager, and so on—and then enter the number. You can enter up to 19 numbers in each of the four drop-down boxes in the Phone area of the dialog box.

**8.** (Optional) Enter up to three e-mail addresses in the **E-mail** text box; in the **Web Page** text box, enter the address for the company or contact's WWW page on the Internet.

**9.** (Optional) In the comment text box, enter any descriptions, comments, or other pertinent information you want. Then select or enter a category to classify the contact.

**10.** Open the **File** menu and choose one of the following commands:

> **Save**   Saves the record and closes the Contact dialog box.
>
> **Save and New**   Saves the record and clears the Contact dialog box so you can enter a new contact.
>
> **Save and New in Company**   Saves the record and clears the Name, Job Title, File As, E-Mail, and comment text boxes so you can enter a new contact within the same company.

You can edit the information about a contact at any time by double-clicking the contact's name in the Contacts list; this displays the contact's information window. Alternatively, you can click within the information listed below a contact's name (such as the phone number or address) to position the insertion point in the text, and then delete or enter text. Press **Enter** to complete the modifications you've made and move to the next contact in the list.

# Viewing the Contacts List

By default, you see the contacts in an Address Cards view. The information you see displays the contact's name and other data such as addresses and phone numbers. The contact's company name, job title, and comments, however, are not displayed by default. Figure 12.2 shows the Contacts list in the default Address Cards view.

You can use the horizontal scroll bar to view more contacts, or you can click a letter in the index to display contacts beginning with that letter in the first column of the list.

Change views here.

Quickly find a contact using the index.

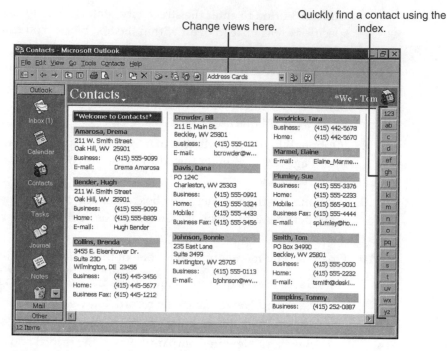

**Figure 12.2**  View your contacts in Address Cards view.

**CAUTION**

**Do I Save View Settings?**  Depending on the changes you make to a view, Outlook might display the Save View Settings dialog box to ask if you want to save the view settings before you switch to a different view. If you choose to save the current settings, Outlook lets you name the view and adds that view to the Current View list. If you choose to discard the current settings, your modifications to the view will be lost. If you choose to update the view, your modifications are saved with that view.

You can change how you view the contacts in the list by choosing one of these options from the Current View drop-down list on the standard toolbar:

**Address Cards**  Displays File As names (last name first, first name last, and so on), addresses, and phone numbers of the contacts, depending on the amount of information you've entered in a card format.

**Detailed Address Cards** Displays File As name, full name, job title, company, addresses, phone numbers, e-mail addresses, categories, and comments in a card format.

**Phone List** Displays full name, job title, company, File As name, department, phone numbers, and categories in a table, organizing each entry horizontally in rows and columns.

**By Category** Displays contacts in rows by categories. The information displayed is the same as what's displayed in a phone list.

**By Company** Displays contacts in rows, grouped by their company. The information displayed is the same as what's displayed in a phone list.

**By Location** Displays contacts grouped by country. The information displayed is the same as what's displayed in a phone list.

# Communicating with a Contact

You can send messages to any of your contacts, arrange meetings, assign tasks, or even send a letter to a contact from within Outlook. To communicate with a contact, make sure you're in the Contacts folder. You do not need to open the specific contact's information window to perform any of the following procedures.

## Sending Messages

To send a message to a contact, you must make sure you've entered an e-mail address in the General tab of the Contact dialog box for that particular contact. If Outlook cannot locate the mailing address, it displays the message dialog box shown in Figure 12.3.

**Figure 12.3** Outlook cannot send the message until you complete the address in the New Message dialog box.

To send a message from the Contacts folder, select the contact and choose **Contacts, New Message to Contact**. In the Untitled - Message dialog box, enter the subject and message and set any options you want. When you're ready to send the message, click the **Send** button. For more information about sending mail, see Lesson 6, "Creating Mail."

## Scheduling a Meeting with a Contact

To schedule a meeting with a contact, the contact must have a valid e-mail address. If no address is listed for the contact, Outlook notifies you with a message box and enables you to enter an address within the message dialog box. If the listed address is not found, Outlook responds with the Check Names dialog box, as described in the previous section.

To schedule a meeting with a contact, select the contact and choose **Contacts, New Meeting with Contact**. The Untitled - Meeting dialog box appears. Enter the subject, location, time and date, and other information you need to schedule the meeting, and then notify the contact by sending an invitation. For more information about scheduling meetings, see Lesson 11, "Planning a Meeting."

## Assigning a Task to a Contact

Tasks are assigned through e-mail. Therefore, you must enter a valid e-mail address for the contact before you can assign him or her a task.

To assign a task to a contact, select the contact and choose **Contacts, New Task for Contact**. The Task dialog box appears. Enter the subject, due date, status, and other information, and then send the task to the contact. For detailed information about assigning tasks, see Lesson 13, "Creating a Task List."

## Sending a Letter to a Contact

Outlook uses the Microsoft Word Letter Wizard to help you create a letter to send to a contact. Within the Word Wizard, you follow directions as they appear on-screen to complete the text of the letter.

To send a letter to the contact, select the contact in the Contact folder and choose **Contacts, New Letter to Contact**. Word opens the Letter Wizard on-screen. The Letter Wizard helps you format and complete the letter (see Figure 12.4). You can click the Office Assistant button if you need additional help. Then all you have to do is follow the directions and make your choices.

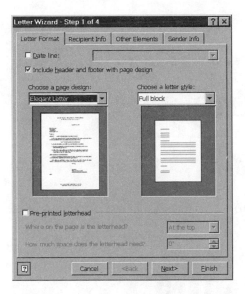

**Figure 12.4** Use Word's Letter Wizard to create a letter to a contact.

In this lesson, you learned to create a Contacts list, view the list, and send mail to someone on your Contacts list. In the next lesson, you'll learn to create a task list.

# Creating a Task List

*In this lesson, you learn to enter a task and record statistics about the task.*

## Entering a Task

You can use the Task folder to create and manage your task list. You can list due dates, status, and priorities, and even set reminder alarms so you don't forget to perform certain tasks.

**Task List**   A task list is simply a list of things you must do to complete your work, plan for a meeting, arrange an event, and so on. Various tasks might include making a phone call, writing a letter, printing a spreadsheet, or making airline reservations

To enter a task, follow these steps:

1. In the Tasks folder, choose **Tasks**, **New Task** or click the **New Task** button on the Toolbar. The Untitled - Task dialog box appears (see Figure 13.1).

2. In the Task tab, enter the subject of the task.

3. (Optional) Enter a date on which the task should be complete, or click the down arrow to open the **Due** drop-down calendar and then choose a due date.

4. (Optional) Enter a start date, or click the down arrow to open the **Start** drop-down calendar and then choose a starting date.

5. From the **Status** drop-down list, choose the current status of the project: Not Started, In Progress, Completed, Waiting on Someone Else, or Deferred.

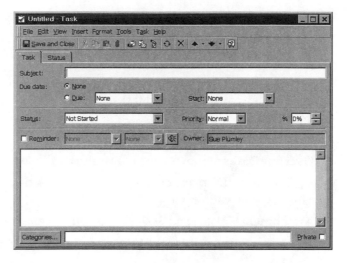

**Figure 13.1**   Enter data such as due dates, priority, and the subject of the task.

**6.** In the **Priority** drop-down list, choose Normal, Low, High priority.

**7.** In the % **Complete** text box, type a percentage or use the spinner arrows to enter one.

**8.** (Optional) To set an alarm to remind you to start the task or complete the task select the **Reminder** check box and enter a date and a time in the associated text boxes.

**9.** Enter any comments, descriptions, or other information related to the task in the comments text box.

**10.** Click the **Categories** button and choose a category, or simply enter your own category in the text box.

**TIP**   **Access Denied**   Select the **Private** check box if you don't want others to see information about your task.

**11.** Click the **Save and Close** button when you're done.

# Viewing Tasks

As in any Outlook folder, you can change how you view tasks in the list using the Current View drop-down list in the Standard Toolbar. By default, the Tasks folder displays tasks in a Simple List view. Following is a description of the views you can use to display the Tasks folder:

**521**

**Simple List**   Lists the tasks, completed check box, subject, and due date.

**Detailed List**   Displays the tasks, priority, subject, status, percent complete, and categories.

**Active Tasks**   Displays the same information as the detailed list but doesn't show any completed tasks.

**Next Seven Days**   Displays only those tasks you've scheduled for the next 7 days, including completed tasks.

**Overdue Tasks**   Shows a list of tasks that are past due.

**By Category**   Displays tasks by category; click the button representing the category you want to view.

**Assignment**   Lists tasks assigned to you by others.

**By Person Responsible**   Lists tasks grouped by the person who assigned the tasks.

**Completed Tasks**   Lists only those tasks completed, along with their due dates and completion dates.

**Task Timeline**   Uses the timeline view to display tasks by day, week, or month. Figure 13.2 shows the tasks assigned within one week.

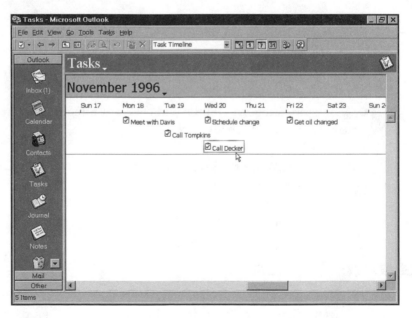

**Figure 13.2**   Double-click a task in timeline view to edit it.

**Save What Settings?** Depending on the changes you make to a view, Outlook might display the Save View Settings dialog box asking if you want to save the view settings before you switch to a different view. Generally, you'll want to discard the current view settings and leave everything the way you found it.

CAUTION

# Managing Tasks

When working with a task list, you can add and delete tasks, mark tasks as completed, and arrange the tasks within the list. You also can perform any of these procedures in most of the task views described in the previous section. For information about printing a task list, see Lesson 16, "Printing in Outlook."

Figure 13.3 shows the Task folder; the following list describes how to manage certain tasks in the list.

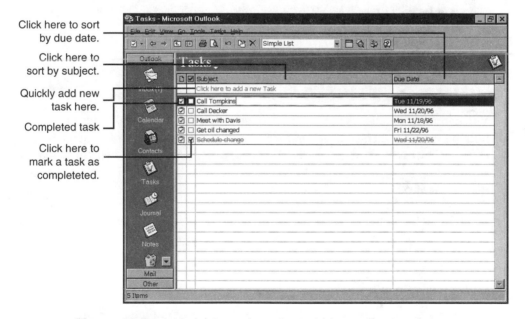

Click here to sort by due date.

Click here to sort by subject.

Quickly add new task here.

Completed task

Click here to mark a task as completeted.

**Figure 13.3** Add, delete, and sort the tasks in your list.

- To quickly add a task, click the top row of the task list where it says "Click Here to Add a New Task" and enter the subject and date.
- To edit a task, double-click the task in the list. The task dialog box appears.

- To mark a task as completed, click the check box in the second column from the left, or right-click the task and choose **Mark Complete** from the shortcut menu. Outlook places a line through the task.

- To delete a task, right-click the task and choose **Delete** from the shortcut menu.

- To assign a task to someone else, right-click the task and choose **Assign Task** from the shortcut menu. Fill in the name of the person to whom you want to assign the task and click the **Send** button to e-mail him or her the task request.

- To assign a new task to someone else, choose **Tasks**, **New Task Request**. Create the task as you normally would, but send the task as an e-mail by clicking the **Send** button.

 **TIP**   **Get Rid of the Default Task**   If you don't want to leave the Start up Microsoft Outlook task on your list, you can right-click the task and choose **Delete**.

# Recording Statistics About a Task

You can record statistics about a task, such as time spent completing the task, billable time, contacts, and so on, for your own records or for reference when sharing tasks with your coworkers. This feature is particularly helpful when you assign tasks to others; you can keep track of assigned tasks and find out when they are completed.

To enter statistics about a task, open any task in the task list and click the **Status** tab. Figure 13.4 shows a completed Status tab for a sample task.

The following list describes the text boxes in the Status tab and the types of information you can enter:

> **Date Completed**   Enter the date the task was completed, or click the arrow to display the calendar and choose the date.
>
> **Total Work**   Enter the amount of time you expect the task to take. When you complete the job, Outlook calculates the actual time spent and enters it in this text box.

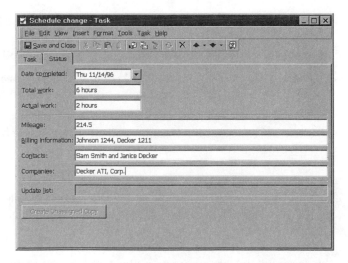

**Figure 13.4** Fill in the status of the task so you can share it with others and keep personal records.

**Actual Work** Enter the amount of time it actually took to complete the job.

**Mileage** Enter the number of miles you traveled to complete the task.

**Billing Information** Enter any specific billing information, such as hours billed, resources used, charges for equipment, and so on.

**Contacts** Enter the names of in-house or outside contacts associated with the task. Separate multiple names with semicolons.

**Companies** Enter the names of any companies associated with the contacts or with the project in general.

**Update List** Automatically lists the people whose task lists are updated when you make a change to your task.

**Create Unassigned Copy** Copies the task so it can be reassigned; use the button to send a task to someone other than an original recipient. If the task is not sent to someone else, the button is unavailable.

To track tasks you've assigned to others and to receive status reports, follow these steps:

**1.** In the Outlook dialog box, choose **Tools**, **Options**. The Options dialog box appears with the Tasks/Notes tab displayed.

2. In the Task Defaults area of the dialog box, check the **Keep Updated Copies of Assigned Tasks on My Task List** check box. This automatically tracks the progress of new tasks that you assign to others.

3. Check the **Send Status Reports When Assigned Tasks Are Completed** check box to automatically receive notification upon the completion of assigned tasks.

4. Click **OK** to accept the changes and close the dialog box.

 **TIP**   **Color Your World**   You can also set colors to represent tasks within the Tasks/Notes tab of the Options dialog box. Outlook offers twenty different colors from which you can choose for overdue tasks and completed tasks.

In this lesson, you learned to enter a task and record statistics about the task. In the next lesson, you will learn to use the Journal.

# Using the Journal

*In this lesson, you learn to create journal entries manually and automatically, and to change views in the Journal.*

## Creating a Journal Entry

You can create a record of various items and documents so you can track your work, communications, reports, and so on. In the journal, you can manually record any activities, items, or tasks you want. You also can automatically record e-mail messages, faxes, meeting requests, meeting responses, task requests, and task responses. Additionally, you can automatically record documents created in the other Office applications: Access, Excel, Office Binder, PowerPoint, and Word.

 **Journal**   A folder within Outlook that you can use to record interactions, phone calls, message responses, and other activities important to your work.

**Item**   An article or object in Outlook, such as a task, appointment, or contact.

You can automatically or manually record items in your journal. You can, for example, choose to automatically record your e-mail messages, meeting requests, task responses, and so on. When you automatically record items in the journal, Outlook records all items you receive. However, if you don't want to record all items, you can have Outlook record only those items you choose by manually adding them to your journal. For example, you might add only the e-mail relating to one account or one client instead of all e-mail you receive.

# Manually Recording an Entry

To manually create a journal entry, follow these steps:

1. In the Inbox folder (or any other folder in Outlook), select the item you want to record in the journal and choose **Tools**, **Record in Journal**. The Journal Entry dialog box appears (see Figure 14.1).

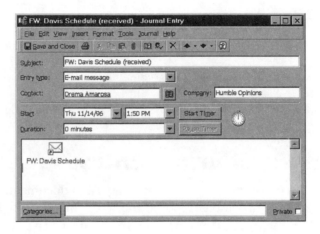

**Figure 14.1**   Record any Outlook item in the Journal.

2. The Subject, Entry Type, Contact, and Company boxes and other information is entered for you from the selected task, contact, or other selected item. However, you can change any of the statistics you want by entering new information in the following text boxes:

    **Subject**   Displays the title or name of the item.

    **Entry Type**   Describes the item based on its point of origin, such as a Word document, Meeting or Appointment, and so on.

    **Contact**   Lists the name(s) of any attendees, contacts, or other people involved with the selected item.

    **Company**   Lists the company or companies associated with the contacts.

    **Start Time**   Displays the date and time of the meeting, appointment, or other item.

    **Start Timer**   Like a stop watch, the timer records the time that passes until you click the Pause Timer button.

    **Pause Timer**   Stops the timer.

    **Duration**   Enter the amount of time for completing the item.

Text box   Displays shortcuts to any text, documents, details, or other information related to the item.

Categories   Enter or select a category in which to place the item.

**3.** Click the **Save and Close** button to complete the entry.

**TIP**   **Time Your Calls**   When making phone calls or meeting with clients, create a journal entry to record the event, and use the Start Timer and Pause Timer buttons to record billable time.

If you want to create a new journal entry, but you don't have a contact, task, e-mail, or other related item for the entry, you can manually record a journal entry by following these steps:

**1.** Change to the Journal folder.

**2.** Choose **Journal**, **New Journal Entry** or click the **New Journal Entry** button on the Standard toolbar. The Journal Entry dialog box appears.

**3.** Enter the information (subject, contact, etc.) you want to record.

**4.** When you finish, click the **Save and Close** button.

# Automatically Recording Entries

You can set options to automatically record items and their related contacts and/or statistics about Microsoft Office documents you create. Suppose you want to keep a record, for example, of all memos you send to your boss. You can record it in your journal. To set the options to automatically record journal entries, follow these steps:

**1.** In the Journal folder, choose **Tools**, **Options**. The Options dialog box appears with the Journal tab displayed, as shown in Figure 14.2.

**2.** In the **Automatically Record These Items** list, check those items you want Outlook to automatically record in your journal. (The items recorded correspond with those people selected in the list of contacts in step 3.)

**3.** In the **For These Contacts** list, check any contacts you want automatically recorded in the Journal. Outlook records any items checked in step 2 that apply to the selected contacts.

**4.** In the **Also Record Files From** list, check the applications for which you want to record journal entries. Outlook records the date and time you create or modify files in the selected program.

**Figure 14.2**  Set options for automatically recording items in your Journal.

**TIP**  **Automatic and Easy**  When you're creating a new contact in Outlook, you can set items to be automatically recorded in the journal by choosing the **Journal** tab in the Contact dialog box and checking the **Automatically Record Journal Entries for This Contact** check box.

# Viewing Journal Entries

By default, the Journal folder displays information in the Timeline view and By Type, as shown in Figure 14.3. However, you can display the entries in various views, as described in the following list.

**Save Settings?**  As in other views, Outlook might display the Save View Settings dialog box to ask if you want to save the view settings before you switch to a different view. You're probably getting used to this dialog box **CAUTION**  by now.

**By Type**  In Timeline view, this option groups journal entries by type, such as e-mail messages, meetings, Word documents, and so on. Double-click a type to display its contents, and then position the mouse pointer over an entry to view its contents or name.

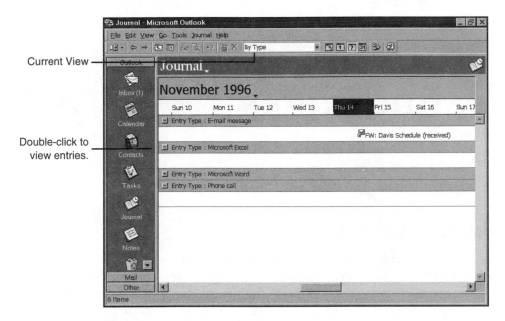

Current View

Double-click to
view entries.

**Figure 14.3** View the journal entries by type.

**By Contact** In Timeline view, this displays the name of each contact that you selected in the Options dialog box. Double-click any contact's name to view recorded entries.

**By Category** If you've assigned categories to your journal entries and other items, you can display your journal entries by category in the timeline view.

**Entry List** Displays entries in a table with columns labeled Entry Type, Subject, Start, Duration, Contact, and Categories.

**Last Seven Days** Displays entries in an entry list, but includes only those entries dated within the last seven days.

**Phone Calls** Lists all entries that are phone calls.

**TIP** **Sort Journal Entries** You can click the heading bar—Subject, Start, or Duration—in any Entry list view to sort the items in that column in ascending or descending order.

In this lesson, you learned to manually and automatically create journal entries and to change views in the Journal. In the next lesson, you'll learn to create notes.

# Creating Notes

*In this lesson, you learn to create, sort, and view notes.*

## Creating Notes

If you've ever used a paper sticky note to remind yourself of tasks, ideas, or other brief annotations, Outlook's Notes are for you. Notes are very similar to paper sticky notes. You can use Notes to write down reminders, names, phone numbers, directions, or anything else you need to remember. In Outlook, all notes are kept in the Notes folder. You'll have to remember to look at the folder so you can view your notes.

To create a note, follow these steps:

1. In the Notes folder, choose **Note**, **New Note** or click the **New Note** button on the Standard toolbar. A note appears, ready for you to type your text (see Figure 15.1).

2. Enter the text for your note.

 **TIP** **The Long and Short of It** Notes don't have to be brief. You can enter pages and pages of text if you want. As you type, the page scrolls for you; use the arrow keys and the Page Up/Page Down keys to move through the note text.

3. When you finish, click the **Close** (X) button to close the note. You can reopen a note and enter as much text or edit text as you need to.

If you press Enter after entering text in the note, you create a line break and a title of sorts at the same time; only the text before the hard return is visible when the note is closed. If you do not add a hard return, but enter the note text so that it automatically wraps from line to line, the entire note text appears below the note in Icons view.

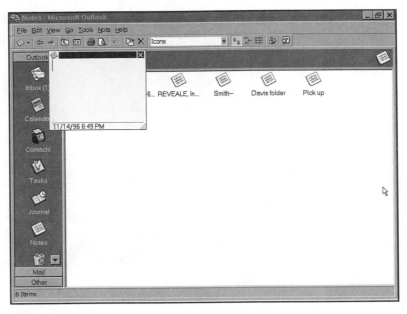

**Figure 15.1** A note automatically includes the date and time it was created.

# Setting Note Options

You can change the default color and size of your notes. You also can change the default font used for your notes. To set note options, follow these steps:

1. In the Notes folder, choose **Tools**, **Options**. The Options dialog box appears with the Tasks/Notes tab displayed (see Figure 15.2).

2. In the Note Defaults area of the dialog box, click the **Color** drop-down arrow and select a new default color for your notes. You can change the color to yellow, blue, green, pink, or white. The default is yellow.

3. Open the **Size** drop-down list and choose **Small**, **Medium**, or **Large** for the size of the notes. The default is Medium.

4. If you would prefer not to show the time and date on your notes, deselect the **Show Time and Date** check box.

5. To change the font, click the **Font** button. The Font dialog box appears. Change the font, font style, size, color, and other options, and then click **OK**.

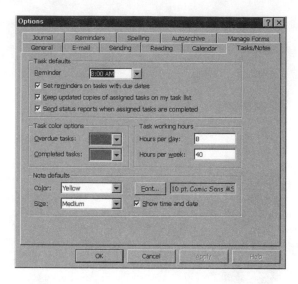

**Figure 15.2**  Customize your notes.

# Managing Individual Notes

To open a note, double-click it in the Notes folder. You can edit the text in an open note as you would edit any text. To move a note, drag its title bar. You also can delete, forward, or print notes; you can change the color of individual notes; and you can specify categories for your notes.

Click an open note's **Control-menu** button to display a menu with the following commands:

**New Note**   Creates a new note but leaves the first note open.

**Save As**   Enables you to save the note and its contents.

**Delete**   Deletes a note and its contents. (You also can delete a note by selecting it in the Notes list and pressing the **Delete** key.)

**Forward**   Enables you to send the note as an attachment in an e-mail message.

**Cut, Copy, Paste**   Enables you to select text from the note and cut or copy it to the Clipboard. The Paste command enables you to paste items on the Clipboard at the insertion point in the note.

**Color**   Choose another color for the individual note.

**Categories** Enter or choose a category.

**Print** Print the contents of the note.

**Close** Closes the note. (You also can click the **Close** (X) button in the note's title bar.) A closed note appears in the Notes folder.

# Viewing Notes

The Notes folder provides various views for organizing and viewing your notes. You also can sort notes in any entry list view by right-clicking the heading bar—Subject, Created, Categories, and so on—and select the sort method.

The default view is Icons, but you can change the view using the Current View drop-down list in the Standard Toolbar. Figure 15.3 shows the Notes folder in the default view.

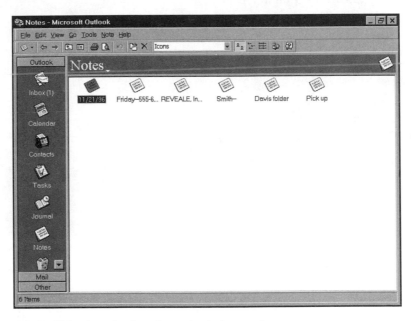

**Figure 15.3** This view displays the notes in Icons view.

You can choose to display your Notes folder in any of the following views:

**Icons**   Displays the notes as note icons with the message (or a portion of the message) displayed below the icon.

**Notes List**   Displays the notes in a list, showing the title and note contents in the Subject column, the creation date and time, and the Categories.

**Last Seven Days**   Displays all notes written in the last seven days, by Subject, creation date, and categories.

**By Category**   Displays the categories; double-click a category to show its contents.

**By Color**   Displays notes by their color. Double-click a color to display the notes.

In this lesson, you learned to create, sort, and view notes. In the next lesson, you will learn to print in Outlook.

# Printing in Outlook

*In this lesson, you learn to print items in Outlook, change the page setup, preview an item before printing it, and change printer properties.*

## Choosing Page Setup

In Outlook, before you print you choose the print style you will use. Each folder—Inbox, Calendar, Contacts, and so on—offers various print styles, and each style displays the data on the page in a different way.

 **Page** In Outlook, this is the area of the paper that will actually be printed on. You might, for example, print two or four pages on a single sheet of paper.

**Print Style** The combination of paper and page settings that control printed output.

You can choose from Outlook's built-in print styles, modify the default print styles, or create your own print styles. These lists show the default print styles available for each folder.

The Inbox, Contacts, and Tasks use the following two styles:

 **Table Style** Displays data in columns and rows on an 8.5 × 11 sheet, portrait orientation, .5-inch margins.

 **Memo Style** Displays data with a header of information about the message and then straight text on an 8.5 × 11 sheet, portrait orientation, .5-inch margins.

The Calendar folder provides the Memo style, plus the following styles:

 **Daily Style**   Displays one day's appointments on one page on an 8.5 × 11 sheet, portrait orientation, .5-inch margins.

 **Weekly Style**   Displays one week's appointments per page on an 8.5 × 11 sheet, portrait orientation, .5-inch margins.

 **Monthly Style**   Displays one month's appointments per page on an 8.5 × 11 sheet, landscape orientation, .5-inch margins.

 **Tri-fold Style**   Displays the daily calendar, task list, and weekly calendar on an 8.5 × 11 sheet, landscape orientation, .5-inch margins.

The Contacts folder provides the Memo style, plus the following styles:

 **Card Style**   Two columns and headings on an 8.5 × 11 sheet, portrait orientation, .5-inch margins.

 **Small Booklet Style**   One-column page that equals 1/8 of a sheet of paper—so that eight pages are on one 8.5 × 11 sheet of paper with .5-inch margins. Then the portrait orientation applies to the 1/8 pages.

 **Medium Booklet Style**   One column that equals 1/4 of a sheet of paper—so that four pages are on one 8.5 × 11 sheet of paper. Portrait orientation with .5-inch margins.

 **Phone Directory Style**   One column, 8.5 × 11 sheet of paper, portrait orientation with .5-inch margins.

 **TIP**   **Page Setup Only Matters in Printing**   No matter how you set up your pages, it will not affect your view of tasks, calendars, or other Outlook items on-screen. Page setup only applies to a printed job.

You can view, modify, and create new page setups in Outlook. To view or edit a page setup, follow these steps:

1.  Change to the folder for which you're setting the page.

2.  Choose **File**, **Page Setup**. A secondary menu appears that lists the available print types.

3.  Select the print type you want to view or edit, and the Page Setup dialog box appears (see Figure 16.1).

4.  Click the **Format** tab to view or edit the page type, to choose options (in some cases), and to change fonts.

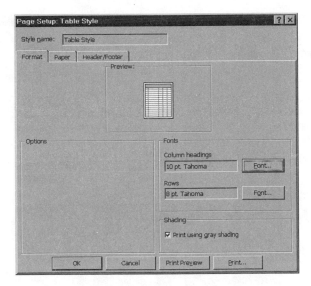

**Figure 16.1** Customize the print type to suit yourself.

**5.** Click the **Paper** tab to view or edit paper size, page size, margins, and orientation.

**6.** Click the **Header/Footer** tab to view or edit headers for your pages.

# Previewing Before Printing

You can choose to preview an item before printing it so you're sure it looks the way you want it to look. If you do not like the way an item looks in preview, you can change the page setup.

Before you display an item in print preview, you must change to the folder containing the item you want to print. Then you can choose to preview the item in any of the following ways:

- Click the **Print Preview** button in the Page Setup dialog box.
- Choose **File**, **Print Preview**.
- Click the **Print Preview** button on the Standard toolbar.
- Click the **Preview** button in the Print dialog box.

Figure 16.2 shows a calendar and task list in Print Preview. You can change the page setup by clicking the **Page Setup** button; the Page Setup dialog box appears. Click the **Print** button to send the job to the printer. Click the **Close** button to exit Print Preview and return to the Outlook folder.

**539**

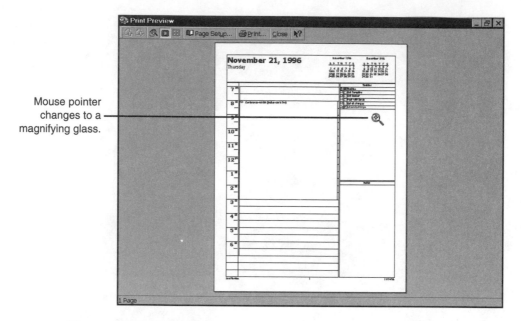

Mouse pointer changes to a magnifying glass.

**Figure 16.2** Preview the item before printing it.

 **TIP** **Enlarge the View** When the mouse pointer looks like a magnifying glass with a plus sign in it, you can click to enlarge the page. When the mouse pointer looks like a magnifying glass with a minus sign in it, you can click to reduce the view again.

# Printing Items

After you choose the print style and preview an item to make sure it's what you want, you can print the item. You can indicate the number of copies you want to print, select a printer, change the print style or page setup, and set a print range.

When you're ready to print an item, follow these steps:

1. Choose **File**, **Print** or click the **Print** button on the Standard toolbar. The Print dialog box appears, as shown in Figure 16.3.

2. In the Printer area of the dialog box, choose a different printer from the **Name** drop-down list if necessary.

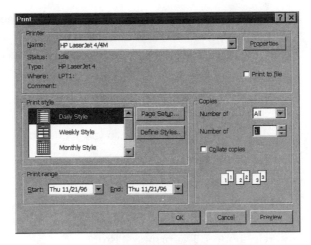

**Figure 16.3** Set the printing options before printing the item.

 **TIP** **In a Hurry?** If your computer is on a network and you notice the Status of the selected printer is Busy or Paused, for example, choose a different printer from the drop-down list.

**3.** In the Print Style area, choose a print style from the list. You also can edit the page setup (with the Page Setup button) or edit or create a new style (with the Define Styles button).

**4.** In the Copies area of the dialog box, choose **All**, **Even**, or **Odd** in Number of Pages and enter the number of copies you want to print. Click the **Collate Copies** check box if you want Outlook to automatically assemble multiple copies.

**5.** Set the print range with the options in that area. (The Print Range options vary depending on the type of item you're printing.)

**6.** Click **OK** to print the item.

# Setting Printer Properties

Whether you're printing to a printer connected directly to your computer or to a printer on the network, you can set printer properties. The properties you set apply to all print jobs you send to the printer until you change the properties again.

**Printer Properties**   Configurations specific to a printer connected to your computer or to the network. Printer properties include paper orientation, paper source, graphics settings, fonts, and print quality.

**CAUTION**

**Access Denied?**   If you cannot change the printer properties to a network printer, it's probably because the network administrator has set the printer's configuration, and you're not allowed access to the settings. If you need to change printer properties and cannot access the printer's Properties dialog box, talk to your network administrator.

To set printer properties, open the Print dialog box (by choosing **File, Print**). In the Printer area, select a printer from the **Name** drop-down list, and then click the **Properties** button. The printers' Properties dialog boxes differ depending on the make and model of printer.

Most likely, you'll be able to set paper size, page orientation, and paper source using options on a Paper tab in the dialog box. In addition, you might see a Graphics tab, in which you can set the resolution, intensity, and graphics mode of your printer. A Fonts tab enables you to set options on TrueType fonts, font cartridges, and so on. You might also find a Device Options tab, in which you can set print quality and other options. For more information about your printer, read the documentation that came with it.

In this lesson, you learned to print items in Outlook, change the page setup, preview an item before printing it, and change printer properties. In the next lesson, you will learn to manage your files and Outlook items.

# Saving, Opening, and Finding Outlook Items

*In this lesson, you learn to save items, open items, and find items in Outlook.*

## Saving Items

Generally, when you finish adding a new task, appointment, meeting, contact, or other item, Outlook automatically saves that item for you or you're prompted to save the item yourself. You also can save most items in Outlook for use in other applications by using the Save As command. After you save an item by naming it, you can open that same item and edit, print, or otherwise use the saved file in Windows applications that support the file type. You might save an item—a journal entry or appointment page, for example—so you can refer to it later, edit the original, or keep it as a record.

**Save As**   When you save an item using the File, Save As command, you can designate a drive, directory, and new file name for that item, as well as a file type.

**File Type**   A file type is the same thing as a file format. When you save a file, you specify a file type that identifies the file as one that can be opened in specific applications. For example, the file extension .DOC identifies a file type that you can open in Word, and the extension .TXT represents a text-only format you can open in nearly any word processor or other application.

To save an item, follow these steps:

**1.** In the folder containing the item you want to save, choose **File**, **Save As**. The Save As dialog box appears (see Figure 17.1).

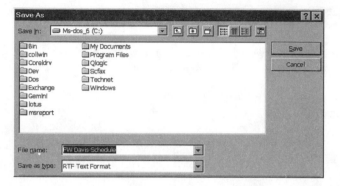

**Figure 17.1** Save items as files for use in other programs, as copies of the originals, or for later use.

**Why Is Save As Dimmed?** When the Save As command is dimmed, you must first select an item—an appointment, meeting, task, note, and so on—before you can save it.

**CAUTION**

**2.** From the **Save In** drop-down list, choose the drive to which you want to save the file. From the folders on that drive, select the one you want to save to.

**3.** In the **Save As Type** drop-down list, choose a file type. You can save the file in the following file types:

**Text Only**   Saves in an ASCII format that you can use in other applications, such as Word, Notepad, and so on.

**RTF Text Format**   Saves in rich text format. You also can use this format in Word, Outlook, or Lotus Notes, for example.

**Outlook Template**   Saves as a template (or style sheet) that you can use as a basis for other items.

**Message Format**   Saves in a format you can use in your e-mail messages.

**4.** Enter a name for the item in the **File Name** text box, or accept the default.

**5.** Click the **Save** button.

# Opening and Using Saved Items

After you save items, you can open and use them in Outlook and other applications. If, for example, you saved a contact as a message file, you can insert that file into a message and send the contact's name, address, and other information to someone through an e-mail message. You can save other items, such as meeting information from your calendar, as a text file you can open in Notepad or Word to edit, format, print, or otherwise modify the file.

## Opening and Using an RTF File

You can open RTF files in many word processing programs—Word, Notepad, WordPad, and so on. To open an RTF file in Outlook or another Windows application, choose **File, Open**. In the Open dialog box, choose **Rich Text Format** (or **RTF Text Format**) in the **Files of Type** drop-down list. The saved files appear in the file list. Select the file and click the **Open** button.

**CAUTION**

**RTF Isn't Listed?** If RTF isn't listed in the application's Files of Type list box, see if Text Only is listed. You can also save Outlook items as Text Only.

Figure 17.2 shows an e-mail message saved as an RTF file and opened in Word. After opening a file, you can format it, cut or copy items to it, insert objects, print, edit, and otherwise manipulate the file. In addition, you can open and read the attachment from within the saved RTF file.

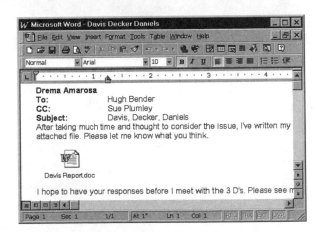

**Figure 17.2** Exchanging data between applications makes your work quicker and easier.

# Opening and Using a Text-Only File

You open a text-only file in much the same way you open an RTF file. In Notepad, for example, choose **File**, **Open** and choose **Text Documents** as the file type in the Open dialog box. Files saved as text-only do not retain any formatting; however, you can select the text and format it in the destination application.

# Using a Message Text File

After you save an item as a message text file, you can insert the item into an e-mail message to send. Suppose you saved a contact's information or an especially long note that you want to share with someone else; you can insert the file as an object into a message and send the e-mail as you normally would. Then the recipient can open the message and the message file.

**TIP**    **Files As Objects**    As described in Lesson 10, you can insert any existing file as an object; therefore, you can insert an RTF, text-only, or message file into any Windows document that supports OLE.

To insert a message file into a message, open the message and choose **Insert, Object**. In the Insert Object dialog box, choose **Create from File**. Enter the path and file name and click **OK**. Figure 17.3 shows a message file in the text of an e-mail.

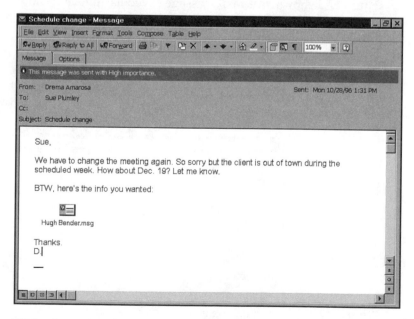

**Figure 17.3**    Open the MSG file by double-clicking its icon.

# Finding Items

Outlook provides a method you can use to locate items on your computer. You can search for messages, files, journal entries, notes, tasks, contacts, appointments, and so on. You can search for specific words, categories, priority, item size, and other criteria that you stipulate. Outlook's Find feature can be especially useful if your folders become full, and locating items on your own is difficult.

 **Criteria** Guidelines you set in the Find dialog box that Outlook uses to find items, such as messages, contacts, or appointments. Included in the criteria you set may be the date an item was created, the title or subject of the item, or specific text within the item.

To find an item in Outlook, follow these steps:

 **1.** Choose **Tools, Find Items** or click the **Find Items** button on the Standard Toolbar. The Find dialog box appears, as shown in Figure 17.4.

 **My Dialog Box Is Different** The Find dialog box in Figure 17.4 was opened from the Inbox. If you open the Find dialog box from Calendar, Tasks, or any other folder, the options in the dialog box relate to the item for which you're searching.

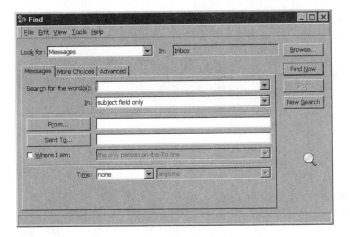

**Figure 17.4** Use the Find dialog box to search for messages, appointments, and other items.

2. In any Find dialog box, choose the item for which you want to search in the **Look For** drop-down list. You can choose Tasks, Notes, Messages, Journal Entries, Files, Contacts, Appointments and Meetings, or Any Type of Outlook Item.

3. Click the **Browse** button to display the Select Folder(s) dialog box, from which you can choose the folder to search.

4. On the first tab, which is named for the item you select in the Look For list, you can enter specific words to search for, fields you want to search, dates, contact names, file types, and so on. The second tab, More Choices, offers additional options to add to the search, such as item size, category, and so on. Set the options you want on both tabs.

 **TIP**   **Narrow the Search**   The more options you select and specify in the Find dialog box, the more you narrow the search; fewer items will match the search criteria. However, when you select more options, the search could take longer.

5. When you're ready to find the item(s), click the **Find Now** button. The Find dialog box extends to display a list of items Outlook finds that match the search criteria. In addition to the name of the item, the search results also show the folder in which you'll find the item, along with other item details.

You can perform a new search by clicking the **New Search** button, which clears the text boxes and previously selected options, and entering new criteria. If you want to pause or stop a search that's taking too long, click the **Stop** button.

 **TIP**   **Fast Find**   When you're in the Inbox, an extra Find command appears on the Tools menu: Find All. With the Find All command, you can choose to find all messages related to the selected message or all messages from the sender of the selected message. The Find dialog box appears, displaying a list of the matching messages.

# Using the Advanced Search

The Find dialog box includes an Advanced tab that contains options you can use to perform more detailed searches than you can with the other options in the dialog box. On the Advanced tab, you can set multiple search criteria such as a category, author, and subject or a message flag and priority setting.

To use the Advanced tab in the Find dialog box, follow these steps:

1. Open the Find dialog box by choosing **Tools, Find Items**.

2. (Optional) Set any criteria you want on the Item tab and More Choices tab.

3. Click the **Advanced** tab.

4. On the Advanced tab, choose the **Field** drop-down list to define more criteria. You can choose from multiple commands, each of which displays a secondary menu. The commands and secondary menus depend on the item for which you're searching. The following are a few of the fields for the Message item:

   **Frequently-Used Fields**   Includes fields such as Categories, Created, Duration, Location, Recurrence, Subject, and so on.

   **Date/Time Fields**   Includes Created, Duration, Start, and so on.

   **All Appointment Fields**   Includes such fields as Importance, Meeting Status, Notes, Recurring, Reminder, Resources, and so on.

   **All Mail Fields**   Includes Categories, Created, Expires, Subject, and so on.

   **All Tasks Fields**   Includes % Complete, Conversation, Due Date, Mileage, Notes, Owner, Priority, and so on.

   **All Journal Fields**   Includes Billing Information, Company, Entry Type, Sensitivity, Start, and so on.

5. After you choose a field, select the condition from the **Condition** drop-down list. Conditions include such constraints as whether the field is empty, and exactly what values or word the field contains. (For example, you might choose the field **Category** and the condition **Contains**.)

6. If you choose a condition that specifies the contents of the field, next you fill in the **Value**. A value might be a name, word, note color, or priority, or other text found in the item.

7. Click the **Add to List** button. Any criteria you set is listed in the Find Items That Match These Criteria list box; more items are added as you select them in the Advanced tab.

8. When you've finished setting your criteria, click the **Find Now** button.

Figure 17.5 shows the Advanced tab before adding the final criterion for which to search. The results of this search will show any messages that contain the words "Time Applied" in the Billing Information field, and do not contain the words "Bender Printing" in the Message text.

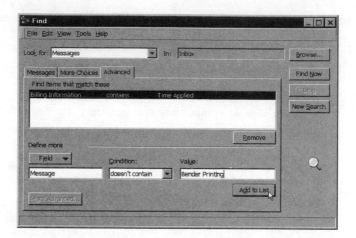

**Figure 17.5**  Set advanced criteria to find specific items.

In this lesson, you learned to save items, open items, and find items in Outlook. In the next lesson, you will learn to integrate items between Outlook folders.

# Integrating Items

*In this lesson, you learn to use various items in Outlook together (to create a task or an appointment from a mail message and to create a document within Outlook, for example).*

## Creating a Task from a Mail Message

You can use a mail message to create a task quickly and easily in Outlook. Instead of printing the message and then opening your Task List to add the information, you can create the task by using drag-and-drop copying. For more information about using the Tasks folder, see Lesson 13, "Creating a Task List."

 **TIP** **You Don't Lose the Message** When you use a message to create another item, Outlook copies the message so that the original message remains in the Inbox.

To create a task from a mail message, follow these steps:

1. Open the **Inbox** folder.
2. Click and drag the unopened mail message from the Inbox window to the Tasks icon on the Outlook Bar. The Task dialog box opens (see Figure 18.1).
3. Change the subject or other data if you want, and then set any options for the task (such as due date, priority, reminders, categories, and so on).
4. Click the **Save and Close** button, and Outlook adds the task to your list.

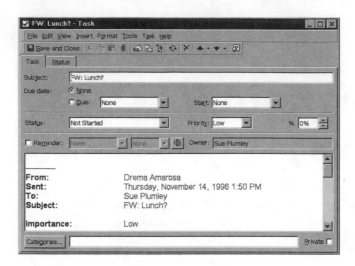

**Figure 18.1** Create a task from an e-mail message.

# Creating an Appointment from a Mail Message

In addition to creating tasks from messages, you can create an appointment from a mail message. When you create the appointment, you can set a time and date for the appointment, invite attendees to the appointment, create a meeting, and otherwise set options for the appointment. For more information about creating appointments, see Lesson 10, "Using the Calendar."

To create an appointment from a mail message, follow these steps:

1. Open the Inbox and locate the mail message you want to use.

2. Drag the unopened message from the Inbox window to the Calendar folder on the Outlook Bar. The Appointment dialog box opens with some information automatically filled in (see Figure 18.2).

3. Add the location to the appointment and make any desired changes in the **Subject**, **Start Time**, or **End Time** boxes, or in any other of the options.

4. Click the **Save and Close** button to complete the appointment.

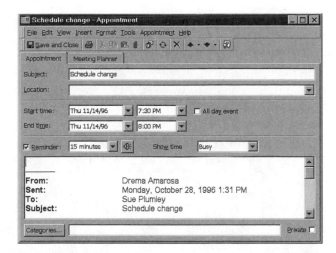

**Figure 18.2** Create an appointment using the data in a mail message.

# Create a Note from Any Item

Just as you can create tasks and appointments from a mail message, you also can create a note from any item in Outlook. Suppose someone e-mailed you information about a product or service that you want to add to a report; you can simply create a note with the information on it. Or suppose you want to call someone at a certain time later in the day. You can create a note from your contact entry so you won't forget.

You can create a note from a mail message, appointment or meeting, contact, task, or journal entry. After you create the note, you can edit the text in the note without affecting the original item.

To create a note from any Outlook item, drag the item into the Notes folder in the Outlook Bar. Outlook creates and displays the note, and you can edit the text if you want. For more information about notes, see Lesson 15, "Creating Notes."

# Using Outlook Templates

Outlook includes many templates on which you can base new messages, appointments, tasks, and so on. You use a template when you want to create a new item. The e-mail templates, for example, supply an Untitled Message window with decorative fonts and graphics you can use to add pizzazz to your message.

To use an Outlook template, follow these steps:

1. Choose **File**, **New**.

2. In the secondary menu that appears, select **Choose Template**. The Choose Template dialog box appears with several templates from which to choose (see Figure 18.3).

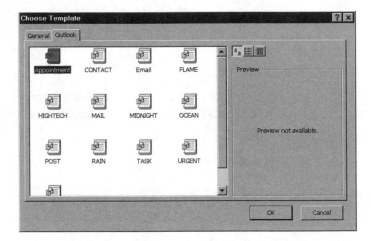

**Figure 18.3** Base your new item on a specific template in Outlook.

3. Select the template you want to use and click **OK**. Outlook displays the message, task, appointment, or other window in which you can create your item.

In this lesson, you learned to use various items in Outlook together—to create a task and an appointment from a mail message and to create a document within Outlook. In the next lesson, you'll learn to archive items.

# Archiving Items

19

*In this lesson, you learn to use AutoArchive and to archive files, retrieve archived files, and delete archived files.*

## Using AutoArchive

You can set an option in Outlook to automatically archive your mail messages into files periodically. The AutoArchive feature cleans your Inbox for you without deleting any messages.

> **TERM** **Archive**   To save items to a file that can be opened at any time and printed, viewed, or otherwise used. You might, for example, want to archive some of your mail messages to keep for your records instead of leaving those messages in your Inbox. Archived items are removed from the folder and copied to an archive file.

To use AutoArchive, follow these steps:

**1.** Choose **Tools, Options**. The Options dialog box appears.

**2.** Click the **AutoArchive** tab.

**3.** Click the **AutoArchive Every** *xx* check box to display the rest of the items in the dialog box (see Figure 19.1).

**4.** Choose from the following options:

**AutoArchive Every** *x* **Days at Startup**   Enter a number for how often (in days) you want Outlook to automatically archive items. If you enter **14**, for example, when you start Outlook on the 14th day, it automatically archives the contents of your folders into an archive file.

**Prompt Before AutoArchive**   If you check this, Outlook displays a dialog box each time it is about to perform the AutoArchive; you can click OK or Cancel to continue or stop the operation.

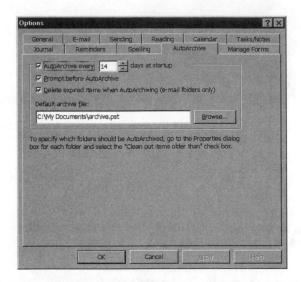

**Figure 19.1** Specify options for automatically archiving items into files.

> **Delete Expired Items When AutoArchiving (E-Mail Folders Only)**
> Check this box to have Outlook delete messages from the Inbox after
> archiving them.

5. In the **Default Archive File** text box, enter a path to where you want to save the file, and name it (if you don't want to use the default).

6. Click **OK** to close the dialog box.

In addition to setting the AutoArchive options in the Options dialog box, each folder—Inbox, Tasks, Calendar, and so on—has additional AutoArchive options you can set.

To set individual folder's AutoArchive options, follow these steps:

1. Right-click the folder in the Outlook Bar to display the shortcut menu.

2. Choose **Properties**. The item's Properties dialog box appears.

3. Choose the **AutoArchive** tab (see Figure 19.2).

4. Set the options you want in the dialog box. You can change the length of time you want the archived files to be saved before they're deleted or saved to another file, and you can enter a path and file name for the second save.

5. Click **OK** to close the dialog box.

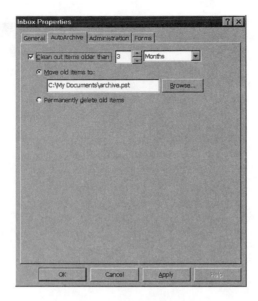

**Figure 19.2**  Set AutoArchive options for individual folders.

# Archiving Manually

You can choose to archive one or two folders or all folders manually whenever you're ready to create an archive file. If you choose to do it yourself, you control exactly how and when archives are created.

To create an archive, follow these steps:

1. Choose **File**, **Archive**. The Archive dialog box appears (see Figure 19.3).
2. Choose one of the following options:

   **Archive All Folders According to Their AutoArchive Settings**   Use this option to save archives of each folder using the settings you select
   in the AutoArchive tab of the folder's Properties dialog box.

   **Archive This Folder and All Subfolders**   Select this option to archive the selected folder.

3. Enter a date in the **Archive Items Older Than** text box, or select a date from the drop-down calendar.
4. In the **Archive File** text box, enter a path and file name with which to save the file.
5. Click **OK** to archive the selected folder(s).

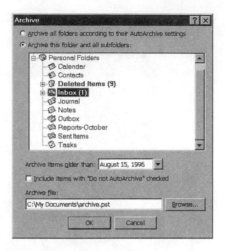

**Figure 19.3**   Enter settings for manual archiving.

# Retrieving Archived Files

You can retrieve an archived file by importing it to the original file. When you retrieve an archived file, it becomes a part of your Outlook folder just as it was before you archived it. Follow these steps to retrieve an archived file:

1. Choose **File, Import and Export**. The Import and Export Wizard dialog box appears.

2. Choose **Import from a Personal Folders File (*PST)** and click the **Next** button.

3. In the second wizard dialog box, enter the path and the file name of the archived file.

4. Select any one of the following options, and then click the **Next** button:

    **Replace Duplicates with Items Imported** to overwrite any copies of the data with imported items.

    **Allow Duplicates to Be Created** to create duplicates of the items instead of overwriting them.

    **Do Not Import Duplicates** to preserve the originals in the folder instead of overwriting them with items from the archived file.

5. In the third wizard dialog box, choose the folder into which you want to import. (The default is to import the archived item to the Personal Folders area; you might have created subfolders into which you want to import.)

6. Click the **Finish** button, and Outlook imports the archived files.

# Deleting Archived Files

The easiest way to delete archived files is by using the Windows Explorer. However, you can also delete files from the Find Files and Folders dialog box or from My Computer (both Windows applications).

To delete an archived file, follow these steps:

1. Open the Explorer and locate the files. Archived files are saved with a .PST extension in the My Documents folder (by default) or any other folder you designate.
2. Open the folder containing the files and select the file(s) you want to delete.
3. Press the **Delete** key, or drag the file(s) to the Recycle Bin.
4. Empty the Recycle Bin by right-clicking the **Bin** and choosing **Empty Recycle Bin**.
5. Close the Explorer by clicking the **Close** (X) button.

In this lesson, you learned to use AutoArchive and to archive files, retrieve archived files, and delete archived files. In the next lesson, you will learn to customize Outlook.

# Customizing Outlook

*In this lesson, you learn to set e-mail, calendar, and other options in Outlook.*

## Setting General Options

General options include choices that can make your work more comfortable or efficient. For example, you can choose to view large toolbar buttons if you have trouble seeing or clicking the small icons, or you can choose to empty the Deleted Items folder automatically when you exit Outlook.

To customize general options, follow these steps:

1. Choose **Tools**, **Options**. The Options dialog box appears.
2. Click the **General** tab.
3. In the General Settings area, check the boxes of the options you want to activate, which are listed here:

    Warn Before Permanently Deleting Items

    Empty the Deleted Items Folder Upon Exiting

    When Selecting Text, Automatically Select Entire Word

    When Online, Synchronize all Folders Upon Exiting

    Provide Feedback with Sound

    Large Toolbar Icons

4. In the Startup Settings area, choose **Prompt for a Profile to Be Used** or **Always Use This Profile**.

**Profile**   A group of settings that control how your mail is delivered, received, and stored in Outlook, and the software used to transfer your mail, such as Microsoft Mail, Microsoft Exchange, Lotus Notes, and so on.

**5.** When you finish setting the options on this tab, do one of the following things:

> Click **Apply** to set these options, and then click another tab to customize the options on it.
>
> Click **OK** to accept the changes and close the Options dialog box.
>
> Click **Cancel** to void any changes you made and close the dialog box.

# Setting E-Mail Options

Use the E-Mail tab to set options that govern how the program deals with new mail and how new mail is processed. Figure 20.1 shows the Options dialog box with the E-Mail tab displayed.

To set e-mail options, follow these steps:

**1.** Choose **Tools**, **Options**. The Options dialog box appears.

**2.** Click the **E-Mail** tab.

**3.** In the **Check for New Mail On** list box, check all types of e-mail you want to receive.

**TIP   Check for New Mail?**   The mail types listed in the Check for New Mail On list box are added when you add a new profile to Outlook. You add a profile by choosing **Tools**, **Services**.

**4.** In the When New Items Arrive area, choose the options you want to apply to your setup.

**5.** In the Settings for Automatic Processing of Mail area, check the boxes next to the options you want to apply (described here):

> **Process Delivery, Read, and Recall, Receipts on Arrival**   When this is checked, Outlook automatically records status when an item is delivered, read, or recalled.

**Process Requests and Responses on Arrival**   When this is checked, Outlook automatically places meeting requests on your Calendar and responses to meeting requests in your Meeting Planner.

**Delete Receipts and Blank Responses After Processing**   When this is checked, Outlook automatically deletes responses to meeting requests that have no comments when mail is delivered, read, or recalled.

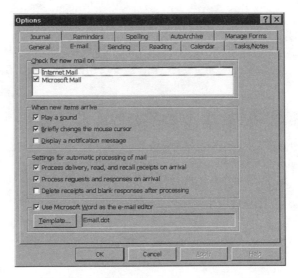

**Figure 20.1**   Customize e-mail options to suit your needs.

**6.** When you're done, click **Apply** to save the changes and view another tab, or click **OK** to save the changes and close the dialog box.

# Setting Sending Options

Sending options allow you to control the font used for new messages, tracking options, and choices for dealing with sent items. Follow these steps to set sending options:

**1.** Choose **Tools**, **Options**. The Options dialog box appears.

**2.** Click the **Sending** tab (see Figure 20.2).

**3.** In the When Composing New Messages area, click the **Font** button to choose a different font for message text.

**4.** Under Tracking Options, choose when you want to be notified about mail you've sent.

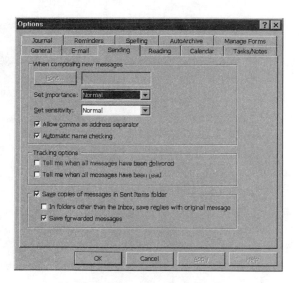

**Figure 20.2** Set options for sending mail.

**5.** In Save Copies of Messages in "Sent Items" Folder, choose the options you want to use for saving messages.

**6.** When you're done, click **Apply** to save the changes and view another tab, or click **OK** to save the changes and close the dialog box.

**TIP** **Reading Options** Take a look at the Reading tab in the Options dialog box. It contains options you can use to choose fonts for message replies that you send and for forwarded messages.

# Setting Calendar Options

If you work during unusual days or hours, you can change your default Calendar work week in the Calendar tab of the Options dialog box. Suppose your work week runs from Tuesday through Saturday, and your work day is from 4 am to 12 noon. You can make changes to the Calendar so that it reflects your actual work week. You can also set your time zone and add holidays to your calendar.

To set Calendar options, follow these steps:

**1.** Choose **Tools, Options**. The Options dialog box appears.

**2.** Click the **Calendar** tab (see Figure 20.3).

**563**

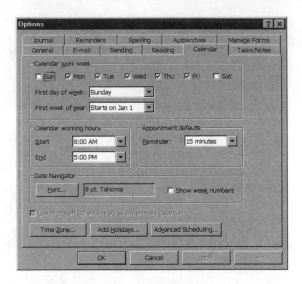

**Figure 20.3**  Set your calendar work week to suit your schedule.

3. In the Calendar Work Week area, choose the days of the week you usually work (the default is Monday through Friday). You also can set the first day of your week and the first week of your year.

4. In the Calendar Working Hours area, set your starting and ending time (the default is 8 am to 5 pm).

5. To set the time zone for your area, click the **Time Zone** button, and then choose the zone that describes your location.

6. To add holidays to your calendar, click the **Add Holidays** button. Then check the box representing your country (US is default) and click **OK**. Outlook imports the US holidays to the calendar.

7. When you're done, click **Apply** to save the changes and view another tab, or click **OK** to save the changes and close the dialog box.

In this lesson, you learned to set e-mail, calendar, and other options in Outlook.

# Access

# What Is a Database?

*In this lesson, you learn some basic database concepts and find out how Microsoft Access handles them.*

## What Are Databases Good For?

Strictly speaking, a database is any collection of information. Your local telephone book, for example, is a database, as is your Rolodex file and the card catalog at your local library. With a computerized database in Microsoft Access, you can store information as these three examples do, but you can also do much more. For instance, if you keep a list of all your business customers in an Access database, you can:

- Print out a list of all customers who haven't bought anything in the last 60 days, along with their phone numbers, so you can call each one.
- Sort the customers by ZIP code and print out mailing labels in that order. (Some bulk-mailing services require you to presort by ZIP code to get the cheaper mailing rate.)
- Create a simple on-screen order entry form that even your most technically unskilled employee can use successfully.

These examples only scratch the surface of what you can do. With Access, you can manipulate your data in almost any way you can dream up.

## How Access Stores Your Data

In Access, the first thing you do is create a database file. That file holds everything you create for that database—not only all the data, but also the customized forms, reports, and indexes. If you have two or more businesses, you may want to create two or more separate databases (one for each business).

# Tables

The heart of each database is its tables. A table is a lot like a spreadsheet. Figure 1.1 shows a data table (or just "table" for short).

Each column is a field.

Each row is a record.

The insersection of a row and column is a cell.

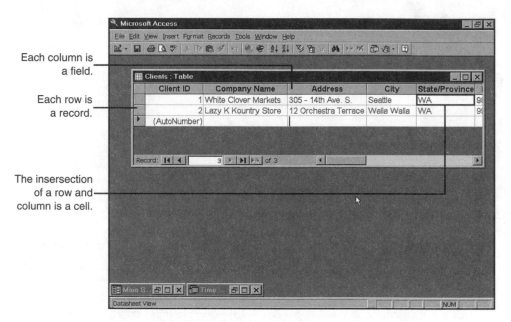

**Figure 1.1** A typical table in Access.

Access stores each database entry (such as each client or each inventory item) in its own row; this is a *record*. For example, all the information about White Clover Markets, including the Address, City, State, and ZIP code, forms a single record (see Figure 1.1).

Each type of detail is kept in its own column: a *field*. For example, Client ID is one field, and Company Name is another. All the company names in the entire table are collectively known as the Company Name field.

At the intersection of a field and a row is the individual bit of data for that particular record; this area is a *cell*. For example, in the cell where the City column and the White Clover Markets record intersect, you find Seattle.

You'll learn how to create tables in Lessons 6 and 7. Each database file can have many tables. For instance, you might have one table that lists all of your customers and another table that lists information about the products you sell. A third table might keep track of your salespeople and their performance.

# Forms

All the data you enter into your database ends up in a table for storage. You can enter information directly into a table, but it's a little bit awkward to do so. Most people find it easier to create a special on-screen form in which to enter the data. A form resembles any fill-in-the-blanks sheet that you might complete by hand, such as a job application. You'll learn how to create a form in Lesson 12.

Access links the form to the table and stores the information you put into the form in the table. For instance, take a look at Figure 1.2. Access will store the client data entered on this form in the table shown in Figure 1.1.

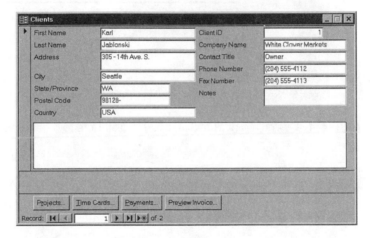

**Figure 1.2** Forms make data entry more convenient.

 **TIP** **Multitable Forms** You can use a single form to enter data into several tables at once, as you'll learn in later lessons.

# Reports

While forms are designed to be used on-screen, reports are designed to be printed. Reports are specially formatted collections of data, organized according to your specifications. For instance, you might want to create a report of all your clients like the one shown in Figure 1.3.

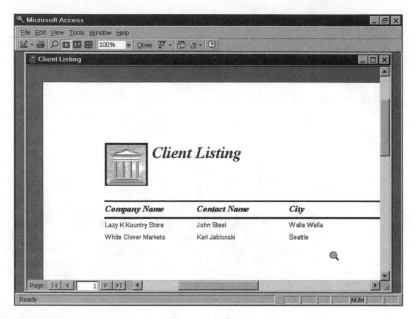

**Figure 1.3**  You might print this report to distribute to other employees.

TIP  **Print Preview**  Although you create reports so that you can print them, you can also display them on-screen in Print Preview (as in Figure 1.3). You'll learn how to view and print reports in Lesson 19.

## Queries

A *query* provides you with a way of weeding out the information you don't want to see, so that you can more clearly see the information you do need. You can think of it as a sieve you dump your data into: the data you don't want falls through the holes in the sieve, leaving only the data you're interested in.

Many people are afraid of queries because of the technical terms associated with them (such as values, criteria, and masks). But there's no need to be wary. In Lesson 16, you'll learn to create and use a simple query.

## How the Parts Fit Together

Even though you create tables, reports, forms, and queries in separate steps, they're all related. As I mentioned earlier, tables are the central focus of all activities—all the other objects do something to or with the table data. Reports summarize and organize the table data; forms help you enter information into the table; queries help you find information you want to use in the table. In future lessons, you'll learn how each part relates to the whole database.

# Access Wizards Make Databases Easy

Throughout this book, you will use the Access wizards. What's a wizard? It's a mini program that "interviews" you, asking you questions about what you want to accomplish. Then it takes your answers and creates the table, report, query, or whatever, according to your specifications. Figure 1.4 shows a sample wizard screen.

Each time you create a new object, such as a table or a form, you have the choice of creating it "from scratch" in a Design view or with a wizard to help you.

I recommend that beginners use wizards as much as possible. I use them because they're so convenient. Leave the tough stuff—the Design view creations—to those with lots of leisure time.

In this lesson, you learned some basic facts about databases and Access. In the next lesson, you'll learn some strategies for planning your database. Don't skip Lesson 2! Ten minutes worth of up-front planning can save you hours of back-tracking later.

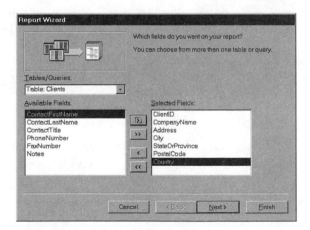

**Figure 1.4**   Wizards make it easy to create all kinds of database objects.

# Planning Your Database

*In this lesson, you learn some principles of good database design to help you plan your course of action.*

## Planning Is Important!

How many times have you dived enthusiastically into a new craft or skill without really knowing what you were doing? Your first attempt was probably pretty poor, whether the pursuit was pottery or computer programming. But as you worked, you probably made notes to yourself of what you'd do differently next time, and the next time you did better.

With something as important as your database, however, you can't afford to learn by experimentation and trial and error. So in this lesson, I'll give you a crash course in the database planning that most people learn the hard way.

Before you create your database, you should ask yourself the following questions:

- What data do I want to store, and what is the best way to organize it? This determines what tables you'll need.
- What data entry actions do I perform in the course of my business or hobby? This determines the forms you'll need.
- What information do I want to know about the status of the business or hobby? This answer will tell you what reports you'll want.

# Determining What Tables You'll Need

How many tables will you need? Technically, you will only need one. That's the minimum a database can function with. However, the biggest mistake most people make with Access is to put too much information in one table. Access is a relational database program; unlike more simple database programs, it's meant to handle lots of tables and create relationships among them. Figure 2.1 shows a list of tables in a database that keeps track of the employee hours spent on various projects.

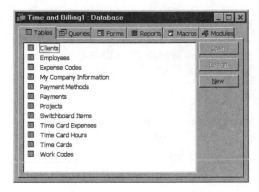

**Figure 2.1** Access really shines when you take advantage of its capability to store many tables.

 TIP **Plan Tables Now!** You should plan your tables before you create your database because changing a table's structure once it's been filled with data is difficult.

Another big mistake people make is to try to make each table look like a stand-alone report. For instance, they might repeat a customer's name and address in all eight tables because they want that information readily available when it's required. This is a waste! You can easily create a report or form that includes this information whenever you need it. You really only need the information in one table.

# Normalizing Your Database

When a database suffers from poor table organization, experts say it's not *normalized*. There are rules that govern how a relational database should store its tables. Those rules are called the rules of Data Normalization.

 **TERM**    **Data Normalization**  The process of making tables as efficient and compact as possible to eliminate the possibility for confusion and error.

There are five normalization rules, but the latter ones are fairly complicated and are used mostly by database professionals. In this lesson, I'll explain the first two normalization rules, which are all a beginner really needs to understand in order to avoid major mistakes.

 **TIP**   **Normalized Wizards**  Luckily, database professionals had a hand in creating Access's Database Wizard, so any tables you create using this feature (see Lesson 4) will be normalized.

## Rule #1: Avoid Repeated Information

Let's say that you want to keep contact information on your customers along with a record of each transaction they make. If you kept it all in one table (like the one shown below), you would have to repeat the customer's full name, address, and phone number each time you entered a new transaction! And it would also be a nightmare if the customer's address changed; you would have to make the change to every transaction.

| Customer Name | Customer Address | Customer Phone | Order Date | Order Total |
|---|---|---|---|---|
| ABC Plumbing | 201 W. 44th St. | (317) 555-2394 | 2/5/96 | $155.90 |
| ABC Plumbing | 201 W. 44th St. | (317) 555-2394 | 5/14/96 | $90.24 |
| ABC Plumbing | 201 W. 44th St. | (317) 555-2394 | 7/9/96 | $224.50 |
| Jack's Emporium | 1155 Conner Ave. | (317) 555-4501 | 6/6/95 | $1,592.99 |
| Jack's Emporium | 1155 Conner Ave. | (317) 555-4501 | 7/26/96 | $990.41 |
| Millie's Pizza | 108 Ponting St. | (317) 554-2349 | 8/29/96 | $39.95 |

A better way is to assign each customer an ID number. Include that ID number in a table that contains names and addresses (see the Customers Table, below). Then you can include the same ID number as a link in a separate table that contains transactions (see the Orders Table).

Customers Table

| Customer ID | Customer Name | Customer Address | Customer Phone |
|---|---|---|---|
| 1 | ABC Plumbing | 201 W. 44th St. | (317) 555-2394 |
| 2 | Jack's Emporium | 1155 Conner Ave. | (317) 555-4501 |
| 3 | Millie's Pizza | 108 Ponting St. | (317) 554-2349 |

Orders Table

| Customer ID | Order Date | Order Total |
|---|---|---|
| 1 | 2/5/96 | $155.90 |
| 1 | 5/14/96 | $90.24 |
| 1 | 7/9/96 | $224.50 |
| 2 | 6/6/95 | $1,592.99 |
| 2 | 7/26/96 | $990.41 |
| 3 | 8/29/96 | $39.95 |

## Rule #2: Avoid Redundant Data

Let's say you want to keep track of which employees have attended certain training classes. There are lots of employees and lots of classes. One way to do this would be to keep it all in a single Personnel table, like this:

| Employee Name | Employee Address | Employee Phone | Training Date | Class Taken | Credit Hours | Passed? |
|---|---|---|---|---|---|---|
| Phil Sharp | 211 W. 16th St. | (317) 555-4321 | 5/5/96 | Leadership Skills | 3 | Yes |
| Becky Rowan | 40 Westfield Ct. | (317) 555-3905 | 5/5/96 | Customer Service | 2 | Yes |
| Nick Gianti | 559 Ponting St. | (317) 555-7683 | 6/15/96 | Public Speaking | 9 | Yes |
| Martha Donato | 720 E. Warren | (317) 555-2930 | 5/5/96 | Public Speaking | 9 | No |
| Cynthia Hedges | 108 Carroll St. | (317) 555-5990 | 6/15/96 | Customer Service | 2 | Yes |
| Andrea Mayfair | 3904 110th St. | (317) 555-0293 | 6/15/96 | Leadership Skills | 3 | Yes |

But what if an employee takes more than one class? You'd have to add a duplicate line in the table to list it, and then you'd have the problem described in the previous section—multiple records with virtually identical field entries. And what if the only employee who has taken a certain class leaves the company? When you delete that employee's record, you delete the information about the class's credit hours, too.

A better way would be to create separate tables for Employees, Classes, and Training. Here are some examples of what such tables might look like.

Employee Table

| Employee ID | Employee Name | Employee Address | Employee Phone |
|---|---|---|---|
| 1 | Phil Sharp | 211 W. 16th St. | (317) 555-4321 |
| 2 | Becky Rowan | 40 Westfield Ct. | (317) 555-3905 |
| 3 | Nick Gianti | 559 Ponting St. | (317) 555-7683 |
| 4 | Martha Donato | 720 E. Warren | (317) 555-2930 |
| 5 | Cynthia Hedges | 108 Carroll St. | (317) 555-5990 |
| 6 | Andrea Mayfair | 3904 110th St. | (317) 555-0293 |

Class Table

| Class ID | Class | Credits |
|---|---|---|
| C1 | Leadership Skills | 3 |
| C2 | Customer Service | 2 |
| C3 | Public Speaking | 9 |

Training Table

| Employee ID | Date | Class | Passed? |
|---|---|---|---|
| 1 | 5/5/96 | C1 | Yes |
| 2 | 5/5/96 | C2 | Yes |
| 3 | 6/16/96 | C3 | Yes |
| 4 | 5/5/96 | C3 | No |
| 5 | 6/15/96 | C2 | Yes |
| 6 | 6/15/96 | C1 | Yes |

# Summary: Designing Your Tables

Don't be overwhelmed by all this information about database normalization. Good table organization boils down to a few simple principles:

- Each table should have a theme, such as Employee Contact Information or Customer Transactions. Try to restrict yourself to only one theme per table.
- If you see that you might end up repeating data in a table in the future, plan now to separate the information that will be repeated into its own table.

- If there is a list of reference information you want to preserve (such as the names and credit hours for classes), put it in its own table.
- Wherever possible, use ID numbers, as they'll help you link tables together later and help you avoid typing errors that come from entering long text strings (such as names) over and over.

# What Forms Will You Use?

As explained in Lesson 1, forms are data entry tools. You can arrange fields from several tables on a form, and you can easily enter data into those fields on a single screen. For instance, a timesheet form for an employee might contain fields from the Employees, Projects, and Work Codes tables. Figure 2.2 shows such a form.

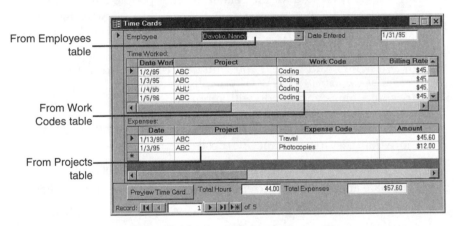

**Figure 2.2**   A form can link several tables.

When thinking about what forms you'll need, the question is really "what actions will I perform?" The following list describes some actions that might require a form:

- Hiring employees (and entering their information in the database)
- Selling goods or services
- Making purchases
- Collecting the names and contact information for volunteers
- Keeping track of inventory

**CAUTION**

**I Can't Predict What Forms I'll Need!**  Although it's important to have effective forms, you can make changes to forms at any time fairly easily (unlike tables), so you don't have to know exactly what forms you want before you start. You'll learn to create forms in Lesson 12.

# What Reports Will You Want to Produce?

A report satisfies your need for information about your data. It's usually printed (unlike tables and forms, which are usually used on-screen only). For instance, you may want a report of all people who have not paid their membership dues, or all accounts with a balance owed of more than $1,000.00. (You can find this information with a query, too, as you'll learn in Lesson 16.)

A report is usually created for the benefit of other people who aren't sitting with you at your computer. For instance, you might print a report to hand out to your board of directors to encourage them to keep you on as CEO! A report can pull data from many tables at once, perform calculations on the data (such as summing or averaging), and present you with neatly formatted results.

Here are some things you can do with reports:

- Print a list of all your personal possessions with a replacement value of more than $50, for insurance purposes.
- Show a list of all club members who have not paid their dues.
- Calculate and show the current depreciated value of all capital equipment.
- List the commissions paid to each of your top 50 salespeople in the last quarter, compared to the company-wide average.

You can create new reports at any time; you do not have to plan them before you create your database. However, if you know you will want a certain report, you might design your tables in the format that will be most effective for that report's use.

In this lesson, you planned your database tables, forms, and reports. In the next lessons, you'll learn to start and exit Access.

# Starting and Exiting Access

*In this lesson, you learn to start and exit Microsoft Access.*

## Starting Access

There may be several ways you can start Access, depending on how you've installed it. The most straightforward way is to use the Start menu. Follow these steps:

1. Click the **Start** button, and the Start menu appears.
2. Highlight or point to **Programs**. A list of your program groups appears.
3. Click **Microsoft Access**, and Access starts.

**TIP**   **Moving Programs Around on the Start Menu**   If you would prefer to have Access in a different program group, right-click the **Start** button and select **Explore** from the shortcut menu. Then use the Explorer to find and move the Microsoft Access shortcut to a different program group.

## Other Ways to Start Access

Here are some other ways to start Access. Some of these require more knowledge of Windows 95 or Windows NT Workstation and Microsoft Office; if you're confused by them, stick with the primary method explained in the preceding steps.

- You can create a shortcut icon for Access and place it on your desktop. You can then start Access by double-clicking the icon.

- When you're browsing files in the Windows Explorer program, you can double-click any Access data file to start Access and open that file. Access data files have an .MDB extension and a little icon next to them that resembles the icon that's next to Microsoft Access on the Programs menu.

- If you can't find Access, you can search for it. Click the **Start** button, select **Find**, and select **Files**. In the **Named** box, type **msaccess.exe**. Then open the **Look In** list, select **My Computer**, and click **Find Now**. When the file appears in the list below, double-click it to start Access.

When you start Access, the first thing you'll see is a dialog box prompting you to create a new database or open an existing one (see Figure 3.1). For now, click **Cancel**. (We won't be working with any particular database in this lesson.)

**Figure 3.1** This Microsoft Access dialog box appears each time you start Access.

# Parts of the Screen

Access is much like any other Windows program: it contains menus, toolbars, a status bar, and so on. Figure 3.2 points out these landmarks. Notice that in Figure 3.2, many of the toolbar buttons are grayed out (which means you can't use them right now). There's also nothing in the work area. That's because no database file is open. As you will see, the Access screen will become a much busier place in later lessons when you begin working with a database. The buttons will become available, and your database will appear in the work area.

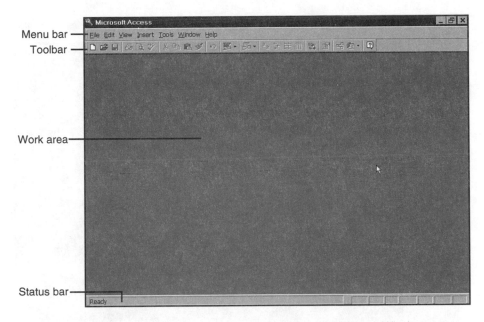

Menu bar
Toolbar
Work area
Status bar

**Figure 3.2** Access has the same interface landmarks as any Windows program.

# Understanding Access Toolbars

If you have used Windows programs before, you are probably familiar with toolbars. They're rows of buttons that represent common commands you can issue. Toolbar buttons are often shortcuts for menu commands.

The toolbar changes depending on what type of object you're currently working with (a table, a form, and so on) and what you're doing to it. More toolbars sometimes appear when you're doing special activities, such as drawing. To find out what a toolbar button does, point at it with your mouse pointer. Its name appears next to the pointer in a ScreenTip (see Figure 3.3). You can use ScreenTips even when a button is unavailable (grayed out).

 **TIP** **Customizing Toolbars** You can choose which toolbars are displayed at any time, and you can even add buttons to and remove buttons from any toolbar. Right-click any toolbar and a shortcut menu appears. Use that list to choose which toolbars are displayed, or click **Customize** to open a dialog box in which you can customize a toolbar's buttons.

Close button

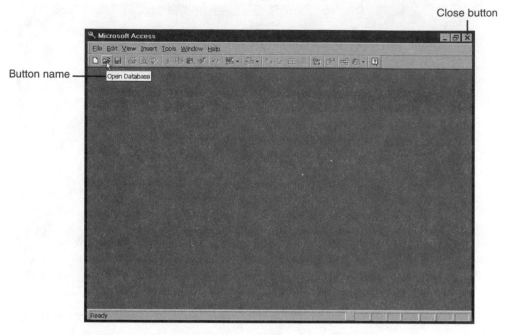

Button name —— Open Database

**Figure 3.3** To find out what a toolbar button does, point at it.

# Exiting Access

When you finish working with Access, you should exit to free up your
computer's memory for other tasks. Here are several ways to exit Access:

- Press **Alt+F4**.
- Select **File**, **Exit**.
- Click the Access window's **Close** (X) button (see Figure 3.3).

TIP **Alt+F4? File, Exit?** In this book, I use a kind of shorthand to tell you which
keys to press and which menu commands to select. When you see "press
**Alt+F4**," it means "hold down the Alt key on the keyboard and press the F4
key." When you see "select **File**, **Exit**," it means "click the word File on the
menu bar, and then click the Exit command on the menu that appears."

In this lesson, you learned to start and exit Access, and you learned about the
main parts of the screen, including the toolbar buttons. In the next lesson, you'll
learn how to create a new database.

**582**

# Creating a
# New Database

*In this lesson, you learn how to create a blank database. You also
learn how to create a database with pre-made tables, reports, and forms using the Database Wizard.*

## Choosing the Right Way to Create Your Database

Before you create your database, you have an important decision to make.
Should you create a blank database from scratch, and then manually create
all the tables, reports, and forms you'll need? Or should you use a Database
Wizard, which does all that for you?

**Database Wizard**   Access comes with several Database Wizards. These
are mini-programs that question you about your needs and then create a
database structure that matches them. (You will enter the actual data yourself.)

The answer depends on how well the available wizards match your needs. If
there is a Database Wizard that is close to what you want, it's quickest to use it
to create your database, and then modify it as needed. (Of course, you won't
know which wizards are available until you open the list of them, later in this
lesson.) If you're in a hurry, using a wizard can save you lots of time.

On the other hand, if you want a special-purpose database that isn't similar to any of the wizards, or if you're creating the database primarily as a training exercise for yourself, you should create the blank database.

# Creating a Blank Database

Creating a blank database is very simple because you're just creating an outer shell at this point, without any tables, forms, etc. This section outlines two ways to do that.

If you just started Access, and the Microsoft Access dialog box is still displayed (see Figure 4.1), follow these steps:

1. Click **Blank Database**.
2. Click the **OK** button.

**Figure 4.1** When you first start Access, you can start a new database quickly from the Microsoft Access dialog box.

If the dialog box is gone, you can't get it back until you exit from Access and restart it. But you don't need that dialog box to start a new database. At any time you can follow these steps:

1. Select **File**, **New** or click the **New** button on the toolbar. The New dialog box appears (see Figure 4.2).
2. Click the **General** tab if necessary to bring it to the top. Then double-click the **Blank Database** icon, and the File New Database dialog box appears.

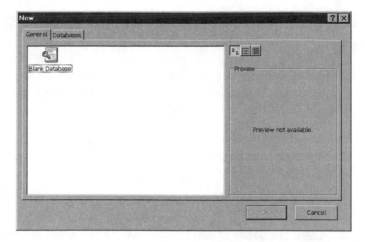

**Figure 4.2** The New dialog box's different tabs give you options to create different kinds of databases.

3. Type a name for your new database (preferably something descriptive) in the **File Name** box. For example, I typed "Kennel Records." Then click **Create**. Access creates the new database, as shown in Figure 4.3.

Your database is completely blank at this point. You can click any of the tabs in the database window (see Figure 4.3), but you won't find anything listed on any of them. Later, you'll learn to create tables (Lessons 6 and 7), forms (Lesson 12), queries (Lesson 16), and reports (Lesson 18) to fill these tabbed windows.

**Figure 4.3** A new, blank database window.

# Creating a Database with Database Wizard

A Database Wizard can create almost all the tables, forms, and reports you will ever need, automatically! The trick is choosing the right wizard to suit your purpose. Follow these steps:

1. If you just started Access, and the Microsoft Access dialog box is still on-screen, click **Database Wizard** and click **OK**. Or, if you've already closed the dialog box, select **File**, **New Database**. Either way, the New dialog box appears.

2. Click the **Databases** tab to display the list of wizards.

3. Click one of the Database Wizards. (They're the icons with the magic wands across them.) For this example, choose **Contact Management**. A preview appears in the Preview area.

4. When you've found the wizard you want, click **OK**. The File New Database dialog box appears.

5. Type a name for the database and click **Create** to continue. The wizard starts, and some information appears explaining what the wizard will do.

6. Click **Next** to continue. A list of the tables to be created appears (see Figure 4.4). The tables appear on the left, and the selected table's fields on the right.

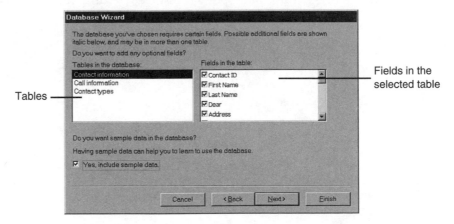

**Figure 4.4**  These are the tables and fields that this wizard will create automatically for you.

**7.** Click a table and examine its list of fields. Optional fields are in italic. To include an optional field, click it to place a check mark next to it.

**CAUTION**

**I Don't Want These Tables and Fields!**   Sorry, that's the price you pay for going with a prefabricated wizard. You can't deselect any fields except the optional (italicized) ones. But you can delete the tables and fields you don't want later. See Lesson 9 to learn how to delete individual fields or an entire table. If the tables and fields seem to be totally inappropriate, perhaps you are using the wrong wizard for your needs. If so, click **Cancel** and try another.

**8.** (Optional) If you are creating this database for a learning experience only, click the **Yes, Include Sample Data** check box. This tells Access to enter some dummy records into the database so you can see how they will work in the database.

**9.** Click **Next** to continue. The wizard asks you what kind of screen display style you want.

**10.** Click a display style in the list and examine the preview of that style that appears. When you have decided on a style, click it and click **Next**. The wizard asks you for a style for printed reports.

**11.** Click a report style and examine the preview of it. When you have decided on a style, click it and click **Next**.

**12.** The wizard asks what title you want for the database. The title will appear on reports, and it can be different from the file name. Enter a title (see Figure 4.5).

**13.** (Optional) If you want to include a picture (such as your company logo) on your forms and reports, click the **Yes, I'd Like to Include a Picture** check box. Then click the **Picture** button, choose a graphics file (change the drive and/or folder if needed), and click **Open** to return to the wizard.

**14.** Click **Next** to continue. When you get to the Finish screen, click **Finish**. The wizard goes to work creating your database. (It may take several minutes.)

When the database is finished, the Main Switchboard window appears (see Figure 4.6). The Switchboard will open automatically whenever you open the database.

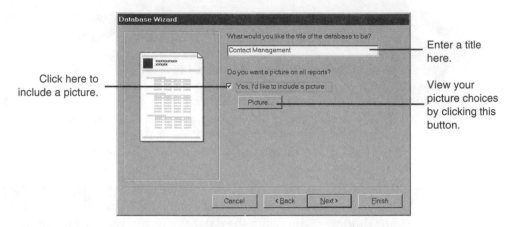

**Figure 4.5** Enter a title for the database and choose a graphic to use for a logo (if you want).

All of the databases created by a Database Wizard include the Main Switchboard. The Main Switchboard is nothing more than a fancy form with some programming built in. It lets you perform common tasks with the database by clicking a button. We won't be working with the Main Switchboard, so click the Main Switchboard window's **Close** (X) button to get rid of it.

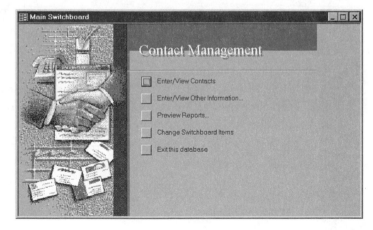

**Figure 4.6** The Switchboard window is a bonus provided by the Database Wizards.

CAUTION

**I Hate That Switchboard!**   To prevent the Switchboard from opening when you open the database, select **Tools**, **Startup**. Open the **Display Form** drop-down list, select **[None]**, and click **OK**.

Once you close the Switchboard window, you'll see the database window. If it's minimized, double-click its title bar (bottom left corner of the screen) to open it again. Click the **Tables** tab, and you see that several tables have been created for you. Click the other tabs to see the other objects created as well.

Even though you may have all the tables, reports, and forms you need, you may still want to go through the lessons in this part in sequential order to learn about creating and modifying these objects. If you're in a hurry to enter data, though, skip to either Lesson 9 (where you learn to enter data in a table) or the end of Lesson 12 (where you learn to enter data using a form).

In this lesson, you learned to create a database from scratch and using a Database Wizard. In the next lesson, you'll learn how to save, close, and open a database.

# Saving, Closing, and Opening a Database

*In this lesson, you learn to save your database, close it, and reopen it.*
*You also learn how to find a misplaced database file.*

## Saving a Database

You need to save your work so that you don't lose anything you've typed after you turn off the computer. When you created the database, you saved it by naming it. When you enter each record, Access automatically saves your work. (You'll learn to enter records in Lesson 9.) In Access, you really don't need to save your work until you're ready to close your database.

When you change the structure of a table, form, or other object, however, Access will not let you close that object or close the database without confirming whether or not you want to save your changes. You'll see a dialog box like the one in Figure 5.1; just click **Yes** to save your changes.

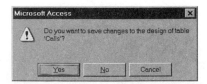

**Figure 5.1** When you make changes to an object's structure, Access asks whether it should save your changes.

Notice that the Save and Save As commands on the File menu aren't even available most of the time; they're grayed out. When you have a particular object (such as a table) highlighted in the Database window, the Save As/Export command is available. You can use this command to save your table in a different format that another program (such as Excel) can read.

 **TIP** **Using Tables in Other Programs**  Another way to copy a table to another application or another database is with the Copy and Paste commands. Highlight the table in the Database window and select **Edit**, **Copy**. Then open a different database or application and select **Edit**, **Paste**. A dialog box opens, giving you the options of pasting the table structure only or the structure and the data. You can also choose to append the data to an existing tables, if the fields match up.

# Closing a Database

When you finish working with a database, you should close it. When you finish using Access, exit the program (see Lesson 3), and the database closes along with the program. But what if you're not ready to close Access? If you want to close one database and then open another, close the database using one of these methods:

- Double-click the **Control-menu** icon in the upper-left corner of the database window (see Figure 5.2).
- Click the database window's **Close** (X) button in the upper-right corner.
- Select **File, Close**.
- Press **Ctrl+F4**.
- Press **Ctrl+W**.

 **Can't I Have More Than One Database Open?**  Sure you can. In fact, you might want several open so that you can transfer data between them. However, if your computer is short on memory (less than 16 megabytes), you'll **CAUTION**  want to close all files you're not using so Access will run faster.

Select Close
from the File
menu.

Double-click here.

Click here.

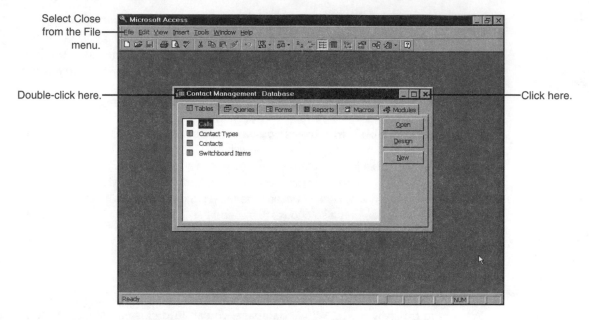

**Figure 5.2**   There are several ways to close a database.

# Opening a Database

When you start Access the next time you want to use your database, you won't create a new datatbase from scratch as you did in Lesson 4. You'll open your existing one.

The easiest way to open a database you've recently used is to select it from the File menu. Follow these steps:

**1.** Open the **File** menu. At the bottom of the menu, Access lists up to four databases you've recently used.

**2.** Click the database you want to open.

If the database you want to open isn't listed, you'll need to use the following procedure instead:

**1.** Select **File**, **Open** or click the **Open** button on the Standard toolbar. The Open dialog box appears (see Figure 5.3).

Folder name—
File names—

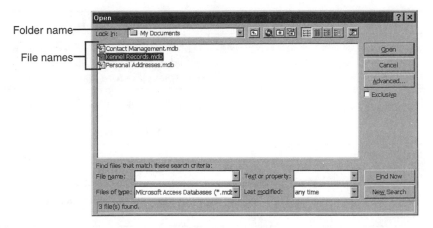

**Figure 5.3** Open a different database file with this dialog box.

**2.** If the file isn't in the currently displayed folder, change drives and folders as necessary. (Refer to the next section, "Changing the Drive or Folder" for details.)

**3.** Double-click the file to open it.

## Changing the Drive or Folder

Windows 95 and Windows NT Workstation applications provide a different dialog box for opening files than you may be used to with Windows 3.1 applications. It takes a bit of getting used to. Figure 5.3 shows the dialog box; Table 5.1 explains the buttons you see in it.

**Table 5.1** Buttons for Changing Drives and Folders in Dialog Boxes

| Button | Purpose |
| --- | --- |
| My Documents | Shows every drive that your computer has access to, plus your Network Neighborhood and Briefcase. Use this to choose a different drive. |
| (up one level icon) | Moves to the folder "above" the one shown in the Look In box (that is, the folder that the current one is inside of). |

| Button | Purpose |
| --- | --- |
| | Shows the C:\WINDOWS\FAVORITES folder, no matter which folder was displayed before. |
| | Adds a shortcut for the currently displayed folder to the C:\WINDOWS\ FAVORITES folder. |
| | Shows the folders and files in the currently displayed folder in a list. |
| | Shows details about each file and folder. |
| | Shows the properties of the selected file. |
| | Shows a preview (if available) of the selected file. |
| | Opens a shortcut menu of settings that affect the way the dialog box shows the files or that affect the selected file. |

**Network Neighborhood and Briefcase** These are two special locations that you may have available on the list of folders. Network Neighborhood gives you access to computers on your local area network, and Briefcase manages files between your laptop and your main computer.

# Finding a Database File

If you're having trouble locating your file, Access can help you look. Follow these steps.

**1.** Select **File, Open Database** if the File Open dialog box is not on-screen.

**2.** In the **File Name** box at the bottom of the dialog box, type the name of the file you're looking for. (Refer to Figure 5.3.)

**Wild Cards** You can use wild cards if you don't know the entire name of the file you're looking for. An **\*** wild card stands in for "any unkown characters," and a **?** wild card stands in for "any single unknown character." For instance, if you know the file begins with P, you could use **P\*.mdb** to find all Access files that begin with P.

**3.** (Optional) If desired, enter any of these other search criteria:

- If you're looking for a different file type, choose it from the **Files of Type** drop-down list.
- If you're looking for a file containing certain text, type it in the **Text or Property** box.
- If you know when you last modified the file, choose the time interval from the **Last Modified** drop-down list.

**4.** Click the **Advanced** button, and the Advanced Find dialog box appears (see Figure 5.4).

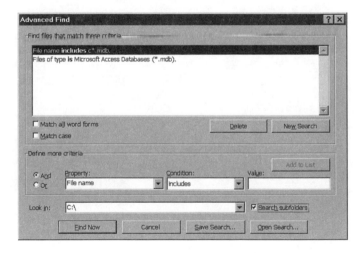

**Figure 5.4** Use the Advanced Find dialog box to select which folders and drives to look in.

**5.** In the **Look In** section at the bottom of the Advanced Find dialog box, narrow down the search area as much as possible:

- If you are sure the file is in a certain folder, type that folder's path in the **Look In** box (for example, C:\WINDOWS).

**595**

- If you are sure the file is on a certain drive, select that drive from the **Look In** list.

- If you don't know which drive contains the file, select **My Computer** from the **Look In** list.

6. Click to select the **Search Subfolders** check box if necessary.

7. Click the **Find Now** button. The Open dialog box reappears, listing all files that were found that matched your criteria.

8. Double-click the desired file to open it.

In this lesson, you learned how to save, close, and open a database. In the next lesson, you will learn how to create a table using Table Wizard.

# Creating a Table with the Table Wizard

*In this lesson, you learn to create a table using the Table Wizard. (To learn how to create a table from scratch, see Lesson 7).*

## Why Create a Table?

Tables are the basis for the whole database. Tables hold your data. Everything else is just dress-up. If you created an empty database in Lesson 4, you'll need to create tables now following the plan you developed in Lesson 2. If you used the Database Wizard to create your tables, you can create new tables here to augment them, or you can skip to Lesson 8, where you'll learn to modify and customize the tables.

When you create a table, you can create it "from scratch," or you can use the Table Wizard. This lesson covers the Table Wizard; Lesson 7 covers the less-automated method.

The Table Wizard can save you lots of time by creating and formatting all the right fields for a certain purpose. Access comes with dozens of pre-made business and personal tables from which to choose. You can pick and choose among all the fields in all the pre-made tables, constructing a table that's right for your needs. Even if you can't find all the fields you need in pre-made tables, you may want to use the Table Wizard to save time, and then add the missing fields later (see Lesson 8).

**Table Wizards** There are three Table Wizards: the standard one, the Import Table Wizard, and the Link Table Wizard. In this lesson, you'll be working with only the standard Table Wizard.

**How Can I Know Beforehand?** You won't know exactly what pre-made fields Access offers until you start the Table Wizard and review the listings; if you find that none of the available tables meets your needs, you can click **Cancel** at any time and start creating your own table (see Lesson 7).

# Creating a Table Using the Table Wizard

If the fields you want to create are similar to any of Access's dozens of pre-made ones, the Table Wizard can save you a lot of time and effort. With the Table Wizard, you can copy fields from any of the dozens of sample tables. To create a table using the Table Wizard, follow these steps:

1. Select **Insert, Table** from the menu bar along the top of the screen. Or in the Database window, click the **Tables** tab and click **New**. The New Table dialog box appears (see Figure 6.1).

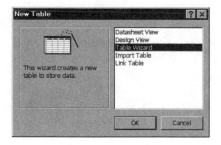

**Figure 6.1** Indicate how you want to create the new table.

**TIP** **Use the Toolbar** Instead of following step 1, you can click the **New Object** drop-down arrow on the toolbar. A drop-down list of the available object types appears. Select **New Table** from that list.

2. Click **Table Wizard** and click **OK**. The Table Wizard window appears (see Figure 6.2).

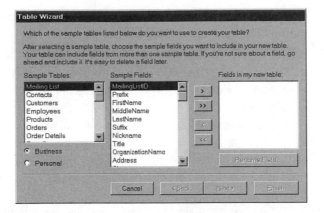

**Figure 6.2**  Choose your table's fields from those that come with any of the pre-made tables.

**3.** Click a table in the **Sample Tables** list. Access then displays its fields in the Sample Fields list.

TIP  **Business or Pleasure?**  There are two separate lists of tables. By default, you see the Business list. To see the Personal list, click the **Personal** option button below the Sample Tables list (see Figure 6.2).

**4.** If you see a field that you want to include in your new table, select it in the **Sample Fields** list. Then click the > button to move it to the Fields in My New Table list. To move the entire contents of the selected Sample Table to your list, click the >> button.

TIP  **Name Change!**  If you see a field that is close to what you want, but you prefer a different name for it, first add it to your list (as described in steps 3 and 4). Then click the field name to select it, click the **Rename Field** button, type a new name, and click **OK**. This renames the field on your list only—not on the original.

**5.** Repeat steps 3 and 4 to select other fields from other sample tables until the list of fields in your new table is complete. (You can remove a field from the list by clicking the < button, and you can remove all the fields and start over by clicking the << button.) When you're finished adding fields, click **Next** to continue.

**599**

6. Next the wizard asks for a name for the table. Type a more descriptive name to replace the default one.

7. Click **Yes, Set a Primary Key for Me** to have the wizard choose your primary key field, or **No, I'll Set the Primary Key** to do it yourself. If you choose Yes, skip to step 10.

**Primary Key Field** The designated field for which every record must have a unique entry. This is usually an ID number, because most other fields could conceivably be the same for more than one record (for instance, two people might have the same first name).

8. A dialog box appears (see Figure 6.3) asking which field will be the primary key. Open the drop-down list and select the field.

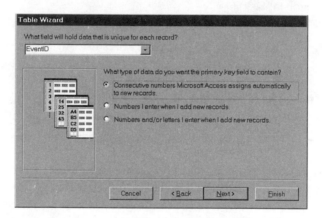

**Figure 6.3** You can set your own primary key for the table.

9. Choose a data type for the primary key field:

   • **Consecutive numbers Microsoft Access assigns automatically to new records.** Choose this if your primary key field is a simple record number. (That is, if you're numbering the records you enter consecutively as you enter them.)

   • **Numbers I enter when I add new records.** Choose this if you want to enter your own numbers. Access will not allow you to enter any letters. This choice works well for unique ID numbers such as driver's license numbers.

- **Numbers and/or letters I enter when I add new records.** Choose this if you want to include both numbers and letters in the field. For instance, if your primary key field will contain vehicle identification numbers for the cars in your fleet, you will need to enter both numbers and letters.

**10.** Click **Next** to continue.

**11.** If you already have at least one table in this database, a screen appears asking about the relationship between tables. Just click **Next** to move past it for now.

**12.** At the Finish screen, click one of the following options:

- **Modify the table design**. This takes you into Table Design view, the same as if you had created all those fields yourself. Choose this if you have some changes you want to make to the table before you use it.

- **Enter data directly into the table**. This takes you to Table Datasheet view, where you can enter records into the rows of the table. Choose this if the table's design seems perfect to you as-is.

- **Enter data into the table using a form the wizard creates for me**. This jumps you ahead a bit in this part of the book; it leads you right into the Form Wizard covered in Lesson 12. Leave this one alone for now if you want to continue following along with the lessons in this part in order.

**13.** Click **Finish**, and you're taken to the area of Access that you indicated you wanted to go (in step 12).

If you decide you don't want to work with this table anymore for now (no matter what you selected in step 12), click the **Close** (X) button for the window that appears.

Now you have a table. In the Database window, when you click the **Tables** tab, you can see your table in the list (see Figure 6.4).

**Figure 6.4** Now you have a table on your Tables tab.

# Now What?

From here, there are a number of places you can go:

- To learn how to create a table from scratch, go on to Lesson 7, "Creating a Table Without a Wizard."

- To modify the table you just created, jump to Lesson 8, "Modifying a Table."

- To enter data into your table, skip to Lesson 9, "Entering Data in a Table."

- To create a data entry form for easier data entry, check out Lesson 12, "Creating a Simple Form." (Don't do this yet if you still want to modify your table.)

In this lesson, you learned to create a new table using the Table Wizard. In the next lesson, you'll learn how to create a table without the wizard.

# Creating a Table Without a Wizard

*In this lesson, you learn to create a table in Table Design view.*

## Why Not Use a Wizard?

Access's wizards are very useful, but they do not offer the flexibility you have when performing the equivalent tasks "from scratch." For instance, if you want to create a table that contains special fields not available in a wizard, you are better off creating that table in Table Design view. You'll learn to do that in this lesson.

## Creating a Table in Table Design View

To create a table in Table Design view, follow these steps:

1.  Select **Insert**, **Table** or, from the Database window, click the **Table** tab and click the **New** button. The New Table dialog box appears (see Figure 7.1).

**Figure 7.1**  Start your new table in Design View.

**TIP** 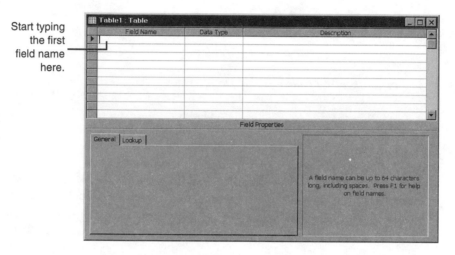 **Quick! A New Object!**   Instead of step 1, you can click the **New Object** drop-down arrow on the toolbar. A drop-down list appears, showing the available object types. Select **New Table** from that list.

2. Click **Design View** and click **OK**. Table Design view opens (see Figure 7.2).

Start typing the first field name here.

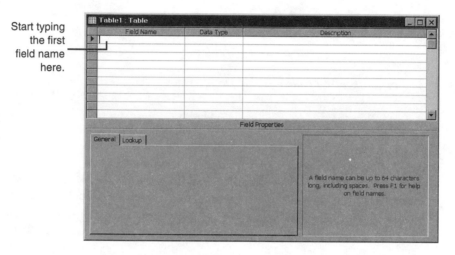

**Figure 7.2**   From Table Design view, you can control the entire table creation process.

3. Type a field name on the first empty line in the **Field Name** column. Then press **Tab** to move to the Data Type column.

**TERM**

**Field Naming Rules**   Field names—and all other objects in Access for that matter—can contain up to 64 characters and can include spaces and any symbols except periods (.), exclamation marks (!), accent grave symbols (`), or square brackets ([]). However, you may want to stick with short, easy-to-remember names.

4. When you move to the Data Type column, an arrow appears there for a drop-down list. Open the **Data Type** drop-down list and select a field type. (See the section "Understanding Data Types and Formats" later in this lesson if you need help deciding which field type to use.)

5. (Optional) Press **Tab** to move to the Description column, and then type a description of the field. (The table will work fine even without a description.)

6. In the bottom half of the dialog box, you see Field Properties for the field type you selected (see Figure 7.3). Make any changes desired to them. (See "Understanding Data Types and Formats" later in this lesson for help.)

Field properties—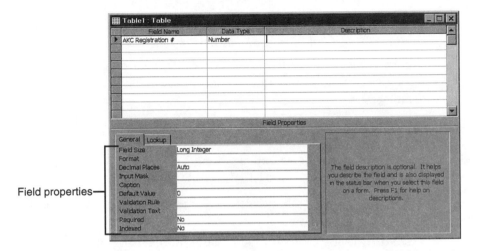

**Figure 7.3**   The Field Properties change depending on the field type.

**TIP**   **Switching Between Views**   At any time after you've entered the first field, you can switch to Datasheet view to see how your table is going to look. Just select **View**, **Datasheet**. You may be asked to save your work before you enter Datasheet view. If so, click **Yes**, enter a name, and click **OK**.

7. If you have more fields to enter, repeat steps 3 through 6.
8. Click the Table Design window's **Close** (X) button.
9. When you are asked if you want to save your changes to the table, click **Yes**. The Save As dialog box appears.
10. Type a name for the table in the **Table Name** text box and click **OK**.

**No Primary Key!**   When you close Table Design view, you may get a message that no primary key has been assigned. See the section "Setting the Primary Key" later in this lesson to learn what to do.

**CAUTION**

**605**

# Understanding Data Types and Formats

Each field must have a type so that Access will know how to handle its contents. Here are the types you can choose from:

**Text** Plain, ordinary typed text, which can include numbers, letters, and symbols. A Text field can contain up to 255 characters.

**Memo** More plain, ordinary text, except this one doesn't have a maximum field length. So you can type an almost infinite amount of text (64,000 characters).

**Number** A plain, ordinary number (not a currency value or a date). Access won't allow any text in a Number field.

**Date/Time** Just that—a date or a time.

**Currency** A number formatted as an amount of money.

**AutoNumber** A number that Access automatically fills in for each consecutive record.

**Yes/No** The answer to a true/false question. It can contain either of two values, which might be Yes or No, True or False, On or Off.

**OLE Object** A link to another database or file. This is an advanced feature that I don't cover in this book.

**Hyperlink** A link to a location on the World Wide Web. (See Lesson 6 in Part 7 of this book for more information.)

**Lookup Wizard** Lets you create a list to choose a value from another table or list of values in a combo box for each record. It is another advanced feature that I won't cover here.

In addition to a field type, each field has formatting options you can set. They appear in the bottom half of the dialog box in the Field Properties area. The formatting options change depending on the field type, and there are too many to list here. But these are some of the most important ones you'll encounter:

**Field Size** The maximum number of characters a user can input in that field.

**Format** A drop-down list of the available formats for that field type. You can also create custom formats.

**Default Value** If a field is usually going to contain a certain value (for instance, a certain ZIP code for almost everyone), you can enter it here to save time. It will always appear in a new record, and you can type over it in the rare instances when it doesn't apply.

**Decimal Places** For number fields, you can set the default number of decimal places a number will show.

**Required** Choose **Yes** or **No** to tell Access whether a user should be allowed to leave this field blank when entering a new record.

# Setting the Primary Key

Every table must have at least one field that has a unique value for each record. For instance, in a table of the dogs your kennel owns, you might assign an ID number to each dog, and have an ID # field in your table. Or you might choose to use each dog's AKC (American Kennel Club) registration number. This unique identifier field is known as the Primary Key field.

You must tell Access which field you are going to use as the Primary Key so that it can prevent you from accidentally entering the same value for more than one record in that field. To set a primary key, follow these steps:

**1.** In Table Design view, select the field that you want to use for the primary key.

 **2.** Select **Edit**, **Primary Key** or click the **Primary Key** button on the toolbar. A key symbol appears to the left of the field name, as shown in Figure 7.4.

Key symbol———

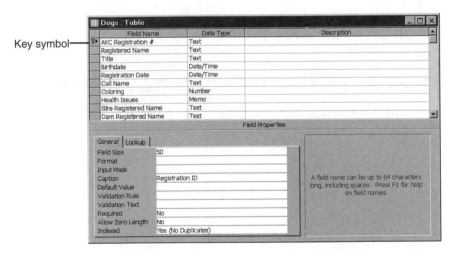

**Figure 7.4** The primary key field is marked by a key symbol.

**Primary Key Field**   The designated field for which every record must have a unique entry. This is usually an ID number, because most other fields could conceivably be the same for more than one record (for instance, two people might have the same first name).

# Switching Between Design and Datasheet Views

When working with tables, you can use one of two available views: Design view or Datasheet view.

 One easy way to switch between the views is to click the **View** drop-down arrow on the toolbar (it's the leftmost button). Then select the view you want from the drop-down list that appears.

The following steps teach you another way to switch between views:

1. Open the **View** menu.
2. Select **Table Design** or **Datasheet**, depending on which view you are currently in.
3. If you're moving from Table Design view to Datasheet view, you may be asked to save your work. If so, click **Yes**.
4. If you're asked for a name for the table, type one and click **OK**.

# Creating a Table in Datasheet View

Some people prefer to create a table in Datasheet view. However, Access designed Datasheet view for data entry and viewing, not for table structure changes. I do not recommend creating the table this way, because you do not have access to as many controls as you do with Table Design view.

To create a table in Datasheet view, follow these steps:

1. Select **Insert, Table**.
2. Click **Datasheet View** and click **OK**. A blank table opens, as shown in Figure 7.5.

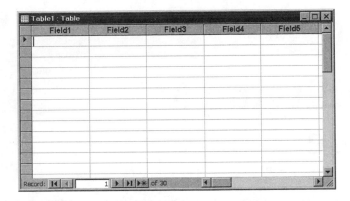

**Figure 7.5** Creating a new table in Datasheet view gives you a quick, generic table.

**How Do I Set the Field Names?** When you create a table in Datasheet view, the fields have generic names such as Field1. To change a field name, click the present name to select the column. Then select **Format**, **Rename Column**, type the new name, and press **Enter**.

**3.** Make any necessary changes to the design of the table (as explained in Lesson 8, "Modifying a Table").

**4.** When you finish making changes, click the table's **Close** (X) button. Access asks if you want to save the design changes.

**5.** Click **Yes**. When Access asks for a name for the table, type one and click **OK**.

In this lesson, you learned to create a table without the help of a wizard. Before you enter data into your table, you should make sure it's exactly the way you want it. In the next lesson, you'll learn how to make any needed changes to your table.

# Modifying a Table

8

*In this lesson, you learn how to change your table by adding and removing fields and hiding columns.*

Now that you've created a table, you may be eager to begin entering records into it. You'll learn to do that in Lesson 9. Before you begin, you should make certain that your table is structured exactly as you want it, so you won't have to backtrack later.

## Editing Fields and Their Properties

No matter how you create your table (whether with or without the Table Wizard), you can modify it using Table Design view. If you create the table without Table Wizard, Table Design view will look very familiar to you.

To enter Table Design view, do one of the following:

- From the Database window, click the **Table** tab, select the table you want to work with, and click the **Design** button.
- If the table appears in Datasheet view, select **View, Table Design.**

 Don't forget, you can quickly change views with the View button at the far left end of the Standard toolbar. Click the **View** drop-down arrow and select a view from the list that appears.

Once you're in Table Design view (see Figure 8.1), you can edit any field, as you learned in Lesson 7, "Creating a Table Without a Wizard." Here is the general procedure:

**1.** Click any field name in the **Field Name** list.

2. If desired, click the field's Data Type area and select a new data type from the drop-down list.

3. In the Field Properties area (the bottom half of the Table Design screen), click any text box in order to change its value. Some text boxes have drop-down lists, which you can activate by clicking in the box.

4. Repeat steps 1–3 for each field you want to change.

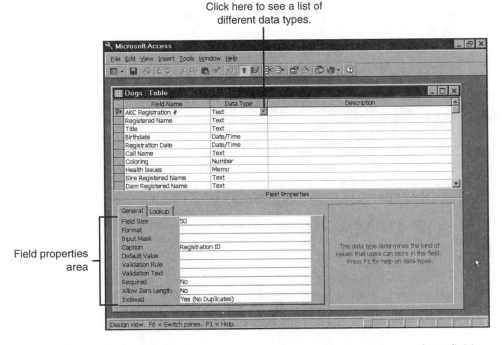

**Figure 8.1**  In Table Design view, you can modify the attributes of any field.

**I Need More Help!**  For those who created their table without a wizard (Lesson 7), the above steps will be self-explanatory. However, if you used Table Wizard, you may be lost right now. Review Lesson 7 to get up-to-speed.

# Adding Fields

Before you enter data into your table (see Lesson 9), you should make very sure that you have included all the fields you'll need. Why? Because if you add a field later, you'll have to go back and enter a value in that field for each record that you've already entered. In addition, if you change the field length, you risk truncating or invalidating data that's already been entered.

You can add a field in either Table Design view or Datasheet view. Try it in Table Design view first, since you're already there:

**1.** Select the field before which you want the new field to appear.

**2.** Click the **Insert Rows** button on the toolbar or select **Insert, Row**. A blank row appears in the Field Name list.

**3.** Enter a name, type, description, and so on for the new field. (Refer to Lesson 7 if necessary.)

# Deleting Fields

If you realize that you don't need one or more fields that you've created, now is the time to get rid of them. Otherwise, you'll needlessly enter information into each record that you will never use.

**CAUTION**

**Don't Remove Important Fields!** Be very careful about deleting fields once you start entering records in your table. When you delete a field, the information for each record stored in that field is deleted, too. The best time to experiment with deleting fields is *now*, before you enter any records.

You can erase fields in either Table Design view or Datasheet view. To delete a field in Table Design view, follow these steps:

**1.** Switch to Table Design view if you're not already there.

**2.** Select a field.

**3.** Do one of the following:

   • Press the **Delete** key on your keyboard.

   • Click the **Delete Rows** button on the toolbar.

   • Select **Edit, Delete Row**.

If you prefer, you can delete the field in Datasheet view. Whereas there's an advantage to using Table Design view to add fields, there's no significant difference when you delete fields. You can accomplish a field deletion easily in either view. Follow these steps to delete a field in Datasheet view.

1. Switch to Datasheet view if you're not already there.
2. Select the entire column for the field you want to delete.
3. Select **Edit, Delete Column**.

# Hiding a Field

If your table includes a field that you don't want to use at the moment but that you will want later, you may want to hide it instead of deleting it. There are two advantages to hiding a field:

- If you have entered any records, you can preserve the data you've entered into that field.
- The Field Properties you set when you created the field will remain intact, so you don't have to re-enter them later.

You must hide a field using Datasheet view; you cannot hide it using Table Design view. Follow these steps:

1. Switch to Datasheet view, if you aren't there already.
2. Select the field(s) you want to hide.
3. Select **Format, Hide Columns**. The columns disappear.

To unhide the column(s) later, follow these steps:

1. Select **Format, Unhide Columns**. The Unhide Columns dialog box appears (see Figure 8.2). Fields with a check mark beside them are displayed; fields without a check mark are hidden.

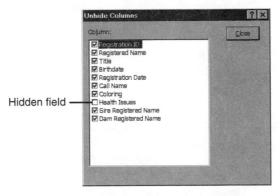

**Figure 8.2** You can either unhide or hide fields from the Unhide Columns dialog box.

**2.** Click the check box of any field that you want to change. Clicking the box switches between hidden and unhidden status.

**3.** When you're finished, click the **Close** button.

Hidden fields are still very much a part of your database. To verify that, switch to Table Design view. You'll still see them in Table Design view, along with all the other fields.

# Deleting a Table

Now that you've created a table and worked with it a bit, you may discover that you made so many mistakes creating it that it would be easier to start over. (Don't feel bad; that's what happened to me the first time.) Or you may have several tables by now, and you might decide that you don't need all of them. Whatever the reason, it's easy to delete a table. Follow these steps:

**1.** From the Database window, click the **Tables** tab.

**2.** Select the table you want to delete.

**3.** Select **Edit, Delete** or press the **Delete** key on your keyboard.

**4.** A message appears asking if you are sure you want to do this. Click **Yes**.

 **TIP**  **Cut versus Delete**  You can also cut a table. Cutting is different from deleting, because the table isn't gone forever; rather, Access moves it to the Clipboard. From there, you can paste it into a different database or into some other application. However, because the Clipboard holds only one item at a time, you will lose the table when you cut or copy something else to the Clipboard.

In this lesson, you learned how to modify your table by adding and removing fields, hiding fields, and editing the information about each field. In the next lesson, you'll begin entering data into a table.

# Entering Data into a Table

*In this lesson, you learn how to add records to a table, how to print the table, and how to close it*

At this point, you have created your table structure and you've fine-tuned it with the settings you want. It's finally time to enter records! Open the table and start.

**TIP**    **Other Ways to Enter Records**    Entering records directly into a table, which you'll learn to do in this lesson, is not always the best way to enter records. If you have many records to enter, it's often more efficient in the long run to take the time to create a form with which to do your data entry. You'll learn to create a form in Lesson 12.

## Entering a Record

If you read Lessons 1 and 2 (and I hope you did!), you know that a record is a row in your table. It contains information about a specific person, place, event, or whatever. You enter a value for each record into each field (column) in your table.

First you must open the table. Remember that to open a table, you can double-click it in the Database window, or click it once and then click **Open**. Then follow these steps to enter a record:

**There's a Number in the First Column!**    If you've set up the first field to be automatically entered (for instance, a sequentially numbered field with Autonumber), start with the second field instead.

CAUTION

**1.** Click in the first empty cell in the first empty column.

**Cell**   The intersection of a row and a column. It's where you enter the data for a particular field for a particular record. Sometimes, the word field is used to mean the entry in a field for an individual record, but "field" actually refers to the entire column. Cell is the proper name for an individual block.

**2.** Type the value for that field.

**3.** Press **Tab** to move to the next field, and then type its value.

**4.** Continue pressing **Tab** until you get to the last field. When you press Tab in the last field, the insertion point moves to the first field in the next line, where you can start a new record.

**Insertion Point**   When you click a field, you see a blinking vertical line, called an insertion point, which tells you that is the place where anything you type will appear.

**5.** Continue entering records until you've filled them all.

# Some Data Entry Tricks

Sure, you *can* enter all your data with nothing more than the Tab key and some typing. But here are a few keyboard tricks that will make the job easier:

- To insert the current date, press **Ctrl+;** (semicolon). To insert the current time, press **Ctrl+:** (colon).

- If you have defined a default value for a field (in Table Design view), you can insert it by pressing **Ctrl+Alt+Spacebar**.

- To repeat the value from the same field in the previous record, press **Ctrl+'** (apostrophe).

# Moving Around in a Table

In the preceding steps, you pressed Tab to move from field to field in the table. There are other ways to move around, and you might actually find them to be more convenient. For instance, you can click in any field at any time to place the insertion point there. Table 9.1 summarizes the many keyboard shortcuts for moving around in a table.

**Table 9.1**   Table Movement Keys

| To Move To | Press |
| --- | --- |
| Next field | Tab |
| Previous field | Shift+Tab |
| Last field in the record | End |
| First field in the record | Home |
| Same field in the next record | Down arrow |
| Same field in the previous record | Up arrow |
| Same field in the last record | Ctrl+Down arrow |
| Same field in the first record | Ctrl+Up arrow |
| Last field in the last record | Ctrl+End |
| First field in the first record | Ctrl+Home |

# Printing a Table

Normally, you will not want to print a table—it won't look very pretty. A table is just a plain grid of rows and columns. Instead, you'll want to create and print a report that contains exactly the data you want (see Lesson 18).

However, sometimes you may want a quick printout of the raw data in the table. In that case, follow these steps:

1. Open the table.

2. Click the **Print** button on the Standard toolbar. Access prints the table.

TIP   **More Printing Control**   You can set some printing options before you print if you want. Instead of clicking the Print toolbar button, select **File**, **Print.** Then choose your printing options from the Print dialog box and click **OK.** Access prints the table according to your specifications.

# Closing a Table

By now you have probably discovered that a table is just another window; to close it you simply click its **Close** (X) button or double-click its **Control-menu** icon (see Figure 9.1).

Control-menu icon                                                  Close button

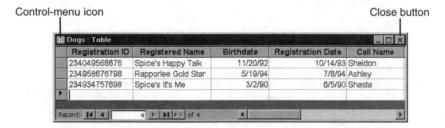

**Figure 9.1**   Close a table the same way you would close any window.

In this lesson, you learned to enter records into a table, to print the table, and to close it. In the next lesson, you'll learn to edit your table data.

# Editing Data in a Table

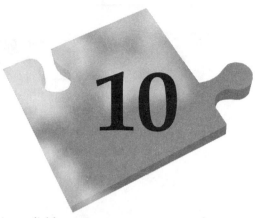

*In this lesson, you learn how to change information in a field, select records, and insert and delete records.*

Very few things are done perfectly the first time around. As you're entering records into your table, you may find you need to make some changes. This lesson shows you how.

## Changing a Cell's Content

Editing a cell's content is easy. You can either replace the old content completely or edit it. Which is better? It depends on how much you need to change; you make the call.

## Replacing a Cell's Content

If the old content is completely wrong, it's best to enter new data from scratch. To replace the old content in a field, follow these steps:

**1.** Select the cell whose contents you want to replace. Do this by clicking it or by moving to it with the keyboard (see Table 9.1 in Lesson 9).

If you are going to select the cell by clicking it, position the mouse pointer at the left edge of the field sox the mouse pointer becomes a plus sign (see Figure 10.1). Then click once to select the entire content.

**2.** Type the new data. The new data replaces the old data.

Mouse pointer

**Figure 10.1** To select a field's entire content, make sure the mouse pointer is a plus sign when you click.

# Editing a Cell's Content

If you need to make a small change to a cell's content, there's no reason to completely retype it. Instead, edit the content. Follow these steps to learn how:

**1.** Position the mouse pointer in the cell so the mouse pointer looks like an I-beam (see Figure 10.2).

**2.** Click once, and an insertion point appears in the cell.

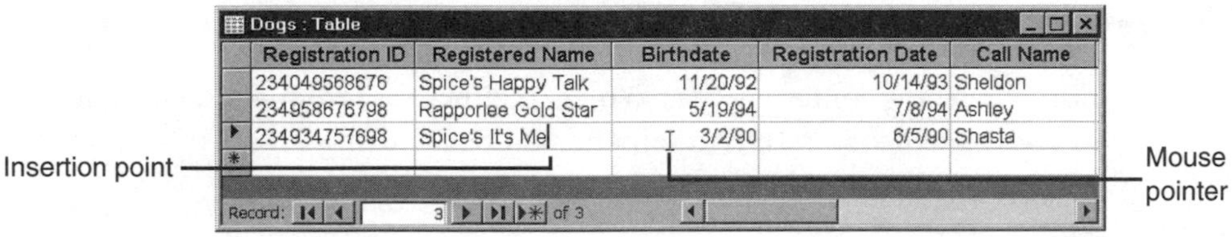

Insertion point

Mouse pointer

**Figure 10.2** Click in a cell to place the insertion point in it.

**3.** Use the arrow keys to move the insertion point to the location in the cell where you want to start editing. Table 10.1 lists a number of key combinations you can use to move within the cell.

**4.** Press **Backspace** to remove the character to the left of the insertion point, or press **Delete** to remove the character to the right of it. Then type your change.

**Table 10.1** Moving Around Within a Cell

| To Move... | Press... |
| --- | --- |
| One character to the right | → |
| One character to the left | ← |

| To Move... | Press... |
|---|---|
| One word to the right | Ctrl+→ |
| One word to the left | Ctrl+← |
| To the end of the line | End |
| To the end of the field | Ctrl+End |
| To the beginning of the line | Home |
| To the beginning of the field | Ctrl+Home |

# Selecting Records

In addition to editing individual cells in a record, you may want to work with an entire record. To do this, click in the gray square to the left of the record (the record selection area). Access highlights the entire record—displaying white letters on black—as shown in Figure 10.3.

Record selection area ⎯

A triangle marks the
selected record.

**Figure 10.3**   The selected record.

You might want to select several records as a group to perform an action on all of them at once. To do so, select the first record, press and hold down **Shift**, and select the other records. You can select only adjacent groups of records; you can't pick them from all over the list.

TIP   **Selecting All Records**   There are several quick ways to select all records at once. You can click the blank box at the intersection of the row and column headings; you can press **Ctrl+A;** or you can choose the **Edit**, **Select All Records** command.

**621**

## Understanding Record Selection Symbols

When you select a record, a triangle appears in the record selection area (see Figure 10.3). In addition to the triangle, you might see either of these icons in that area:

 Being entered or edited

 New Record

 **Only One Triangle**  If you select several records, only the first one you click will have the triangle symbol beside it. That doesn't matter, though; they're all equally selected.

CAUTION

# Inserting New Records

Access inserts new records automatically. When you start to type a record, a new line appears below it, waiting for another record (as you see in Figure 10.3). You can't insert new records between existing ones. You must always insert new records at the end of the table.

 **What If I Want the Records in a Different Order?**  It's easy to sort your records to put them in any order you want. You'll learn how to sort in Lesson 15, "Sorting and Filtering Data."

CAUTION

# Deleting Records

If you find that one or more records is outdated or doesn't belong in the table, you can easily delete it. You can even delete several records at a time. Here's how:

1. Select the record(s) you want to delete.
2. Do any of the following:

- Click the **Delete Records** button on the toolbar.
- Press the **Delete** key on the keyboard.
- Select the **Edit, Delete** command.
- Select the **Edit, Delete Record** command.

**Delete versus Delete Record**   If you select the entire record, there's no difference between these two commands. However, if you select only a portion of the record there is a difference: Delete removes only the selected text, while Delete Record removes the entire record. You cannot undo a deletion, so be careful what you delete.

# Moving and Copying Data

As with any Windows program, you can use the Cut, Copy, and Paste commands to copy and move data. Follow these steps:

**1.** Select the field(s), record(s), cell(s), or text that you want to move or copy.

**2.** Open the **Edit** menu and select **Cut** (to move) or **Copy** (to copy). Or, click the **Cut** or **Copy** button on the Standard toolbar.

**3.** Position the insertion point where you want to insert the cut or copied material.

**4.** Select **Edit, Paste** or click the **Paste** button on the Standard toolbar. Access places the cut or copied material in that location.

**TIP**   **Moving and Copying Entire Tables**   You can move and copy entire objects—not just individual fields and records. From the Database window, select the table, report, query, and so on, that you want to move or copy. Then execute the **Cut** or **Copy** command, move to where you want the object to go (for example, in a different database), and execute the **Paste** command.

In this lesson, you learned to edit data in a field, to insert and delete fields, and to copy and move data from place to place. In the next lesson, you'll learn about table formatting.

# Formatting a Table

11

*In this lesson, you learn to improve the look of a table by adjusting the row and column sizes, changing the font, and choosing a different alignment.*

## Why Format a Table?

Most people don't spend a lot of time formatting Access tables simply because they don't have to look at or print their tables. They use data entry forms (Lesson 12) to see the records on-screen and reports (Lesson 18) to print their records. The tables are merely holding tanks for raw data.

However, creating forms and reports may be more work than you want to tackle right now. For instance, if your database is very simple, consisting of one small table, you may want to add enough formatting to your table to make it look fairly attractive. Then you can use it for all your viewing and printing—foregoing the fancier forms and reports.

Even if you decide later to use a form or report, you might still want to add a bit of formatting to your table so it will be readable if you ever need to look at it.

## Changing Column Width and Row Height

One of the most common problems with a table is that you can't see the complete contents of the fields. Fields often hold more data than will fit across a column's width, so the data in your table appears to be truncated, or cut off.

There are two ways to fix this problem: make the column wider so it can display more data, or make the row taller so it can display more than one line of data.

# Changing Column Width

Access offers many different ways to adjust column widthin a table; you can choose the method you like best.

One of the easiest ways to adjust column width is to simply drag the column headings. Follow these steps:

**1.** Position the mouse pointer between two field names (column headings). The mouse pointer turns into a vertical line with left- and right-pointing arrows (see Figure 11.1). You'll be adjusting the column on the left; the column on the right will move to accommodate it.

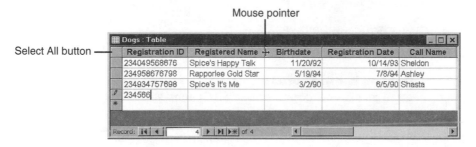

**Figure 11.1**  Position the mouse pointer between two column headings.

**2.** Press and hold the mouse button and drag the column to the right or left to increase or decrease the width.

**3.** Release the mouse button when the column is the desired width.

Another more precise way to adjust column width is to use the Column Width dialog box. Follow these steps:

**1.** Select the column(s) whose width you want to adjust. If you want to adjust all columns, select them all by clicking the Select All button (see Figure 11.1).

**2.** Select **Format, Column Width**. The Column Width dialog box (shown in Figure 11.2) appears.

**3.** Do one of the following to set the column width:

- Adjust the column to exactly the width needed for the longest entry in it by clicking **Best Fit**.

- Set the width to a precise number of field characters by typing a value in the **Column Width** text box.
- Reset the column width to its default value by selecting the **Standard Width** check box.

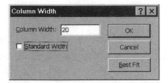

**Figure 11.2**   Adjust column width precisely here.

**4.** Click **OK** to apply the changes.

**TIP**   **Column Width Shortcut**   Instead of selecting Format, Column Width, you can right-click the column and select **Column Width** from the shortcut menu that appears.

# Changing Row Height

If you don't want to make a column wider but still want to see more of its contents, you can make the rows taller.

**Which Rows Should I Adjust?**   It doesn't matter which row you've selected; the height you set applies to all rows. You can't adjust the height of individual rows.

**CAUTION**

One way to make rows taller is to drag one of their dividers, just as you dragged a column in the preceding section. Position the mouse pointer between two rows in the row selection area; then drag up or down.

Another way is with the Row Height dialog box. It works the same as the Column Width dialog box except there's no Best Fit option. In this dialog box you have two choices. Right-click the column, select **Row Height**, and enter a new height. Or, select **Format, Row Height**, enter the new height, and click **OK**.

# Changing the Font

Unlike in other Access views (like Report and Form), you can't format individual fields or entries differently from the rest. You can choose a different font, but it automatically applies to all the text in the table, including the column headings.

Font changes you make in Datasheet view will not appear in your reports, queries, or forms; they're for Datasheet view only.

**CAUTION**

**Why Would I Change the Table Font?**  You might want to make the font smaller so you can see more of the field contents on-screen without having to adjust column width. Or you might make the font larger so you can see the table more clearly.

To choose a different font, follow these steps:

**1.** Select **Format, Font**. The Font dialog box appears (see Figure 11.3).

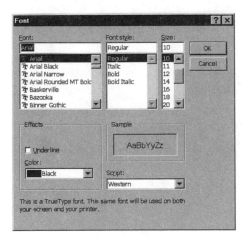

**Figure 11.3**  The Font dialog box lets you set one font for the entire table.

**2.** Choose a font from the **Font** list box.

**3.** Choose a style from the **Font Style** list box.

**4.** Choose a size from the **Size** list box.

5. Choose a color from the **Color** drop-down list.

6. (Optional) Click the **Underline** check box if you want underlined text.

7. You can see a sample of your changes in the Sample area. When you're happy with the look of the sample text, click **OK**.

 **TIP**   **More Cell Appearance Changes**   Another way you can change the look of your table is with the Cells Effects dialog box. Select **Format**, **Cells** to see it. You can change the background color, the color of the gridlines between each row and column, and whether or not the lines show.

In this lesson, you learned how to format a table. In the next lesson, you'll learn how to create a simple data entry form.

# Creating a
# Simple Form

*In this lesson, you learn to create a form, both with and without the Form Wizard.*

## Why Create Forms?

As you saw in Lessons 9 and 10, you can do all your data entry and editing in a table, but that may not be the best way. For one thing, unless you set your field widths very wide (see Lesson 11), you probably won't be able to see everything you type in the field. Also, if you have data you want to enter into several tables, you have to open each table individually.

A better data entry method is to create a form. With a form, you can allot as much space as needed for each field, and you can enter information into several tables at once. You can also avoid the headaches that occur when you try to figure out which record you're working with on a table; each form shows only one record at a time.

There are three ways to create a form:

- AutoForm is great when you want an extremely quick, generic form that contains all the fields in a single table.
- Form Wizard provides a compromise between speed and control; you can create a form by following a series of dialog boxes and choosing which fields the form will contain.

- Creating a form from scratch is the most difficult way, but it's the method that provides the most control.

Each of these is explained in this lesson.

# Creating a Form with AutoForm

The easiest way to create a form is with AutoForm. AutoForm simply plunks the fields from a single table into a form; it's the least flexible form, but it's very convenient. Follow these steps:

**1.** From the Database window, click the **Forms** tab.

**2.** Click the **New** button. The New Form dialog box appears (see Figure 12.1).

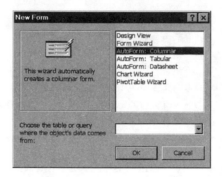

**Figure 12.1** Choose how you want to create your form.

**3.** Click **AutoForm: Columnar** to create a columnar form (the most popular kind). This creates a form that contains your fields in a single column. Alternatively, you can click **AutoForm: Tabular** for a form that looks like a table or **AutoForm: Datasheet** for a form that looks like a datasheet.

**4.** Open the drop-down list at the bottom of the dialog box and choose the table this form will be associated with.

**5.** Click **OK**, and the form appears, ready for data entry.

If the form created by AutoForm is not what you want, delete it and try again with the Form Wizard (as explained in the next section). To delete the form, simply close it and answer **No** when asked if you want to save your changes.

# Creating a Form with Form Wizard

The Form Wizard offers a good compromise between the automation of AutoForm and the control of creating a form from scratch. Follow these steps to use the Form Wizard:

1. From the Database window, click the **Forms** tab.
2. Click the **New** button. The New Form dialog box appears (see Figure 12.1).
3. Click **Form Wizard**.

**Don't I Have to Pick a Table?**  When using the Form Wizard, you don't have to choose a table from the drop-down list in the New Form dialog box; you'll choose it in step 5.

**CAUTION**

4. Click **OK** to start the Form Wizard (see Figure 12.2).

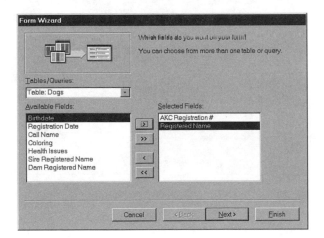

**Figure 12.2**  The Form Wizard lets you choose which fields you want to include, from as many different tables as you like.

5. Open the **Tables/Queries** drop-down list and choose a table or query from which to select fields.
6. In the **Available Fields** list, click a field that you want to include on the form, and then click the **>** button to move it to the Selected Fields list.
7. Repeat step 6 until you've selected all the fields you want to include from that table. If you want to include fields from another table or query, repeat steps 5 and 6 to choose another table and other fields.

> **TIP** **Selecting All Fields** You can quickly move all the fields from the Available Fields list to the Selected Fields list by clicking the **>>** button. If you make a mistake, you can remove a field from the Selected Fields list by clicking it and clicking the **<** button.

8. Click **Next** to continue. You'll be asked to choose a layout: **Columnar** (the most common), **Tabular**, **Datasheet**, or **Justified**. Click each of the buttons to see a preview of that type. When you've made a decision, click the one you want and click **Next**.

9. The wizard asks to choose a style. Click each of the styles listed to see a preview of it; click **Next** when you've chosen the one you want.

10. Enter a title for the form in the text box at the top of the dialog box.

11. Click the **Finish** button, and the form appears, ready for data entry, as shown in Figure 12.3. The first record in the table appears in it.

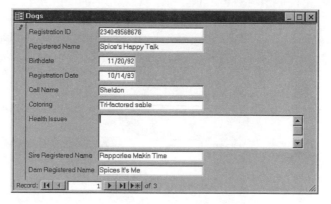

**Figure 12.3** The Form Wizard's simple but usable form.

# Creating a Form from Scratch

The most powerful and most difficult way to create a form is with Form Design. In Form Design view, you decide exactly where to place each field and how to format it. The following steps initiate your use of Form Design view; you'll learn more about this view in Lesson 13.

1. From the Database window, click the **Forms** tab.

2. Click the **New** button, and the New Form dialog box appears.

**3.** Click **Design View**.

**4.** Select a table or query from the drop-down list at the bottom of the dialog box. This is important! You won't have the opportunity to change your selection later.

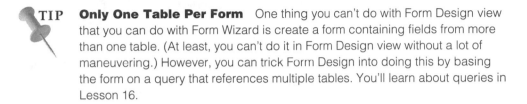

**TIP** **Only One Table Per Form** One thing you can't do with Form Design view that you can do with Form Wizard is create a form containing fields from more than one table. (At least, you can't do it in Form Design view without a lot of maneuvering.) However, you can trick Form Design into doing this by basing the form on a query that references multiple tables. You'll learn about queries in Lesson 16.

**5.** Click **OK**. A Form Design screen appears, as shown in Figure 12.4. You're ready to create your form.

In the next lesson, you'll  Field List   Toolbox
learn to create other   button   button
areas besides Detail.

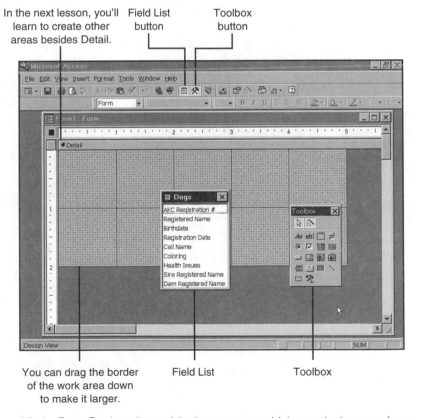

You can drag the border        Field List              Toolbox
of the work area down
to make it larger.

**Figure 12.4** Form Design view: a blank canvas on which you design your form.

**633**

> **TIP**  **Toolbox and Field List**  You'll want to use the Form Design toolbox and the Field List shown in Figure 12.4. If they're not visible, click the **Toolbox** button and/or the **Field List** button in the toolbar.

# Adding Fields to a Form

The basic idea of the Form Design screen is simple: it's like a light table or pasteup board where you place the elements of your form. The fields you add to a form will appear in the Detail area of the form. The Detail area is the only area visible at first; you'll learn to add other areas later in the next lesson.

To add a field to the form, follow these steps:

1. Display the Field List if it's not showing by clicking the **Field List** button or selecting **View**, **Field List**.
2. Drag a field from the Field List onto the Detail area of the form (see Figure 12.5).
3. Repeat step 2 to add as many fields as you want to the form.

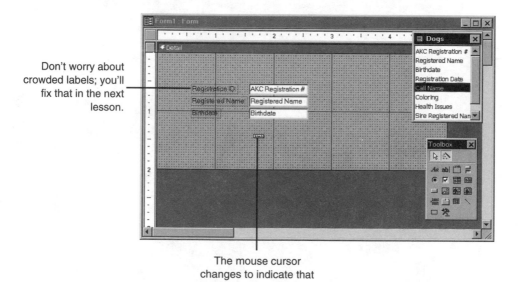

Don't worry about crowded labels; you'll fix that in the next lesson.

The mouse cursor changes to indicate that a field is being placed.

**Figure 12.5**  Drag fields from the Field List to the grid.

You can drag more than one field to the form at once. In step 2, instead of clicking a single field and then dragging it, do one of the following before you drag:

- To select a block of fields, click the first one you want, press and hold **Shift**, and click the last one.

- To select non-adjacent fields, hold down **Ctrl** and click on each one you want.

- To select all the fields on the list, double-click the **Field List** title bar.

You can move objects around on a form after you've initially placed them; you'll learn how to do this in Lesson 13. Don't worry if your form doesn't look very professional at this point. In the next several lessons, you'll learn how to modify and improve your form.

**TIP**   **Using Snap to Grid**   If you find it hard to align the fields neatly, select **Format**, **Snap to Grid** to place a check mark next to that command. If you want to align the fields on your own, select it again to turn it off.

If you are satisfied with your form, close it by clicking its **Close** (X) button. When asked if you want to save your changes, choose **Yes**. Type a name for the form in the text box provided and click **OK**. If, on the other hand, you want to make more modifications to your form, leave it open and skip to Lesson 13 now.

# Entering Data in a Form

The whole point of creating a form is so you can enter data into your tables more easily. The form acts as an attractive "mask" that shields you from the plainness of your table. Once you create a form, follow these steps to enter data into it:

**1.** Open the form, and then do one of the following:

- If your form appears in Form Design view, select the **View**, **Form** command or click the **View** drop-down arrow and select **Form View** to enter Form view.

- If the form isn't open at all, click the **Form** tab in the Database window and double-click the form's name or click the **Open** button.

**2.** Click the field you want to begin with and type your data.

**3.** Press **Tab** to move to the next field. If you need to go back, you can press **Shift+Tab** to move to the previous field. When you reach the last field, pressing Tab moves you to the first field in a new, blank record.

To move to the next record before you reach the bottom field, or to move back to previous records, click the right and left arrow buttons on the left end of the status bar.

**4.** Repeat steps 2 and 3 to enter all the records you want. Each record is saved automatically as you enter it.

 **TIP** **Data Entry Shortcuts** See the section "Some Data Entry Tricks" in Lesson 9 for some shortcut ideas. They work equally well in forms and tables.

In this lesson, you created a simple form and added data to it. In the next lesson, you'll learn how to make changes to your form to better suit your needs.

# Modifying Your Form

*In this lesson, you learn to modify a form. You can use any form, created in any of the ways you learned in Lesson 12.*

This lesson is about making changes to forms. At this point, you might have a very rough form that you created from scratch, or you might have a polished, good-looking form that the Form Wizard created for you. The steps are the same no matter what you're starting with. (The examples in this lesson use a form created with Form Wizard.)

## Moving Fields

The most common change to a form is moving fields around. You might want to move several fields down so you can insert a new field, or you might want to just rearrange the order in which the fields appear. From Form Design view, follow these steps:

1. Click a field's name to select it. Selection handles appear around it (see Figure 13.1). You can select several fields by holding down **Shift** and clicking each one.

2. Position the mouse pointer so that it becomes a hand (see Figure 13.1). If you're moving more than one field, you can position the mouse pointer on any of the selected fields.

3. Press and hold down the left mouse button and drag the field to a different location.

4. When the field is at the desired new location, release the mouse button.

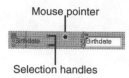

Mouse pointer

Selection handles

**Figure 13.1** To move a field, select it and drag it with the open hand mouse pointer.

**The Label Moved Without the Field Attached!** Be careful when you position your mouse pointer over the field you want to move. Make sure the pointer changes to an *open* hand. If you position the mouse pointer over the top left selection handle for either the label or the field, the mouse pointer changes to a hand with a pointing finger, and when you drag, the label (or the field box) moves independently. This can be handy for special situations, but it's probably not what you want right now.

# Adding Text

The next most common change is adding text to the form. You might add titles, subtitles, or explanatory text, for example. To do so, follow these steps:

1. If the Toolbox is not displayed, select **View**, **Toolbox** or click the **Toolbox** button on the toolbar.

2. Click the **Label** tool in the toolbox (the one with the italicized letters *Aa* on it). The mouse pointer changes to a capital A with a plus sign next to it (see Figure 13.2).

3. Click anywhere on the form where you want to create the new text. A tiny box appears. (The box will expand to hold the text as you type.)

4. Type the text.

5. Press **Enter** or click anywhere outside the text area to finish.

**Text Dragging** Don't worry about positioning the text as you create it. You can move text in the same way that you move fields. Just click it, position the mouse pointer so that the open hand appears, and then drag it to where you want it.

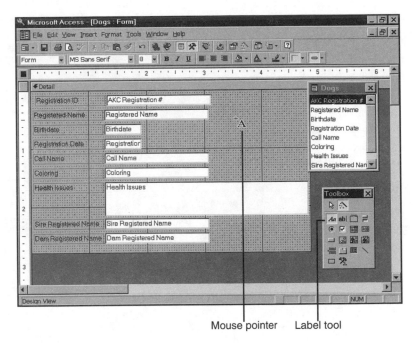

Mouse pointer    Label tool

**Figure 13.2**  Select the Label tool in the toolbox.

# Viewing Headers and Footers

You have been working with the Detail area so far, but there are other areas you can use, as shown in Figure 13.3. To display these areas, follow these steps:

1. To view the Page Header/Footer, select **View**, **Page Header/Footer**.

2. To view the Form Header/Footer, select **View**, **Form Header/Footer**.

3. To turn either area off, repeat step 1 or 2 as appropriate.

After you display any of these headers and footers, you can add text to them the same way that you learned to add text in the preceding section. For instance, you might add a title for the form in the Form Header area.

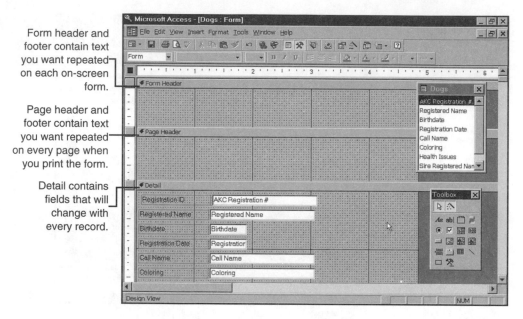

Form header and footer contain text you want repeated on each on-screen form.

Page header and footer contain text you want repeated on every page when you print the form.

Detail contains fields that will change with every record.

**Figure 13.3** Each form can have several areas.

# Changing Field Lengths

Suppose you want the Registration ID field area to be capable of displaying more characters. You just drag the field entry area to make it longer so more characters will show. Follow these steps to see how it works:

1. Click the field entry area to select it. Selection handles appear around it.
2. Position the mouse pointer at the right edge of the field entry area so the mouse pointer turns into a double-headed arrow (see Figure 13.4).
3. Drag the field to its new length and release the mouse button.

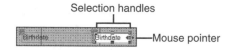

Selection handles

Mouse pointer

**Figure 13.4** You can change the size of the field entry area by dragging it.

You can resize the labels for each field in the same way: position the mouse pointer at the left end of one of them and drag until the box containing the label is the desired length.

# Formatting Text on a Form

After you place all your information on the form (that is, the fields you want to include and any titles or explanatory text), the next step is to make the form look more appealing.

All the formatting tools you need are on the Formatting toolbar (the second toolbar from the top in Form Design view). Table 13.1 shows the controls and describes each one. To use a control, select the element you want to format, and then click the appropriate toolbar button.

Some controls, like the font and size, display drop-down lists. You click the down arrow next to the button, and then select from the list. Other controls are simple buttons, such as Bold and Italic. Still other controls—the coloring and border buttons, for example—are a combination of a button and a drop-down list. You click the button to apply the current value, or you click the down arrow next to the button to change the value.

**Table 13.1** Controls on the Formatting Toolbar

| *Button* | *Function* |
|---|---|
| CustomerID ▾ | Lists the fields in the table you are using |
| Arial ▾ | Lists the available fonts |
| 10 ▾ | Lists the available sizes for the selected font |
| **B** | Toggles Bold on/off |
| *I* | Toggles Italics on/off |
| U | Toggles Underline on/off |

*continues*

**Table 13.1** Continued

| Button | Function |
| --- | --- |
| | Left-aligns text |
| | Centers text |
| | Right-aligns text |
| | Fills the selected box with the selected color |
| | Colors the text in the selected box |
| | Colors the outline of the selected box |
| | Adds a border to the selected box |
| | Adds a special effect to the selected box |

**TIP** **Changing the Background Color** You can change the color of the background on which the form sits, too. Just click the header for the section you want to change (for instance, **Detail**) to select the entire section. Then use the **Fill/Back color** control to change the color.

**TIP** **AutoFormat** Here's a shortcut for formatting your form. If you created the form with Form Wizard, you already saw AutoFormat at work. To see it again, select **Format**, **AutoFormat**. You'll be asked to choose from among several predesigned color and formatting schemes.

# Changing Tab Order

When you enter data on a form, you press **Tab** to move from one field to the next, in the order they're shown in the form. This progression from field to field is the tab order. When you first create a form, the tab order runs from top to bottom.

When you move and rearrange fields, the tab order doesn't change automatically. For instance, if you had 10 fields arranged in a column, and you rearranged them so that the 10th one was at the beginning, the tab order would still show that field in 10th position even though it would be at the top of the form. This makes it more difficult to fill in the form, so you'll want to adjust the tab order to reflect the new structure of the form.

**TIP** **Tab Order Improvements** To make data entry easier, you might want to change the tab order to be different from the obvious top-to-bottom structure. For instance, if 90 percent of the records you enter skip several fields, you might want to put those fields you don't use last in the tab order so you can skip over them easily.

Follow these steps to adjust the tab order:

1. Select **View**, **Tab Order**. The Tab Order dialog box appears (see Figure 13.5).

**Figure 13.5** Use the Tab Order dialog box to control the tab order in your form.

2. The fields appear in their tab order. To change the order, click a field and then drag it up or down on the list.
3. To quickly set the tab order based on the fields' current positions in the form (top-to-bottom), click the **Auto Order** button.
4. Click **OK**.

In this lesson, you learned to improve a form by moving fields, adding text, adding formatting, and adjusting the tab order. In the next lesson, you'll learn to search your database to find specific information.

# Searching for Data

*In this lesson, you learn the most basic ways to search for data in a database using the Find and Replace features.*

## Using the Find Feature

The Find feature is useful for locating a particular record that you have previously entered. For instance, if you keep a database of customers, you might want to find a particular customer's record quickly when he is ready to make a purchase so you can verify his address. Or, to continue the dog kennel example we've been using, you could quickly find the record for the dog with the call name of Sheldon in order to look up his birth date.

TIP **Finding More Than One Record** If you need to find several records at once, Find is not the best tool. It finds only one record at a time. A better tool for finding multiple records is a filter, which you'll learn about in Lesson 15.

To find a particular record, follow these steps:

**1.** Switch to either Datasheet view or Form view. Either one supports the Find feature.

**2.** Click in the field that contains the data you want to find, if you know which field it is. For instance, if you're going to look for a customer based on his last name, click in the **Name** field.

 **3.** Click the **Find** tool in the toolbar, or select **Edit**, **Find**, or press **Ctrl+F**. The Find dialog box appears (see Figure 14.1).

**Figure 14.1** Use the Find dialog box to find data in a record.

**4.** Type the text or numbers that you want to find in the **Find What** text box.

**5.** Open the **Match** drop-down list and select one of the following:

**Whole Field** finds fields where the specified text is the only thing in that field. For instance, the search text "Smith" would not match "Smithsonian."

**Start of Field** finds fields that begin with the specified text. For instance, the search text "Smith" would match "Smith" and "Smithsonian," but not "Joe Smith."

**Any Part of Field** finds fields that contain the specified text in any way. So the search text "Smith" would match "Smith," "Smithsonian," and "Joe Smith."

**6.** If you want to search only forward from the current record, open the **Search** drop-down list and select **Down**. If you want to search only backward, select **Up**. (The default is All, which searches all records.)

**7.** To limit the match to only entries that are the same case (upper and/or lower), select the **Match Case** check box. As a result, the search text "Smith" would not match "SMITH" or "smith."

**8.** To find only fields with the same formatting as the text you type, select **Search Fields As Formatted**. With this option on, "12/12/95" would not find "12-12-95," even though they represent the same date, because they're formatted differently. The Search Fields as Formatted option is available only if you select **Search Only Current Field** (see step 9).

**TIP** **Don't Slow Down** Don't use the Search Fields as Formatted option unless you specifically need it, because it makes your search go more slowly.

9. To limit the search to the field where you clicked when you started this procedure, select the **Search Only Current Field** check box. (Do this whenever possible because it makes the search faster.) However, if you don't know what field the data is in, you shouldn't check this.

10. Click **Find First** to find the first match for your search.

11. If necessary, move the Find dialog box out of the way by dragging its title bar so you can see the record it found. Access highlights the field entry containing the found text (see Figure 14.2).

When the Search Only Current Field option is on,
the title bar shows which field is being searched.

Access highlights
the found text.

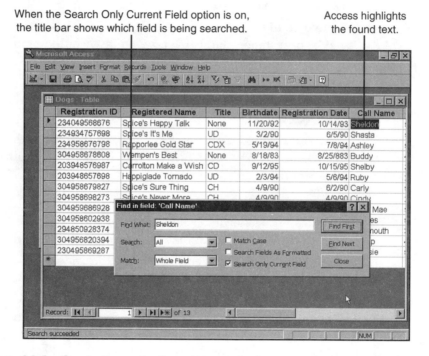

**Figure 14.2** One instance at a time, Access displays records that contain the selected text.

12. To find the next occurrence, click **Find Next**. If Access cannot find any more occurrences, it tells you **The search item was not found**. Click **OK** to clear that message.

13. When you finish finding your data, click **Close** to close the Find dialog box.

# Using the Replace Feature

Replacing is a lot like finding; it finds the specified text, too. But as an extra bonus, it replaces the found text with text that you specify. For instance, if you found that you misspelled a brand name in your inventory, you could replace the word with the correct spelling. Or, in our dog kennel example, you could find the dog named Sheldon and change his name to Sherman, if his new owners changed his name.

To find and replace data, follow these steps:

**1.** Select **Edit**, **Replace** or press **Ctrl+H**. The Replace dialog box appears (see Figure 14.3).

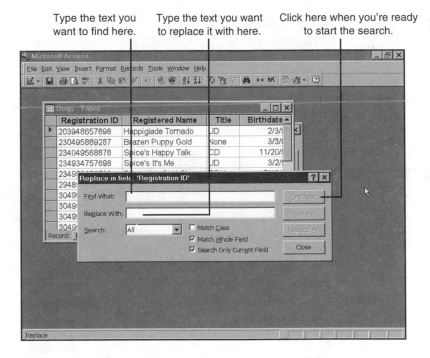

Type the text you want to find here.

Type the text you want to replace it with here.

Click here when you're ready to start the search.

**Figure 14.3** You can find specific text and replace it with different text.

**2.** Type the text you want to find in the **Find What** text box.

**3.** Type the text you want to replace it with in the **Replace With** text box.

**4.** Select any options you want, as you learned to do with the Find dialog box in the previous section.

**CAUTION**

**There's No Match** Compared to the Find dialog box, the one thing that the Replace dialog box lacks is the Match drop-down list. The Replace feature always uses the Any Part of Field option for matching.

**5.** Click **Find Next**, and Access finds the first occurrence of the text.

**6.** If necessary, drag the title bar of the Replace dialog box to move the box so you can see the text that Access found.

**7.** Click the **Replace** button to replace the text.

**8.** Click **Find Next** to find other occurrences if desired, and replace them by clicking the **Replace** button.

**TIP** **Replace All** If you are certain you want to replace every occurrence of the text in the entire table, click **Replace All**. It's quicker than alternating repeatedly between Find Next and Replace. Be careful, though! You may not realize all the things that might be changed. After all, you wouldn't want to change "will" to "would" and later find that "willfully" had been changed to "wouldfully."

**9.** When you finish replacing, click **Close**.

# Other Ways to Find Data

The Find and Replace features work well on individual records, but there are several more sophisticated ways of locating data in your database, as you'll learn in upcoming lessons. They include:

- **Sorting** Rearranging the data on-screen so it's easier to skim through the list to find what you want. See Lesson 15.

- **Filtering** Narrowing down the list to eliminate the data you know you don't want to see. See Lesson 15.

- **Querying** Creating a more formal filter with complex criteria that you can save and apply again and again. See Lessons 16 and 17.

- **Reporting** Creating a printed report containing only the records and fields that you're interested in. See Lessons 18 and 19.

In this lesson, you learned to find and replace data in a database. In the next lesson, you'll learn about two other ways of locating data: sorting and filtering.

# Sorting and Filtering Data

15

*In this lesson, you learn how to find data by sorting and filtering.*

Access has many ways of finding and organizing data, and each is good for a certain situation. As you learned in Lesson 14, Find and Replace are great features when you're working with individual instances of a particular value (finding Mr. Smith's record quickly, for example). This chapter explains two other ways of finding what you need.

## Sorting Data

Even though you enter your records into the database in some sort of logical order, at some point, you'll want them in a different order. For instance, we might enter the dogs in our kennel according to registration number, but later we might want to look at the list in order of the dogs' birth dates, from oldest to youngest.

The Sort command is the perfect solution to this problem. With Sort, you can rearrange the records according to any field you like. You can sort in either ascending order (A to Z and 1 to 10) or descending order (Z to A and 10 to 1).

TIP    **Which View?**    You can sort in either Form view or Datasheet view. I prefer Datasheet view because it shows many records at once.

Follow these steps to sort records:

   **1.** Click anywhere in the field by which you want to sort.

**2.** Click the **Sort Ascending** button or the **Sort Descending** button on the toolbar. Or if you prefer, select **Records**, **Sort**, and then choose **Ascending** or **Descending** from the submenu. Figure 15.1 shows our table of dogs sorted in Ascending order by birth date.

Access sorted the table by this column.

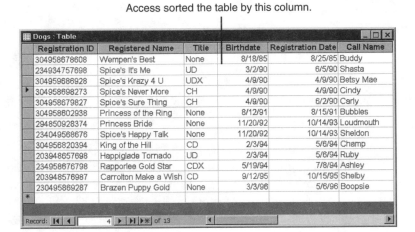

| Registration ID | Registered Name | Title | Birthdate | Registration Date | Call Name |
|---|---|---|---|---|---|
| 304958678608 | Wempen's Best | None | 8/18/85 | 8/25/85 | Buddy |
| 234934757698 | Spice's It's Me | UD | 3/2/90 | 6/5/90 | Shasta |
| 304959686928 | Spice's Krazy 4 U | UDX | 4/9/90 | 4/9/90 | Betsy Mae |
| 304958698273 | Spice's Never More | CH | 4/9/90 | 4/9/90 | Cindy |
| 304958679827 | Spice's Sure Thing | CH | 4/9/90 | 6/2/90 | Carly |
| 304958602938 | Princess of the Ring | None | 8/12/91 | 8/15/91 | Bubbles |
| 294850928374 | Princess Bride | None | 11/20/92 | 10/14/93 | Loudmouth |
| 234049568676 | Spice's Happy Talk | None | 11/20/92 | 10/14/93 | Sheldon |
| 304956820394 | King of the Hill | CD | 2/3/94 | 5/6/94 | Champ |
| 203948657698 | Happiglade Tornado | UD | 2/3/94 | 5/6/94 | Ruby |
| 234958676798 | Rapporlee Gold Star | CDX | 5/19/94 | 7/8/94 | Ashley |
| 203948576987 | Carrolton Make a Wish | CD | 9/12/95 | 10/15/95 | Shelby |
| 230495869287 | Brazen Puppy Gold | None | 3/3/96 | 5/6/96 | Boopsie |

Record:  ◄ ◄   4   ► ►I ►* of 13

**Figure 15.1**   Access sorted this table in Ascending order by the Birthdate column.

**3.** If you want to restore the records to their presorted order, select **Records**, **Remove Filter/Sort**.

**What Is Presorted Order?**   If you defined a Primary Key field when you created your database (see Lesson 4), the records appear sorted in ascending order according to that field by default. This is the order they revert to when you remove a sort (as in step 3). If you save the datasheet or form without removing the sort, the sort order becomes part of that object.

# Filtering Data

Filtering is for those times when you want to get many of the records out of the way so that you can see the few that you're interested in. Filtering temporarily narrows down the number of records that appear, according to criteria you select.

**Filters Versus Queries** Queries also narrow down the records displayed, as you'll learn in Lesson 16. Using a filter is easier and quicker than using a query, but you can't save a filter as a separate object for later use. (However, you can save a filter as a query, as you'll learn later in this lesson.)

There are three ways to apply a filter: Filter By Selection, Filter by Form, and Advanced Filter/Sort. The first two are the most common for casual users, as you will discover in the following sections. The third method is for advanced users only.

 **TIP** **Sorting and Filtering** Neither of the filtering methods you'll learn in this lesson allow you to sort at the same time that you filter. However, it's easy enough to sort the filtered records using the same sorting process you learned earlier in this lesson.

# Filter by Selection

Filtering by selection is the easiest method of filtering. But before you can use it, you have to locate an instance of the value you want the filtered records to contain. For example, if you want to find all the dogs in your table that have earned the title of "CD" (Companion Dog), you must first locate a record that meets that criteria. You then base the rest of the filter on that record.

To filter by selection, follow these steps:

1. In a field, find one instance of the value you want all filtered records to contain.

2. Select the value using one of these methods:
   - To find all records in which the field value is identical to the selected value, select the entire field entry.
   - To find all records in which the field begins with the selected value, select part of the field entry beginning with the first character.
   - To find all records in which the field contains the selected value at any point, select part of the field entry beginning after the first character.

 3. Click the **Filter by Selection** button on the toolbar or select **Records, Filter, Filter by Selection**. Access displays the records that match the criterion you selected.

Figure 15.2 shows the Dogs table filtered to show only dogs that have earned the "CD" title.

Access filtered the table by this column.

| Registration ID | Registered Name | Title | Birthdate | Registration Date | Call Name |
|---|---|---|---|---|---|
| 294850928374 | Princess Bride | CD | 11/20/92 | 10/14/93 | Loudmouth |
| 234049568676 | Spice's Happy Talk | CD | 11/20/92 | 10/14/93 | Sheldon |
| 304956820394 | King of the Hill | CD | 2/3/94 | 5/6/94 | Champ |
| 203948576987 | Carrolton Make a Wish | CD | 9/12/95 | 10/15/95 | Shelby |

Dogs : Table

Record: 1 of 4 (Filtered)

**Figure 15.2**   The result of a filter is a list of records that match the criterion.

**TIP**   **Filtering by More Than One Criterion**   With Filter by Selection, you can filter by only one criterion at a time. However, you can apply successive filters after the first one to further narrow the list of matching records.

You can also filter for records that don't contain the selected value. After selecting the value, right-click it and select **Filter Excluding Selection**.

You can cancel a filter by clicking the **Remove Filter** button (which is the same as the Apply Filter button) or by selecting **Records**, **Remove Filter/Sort**.

# Filter by Form

Filtering by form is a more powerful filtering method than filtering by selection. With filter by form, you can filter by more than one criterion at a time. You can also set up "or" filters, which find records that match any one of several criteria. You can even enter logical expressions (such as "greater than a certain value").

To filter by form, follow these steps:

**1.** In Datasheet or Form view, click the **Filter by Form** button on the toolbar or select **Records**, **Filter**, **Filter by Form**. A blank form appears, resembling an empty datasheet with a single record line.

**2.** Click in the field you want to set a criterion for, and a drop-down arrow appears. Click the arrow and select the value you want from the list. Or, you can type the value directly into the field if you prefer.

3. Enter as many criteria as you like in various fields. Figure 15.3 shows two criteria, including a criteria that uses a less-than sign (a mathematical operator explained in Lesson 16).

4. If you want to set up an "or" condition, click the **Or** tab at the bottom of the Filter by Form window and enter the alternate criteria into that form. Notice that another Or tab appears when you fill this one, so you can add multiple "or" conditions.

5. After you enter your criteria, click the **Apply Filter** button on the toolbar. Your filtered data appears.

As with Filter by Selection, you can undo a filter by clicking the **Filter** button again or by selecting **Records**, **Remove Filter/Sort**.

Click here to create an "or" criterion.
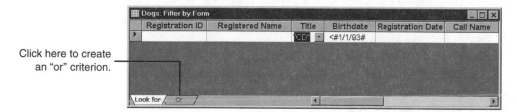

**Figure 15.3** This query finds all dogs that were born before 1/1/93 and have a "CD" (Companion Dog) title.

# Saving Your Filtered Data As a Query

Using filters is a convenient alternative to creating a simple query from scratch. You can save a filter as a query and use it as you would use a query; it even appears on your Queries list in the Database window. (You'll learn more about working with queries in Lesson 16.) To save a filter as a query, follow these steps:

1. Display the filter in Query by Form view.

2. Select **File**, **Save As Query** or click the **Save** button on the toolbar. Access asks for a name for the new query.

3. Type a name and click **OK**. Access saves the filter.

In this lesson, you learned how to sort and filter your database. In the next lesson, you'll begin learning about queries, which provide a more sophisticated way of isolating and organizing information.

# Creating a Query

*In this lesson, you learn how a query can help you find the information you need, and you learn to create a simple query using the Simple Query Wizard. You also learn how to save and print any query's results, and you learn about other Query Wizards that Access provides for special situations.*

## What Is a Query?

As you learned in Lesson 15, Access offers many ways to help you narrow down the information you're looking at, including sorting and filtering. A query is simply a more formal way to sort and filter. Queries enable you to specify:

- Which fields you want to see.
- The order in which the fields should appear.
- Filter criteria for each field (see Lesson 15).
- The order in which you want each field sorted (see Lesson 15).

 **TIP**   **Saving a Filter**   When the primary purpose of the query is to filter, you might find it easier to create a filter and save it as a query. See Lesson 15 for details.

In this lesson, you'll create a very simple query, which may not do everything you want it to do. But in the next lesson (Lesson 17), you'll learn how to modify it to make it more powerful.

# Creating a Simple Query Using Query Wizard

The easiest way to create a query is with a Query Wizard, and the easiest Query Wizard is the Simple Query Wizard. (The other Query Wizards are "special-use" ones that you'll probably never need; they're described later in this lesson.)

The Simple Query Wizard lets you select the fields you want to display—that's all. You don't get to set criteria for including individual records, and you don't get to specify a sort order. (You'll learn to do those things in Lesson 17.) This kind of simple query is useful when you want to weed out extraneous fields, but you still want to see every record.

**Select Query**   The query that the Simple Query Wizard creates is a very basic version of a Select query. The Select query is the most common query type. With a Select query, you can select records, sort them, filter them, and perform simple calculations (such as counting and averaging) on the results.

To create a simple Select query with the Simple Query Wizard, follow these steps:

1. Open the database you want to work with and click the **Queries** tab.
2. Click the **New** button. The New Query dialog box appears.
3. Click **Simple Query Wizard** and click **OK**. The first box of the Simple Query Wizard appears (see Figure 16.1). This screen may look familiar; it's similar to the first screen of the Form Wizard you worked with in Lesson 12.
4. In the **Tables/Queries** drop-down list, choose the table from which you want to select fields. For example, I'm going to use the Dogs field.
5. Click a field name in the **Available Fields** list and click the > button to move it to the Selected Fields list. Do the same for any other fields you want to move, or move them all at once with the >> button.
6. Select another table or query from the **Tables/Queries** list and add some of its fields to the Selected Fields list if you want. When you finish adding fields, click **Next**.
7. Next you're asked whether you want a Detail or a Summary query. Choose whichever you want; if you're not sure, stick with **Detail**, the default. If you choose **Summary**, the Summary Options button becomes available,

which you can click to open a dialog box of summary options. When you're finished, click **Next**. The next dialog box appears (see Figure 16.2).

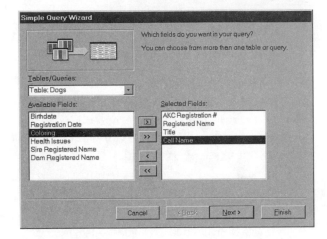

**Figure 16.1** The Simple Query Wizard first asks which fields you want to include.

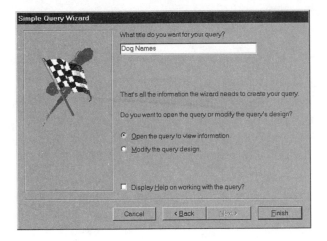

**Figure 16.2** Enter a title for your query.

**Relationships Required** If you are going to use two or more tables in your query, they must be joined with a relationship. See Lesson 21 to learn how to create relationships between tables.

**656**

8. Enter a title for the query in the **What Title Do You Want for Your Query?** text box. I'm going to call mine Dog Names.

9. Click **Finish** to view the query results. Figure 16.3 shows my results.

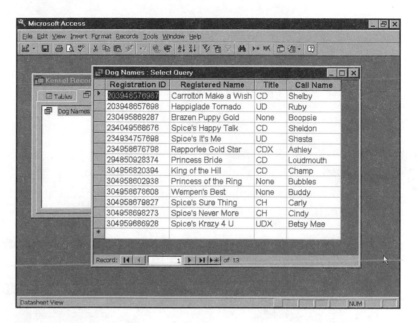

**Figure 16.3** The results of my Select query.

This simple query is actually too simple; it has limited usefulness and doesn't show off any of Access's powerful query features. You could get the same results by hiding certain columns in Datasheet view! Luckily, the Select query is much more powerful than the Simple Query Wizard makes it appear, as you'll see in the next lesson. But before you go there, take a look at a few basics that apply to any query.

# Saving a Query

When you create a query, Access saves it automatically. You don't need to do anything special to save it. Just close the query window and look on the Queries tab of the Database window. You'll see the query on the list.

**TIP** **Close the Query?** You close a query window the same way you close any window—by clicking its **Close** button (the X in the upper-right corner).

# Rerunning a Query

At any time, you can rerun your query. If the data has changed since the last time you ran the query, those changes will be represented.

To rerun a query, follow these steps:

**1.** Open the database containing the query.

**2.** Click the **Queries** tab in the Database window.

**3.** Double-click the query you want to rerun, or click it once and click the **Open** button (see Figure 16.4).

Double-click here to open the Dog Names query.

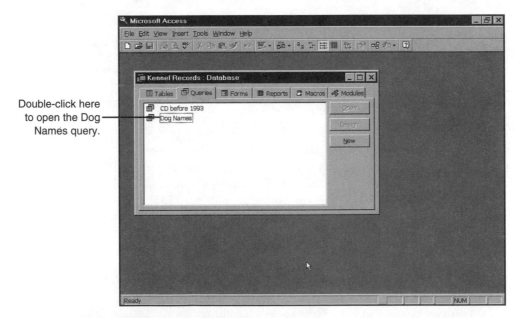

**Figure 16.4** You can redisplay any query by opening it from the Queries tab.

# Working with Query Results

Query results appear in Datasheet view, as shown in Figure 19.3. You can do anything to the records that you can do in a normal Datasheet view (see Lesson 10), including copy and delete records and change field entries.

For example, let's say you wanted to update a sales database to change the Last Contacted field (a date) to today for every record. From your query results window, you could make that change. Or perhaps you want to delete all records for customers who haven't made a purchase in the last two years. You could delete the records from the query results window, and they would disappear from the table too.

Of course, with the latter example, it would be easier if the records were sorted according to the field in question—and the Simple Query Wizard you learned about in this lesson won't let you sort. However, in Lesson 17, you'll learn about some other, more powerful Query Wizards that let you choose more options.

# Printing Query Results

The query results window not only edits like a datasheet, but also prints like one. To print the query results, do the following:

1. Make sure the query results window is active.
2. Select **File**, **Print** or press **Ctrl+P**. The Print dialog box appears.
3. Select whatever print options you want, and then click **OK**.

 If you don't want to set any print options, you can simply click the **Print** button on the toolbar to print, bypassing the Print dialog box.

# Other Query Wizards

Access's query features are very powerful; they can do amazingly complicated calculations and comparisons on many tables at once. You can create queries with their own dialog boxes for custom entry of special criteria, link a query to external databases (databases in other programs), and much more.

Unfortunately, the process for creating a lot of these powerful queries is quite complicated. It's enough to give casual users a major headache. That's why in this book, I stick to the basic Select type of query, which does almost everything an average user needs to do.

Some intermediate Access Query Wizards can help you experiment with more complex query types without causing too much stress. These Query Wizards appear on the list when you click the New button on the Queries tab. We won't cover any of that in this book, but you may want to try them out yourself:

- **Crosstab Query Wizard**   Displays summarized values (such as sums, counts, and averages from one field) and groups them by one set of facts listed down the left side of the datasheet as row headings and another set of facts listed across the top of the datasheet as column headings.
- **Find Unmatched Query Wizard**   Compares two tables and finds all records that do not appear in both tables (based on a comparison of certain fields).
- **Find Duplicates Query Wizard**   The opposite of Find Unmatched. It compares two tables and finds all records that appear in both.

In this lesson, you learned to create a simple query and to save, edit, and print query results. In the next lesson, you'll learn how to modify the query you created.

# Modifying a Query

*In this lesson, you learn how to modify the query you created in Lesson 16 using Query Design view.*

## Introducing Query Design View

In Lesson 16, you created a very simple query using the Simple Query Wizard. That query selected and displayed fields from a table. There's a lot more you can do with your query when you enter Query Design view.

Query Design view is much like Table Design view and Form Design view, both of which you encountered earlier in this part. In Query Design view, you can change the rules that govern your query results.

### Opening a Query in Query Design View

To open an existing query in Query Design view, follow these steps:

1. Open the database that contains the query you want to edit.
2. Click the **Queries** tab.
3. Click the query you want to edit, and then click the **Design** button.

Figure 17.1 shows the query from Lesson 16 as it looks in Query Design view. You'll learn how to edit it in this lesson. (This query has only one table. If it had more than one, each table would be displayed in a separate box listing its fields.)

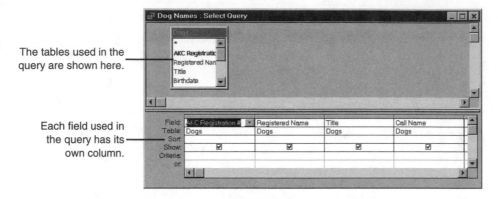

The tables used in the query are shown here.

Each field used in the query has its own column.

**Figure 17.1**   In Query Design view, you can edit a query you've created.

# Starting a New Query in Query Design View

Instead of using the Simple Query Wizard to begin your query (as you did in Lesson 16), you can begin a query from scratch in Query Design view. As you become more familiar with Access queries, you might find that this is faster and easier than using a wizard.

To begin a new query in Query Design view, follow these steps:

1. Open the database in which you want the query.
2. Click the **Queries** tab in the Database window.
3. Click the **New** button.
4. Click **Design View** and click **OK**. The Show Table dialog box appears, listing all the tables in the database.
5. Select the table you want to work with and click the **Add** button.
6. Repeat step 5 for each table you want to add. Don't forget that if you use more than one table, a relationship must already be established between the tables (see Lesson 21).
7. Click **Close** when you finish adding tables. The Query Design view window opens, as in Figure 17.1, but no fields are selected yet.

# Adding Fields to a Query

If you created your query from scratch (as in the preceding set of steps), the first thing you need to do is add the fields you want to work with. You can also use this same procedure to add additional fields to an existing query.

**TIP** **Adding More Tables** You can add additional tables to your query at any time. Just click the **Show Table** button on the toolbar or select **Query**, **Show Table**. Then select the table(s) you want and click **Add**. Click **Close** to return to your query design.

There are three ways to add a field to a query. All methods are easy; try all of them to see which you prefer.

Here's the first method.

**TIP** **Only One Table?** If you are using only one table in the query, you can skip the first two steps in this procedure.

1. Click in the Table row of the first blank column. A down arrow button appears, indicating a drop-down list is available.
2. Open the drop-down list and select a table. The tables available on the list are the same as the table windows that appear at the top of the query design window.
3. Click in the Field row directly above the table name you just chose. A down-arrow button appears, indicating a drop-down list is available.
4. Open the drop-down list and select a field. The fields listed come from the tables you chose for the query. The field's name appears in the Field row, in the column where you selected it.

Here's the second method of adding a field:

1. Scroll through the list of fields in the desired table window at the top of the Query Design box, until you find the field you want to add.
2. Click the field name and drag it into the Field row of the first empty column. The field's name appears in that location.

The third method is to simply double-click the field name in the field list. It moves to the first available slot in the query grid.

# Deleting a Field

There are two ways to delete a field from your query:

- Click anywhere in the column and select **Edit**, **Delete Column**.

- Position the mouse pointer directly above the column so the pointer turns into a down-pointing black arrow. Click to select the entire column, and then press the **Delete** key or click the **Cut** button on the toolbar.

 **Cut versus Delete** If you cut the column instead of deleting it, you can paste it back into the query. Just select the column where you want it, and then click the **Paste** button or choose **Edit**, **Paste**. Be careful, though because the pasted column will replace the selected one; the selected column doesn't move over to make room for it. Select an empty column if you don't want to replace an existing one.

# Adding Criteria

Criteria will be familiar to you if you read Lesson 15, which dealt with filters. You use criteria to choose which records will appear in your query results. For example, I could limit my list of dogs to those whose birth dates were before 8/5/94.

**TIP** **Filters versus Queries** If the primary reason for creating the query is to filter, you may want to create the filter part first using one of the procedures described in Lesson 15, and then save the filter as a query. You can open that query in Query Design view and fine-tune it as needed.

To set criteria for a field that you've added to your query, follow these steps:

**1.** In Query Design view, click the Criteria row in the desired field's column.

**2.** Type the criterion you want to use, as shown in Figure 17.2. Table 17.1 provides some examples you could have entered in Figure 17.2, as well as the subsequent results.

In Figure 17.2, Access added # symbols because you are working with a date. For other types of criteria, Access adds other symbols, such as quotation marks around a text or number string.

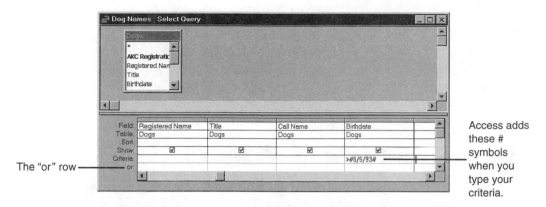

Access adds
these #
symbols
when you
type your
criteria.

The "or" row

**Figure 17.2** Enter criteria into the Criteria row in the appropriate field's column.

**Table 17.1** Sample Criteria for Queries

| Enter This | To Get Records Where This Value Is... |
| --- | --- |
| 8/5/93 | Exactly 8/5/93 |
| <8/5/93 | Before 8/5/93 |
| >8/5/93 | After 8/5/93 |
| >=8/5/93 | On or after 8/5/93 |
| <=8/5/93 | On or before 8/5/93 |
| Not <8/5/93 | Not before 8/5/93 |
| Not >8/5/93 | Not after 8/5/93 |

 **TIP** **Text, Too** You can also enter text as a criteria. The **<** and **>** (before and after) operators apply to alphabetical order with text. For instance, **<C** finds text that begins with A or B.

Did you notice the "or" row under the Criteria row in Figure 17.2? You can enter more criteria using that line. The query will find records where any of the criteria is true. When you enter criteria into the "or" row, another "or" row appears, so you can enter more.

CAUTION

**What About "And"?** When you have two criteria that must both be true, you can put them both together in a single Criteria row with the word "And." For instance, you might want birth dates that were between 12/1/93 and 12/1/95. You could put all of that in a single Criteria row, like this: >12/1/93 And <12/1/95.

# Sorting a Field in a Query

After all this complicated criteria discussion, you will be happy to know that sorting is fairly straightforward. To sort any field, just follow these steps from the query results window:

1. Click in the Sort row for the field you want to sort. A drop-down arrow appears.

2. Open the drop-down list and select **Ascending** or **Descending**.

Later, if you want to cancel sorting for this field, repeat these steps, but select **(not sorted)**. Refer to Lesson 15 for more information about sorting.

# Showing or Hiding a Field

Some fields are included in your query only so you can filter or sort based on them. You may not necessarily be interested in seeing that field in the query results. For instance, you may want to limit your query to all dogs born before 8/5/93, but you don't want each dog's birth date to appear in the query.

To exclude a field from appearing in the query results, just deselect its check box in the Show row. To include it again, select the check box again.

# Viewing Query Results

 When you're ready to see the results of your query, click the **Run** button on the Query Design toolbar or select **Query, Run**. Your results appear in a window that resembles a datasheet (see Figure 17.3).

**Figure 17.3** The results of a kennel query based on birth dates.

In this lesson, you learned to modify and strengthen your queries. In the next lesson, you'll learn how to create a simple, attractive report suitable for printing and distributing to others.

# Creating a Simple Report

18

*In this lesson, you learn how to create reports in Access using AutoReport and Report Wizard.*

## Why Create Reports?

You've learned many ways to organize and view your data, but until now each method has focused on on-screen use. Forms help with data entry on-screen, and queries help you find information and display the results on-screen.

You can print any table, form, or query, but the results will be less than professional-looking because those tools are not designed to be printed. Reports, on the other hand, are specifically designed to be printed and shared with other people. With a report, you can generate professional results that you can be proud of, whether you're distributing them on paper or publishing them on the Internet.

There are several ways to create a report, ranging from easy-but-limited (AutoReport) to difficult-but-very-flexible (Report Design view). The intermediate choice is Report Wizard, which offers some flexibility along with a fairly easy procedure.

## Using AutoReport to Create a Report

If you want a plain, no-frills report based on a single table or query, AutoReport is for you. You can go back and improve its appearance later, when you learn about customizing reports in Lesson 19.

You can create either a Tabular or a Columnar report. A tabular report resembles a datasheet, and a columnar report resembles a form. They are equally easy to create.

To create a report with AutoReport, follow these steps:

1. Open the database containing the table or query on which you want to report.
2. Click the **Reports** tab in the Database window, and then click the **New** button. The New Report dialog box appears (see Figure 18.1).
3. Click **AutoReport: Columnar** or **AutoReport: Tabular**.

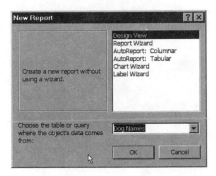

**Figure 18.1**   Choose one of the AutoReports from this window.

4. In the drop-down list at the bottom of the dialog box, select the table or query on which you want to base the report.

**Multiple Tables?**   AutoReports can use only one table or query. If you want to create an AutoReport that uses several tables, first create a query based on those tables, and then base the AutoReport on the query.

**CAUTION**

5. Click **OK**. The report appears in Print Preview. See the section "Viewing and Printing Reports in Print Preview" later in this lesson to learn what to do next.

As you can see in Print Preview, the AutoReports' output is not much better than a raw printout from a table or form. If you want a better-looking report, try Report Wizard, which is explained in the following section.

# Creating a Report with Report Wizard

The Report Wizard offers a good compromise between ease of use and flexibility. With Report Wizard, you can use multiple tables and queries and choose a layout and format for your report.

Follow these steps to create a report with Report Wizard:

**1.** Open the database containing the table or query on which you want to report.

**2.** Click the **Reports** tab in the Database window, and then click the **New** button. The New Report dialog box appears (see Figure 18.1).

**3.** Click **Report Wizard** and click **OK**. The Report Wizard starts (see Figure 18.2).

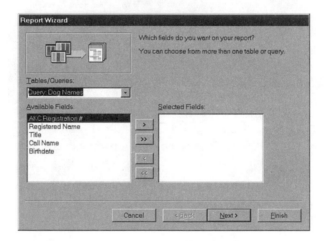

**Figure 18.2** The first Report Wizard screen.

TIP **Multiple Tables/Queries Allowed** You don't need to select a table or query from the drop-down list in the New Report dialog box in step 3 because you'll be selecting tables and queries in step 4 as part of the wizard.

**4.** Open the **Tables/Queries** drop-down list and select one of the tables or queries from which you want to include fields.

5. Click a field in the **Available Fields** list, and then click the > button to move it to the Selected Fields list. Repeat this step to select all the fields you want, or click >> to move all the fields over at once.

6. If necessary, select another table or query from the **Tables/Queries** list and repeat step 5. When you finish selecting fields, click **Next**. The next screen of the wizard appears (see Figure 18.3).

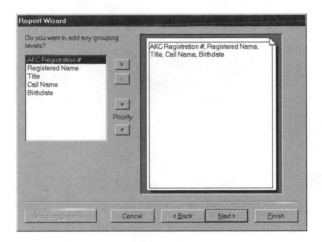

**Figure 18.3** Set your report's grouping.

7. If you want the records grouped by any of the fields you selected, click the field and click the > button. If you want to select more than one grouping levels, select them in the order you want them. Then click **Next** to move on.

**Grouping?** The instructions on the screen are a bit cryptic. By default, there are no groups. You have to select a field and click the > button to create a grouping. For instance, if I had several dogs with the same birthday, I could identify them by grouping my dogs using the Birth Date field. Grouping sets off each group on the report. If you select a field to group by, the Grouping Options button becomes active, and you can click it to specify precise grouping settings.

8. Next you're asked what sort order you want to use (see Figure 18.4). If you want sorted records, open the top drop-down list and select a field to sort by. You can select up to four sorts from the drop-down lists. Then click **Next**.

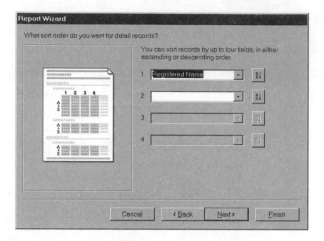

**Figure 18.4** Set the sort order.

**TERM**

**Ascending or Descending?** By default, Access sorts in ascending order (A–Z). Click the **AZ** button next to the box to change the sort order to descending (Z–A) if you want. See Lesson 15 for more information about sorting.

**9.** In the next dialog box (shown in Figure 18.5), choose a layout option from the Layout area. When you click an option button, the sample in the box changes to show you what you've selected.

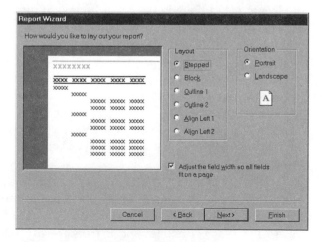

**Figure 18.5** Choose the layout of your report.

**CAUTION**

**Where Are All the Layouts?** If you didn't choose any groupings in your report, your layout choices will be limited to three: Columnar, Tabular, and Justified. The layouts shown in Figure 18.5 are unique to grouped reports.

**10.** Choose the orientation for your printed report: **Portrait** (across the narrow edge of the paper) or **Landscape** (across the wide edge of the paper). Then click **Next** to continue.

**11.** In the next wizard dialog box, you're asked to choose a report style. Several are listed; click one to see a sample of it. When you're satisfied with your choice, click **Next**.

**12.** Finally, you're asked for a report title. Enter one in the **Report** text box and click **Finish** to see your report in Print Preview (see Figure 18.6).

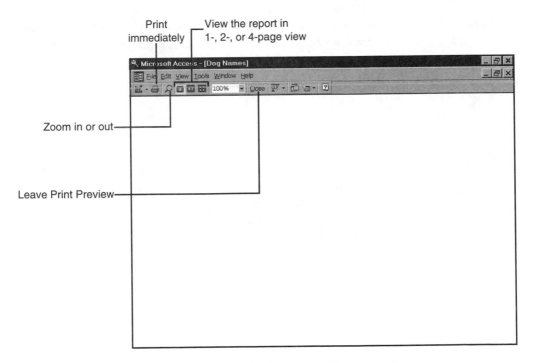

**Figure 18.6** Here's a very simple report with no grouping.

# Viewing and Printing Reports in Print Preview

When you finish a report with either Report Wizard or AutoReport, the report appears in Print Preview (as shown in Figure 18.6). From here, you can print the report if you're happy with it, or you can go to Report Design view to make changes if you aren't. (You'll learn more about the latter in Lesson 19).

If you want to print the report and specify any print options (such as number of copies), open the **File** menu and select **Print**. If you want a quick hard copy, click the **Print** button on the toolbar. Click the button appropriate to what you want to do. Figure 18.6 points out some of the other useful buttons available in Print Preview. To go to Report Design view, click **Close**. (Report Design view is actually open, it's just obscured by the Print Preview window.)

In this lesson, you learned to create and print a simple report. In the next lesson, you'll learn how to work in Report Design view to customize your report.

# Customizing a Report

*In this lesson, you learn to use Report Design view to make your report more attractive.*

## Entering Report Design View

When you finish previewing a report you've created, close Print Preview and you're automatically in Report Design view. If you want to come back to Report Design view later from the Database window, perform these steps:

1. Click the **Reports** tab.
2. Click the report you want to modify.
3. Click the **Design** button. The report appears in Design view, as shown in Figure 19.1.

Report Design view might seem familiar to you; it looks a lot like Form Design view. Almost everything you learned about editing forms in Lesson 13 applies also to reports. As in Form Design view, there is a toolbox of common editing tools.

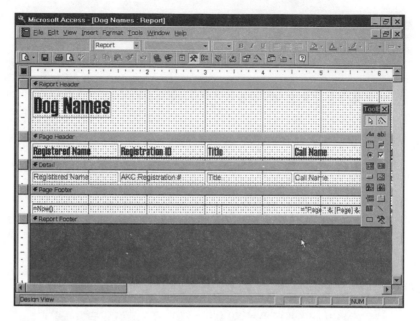

**Figure 19.1** The report created in the previous lesson, as it looks in Design view.

# Working with Objects on Your Report

Working with report objects in Report Design view is exactly the same as working with objects in Form Design view. An object is any control, such as a field name or a title. Turn back to Lesson 13 for the full story, or follow the brief review here:

**Selecting objects** Just like in Form Design view, you select an object on your report by clicking it. Selection handles (little squares in the corners) appear around it. See Lesson 14 for more details.

**Moving objects** To move an object, first select it. Position the mouse pointer over a border so the pointer turns into an open black hand. Then click and drag the object to a new location.

**Resizing objects** First, select the object. Then position the mouse pointer over one of the selection handles and drag the handle to resize the object.

**Formatting text objects** Use the Font and Font Size drop-down lists on the toolbar to choose fonts; then use the Bold, Italic, and Underline toolbar buttons to set special attributes.

You can also add graphic lines and objects to reports, just as you do forms.

 **TIP** **Access on the Web** You can assign hyperlinks to objects on your forms and reports, as you'll learn in Part VII of this book. They aren't "hot" (that is, they don't actually link) on the printouts, but if you save a report in Microsoft Word format, the hyperlinks can be activated when you open the document in Word.

# Adding and Removing Fields

You can add more fields to your report at any time. Follow these steps to add a field to your report:

1. If you don't see the Field List, select **View**, **Field List** or click the **Field List** button on the toolbar. A floating box appears listing all the fields in the table you're using.

2. Drag any field from the Field List into the report. Place it anywhere you want in the Detail area.

Don't worry if the field isn't in the right place or if it overlaps another field; you'll learn to fix that in the next section. To delete a field, click it and press the **Delete** key. This deletes the reference to the field from the report, but it remains in the table from which it came.

# Arranging Your New Fields

When you add a field to your report, you're actually adding two things: a label and a text box. These two elements are bound together: the label describes the text box, and the text box represents the actual field that will be used (see Figure 19.2). You can change the label without affecting the text box; for instance, you could change the label on the Coloring field to Dog Color without affecting the contents. To change a label, just click it and retype it.

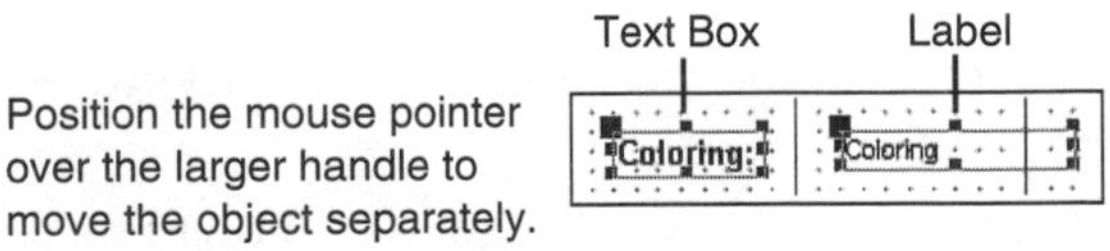

Position the mouse pointer over the larger handle to move the object separately.

Text Box        Label

Coloring:      Coloring

**Figure 19.2** The text box and its label.

By default, when you move the text box, the label follows. When you position the mouse pointer over the border of the text box, and the pointer changes to an open hand, that's your signal that the label will follow the text box when you drag it.

However, you can also move the text box and the label separately. Notice that in the upper-left corner of each, there is a selection handle (square) that's bigger than the others. When you position the mouse pointer over that handle, the cursor becomes a pointing hand. That's your signal that you can click-and-drag the object separately from the other.

Moving the label separately can come in handy when you don't want the label to appear in its default position (to the left of the text box). For instance, you might want the label to appear above the text box.

# Adding Labels

In the preceding section, you saw how to add a field (a text box and a label bound together). But you can also add labels by themselves, with extra text in them that is not necessarily associated with a particular field. For instance, you might add an informational note about the report in general. To do so, click the **Label** button in the toolbox, and then click anywhere on the report and start typing. When you finish, click anywhere outside the label.

# Adding a Calculated Text Box

The most common thing that text boxes hold is references to fields, as you have seen in this lesson. However, text boxes have another purpose: they can also hold calculations based on values in different fields.

Creating a calculated text box is a bit complicated. First you have to create an unbound text box (that is, one that's not associated with any particular field). Then you have to enter the calculation into the text box. Follow these steps:

1. Click the **Text Box** tool in the toolbox, and then click-and-drag on the report to create a text box.

2. Change the label to reflect what's going to go in that box. For instance, if it's going to be Sales Tax, change it to that. Position the label where you want it.

**3.** Click in the text box and type the formula you want calculated. (See the following section for guidance.)

**4.** Click anywhere outside the text box when you finish.

# Rules for Creating Calculations

The formulas you enter into your calculated text box use standard mathematical controls:

| | |
|---|---|
| + | Add |
| – | Subtract |
| * | Multiply |
| / | Divide |

All formulas begin with an equals sign (=), and all field names appear in parentheses. Here are some examples:

To calculate a total price by multiplying the value in the Quantity field by the value in the Price field, enter **=(Quantity)\*(Price)**.

To calculate a 25% discount off the value in the Cost field, enter **=(Cost)\*.075**.

To add the total of the values in three fields, enter **(Field1)+(Field2)+(Field3)**.

**TIP** **More Room** If you run out of room in the text box when typing your formula, press **Shift+F2** to open a Zoom box, where there's more room.

In this lesson, you learned to customize your report by adding and removing objects, moving them around, and creating calculations. In the next lesson, you'll learn how to create mailing labels.

# Creating Mailing Labels

*In this lesson, you learn how to make mailing labels using names and addresses in a database.*

## Easy Mailing Labels with Access

If you have ever done mass mailings to club members, customers, or even friends, the worst part was probably addressing all those envelopes. Most word processors (such as Word) have mailing label features that enable you to create mailing labels from a list of names, but Access is even better: it lets you create mailing labels directly from an address book database (or any other database).

To create mailing labels, use the Label Wizard. Mailing labels are a type of report, so you'll start the process from the Reports tab of your database.

**Which Database?** Because the example dog kennel database we've worked with in previous lessons does not contain any addresses, I'm going to use a sample database I created using Access's Contact Management template and Access's own sample data. If you want to follow along, you can create this same database by following the steps for creating a new database in Lesson 4.

# Creating Mailing Labels with the Label Wizard

To create mailing labels from a table that contains names and addresses, follow these steps:

1. Open the database you want to work with and click the **Reports** tab.

2. Click the **New** button. The New Report dialog box appears. In it, click **Label Wizard**.

3. Open the drop-down list at the bottom of the box and select the table or query from which to pull the names and addresses. Then click **OK**. The first screen of the Label Wizard appears (see Figure 20.1).

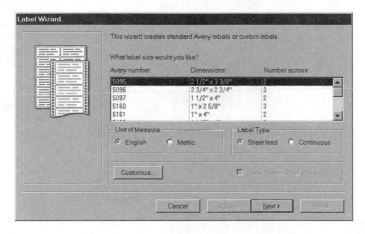

**Figure 20.1**   Label Wizard starts out by asking you what size labels you'll be using.

4. Choose the label type from the list. If only a few labels are listed, make sure the **Show Custom Label Sizes** check box is deselected. (It must be deselected to see the standard label types.)

**CAUTION**

**Don't Know the Avery Number?**   Avery is the largest manufacturer of labels. If you don't know the Avery number for your labels, move through the labels listed until you find one with dimensions that match those of the labels you're using. If the size you are using is not available, you can create a custom label.

5. Click **Sheet Feed** or **Continuous**. (Sheet-fed labels are single sheets; continuous labels are joined to the previous and next sheet at the top, and they have perforated strips on the side that feed through a dot-matrix printer.)

6. Click **Next >** when you've entered your label information.

7. Next you're asked about the appearance of the text (see Figure 20.2). Choose a font from the **Font Name** drop-down list, and choose a font size from the **Font Size** drop-down list.

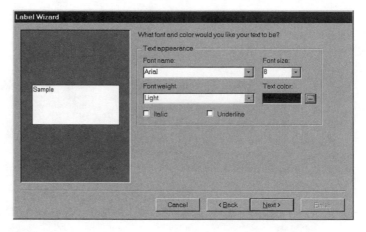

**Figure 20.2**  Choose settings for the text to be printed on the labels.

**Don't Make the Font Too Big!**  If you need to print multiple lines on each label, make sure that the font size you select is small enough that all lines will fit. For mailing labels, 8- or 10-point type works well: it is large enough to be read by U.S. Postal Service machines, but it's small enough that you can fit several lines on each label.

**CAUTION**

8. With some fonts, you can choose a font weight. Open the **Font Weight** drop-down list and choose a different weight if you want. **Normal** will work well in most cases.

9. If you would like color labels (and you have a color printer), choose a different color from the Text Color list. To do so, click the button next to the **Text Color** box, choose from the Color dialog box that appears, and then click **OK** to return.

**Avoid Light Colors!** If you're making labels to be sent through the U.S. Postal Service, keep in mind that their machines can't read light-colored ink such as yellow or pale pink. Choose a dark color to ensure that your addresses will be read correctly.

**CAUTION**

**10.** Click the **Italic** and/or the **Underline** check box if you want the text formatted with either or both of those attributes. Then click **Next >** to continue.

**11.** Next, Access asks which fields to include on the label. Select a field from the **Available Fields** list and click the **>** button to move it to the Prototype label (see Figure 20.3).

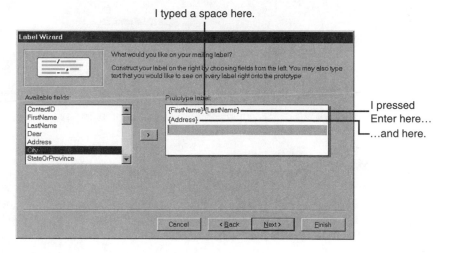

**Figure 20.3** Adding fields to your label.

**12.** Continue selecting fields until all fields you want to use appear on the label. Don't forget to add spaces between fields on the same line (for instance, a space between the first and last name). You can press **Enter** to start a new line on the label. Then click **Next >** to continue.

**TIP** **Adding Other Text** If you want certain text to appear on every label, you can type it as you enter fields. For example, if you want a comma to separate the City and State fields, type it here. You could put **Thanks for your business!** on the labels, or could type the words **Your subscription expires on** right before an Expiration field.

**13.** If you would like your labels sorted by a particular field, select that field on the next screen that appears (see Figure 20.4) and click the > button to move it to the Sort By list. For instance, you might need to sort by ZIP code (Access calls it PostalCode) to do some bulk mailings. Click **Next >** to continue.

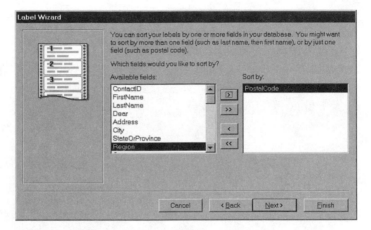

**Figure 20.4** Select which field(s) you want to sort by, if any.

**Order Is Important!** If you pick more than one field to sort by, Access sorts the records first by the first field you select, then by the second, and so on. So it's important to choose the field first that you want to sort by first. If they're in the wrong order, click the << button to remove them all from the Sort By list, and then start over.

**14.** In the last screen, you're asked for a title. Enter one and click **Finish**. Your labels appear in Print Preview, just like any other report. Figure 20.5 shows the labels I've created.

# Printing Labels

You can print by clicking the **Print** button, or you can close the Print Preview box by clicking the **Close** button.

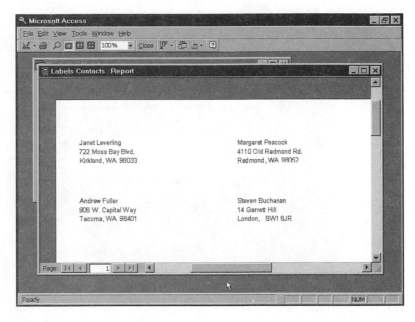

**Figure 20.5** Mailing labels cretaed by the Label Wizaed (displayed in Print Preview).

# Saving Labels

To save your labels, exit from Print Preview. You'll see the labels appear in the Database window on the Reports tab. Unlike with a chart or report, Report Design view does not appear automatically when you close Print Preview.

# Modifying Your Labels

If you want to modify the labels, you can enter Report Design view and make changes just as you would with any report. Just click the labels on the **Reports** tab, and then click **Design**. Your label design appears, as shown in Figure 20.6.

Use all the same editing techniques that you learned in Lesson 19, "Customizing a Report," to make changes to your label.

In this lesson, you learned how to create mailing labels. In the next lesson, you will learn how to create relationships among tables.

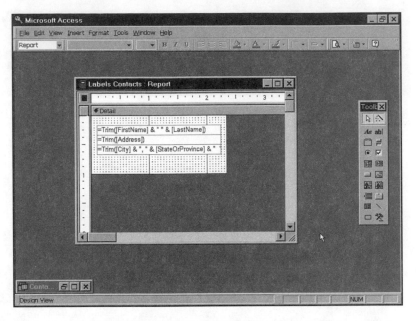

**Figure 20.6**   You can modify your label, just as you would modify any report.

# Creating Relationships Between Tables

*In this lesson, you learn how to link two or more tables together so you can work with them as you would a single table.*

## Why Create Relationships?

In Lesson 2, I encouraged you to make separate tables for information that was not directly related. As you've learned along the way, when you create forms, queries, and reports, you can pull information from more than one table easily. But this works best when there is a well-defined relationship between the tables.

Let's say, for instance, that I have two tables containing information about my customers. One table, called Customers, contains their names and addresses; the other, called Orders, contains their orders. The two tables would have a common field: Customer ID#. All records in the Orders table would correspond to a record in the Customers table. (This is called a "many-to-one" relationship because there could be many orders for one customer.)

As another example, in my dog kennel database, I have several tables describing my dogs and their activities. I have a table listing all the different colorings a dog can have. I could create a relationship between the Dogs table and the Coloring table, matching up each dog's coloring field with one of the accepted colors listed in the Coloring table. This would ensure that I didn't record any dog's coloring as a type that's not allowed.

**More Complicated** Relationships can be extremely complicated and thorny. I'm showing you only simple examples in this lesson because that's probably all you'll need as a casual user. For more information on relationships, see your Access documentation or the book *Using Access 97, Special Edition*, also published by Que Corporation.

# Creating a Relationship Between Tables

To create a relationship between tables, you open the Relationships window and add relationships from there. Follow these steps:

1. From anywhere in the database select **Tools**, **Relationships**.

2. If you have not selected any tables yet, the Show Table dialog box (shown in Figure 21.1) appears automatically. If it doesn't, open the **Relationships** menu and select **Show Table** or click the **Show Table** toolbar button.

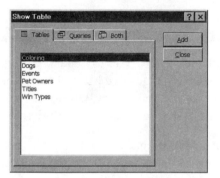

**Figure 21.1** Add tables to your Relationships window.

3. Click a table that you want to use for a relationship, and then click the **Add** button.

4. Repeat step 3 until you've selected all the tables you want to work with. When you're finished, click **Close**. Each table appears in its own box in the Relationships window, as shown in Figure 21.2.

**Make It Bigger** If you can't clearly see all the fields in a table's list, drag the border of its box to make it large enough to see everything. I've done that in Figure 21.2 to make the Dogs table completely visible.

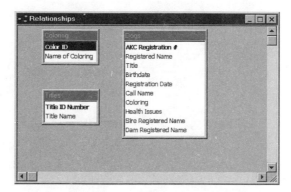

**Figure 21.2** I've added three tables to my Relationships window.

5. Click a field in one table that you want to link to another table. For instance, I'm going to link the Coloring field in my Dogs table to the Color ID field in my Coloring table, so I'm going to click the Coloring field in the Dogs table.

6. Hold down the mouse button and drag away from the selected field. Your mouse pointer will turn into a little rectangle. Drop the little rectangle onto the destination field. For instance, I'm dragging to the Color ID field in the Coloring table. The Relationships dialog box appears (see Figure 21.3).

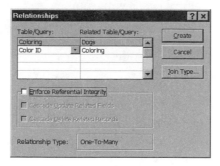

**Figure 21.3** The Relationships dialog box asks you to define the relationship you're creating.

7. Choose any Referential Integrity options you want (see the following section), and then click **Create**. If all goes well, a relationship is created, and you see a line between the two fields in the Relationships window (see Figure 21.4).

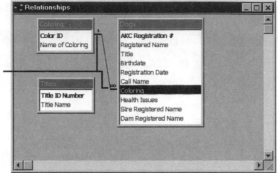

You won't get the Infinity and 1 symbols on this line if you didn't choose Enforce Referential Integrity.

**Figure 21.4** The line represents a relationship between the two fields.

**Relationship Symbols** Notice in Figure 21.4 that next to the Dogs table there's an infinity sign (looks like a sideways 8), and next to the Coloring table there's a 1. These symbols appear in relationships where Enforce Referential Integrity is turned on. The infinity sign means "many"—that means many records in this table can match a single record (hence the 1 sign) in the related Coloring table.

# What Is Referential Integrity?

Referential Integrity keeps you from making data entry mistakes. It says, essentially, that all the information in the two fields should match. If there is an entry in one table in the linked field that doesn't exist in the other, it's a problem that Referential Integrity corrects.

An example will make this clearer. In the Coloring field in my Dogs database, I have a number that matches up with the Color ID field in the Coloring table. The Coloring table lists all the allowable colors for the breed of dog. I don't want my clerks to be able to accidentally enter a number in the Dogs table that doesn't match up with any of the colors in the Coloring table, so I chose to Enforce Referential Integrity. Now Access won't let anyone enter anything in the Coloring field of the Dogs table (the "many" or infinity side) except one of the numbers contained in the Color ID field in the Coloring table (the one side).

What happens if someone tries? It depends on which of the other two check boxes shown in Figure 21.3 were marked.

Here is a summary of the check boxes and their functions:

- **Neither Marked** Access gives an error message that you need a related record in the "[Table Name]" and won't let you make the entry.
- **Cascade Update Related Fields** If this check box is marked and you make a change to the related table (in our example, the Coloring table), the change will be made in the other table (the Dogs table) as well. For instance, if I decided to change a certain coloring number from 7 to 8, and I made the change in the Coloring table (the one side), all the 7s in the Dogs table (the many side) would change to 8s.
- **Cascade Delete Related Fields** If this check box is marked and you make a change to the "one" table (for instance, Coloring) so that the entries in the related table aren't valid anymore, Access deletes the entries in the related table. For instance, if I deleted the record in the Coloring table for Coloring ID number 3, all the dogs from my Dogs table that had coloring number 3 would also be deleted.

The first time you try to use Referential Integrity, you will likely get an error message because there is usually some condition that prevents it from working (as Murphy's Law goes). For instance, when I first created the relationship shown in Figure 21.4 with Enforce Referential Integrity marked, Access wouldn't allow it because the field type for the Coloring field in the Dogs table was set to Text while the Color ID field in the Coloring table was a number. (It didn't matter that I had entered only numbers in the Coloring field in the Dogs table.)

# Editing a Relationship

Once a relationship is created, you can edit it by redisplaying the Relationships dialog box (refer to Figure 21.3). To do so, double-click the relationship's line. From there, you can edit the relationship using the same controls you did when you created it.

# Removing a Relationship

To delete a relationship, just click it in the Relationships window and press the **Delete** key. Access will ask for confirmation. Click **Yes**, and the relationship disappears.

In this lesson, you learned how to create, edit, and delete relationships between tables.

**691**

# Working Together

# Installing Microsoft Office 97

*In this lesson, you learn how to install Microsoft Office 97 on your computer so you can begin using it.*

## What Is Installing?

When you get a new application like Microsoft Office, it comes in a compressed format on a CD or a set of diskettes. You must run a setup program to copy the needed files to your hard disk and decompress the compressed data.

**TIP** **Run from CD**  Office 97 does provide an option to run the Office applications directly from the CD, saving disk space on your PC. However, to set this up, you must still run the setup program, as you'll learn to do later in this lesson.

## Installing Microsoft Office

To install Office on your PC, follow these steps:

1. Close all open applications.
2. Insert the Microsoft Office 97 CD in your CD-ROM drive. A dialog box opens automatically.

**No Dialog Box Opened!**  If no dialog box opened when you inserted the CD, your computer may not be set up to Autorun CDs. Just open the **My Computer** window and double-click the CD drive's icon. Then locate and double-click the **Setup** icon.

CAUTION

3. Click the **Install Microsoft Office** button.

4. At the Welcome dialog box, click **Continue**.

5. In the Name and Organization Information dialog box, enter your name and organization. Then click **OK**.

6. If asked to confirm your name and organization, click **OK** again.

7. If you're asked for the 11-digit CD key, find it on the sticker on the back of the jewel case and enter it. Then click **OK**.

8. Next you see your product ID number. Write it down on your registration card, and then click **OK**.

9. Choose the drive and folder into which Microsoft Office is installed. The default is the Program Files folder on the same drive that Windows is installed on (see Figure 1.1). Click **OK** to accept that, or click **Change Folder** and select a new location.

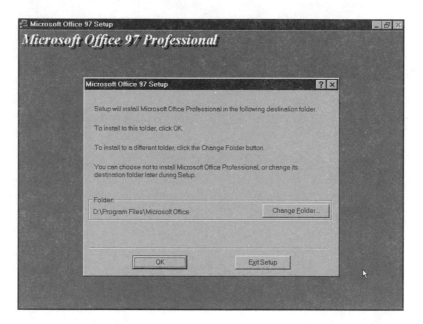

**Figure 1.1** Accept the directory chosen by the installation program by clicking OK, or click Change Folder and choose your own.

10. Choose the type of installation you want:

   • **Typical** installs the most common components. This is the easiest method, and most users will be happy with the options installed.

- **Custom** enables you to choose exactly which components you want. This is for experienced users and those who don't use certain Office products at all.

- **Run from CD-ROM** sets up Office to run mostly from the CD. Because it copies very few files to your hard disk, it's ideal for users who are very short on disk space; however, it requires that the CD be in the drive whenever an Office component is running.

If you chose Typical or Run from CD-ROM, skip to step 14. If you chose Custom, the Microsoft Office 97 Custom dialog box appears (see Figure 1.2).

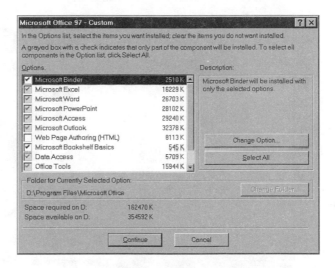

**Figure 1.2** Click the check boxes to select or deselect categories and options.

**11.** You see a series of components with check boxes. A check in a white-background box means all options for that component will be installed. A check in a gray-background box means that only some of the component's options will be installed. Use these methods to choose which components and options you want:

To select all Office components, click the **Select All** button.

To deselect an entire component, click its check box to remove the check mark.

To choose which options of a component are installed, click the component, and then click **Change Option**. A dialog box appears, showing the options for that component, each with its own check box you can use to turn it on or off. Click **OK** to return to the main screen. Refer to Table 1.1 (in the next section) for some ideas about what to select.

**12.** When you finish selecting options, click **Continue**.

**13.** If the installation program finds old Office components, it asks whether you want to remove them. Click **Yes**.

**14.** Wait for the setup program to copy the files (see Figure 1.3). When you see the message **Microsoft Office 97 Setup was completed successfully,** click **OK**. You are now ready to use Microsoft Office.

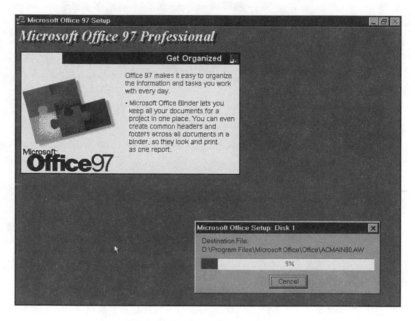

**Figure 1.3** It takes several minutes for the setup program to copy its files; a progress bar at the bottom of the screen shows how far it has progressed.

# Custom Installation: Some Advice

It's hard to know exactly which options to choose in a Custom installation if you're a beginner. Table 1.1 provides some ideas of some components you might want that are not installed by default.

**Table 1.1**   Options Not Installed by Default That You Might Want

| Component | Option | Comments |
| --- | --- | --- |
| Word | Wizards and Templates | If you like using templates, select all of these. Only some are installed by default. |
| Word | Help | If you are a WordPerfect user, install Help for WordPerfect Users. |
| PowerPoint | Content Templates | Three extra templates are available (Business Plan, Corporate Home Page, and Progress Presentation) when you select Additional Content Templates. |
| PowerPoint | Animation Effects Sounds | If you use sounds in your presentations, you may find these sound files useful. |
| PowerPoint | Presentation Translators | If you need to convert presentations from Harvard Graphics for DOS or Lotus Freelance 1.0 through 2.1, install this. |
| Outlook | Lotus Organizer Converters | Install this if you have Organizer files you want to use in Outlook. |
| Excel | Spreadsheet Templates | This installs the Expense Report Template and Purchase Order Template. |
| Excel | Add-Ins | Install the File Conversion Wizard if you have a group of files you will be convert ingto Excel format. |
| Excel | Spreadsheet Converters | The Quattro Pro 1.0/5.0 (Win) converter is not installed by default. |
| Access | Sample Databases | If you want to follow along with the examples in the Access section of this book, or if you want some samples to examine, select these. |
| Web Page Authoring (HTML) | (No options) | If you plan to create Web pages, you will definitely need these tools. |
| Office Tools | Microsoft Office Shortcut Bar | This is not installed by default, although it was in previous releases of Microsoft Office. If you're accustomed to using it, install it. |
| Office Tools | Microsoft Photo Editor | This is a new utility program that scans, edits, and converts images. |

*continues*

**699**

**Table 1.1** Continued

| Component | Option | Comments |
|---|---|---|
| Converters and Filters | Text | I recommend that you install all of these. You never know what file formats you may encounter. |
| Converters and Filters | Graphics | I also recommend that you install all of these. |

# Installing Internet Explorer

If you use the Internet (or if you want to learn), you may find Microsoft's *Web browser*, Internet Explorer 3.0, useful. After you run the Office installation program, an icon appears on your desktop called Setup for Microsoft Internet Explorer 3.0. That icon makes it very easy to install the program.

 **Web Browser**   A Web browser enables you to view graphical content on the Internet. To use it, you must have an Internet connection. You can get an Internet connection by subscribing to The Microsoft Network; the easiest way to get that subscription is to double-click **The Microsoft Network** icon on your desktop and follow the prompts.

Follow these steps to install Internet Explorer:

1. Double-click the **Setup for Microsoft Internet Explorer 3.0** desktop icon.
2. A dialog box asks if you want to install the program. Click **Yes**.
3. Read the licensing agreement, and then click **I Agree**.
4. Wait for the setup program to install the files you need. If the Version Conflict dialog box appears, asking you if you want to keep an existing file, click **Yes**.
5. At the message **Do you want to restart your computer now?**, click **Yes**.

After your computer restarts, you are ready to use Internet Explorer. You can use it through your Microsoft Network account or with any other Internet connection.

In this lesson, you learned how to install Microsoft Office 97 and Internet Explorer 3.0. In the next lesson, you'll learn about the Office 97 Help system.

# Using the Office 97 Help System

*In this lesson, you learn about the various types of help available to you in Microsoft Office programs.*

## Help: What's Available?

Because every person is different, the programs in the MS Office suite offer many different ways to get help with the program. You can:

- Ask the Office Assistant for help.
- Get help on a particular element you see on-screen with the What's This? tool.
- Choose what you're interested in learning about from a series of Help Topics.
- Access the Microsoft On the Web feature to view Web pages containing help information (if you are connected to the Internet).

## Asking the Office Assistant

You have probably already met the Office Assistant; it's the paper clip character that pops up to give you advice. He appears the first time you start each of the Office programs to ask if you need help getting started. Don't let its whimsical appearance fool you, though; behind the Office Assistant is a very powerful Help system.

**No More Answer Wizard**  The Office Assistant replaces the Answer Wizard feature from Microsoft Office for Windows 95.

# Turning the Office Assistant On and Off

By default, the Office Assistant is turned on, and it sits in a little box on top of whatever you're working on, as shown in Figure 2.1. You can turn it off by clicking the **Close** (X) button in its top right corner.

**Figure 2.1** The Office Assistant appears in its own window, on top of the program window.

 To turn the Office Assistant on again, click the **Help** button in the Standard toolbar or select **Help**, **Microsoft Word Help** (or Access, or PowerPoint, or Outlook—whatever program you're using at the moment).

# Kinds of Help Office Assistant Provides

When you first turn on the Office Assistant, a bubble appears next to (or above) its box asking you what kind of help you want (see Figure 2.2). You can do any of the following:

- Type a question in the text box provided to tell the Office Assistant what kind of help you need. (More on this shortly.)
- Select one of the Office Assistant's "guesses" about what you need help with.
- Click the **Tips** button to get any tips that the Office Assistant can provide for the task you're performing.
- Click the **Options** button to customize the way the Office Assistant works. (I'll explain more about this later in this lesson.)
- Click **Close** to close the bubble (but leave the Office Assistant on-screen).

If you close the help bubble, you can reopen it at any time by clicking the **Help** button on the Standard toolbar, by pressing **F1**, by selecting **Help**, **Microsoft Word Help** (or whatever program you're in), or by clicking in the Office Assistant window.

**Figure 2.2**   Office Assistant at your service, asking what you need help with.

TIP   **Extra Tips Along the Way**   Sometimes you'll see a light bulb next to the Office Assistant in its window as in Figure 2.1. This means that the Office Assistant has a suggestion for you regarding the task you're currently perform-ing. To get the suggestion, just click the light bulb. Then click the **Close** button when you finish reading the suggestion.

## Asking the Office Assistant a Question

If you need help on a particular topic, you can type a question into the text box shown in Figure 2.2. Follow these steps to see how it works:

1. If the Office Assistant's help bubble doesn't appear, click the **Help** button on the Standard toolbar.

2. Type a question into the text box. For instance, you might type **How do I print?** to get help on printing your work.

3. Click the **Search** button. The Office Assistant provides some topics that might match what you're looking for. Figure 2.3 shows the Office Assis-tant's answer to the question "How do I print?" in Word. The options may be a little different in the other Office applications.

4. Click the option that best describes what you're trying to do. If you were to choose Print a Document from Figure 2.3, a Help window would appear with instructions for the specified task.

   If none of the options describes what you want, click the **See More...** arrow to view more options, or type a different question into the text box.

The Help window that appears (containing the task instructions) is part of the same Help system you can access with the Help, Contents and Index command. See "Managing Help Topics You've Located" later in this lesson for information about navigating this window.

**Figure 2.3**  The Office Assistant asks you to narrow down exactly what you are trying to accomplish so it can provide the best help possible.

# Using the Help Topics

A more conventional way to get help is through the Contents and Index command on the Help menu. When you open the Help system, you move through the topics listed to find the topic you're interested in.

There are several tabs in the Help system, so you can use Help the way you want it. To access the Help system, select **Help**, **Contents and Index** to produce the Help Topics screen. The following sections explain how to use the tabs and topics contained in Microsoft Help.

## Contents

The Contents tab of the Help system is a series of "books" you can open. Each book has one or more Help topics in it, and some books contain other subbooks! Figure 2.4 shows a Contents screen.

To select a Help topic from the Contents screen, follow these steps:

1. Select **Help**, **Contents and Index**.
2. Click the **Contents** tab.
3. Find the book that describes in broad terms the subject you're looking for help with.

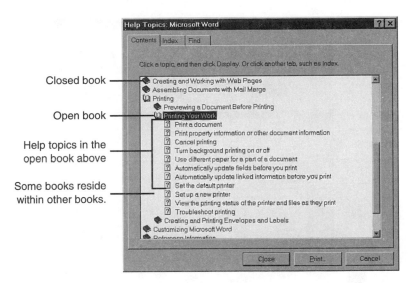

Closed book ——

Open book ——

Help topics in the
open book above

Some books reside
within other books.

**Figure 2.4**  The Help Contents screen is a group of books that contain help information.

4. Double-click the book, and a list of Help topics appears below the book, as shown in Figure 2.4.

5. Double-click a Help topic to display it.

6. When you finish reading a topic, click **Contents** to go back to the main Help screen or click the window's **Close** (X) button to exit Help.

# Index

The Index is an alphabetical listing of every Help topic available. It's like an index in a book.

Follow these steps to use the index:

1. Select **Help, Contents and Index**.

2. Click the **Index** tab.

3. Type the first few letters of the topic you're looking for. The index list jumps quickly to that spot (see Figure 2.5).

4. Double-click the topic you want to see.

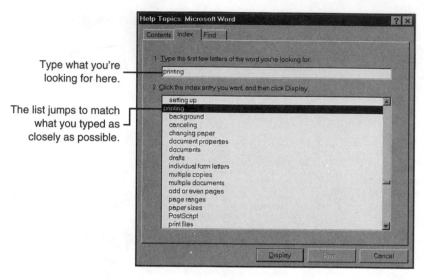

Type what you're
looking for here.

The list jumps to match
what you typed as
closely as possible.

**Figure 2.5** Browse topics alphabetically with the Index.

# Find

The Index is great if you know the name of the Help topic you're looking for—but what if you're not sure? That's where Find comes in handy. Find searches not only the titles of help topics, but their contents, and it retrieves all the topics in which the word(s) you typed appear.

To use Find, follow these steps:

**1.** Select **Help**, **Contents and Index**.

**2.** Click the **Find** tab. The first time you use Find, you'll be asked to build the Find index. Click **Next**, and then click **Finish** to do it.

**3.** Type the topic you're looking for in the top box (1).

**4.** If more than one line appears in the middle box (2), click the one that most closely matches your interest.

**5.** Browse the topics that appear at the bottom (3), and click the one that matches the help you need (see Figure 2.6).

**6.** Click the **Display** button or press **Enter**.

When you're finished reading a topic, you can return to the Find screen by clicking the **Help Topics** button.

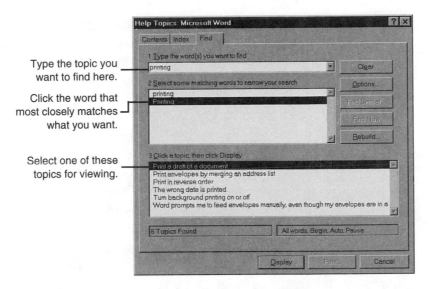

Type the topic you want to find here.

Click the word that most closely matches what you want.

Select one of these topics for viewing.

**Figure 2.6** Use Find to locate all of the Help topics that deal with a certain subject.

# Managing Help Topics You've Located

No matter which of the four avenues you choose for finding a Help topic (the Office Assistant, Contents, Index, or Find), you eventually end up at a Help screen of instructions like the one shown in Figure 2.7. From there, you can read the information on-screen or do any of the following things:

- Click an underlined word to see a definition of it (for instance, see **main document** in Figure 2.7).
- Click a button to jump to another Help screen. For instance, in Figure 2.7, there is a >> button and a button with a curved arrow on it. You can click these to jump to other screens of related information.
- Print a hard copy of the information by clicking the **Options** button and selecting **Print Topic**.
- Copy the text to the Clipboard (for pasting into a program such as Microsoft Word or Windows Notepad) by clicking the **Options** button and selecting **Copy**.
- Return to the previous Help topic you viewed by clicking the **Back** button.
- Return to the main Help Topics screen by clicking the **Help Topics** button.
- Close the Help window by clicking the **Close** (X) button.

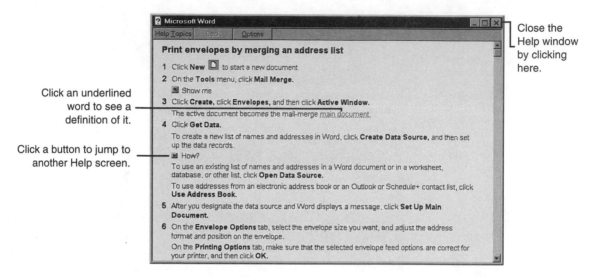

Click an underlined word to see a definition of it.

Click a button to jump to another Help screen.

Close the Help window by clicking here.

**Figure 2.7**   Once you arrive at the information you need, you can read it on-screen, print it, or move to another Help topic.

**Microsoft on the Web**   New for Office 97 is built-in access to Microsoft's Web site, where you can find additional Help information. Establish your Internet connection, and then select **Help, Microsoft on the Web** and choose from the Web pages listed on the submenu to jump directly to one of them.

# Getting Help with Screen Elements

If you wonder about the function of a particular button or tool on the screen, wonder no more. Just follow these steps to learn about this part of Help:

**1.** Select **Help, What's This?** or press **Shift+F1**. The mouse pointer changes to an arrow with a question mark.

**2.** Click the screen element for which you want help. A box appears explaining the element.

In this lesson, you learned about the many ways that Office offers help. In the next lesson, you'll learn about the Shortcut bar.

# Using the Shortcut Bar

*In this lesson, you learn about the Microsoft Office Shortcut Bar and
how it can give you quick access to the programs you use the most.*

## What Is the Shortcut Bar?

The Shortcut Bar is a special toolbar that you can access from Windows 95 or
Windows NT itself, as well as from within each of the Microsoft Office applications. While most toolbars that you have worked with so far are designed to
help you issue commands, the Shortcut Bar is designed to help you start programs. It's shown in Figure 3.1.

**CAUTION**

**It's Not Installed!** The Shortcut Bar is not installed with the Standard
installation of Microsoft Office 97 (see Lesson 1, "Installing Microsoft Office
97"). You must use the Custom installation and choose it as one of the options
you want to install. Go back and reinstall now if you want to use the Shortcut
Bar but don't have it.

There are several sets of tools ("toolbars") you can display on the Shortcut Bar.
The default one is Office, and all the buttons on it start new documents or open
existing ones in Office programs. Table 3.1 shows what each button does. You'll
learn how to display the other toolbars later in this lesson. Just click a button to
use it.

**Figure 3.1**   The Shortcut Bar is available in Windows and all Office applications.

**Table 3.1**   Tools on the Shortcut Bar's Office Toolbar

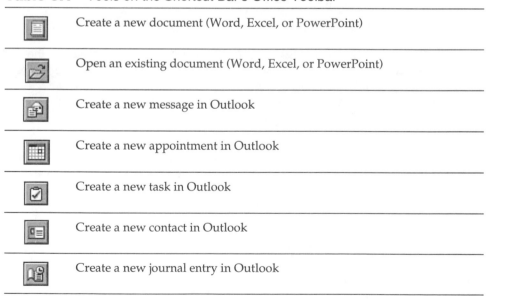

| | |
|---|---|
| | Create a new document (Word, Excel, or PowerPoint) |
| | Open an existing document (Word, Excel, or PowerPoint) |
| | Create a new message in Outlook |
| | Create a new appointment in Outlook |
| | Create a new task in Outlook |
| | Create a new contact in Outlook |
| | Create a new journal entry in Outlook |

Create a new note in Outlook

 Open the Getting Results book on the Microsoft Office CD (The CD must be in your computer's CD-ROM drive.)

# Moving the Shortcut Bar

The Shortcut Bar appears on the right side of the screen by default, but you can easily move it to the bottom or to either side by dragging it. Just drag any portion of the Shortcut Bar that doesn't contain a button. If you drag it away from the edge of the screen, it becomes a floating toolbar, as shown in Figure 3.2.

**Figure 3.2** You can make the Shortcut Bar into a floating toolbar by dragging it away from the edge.

# Customizing the Shortcut Bar

The Office toolbar is useful, but the Shortcut Bar really begins to shine when you customize it for your own needs. You can choose from several levels of customization, ranging from simply displaying another pre-made toolbar to creating brand new toolbars all your own.

## Choosing Which Toolbars Appear

Besides the default Office toolbar, the Shortcut Bar comes with several other toolbars:

* **Favorites** Shows buttons for the contents of your Favorites list.

 **Favorites List** Windows maintains a folder called Favorites within the Windows folder; in it, you can place shortcut links to the files and folders you use most often. In the Open and Save dialog boxes, you'll find buttons for viewing the Favorites folder quickly and for adding items to it. You can also manually copy shortcuts into the Favorites folder using Windows Explorer.

- **Desktop**  Shows buttons representing the contents of your desktop. If you have created shortcut icons on your desktop for programs you use frequently, they appear here.

- **Programs**  Shows buttons representing the contents of your Programs menu. This is useful mainly if you have shortcuts for most of the programs you use directly on the Programs menu. (Microsoft Office places its own programs directly on it.) If most of them are in separate submenus off the Programs menu, icons for the folders will appear, but they will not be readily identifiable.

- **Accessories**  Shows buttons representing the contents of your Accessories submenu (off the Programs menu).

You do not have to choose which toolbar you want to use; you can use them all if you want. To choose which toolbars to display, follow these steps:

1. Right-click the **Shortcut Bar**. A shortcut menu appears containing a list of the available toolbars at the top.

2. Click a toolbar's name to place a check mark next to it. (Toolbars with a check mark are displayed.)

To hide a toolbar, repeat the steps, removing the check mark.

 **TIP**  **Another Way to Display**  You can select which toolbars are displayed from the Toolbars tab of the Customize dialog box. Just click to place a check mark in or to remove the check mark from the check box to the left of each toolbar name.

When you have more than one toolbar set to display, you see only one at a time on the Shortcut Bar, but the others are just a mouse click away. Notice in Figure 3.3 that there are additional icons at either end of the Shortcut Bar; clicking on one of these activates a different toolbar.

These buttons represent different toolbars.                                                    Here are two more toolbars.

**Figure 3.3**  When multiple toolbars are displayed, you can switch among them by clicking a button on the Shortcut Bar.

**CAUTION**

**Which Is Which?**  If you have all (or most) of the toolbars turned on, you might get confused as to which icon represents each toolbar. Luckily, the toolbar buttons come with ScreenTips, the same as in other Office programs. Just point the mouse at a button, and a box appears, telling you which toolbar it represents.

# Creating Your Own Toolbars

Even though I'm a big Microsoft Office fan, I never found a lot of use for the Shortcut Bar—until I discovered how to create my own toolbars. Now I use the Shortcut Bar constantly.

When you create your own toolbar, you decide what buttons it will contain. A toolbar can contain buttons that start other programs (even non-Office ones). It can also contain shortcuts to certain folders and drives that you use often, and even shortcuts to individual documents!

To create a toolbar, follow these steps:

1. Right-click the Shortcut Bar and select **Customize**. The Customize dialog box appears.

2. Click the **Toolbars** tab, and a list of the current toolbars appears (see Figure 3.4).

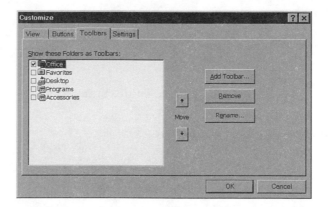

**Figure 3.4**  Create your own toolbars with the Customize dialog box.

3. Click the **Add Toolbar** button. The Add Toolbar dialog box appears.

4. Do one of the following:

   Click the **Create a New, Blank Toolbar Called:** option button and type a name for the new toolbar in the text box below.

   Click the **Make Toolbar for this Folder:** option button and type the path to a folder you want to use as a toolbar, or click the **Browse** button and locate the folder you want.

5. Click **OK** to return to the Customize dialog box. The new toolbar appears on the list of toolbars, with a check mark next to it.

6. If you created a toolbar from an existing folder, you're done; click **OK**. If you created a blank toolbar, continue with the steps in the following section.

## Adding Buttons to a Toolbar

If you created a blank toolbar in the preceding section, you will want to add buttons to it. You can also add buttons to existing toolbars too. If you add a button to a toolbar that's created from a Windows folder (for instance, the Desktop toolbar is created from the contents of the Windows\Desktop folder), you are, in effect, adding a shortcut for the desired program to that folder.

To add a button to a toolbar, follow these steps:

1. If the Customize dialog box is not already open, right-click the **Shortcut Bar** and select **Customize**.

2. Click the **Buttons** tab.

3. Open the **Toolbar** drop-down list and select the toolbar to which you want to add buttons.

4. Click the **Add File** or **Add Folder** button. The Add File (or Add Folder) dialog box appears (Figure 3.5).

5. Move through the drives and folders to find the executable file, folder shortcut, drive shortcut, or data file for which you want to add a button. Figure 3.5 shows a shortcut to Excel being selected.

6. Click the **Add** button to add it to your toolbar.

7. Repeat steps 4 through 6 until you have added all the buttons you want to your toolbar. The buttons appear on a list in the Customize dialog box, as shown in Figure 3.6.

8. Click **OK**, and your new toolbar appears in the Shortcut Bar.

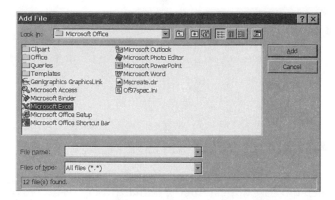

**Figure 3.5**   Browse with the Add File dialog box to locate the executable file for the program you want to add.

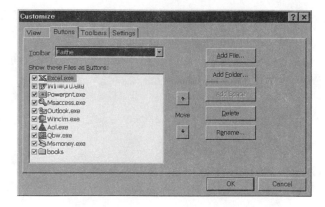

**Figure 3.6**   The buttons now on the toolbar appear as a list.

# Modifying a Toolbar

You can return to the Customize dialog box at any time to fine-tune your toolbars. Just right-click the **Shortcut Bar** and select **Customize**.

You can do any of the following from the Buttons tab:

- If there are any buttons that you do not want to show right now (but you want on-hand for later use), click them to remove the check marks from their boxes.

- If there are any buttons that you want to permanently remove from the toolbar, select them and click the **Delete** button. You might get a message warning you that you are deleting a file, but don't worry; you aren't deleting the real file; you're only deleting the shortcut to it that was created when you added the button to the toolbar.

- To reorder the buttons on a toolbar, click the button you want to move and then click the ↑ or ↓ button to move it.

# Customizing the Shortcut Bar

In addition to changing the buttons that appear on a toolbar and changing which toolbars appear, there are many other options you can set for the Shortcut Bar itself. To access those options, open the Customize dialog box (right-click and choose **Customize**) and click the **View** tab (see Figure 3.7).

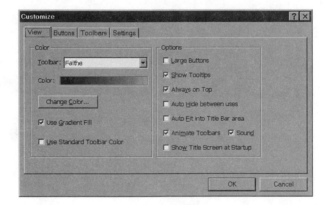

**Figure 3.7**  Specify how you want the Shortcut Bar to behave by selecting these options.

The Color controls take up the left side of the View tab. The controls there are:

- **Toolbar**   Each toolbar has separate color controls, so you must first select the toolbar for which you want to set the color options.
- **Change Color**   Click this button to select a different color for the selected toolbar.
- **Gradient Fill**   This blends the color on the toolbar gradually into gray as it moves from left to right across the toolbar.
- **Use Standard Toolbar Color**   This check box effectively turns off all the other Color controls by forcing the toolbar to use the standard color only (gray).

**716**

On the right side of the View tab are options that affect the entire Shortcut Bar itself:

- **Large Buttons**   Makes the buttons on the toolbar appear larger.
- **Show ScreenTips**   Provides the name of a button when the mouse pointer rests on it.
- **Always on Top**   Keeps the Shortcut Bar visible no matter what window is open over it.
- **Auto Hide Between Uses**   Hides the Shortcut Bar until you move your mouse over its position (for instance, the top of the screen).
- **Auto Fit into Title Bar Area**   Makes the Shortcut Bar small enough so it can overlap the active window's title bar, so it doesn't take up extra space that your application might need to use.

**Good Old Auto Fit**   In previous versions of Microsoft Office, Auto Fit into Title Bar Area was the default. So if you want your Shortcut Bar to look like it did in older versions, make sure this option is turned on.

- **Animate Toolbars**   Makes it look like the toolbars are "moving" when you switch among them.
- **Sound**   Makes a noise when you switch toolbars.
- **Show Title Screen at Startup**   Makes a copyright screen appear when the Shortcut Bar loads.

**TIP**   **Different Sounds**   To change the sounds that the Shortcut Bar makes, use the Sounds options in the Windows Control Panel. All of the sounds associated with Microsoft Office 97 can be changed from there.

# Removing the Shortcut Bar from the StartUp Group

By default, the Shortcut Bar loads when you start Windows because its icon is in the StartUp program group. To prevent the Shortcut Bar from starting automatically, simply use Windows Explorer to move the Microsoft Office Shortcut Bar icon from the C:\Windows\Start Menu\Programs\StartUp folder to the c:\Windows\Start Menu\Programs folder.

When you turn off the Shortcut Bar (see the following section), a message appears asking if you want the Shortcut Bar to appear again the next time you start Windows. Click **No** to remove the Shortcut Bar from the StartUp group.

# Turning Off the Shortcut Bar

If you don't want to use the Shortcut Bar anymore, you should remove it from your StartUp folder as explained in the previous section. But if you just want it stopped for the moment, you can close it by following these steps:

1. Click the **Control-menu** button for the Shortcut Bar. (It's the very leftmost icon on the bar.) A menu opens.

2. Select **Exit**, and the Shortcut Bar closes.

3. Office may ask you whether you want to remove the Shortcut Bar from the StartUp group. Click **Yes** or **No** in answer to the question.

In this lesson, you learned to use the Microsoft Office Shortcut Bar. In the next lesson, you'll learn about the Microsoft Office Binder.

# Using the Microsoft Office Binder

*In this lesson, you learn about the Microsoft Office Binder, which enables you to group related Office documents for convenient access.*

## Introducing the Microsoft Office Binder

Even though the Microsoft Office programs work well together and each program can import information from most of the other programs, they are still separate programs. However, the Binder is a program that attempts to bring all of the Office programs together.

An example will make this clearer. Let's say that you are preparing a report for your boss summarizing your monthly activities. It includes a memo typed in Word, a PowerPoint presentation that you gave to a key client, and a spreadsheet from Excel showing your sales results. One way to integrate all of those pieces seamlessly into a single report would be to import the data from Excel and PowerPoint into Word, and create the "master" report in Word. But the Office Binder offers an alternative. With the Office Binder, you can create a single Binder file that contains all the information from all of the files. Your boss can simply open the binder file in Microsoft Office Binder and look at all your materials without starting any other programs.

As you can see in Figure 4.1, in Microsoft Office Binder, each section of the binder file appears as an icon in a small pane on the left. When you click a file's icon there, the file appears in the main editing window on the right, along with controls for the appropriate program. For instance, in Figure 4.1, a Word file is

selected, so the menus and toolbars shown are those for Microsoft Word.
However, if you clicked on the Excel file, the controls would change to Excel's.

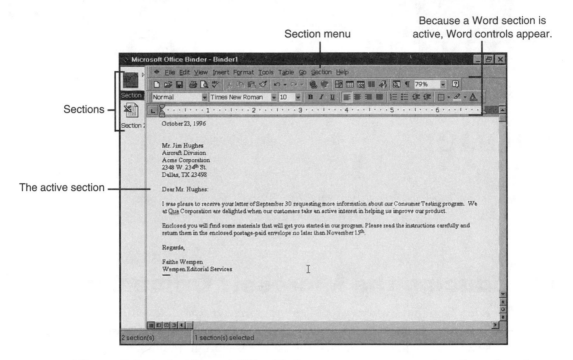

**Figure 4.1** In the Microsoft Office Binder, you can group several sections of varying types and edit each one in its native program.

# Starting a New Binder

When you start the Microsoft Office Binder program, it automatically starts a
new binder. To start the program, follow these steps:

**1.** Click the **Start** button.

**2.** Select **Programs**, **Microsoft Binder**.

If you later want to start another new binder while the program is open, just
select **File**, **New Binder** or press **Ctrl+N**.

Saving and opening binders works the same as saving and opening files in any
other Office program: use **File**, **Open Binder** to open a binder and use **File**, **Save
Binder** to save one.

# Adding a Section to the Binder

The various document files contained in a binder are called sections. You may have noticed in Figure 4.1 that the Word menu bar contained an extra menu: the Section menu. This menu is used to control the Office Binder program itself.

To add a section to the binder, follow these steps:

**1.** Select **Section**, **Add**. The Add Section dialog box shown in Figure 4.2 appears.

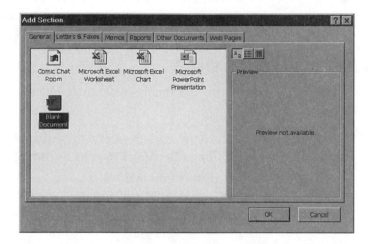

**Figure 4.2**   Select a template from the Add Section dialog box. To create a blank document, select one of the templates on the General tab.

**2.** To create a new blank document, double-click the icon on the General tab that corresponds to the program you want to use. To create a document based on a template or wizard, select one of the other tabs in the dialog box and double-click an icon there.

The new section appears on the section list at the left side of the screen, and the controls for its program open at the top so you can start creating the content.

# Placing an Existing File Into a Binder

If you have a file you have already created, you can place a copy of it inside your binder instead of creating it again from scratch. Follow these steps:

1. Select **Section**, **Add from File**. The Add from File dialog box appears. This is just like the Open dialog box that you work with in all Office programs.

2. Select the file from the dialog box. (Change the drive and folder as needed to locate it.)

3. Click **Add**, and the file appears in the section list in the binder. You can view it or edit it by clicking on it.

# Managing Sections

Once a section appears in your binder, you can do any of the following things with it:

- To move among sections, click the section you want to view, or select **Section**, **Next Section** or **Section**, **Previous Section**.

- To edit a section, click its icon in the Sections pane. Some sections cannot be edited from within the Binder; if you click on such a section (for instance, some PowerPoint presentations), a message appears telling you that you need to use the **Section**, **View Outside** command to edit it.

- To view a section in its full native application (instead of using the native tools and menus within the Binder ), select it and choose **Section**, **View Outside**. To return to the binder, in the native application select **File**, **Close & Return to Binder**.

- To delete a section, just select the section from the Sections list and select **Section**, **Delete**.

- To rename a section, select it and choose **Section**, **Rename**. The name appears highlighted. Type a new name and press **Enter**.

- To copy a section, select it and choose **Section**, **Duplicate**. The Duplicate Section dialog box appears. In the **Insert After** list, choose where you want the copy to appear and click **OK**.

- To rearrange the sections in your binder, select **Section**, **Rearrange**. In the Rearrange Sections dialog box, click a section and click the **Move Up** or **Move Down** button to move the section to a different position. When you're finished, click **OK**.

- To hide a section, select it and choose **Section, Hide**. To unhide a section, choose **Section, Unhide Section**, select the section you want to redisplay from the Unhide Sections dialog box, and click **OK**.

# Printing a Binder's Contents

There are two ways to print data from a binder: you can print the entire binder's contents, or you can print an individual section.

When you print the binder, you can print multiple sections that you select or the entire binder. (Hidden sections will not print; to unhide sections, select **Section, Unhide Section**.) To print multiple sections from a binder, follow these steps:

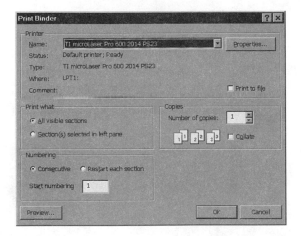

**Figure 4.3**   Print the entire binder or several sections at once from the Print Binder dialog box.

1. If you do not want to print all visible sections in the binder, select the ones you want from the left pane. To select more than one, hold down **Ctrl** and click each one.

2. Select **File, Print Binder**. The Print Binder dialog box opens (Figure 4.3).

3. Open the **Printer** drop-down list and select the printer you want to use.

4. In the Print What section, select **All Visible Sections** or **Section(s) Selected in Left Pane**.

5. In the Numbering section, select **Consecutive** or **Restart Each Section**. The former numbers pages as if all sections together were a single document; the latter treats each section as a separate document.

**6.** If you want the page numbering to start with a number other than 1, enter the number in the **Start Numbering** text box.

**7.** Enter the number of copies you want in the **Copies** box.

**8.** Click **OK**.

The other way to print is to print a section individually. To do this, select **Section, Print**. The controls appear for printing in the native application, which you learned about in the earlier parts of this book. Fill in the dialog box and click **OK**.

# Creating Binder-Wide Headers and Footers

One advantage of using a binder to print a group of documents is that you can establish a single header and footer for the entire grouping. To do so, follow these steps:

**1.** Select **File, Binder Page Setup**. The Binder Page Setup dialog box appears (see Figure 4.4).

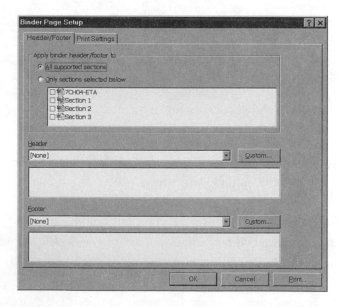

**Figure 4.4**  Use the Binder Page Setup dialog box to construct consistent headers and footers for the entire binder.

2. In the **Apply Binder Header/Footer To** section, select one of the following:

   **All Supported Sections**   Applies the header and footer to all sections contained in the binder except those that the binder can't edit. (For example, the binder can't edit some PowerPoint presentations, but it can include them.)

   **Only Sections Selected Below**   Applies the header and footer to only those sections you selected in the list below (those with check marks next to them).

3. Open the **Header** drop-down list and select one of the pre-formatted headers (such as "Page 1" or "Section 1 of 3"; there are more than a dozen to choose from). Or click the **Custom** button and design your own header, as you learned to do in the individual applications in earlier parts of this book.

4. Open the **Footer** drop-down list and select the footer you want to use, or click the **Custom** button and create your own.

5. Click **OK**.

 **TIP**   **Print Settings?**   There is also a Print Settings tab in the Binder Page Setup dialog box. It contains some of the the same options as the Print Binder dialog box you saw in Figure 4.3. You can set up your print options from it and then click the Print button at the bottom of the Binder Page Setup dialog box to print, as an alternative to the procedure you learned earlier in this lesson.

In this lesson, you learned how to create multi-type documents with the Office Binder. In the next lesson, you'll learn about Object Linking and Embedding (OLE).

# Object Linking and Embedding

*In this lesson, you learn how to create dynamic links and embedding with OLE.*

## What Is Object Linking and Embedding (OLE)?

OLE (pronounced "oh-LAY") stands for Object Linking and Embedding. It is a Windows feature that enables the Windows applications that employ it to transparently share information.

For example, you might create a quarterly report in Microsoft Word that contains an Excel Chart. Each quarter, the Excel data in the chart changes. When it comes time to generate the next quarterly report, you could find the most up-to-date version of the Excel chart and copy-and-paste it into the report, or you could use an OLE link to automatically update the report with the changes made in each supporting document.

### What Is Linking?

When you link an *object* to a *container file*, any changes you make to the object in its native application are automatically made to the object in the container file. The object in the container file remains a mirror image of the object in its native application, regardless of how many times you update the original object.

**Object**   An object is any snippet of data that you want to link to another document. It can be as small as a single character or as large as a huge report with many graphics.

**Container File** A container file is the file that's receiving the object. For example, if I'm linking an Excel chart to a Word document, the Word document is the container file.

# What Is Embedding?

When you embed an object, you insert a copy of it into your document, in the same way you might with the regular Paste command. A link to the source file is not maintained. However, embedding does offer something that regular pasting does not. When you embed an object into a document, a link is maintained to the original application; you can double-click that object at any time to open the application and edit the object.

A good example of an embedded object would be a company logo, created as Microsoft WordArt, that's embedded as part of a letterhead document created in Word. As an embedded object, all the information about the logo is maintained in the letterhead document, so you do not have to worry about managing or locating a separate file for the logo. When you do need to change the logo, you double-click it to open WordArt and edit the logo.

# Linking and Embedding with Paste Special

The easiest way to link and embed is with the Paste Special command on the Edit menu.

When an object is pasted into a document with the regular Paste command, the object is simply dropped in, with no information about its origin. In contrast, when an object is pasted into a document with Paste Special, several pieces of information about the object are stored as part of the container file, including the source file's name and location, the server application, and the location of the object within the source file. This extra information is what makes it possible for the object to be updated whenever the source file is updated.

OLE needs the name of a *source file* to refer back to later in order to link, so you must save your work in the source program before you create a link with OLE. However, if you merely want to embed, and not link, you do not have to have a named source file. The only information OLE needs in order to edit the object later is the name of the *server application* (the application in which it was created).

**TERM**

**Source File** The file from which the information to be pasted originated.

**Server Application** The server application is the native application for the object that's being linked or embedded. For instance, if you embed an Excel worksheet into a Word document, Excel is the server application.

**Container Application** The container application is the application in which the container file (the file to receive the object) is created. For instance, if the container file is a Word document, Microsoft Word is the container application.

To link or embed with Paste Special, follow these steps:

**1.** Copy the desired object to the Clipboard with the **Edit**, **Copy** command.

**2.** Open the container file (the file where you want to paste) and position the insertion point where you want it.

**3.** Select **Edit**, **Paste Special**, and the Paste Special dialog box appears. (The one for Word is shown in Figure 5.1; they are similar in all Office applications.)

Watch this area to preview the results of a selection.

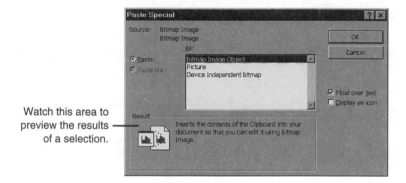

**Figure 5.1** The Paste Special dialog box.

**4.** Choose **Paste** or **Paste Link**, depending on the type of connection you want:

**Paste** Pastes the contents of the Windows Clipboard into the document at the location of the insertion point. The link is not maintained, but you can double-click the pasted material to edit it. (This is embedding.)

**Paste Link** This option is available if the contents of the Clipboard can be linked back to its source file. With this option selected, a link is created between the source file and the container file. If you have not saved the source file, the Paste Link option is not available.

**728**

**5.** Select the format you want to use from the **As** list. The formats listed change depending on the object type. Some formats you might see include:

> **... Object**   A type that ends with the word Object is a recognized OLE-capable format that you can either link or embed. If you want to embed, you should choose a data type that ends with the word "object." For example, in Figure 5.1, you would choose Microsoft Word Document Object.
>
> **Formatted Text (RTF)**   This data type formats text as it is formatted in the source file. If the text is formatted as bold italic, it is pasted as bold italic. This format does not support embedding.
>
> **Unformatted Text**   No formatting is applied to the object when this data type is selected. This format does not support embedding.
>
> **Picture**   This data type formats the object as a Windows metafile picture. It does not support embedding.
>
> **Device Independent Bitmap**   This data type formats the object as a bitmap picture, such as a Windows Paint image. It does not support embedding.

**6.** (Optional) If you want to display the pasted object as an icon instead of as the data itself, select the **Display As Icon** check box. This option is only available if you have selected Paste Link. This is useful for pasting Sounds and MediaClips because you can double-click one to play it later.

**7.** (Optional) If you want the object to appear inline with the rest of the document's text, make sure the **Float Over Text** check box is deselected. When selected, this check box forces the pasted object into the drawing layer of the document, where it can be moved freely over the top of the document.

**8.** Click **OK**. The object is embedded or linked into the container file, depending on the options you chose.

When deciding which options to select in the Paste Special dialog box, pay close attention to the notes that appear in the Result area. These notes tell you what will happen if you choose OK with the present set of options.

# Linking or Embedding an Entire File

If you want to link an entire file to your document, an entire Excel spreadsheet, for example, you can use the Object command. It appears on the Insert menu of most Windows applications.

Unlike with Edit Paste, you do not have to open the source file to retrieve the object. You can perform the entire procedure without leaving the client application. Follow these steps to learn how:

1. Start the client application (the one to receive the object), and then create or open the container file. You'll use Microsoft Word as the client application in this example.

2. Select **Insert**, **Object**. The Object dialog box appears.

3. Click the **Create from File** tab at the top of the dialog box. The dialog box changes to show a File Name list box (see Figure 5.2).

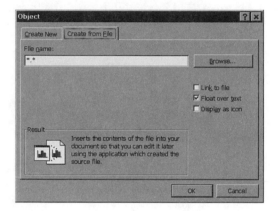

**Figure 5.2** Use the Object dialog box's Create from File tab to choose an existing file to link or embed.

4. Click the **Browse** button, and select the name of the file you want to insert and link or embed in the container file. For example, use an Excel worksheet. Navigate through the directories and subdirectories to locate the file if it does not appear in the current directory. When you locate the file, double-click it.

5. If you want to link, make sure the **Link to File** check box is selected. This will create an active link between the source file and the destination file. If you merely want to embed, not link, make sure it's deselected.

6. Select or deselect the **Float Over Text** and **Display As Icon** check boxes as desired. (See the descriptions of these controls earlier in this lesson.)

7. Click **OK**. The dialog box closes, and the source file is inserted into the container file.

**CAUTION**

**Whole Files Only**  Remember that using the Insert Object command links or embeds an entire file to the container file. You cannot use this command to link an individual object (such as a range of Excel cells) to the container file. Use the steps in the "Linking and Embedding with Paste Special" section earlier in this lesson for that.

# Creating a New Embedded File

The Insert Object command can also help you create a brand new file and embed it at the same time. (You can't link with this procedure because to link you must already have a named file that the object is coming from.) For example, let's say you want to insert an Excel spreadsheet into your Word document, but you haven't created the spreadsheet yet. You can do it all at once with the following procedure:

**1.** Open the container document and position the insertion point where you want the linked or embedded file to go.

**2.** Select **Insert, Object**, and the Object dialog box appears (see Figure 5.3).

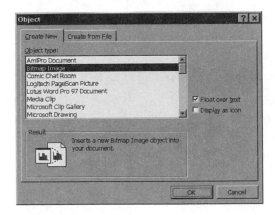

**Figure 5.3**  Select the type of file you want to create.

**3.** In the **Object Type** list, select the type of object you want to create.

**4.** Click **OK**. The application you selected opens within Word, and you can create the object.

**5.** When you're finished working with the object, select **File, Exit and Return to** *application* (the exact name of the command depends on the container application). The object is now embedded in your container file.

# Editing Embedded Objects

Editing an embedded object is where the greatest advantage of embedding comes into play. You do not have to remember the name and location of the source file that you used to create the embedded object. You simply double-click on the object and the source application starts, enabling you to edit the object.

Follow these steps to edit an embedded object:

1. Open then document containing the embedded object you want to edit.
2. Double-click the object or choose **Edit, Object**. The native application of the embedded object starts and displays the object.
3. Edit the object using the server application's tools and commands.
4. Click a portion of the container document or select **File, Exit and Return to** *application* from the object's native application. The object's native application closes, and you are returned to the container document.

**CAUTION**

**Modified Launch**  Some objects perform a function or action when you double-click them, instead of opening the source file for editing. For example, Windows Sound Recorder objects play a sound when double-clicked. To edit objects like this, hold down the **Alt** key and double-click the object.

# Editing Linked Objects

Once you have created a linked object, you may want to edit and update the information in the object. At this stage, you'll realize the full benefit of an OLE link because you can edit the object one time, and it will be updated in every document that it is linked to.

There are two ways to edit a linked object. The first is to start at the source file, using the server application to make changes to the object. The second is to start at the container file and let the link information lead you to the correct source file and server application. With the second method, you do not have to remember the name of the source file or even which server application created it. In the next sections, you'll learn how to edit objects using these two methods.

# Editing from the Source File

To edit a linked object starting from the source file, follow these steps:

1. Start the server application, and then open the source file that contains the object you want to edit.
2. Edit and make changes to the object.
3. Save the document and close the server application.
4. Switch to (or start) the client application and open the container file. The changes should automatically be reflected in the container file.

If the changes are not reflected, the document may not be set up to automatically update links. Skip to "Managing a Link's Update Settings" later in this lesson to learn how to update the links.

**CAUTION**

**Now You See It, Now You Don't**  Some client applications let you edit or make changes directly to the object that is linked to the container file without starting the server application. This can cause problems because the source file is not being changed, only the image of the object. The changes you make to the image will be wiped out when the object is updated via the source file. You will not have this problem with Microsoft Office products, but it may occur with other non-Microsoft applications.

# Editing from the Container File

Editing from the container file is quick and easy because you do not have to find and open the server application manually. To edit a linked object from the container file, follow these steps:

1. From the container file, double-click the linked object you want to update. The server application starts and displays the source file.
2. Edit the object in the source file, making as many changes as necessary.
3. Choose **File, Save** in the server application.
4. Choose **File, Exit** in the server application. You're returned to the container file, which reflects the changes you made to the linked object.

If double-clicking the object does not start the server application, open the Links dialog box by choosing **Links** from the **Edit** menu. Select the link you want to edit and click the **Open Source** button. The server application starts and displays the source file.

# Managing a Link's Update Settings

Once you have created a linked object, you can control when changes to the source file are updated in the container file(s). You can update a link manually or automatically. If a link is set to be updated manually, you must remember to follow the update steps each time you change the source file that contains the linked object. With the automatic setting enabled (the default update setting), the changes you make to the source file are automatically updated each time you open the container file.

To set a linked object to be manually updated, follow these steps:

1. Open the container file that contains the object link you want to update.
2. Choose **Edit, Links**. The Links dialog box appears (see Figure 5.4). For the linked objects in your document, the list indicates the link name, the path name of the source file, and whether the link is set to update automatically or manually.

**Figure 5.4** You can control each individual link in your document.

3. Select the link you want to update.
4. Change the Update setting to **Manual**.
5. Update the link by clicking the **Update Now** button in the Links dialog box. The object is then updated with any changes that were made to the source file.
6. Click **OK** to close the dialog box.
7. Choose **File, Save** to save the document and the changes to the link settings.

With the link set for manual update, you must repeat step 5 of this procedure each time you want the linked object to reflect changes made in the source file.

# Locking and Unlocking Links

In addition to setting link update options to manual and automatic, you can lock a link to prevent the link from being updated when the source file is changed. A locked link will not be updated until it is unlocked.

To lock or unlock a link, follow these steps:

1. Open the document containing the linked object.
2. Choose **Edit**, **Links**. The Links dialog box appears (see Figure 5.4).
3. Select the link you want to lock.
4. To lock the link, select the **Locked** check box. To unlock the link, make sure the check box is empty.
5. Click **OK** to close the dialog box.

# Breaking Links

If at some point, you decide that you want a linked object in your document to remain fixed and no longer be updated by its source file, you can break (or cancel) the link. This does not delete or alter the object, it merely removes the background information that directly ties the object to its source file. The object becomes like any other object that was placed by Windows Copy and Paste operation.

To break or cancel a linked object, follow these steps:

1. Open the container file that contains the object whose link you want to break.
2. Select **Edit**, **Links** (or **Link Options** in some applications). The Links dialog box appears, showing linked object information.
3. Select the link name of the object you want to break.
4. Click **Break Link** (or **Delete** in some applications). A warning box may appear cautioning that you are breaking a link. Click **OK** or **Yes** to confirm your choice.

In this lesson, you learned how to create and manage OLE links and embedding. In the next lesson, you'll learn how to use Microsoft Office applications on the Internet.

# Using Office Applications on the Internet

*In this lesson, you learn how to take advantage of Office 97's new Internet capabilities to link your work to the Internet.*

## Some Internet Basics

The Internet is a vast collection of connected computer networks, and the most popular component of it is the *World Wide Web* (WWW or Web). Most Web files are stored in a format called *Hypertext Markup Language*, or HTML.

Most of the Office 97 applications enable you to interact with the Internet in two ways. You can read and edit Internet information in Office applications, and you can post Office application data to the Internet.

To provide information to incoming users (that is, visitors to your Web site), you can make your work available by saving it in HTML format and copying the files to an Internet host (a computer that's directly connected to the Internet). If your company provides an Internet connection through its LAN, it probably also has a host computer where you can save HTML files somewhere on the network. If you use a modem to connect to the Internet, the local host that you dial in to may provide space on its server for your HTML files.

You can also set up *hyperlinks* to other *URLs* (Web addresses) within an Office document, presentation, spreadsheet, or database, so that your users can have outgoing access to Web sites. When your user clicks a hyperlink as he is using the file, his Web browser program opens over the top of your Office application, and the specified URL is displayed.

**Uniform Resource Locator (URL)**   An URL is a Web address. It's like a phone number, but it's for the Internet instead of the phone system. Most URLs begin with http://, followed by the site's name (for instance, **http://www.mcp.com**). Some URLs also contain specific directory and file names. For example, in the URL **http://www.mcp.com/Pub/index.htm**, Pub/ is a directory, and index.htm is a file name.

**Hyperlink**   A hyperlink is a bit of text or a picture that you can click to access a particular site quickly. When you click a hyperlink, your Web browser program opens (if you have one set up) and displays the specified URL's data.

# Saving an Object in HTML Format

The simplest way to make your work information available on the Web is to export a file in HTML format. It's a two-step process: first you export the file, and then you copy it to the Web server. The following sections describe how to accomplish the first part—exporting—in each program.

**No Link!**   Keep in mind that when you export a file to HTML, no link is maintained between the file and the HTML document. That means that if your file changes, you will need to export it to HTML again to update your HTML document.

CAUTION

## Exporting to HTML Format in Word

In Word, saving to HTML is very straightforward. You save it in almost exactly the same way that you do any other file, and the entire Word file is saved in a single HTML file. To save a file in HTML format in Word, follow these steps:

1. Open the document in Word.
2. Select **File, Save as HTML**. The Save As HTML dialog box opens. (It's the same as any other Save dialog box in an Office program, except the file type is set to HTML Document.)
3. Change the drive and folder if needed.
4. Type a file name in the **File Name** text box. Word adds the HTML extension automatically.
5. Click **Save**.

# Exporting to HTML Format in PowerPoint

PowerPoint starts with the same command as Word: File, Save as HTML. However, instead of opening a simple Save As HTML dialog box, PowerPoint starts a multiscreen wizard that walks you through the questions you need to answer. Follow these steps:

1. Select **File, Save As HTML**. The Save As HTML Wizard opens to walk you through the process. Click **Next** to begin.

2. Choose an existing layout from the **Load Existing Layout** list, or leave the **New Layout** button selected. (If you haven't created any layouts yet, you don't have any choice; you must use Layout.) Then click **Next**.

3. Choose one of the following page styles, and then click **Next**.

    • **Standard** is a simple one-pane view that will be displayed correctly by almost all browsers.

    • **Browser Frames** is fancier, but it might not be displayed correctly if the user viewing the presentation is not using a recent version of Netscape or Internet Explorer.

4. From the choices below, choose a graphic type for your graphics to be exported to. Then click **Next** to continue.

    • GIF and JPEG are both equally acceptable standard formats for graphics. GIF is slightly more common, but JPEG is slightly smaller and more recognized on the Internet. These formats do not support animation, so any animation you have assigned will be lost.

    • PowerPoint Animation format requires users to download a special PowerPoint viewer, but it ensures that your animations and effects will remain true to your original planning.

5. Choose a screen size that your presentation should be optimized for display on. The standard in VGA systems has long been 640×480, but lately many people have been switching to 800×600 resolution. Then click **Next**.

6. When prompted, enter your e-mail address and/or your Web page address. (These will be available to your users as they view your presentation.) Then click **Next**.

7. Next you're asked about colors. Click **Use Browser Colors** to go with the users' defaults, or click **Custom Colors** and choose your own. Click **Next** to Continue.

8. Click the option button next to the button style you want, and then click **Next**.

9. Click the option button next to the button placement you want, and then click **Next**.

10. In the **Create HTML Folder In** text box, enter the folder in which you want to store your converted HTML documents. (The default is My Documents.) Click **Next**.

11. Click the **Finish** button to complete the process.

12. A dialog box appears, asking you to name these settings in case you want to reuse them in the future. Enter a name and click **Save**. From now on, that name will be available at step 2 in the list of layouts. If you don't want to save the settings, click **Don't Save**.

13. Wait for PowerPoint to save the file. When you see the message **The presentation was successfully saved as HTML**, click **OK**.

After you have saved a presentation in HTML format, you must copy it to the server on which you want to make it available. If you use a modem to connect to an Internet service provider, establish your modem connection and use an FTP program to upload the files to the appropriate directory on the server. If you use a LAN or intranet, consult your system administrator to find out where to put the files.

# Exporting to HTML Format in Excel

Unlike in Word or PowerPoint, you do not have to save an entire Excel file (workbook) in HTML format; you can save individual ranges that you specify. (Of course, you are free to specify the entire sheet as the range if you want.) Follow these steps to export to HTML from Excel:

1. Open the workbook in Excel.

2. Select one of the ranges you want to export.

3. Choose **File, Save as HTML**. The Internet Assistant Wizard opens (see Figure 6.1).

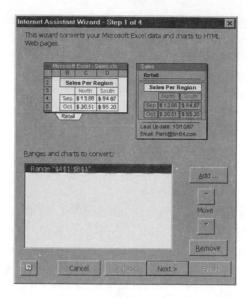

**Figure 6.1** Excel uses the Internet Assistant Wizard to convert data to HTML format.

**4.** If there are other ranges you want to select for conversion, or if the selected range is wrong, click the **Add** button. Select the range or type it in the text box provided, and then click **OK** to return to the Internet Assistant Wizard.

**5.** When you finish selecting ranges, click **Next** to continue.

**6.** Next you're asked to choose where the table will go. Click **Create an Independent, Ready-to-View HTML Document...** and click **Next**.

**7.** When prompted, fill in a title, header, and other information and click **Next**.

**8.** Finally, the wizard prompts you to enter a file name to save it under in the **File Path** text box. Enter a name and click **Finish**.

# Exporting to HTML Format in Access

Access provides a quick way to save multiple objects at a time in HTML format: the Publish to the Web option. It enables you to select multiple objects and simultaneously save them to your local hard disk. There is also an option for saving them directly to the server. If your server is using Microsoft software (Microsoft Web Server or Personal Web Server), you can even use the Publish to the Web Wizard to set up dynamic links to your Access database, so that the person accessing it from the Internet or intranet always sees the most recently updated data. Follow these steps to check it out:

1. Open the database containing the objects you want to publish.

2. Select **File**, **Save As HTML**. The Publish to the Web Wizard appears.

3. Click **Next** to continue. You're asked which objects from the database you want to publish on the Web.

4. Place a check mark beside the name of each object in the database that you want to save in HTML format. (There is a separate tab for each object type.) Then click **Next**.

5. (Optional) If you want to use an HTML file as a template for formatting, enter it in the **What HTML Document** text box or click the **Browse** button to locate it. Or, if you want to use a different template with different objects, select that check box. Click **Next** to continue.

6. If you clicked the check box in step 5, an extra screen appears asking you to specify which templates go with which documents. Select specific objects from the list, and then click the **Browse** button to find the HTML file to use a template for them. When you're finished choosing templates, click **Next** to move on.

7. Next you're asked whether you want static (HTML) or dynamic (HTX/ IDC or ASP) pages. *Dynamic* pages are updated automatically when your Access database is updated, but they require your server to be running Microsoft server software. *Static* pages are ordinary exported HTML files. Choose one or the other, or click the check box below the options to indicate you want some of each type.

8. If you selected the check box in step 7, an extra screen appears in which you must specify which pages should be static and which dynamic. Click an object on the list, and then click the **HTML**, the **HTX/IDC**, or the **ASP** option button to indicate its status. (HTML is static; the other two are dynamic formats.) Repeat for all objects on the list, and then click **Next** to move on.

 **TIP**    **Use Dynamic Sparingly**   It takes longer for a user to access dynamic pages than it does to access static ones because the server has to check your Access database. If you do not expect the information for a particular object to change frequently, it's better to save it as a static page.

9. If you chose Dynamic for any of your pages, a screen appears asking you for information about the server—its Data Source Name and (optionally) the user name and password you use to connect to it. You can also enter ActiveX Server Output information here. Enter the information and click **Next**.

10. Next you're asked about storage. By default, all HTML files will be saved on your hard disk. Specify the drive and folder in the text box labeled **I Want to Put My Web Publications in This Folder**.

11. If you want the HTML files saved on a server, too (in addition to the copy kept on your hard drive), click one of the Yes buttons at the bottom of the current dialog box. (They are not available if you are not currently connected to your server.) The Yes buttons include the following:

    • **Yes, I Want to Run the Web Publishing Wizard to Set Up a New Web Publishing Specification.** Use this one the first time, to set up the information for your server. If you choose this, the Web Publishing Wizard starts, and you must walk through its series of dialog boxes and supply the needed information.

**CAUTION**

**Server Info?** If you are not sure about your server information, ask your system administrator or service provider. Don't try to guess about this information.

    • **Yes, I Want to Use an Existing Web Publishing Server Whose 'Friendly Name' Has Been Set Up Previously.** After you have set up your server's information, use this to use the same server you used last time. Select your server's Friendly Name from the drop-down list.

**TERM**

**Friendly Name** When you use the Web Publishing Wizard to set up your server's information, you're prompted to enter a Friendly Name for it. This is simply a plain-English name that you can readily identify with that server. For instance, I might call the Macmillan Publishing server "Macmillan."

12. Click **Next** to move on when you're finished specifying the storage locations.

**13.** Next you're asked whether you want to create a home page. If you select the **Yes, I Want to Create a Home Page** check box, a home page HTML file will be added to the storage location(s) you specified in step 10.

**14.** If you marked the check box in step 12, enter a title for the page in the **What File Name** text box. This is the name the file will be saved as (for example, Default.htm). This file will contain hyperlinks to all the other objects' pages you're creating. Then click **Next**.

**15.** Next, you're asked whether you want to save your wizard's answers in a Web Publication profile. Click **Yes** and enter the profile name, or click **No**.

**16.** Click **Finish**. Access generates the HTML files you specified and posts them to the location(s) you chose.

# Inserting Hyperlinks

You learned earlier in this lesson how to make your work available on the Internet. But what about the reverse: making the Internet available to users of your documents?

The key to this kind of Internet connectivity is hyperlinks. A hyperlink is an address that points to a specific "page" of information on the Internet. You can insert hyperlinks directly into any Office file. Then when your reader clicks one, his or her Web browser opens and displays the HTML file at that specified address. (The user's Internet connection must be "on" for this to happen, of course. In other words, that person's computer must be connected to the Internet at the moment, whether through a LAN or through a modem connection.)

## Inserting Hyperlinks in Word or Excel

Word is the simplest of all the Office programs when it comes to hyperlinks. Just type the URL into the document, and Word recognizes it as such and converts it into a hyperlink automatically. (It keys in on the http:// part.) Hyperlinks appear underlined and in blue type. What could be simpler?

 Another way to insert hyperlinks (that works in both Word and Excel) is to use the **Insert, Hyperlink** command or to click the **Insert Hyperlink** toolbar button. When you do so, the Insert Hyperlink dialog box appears (see Figure 6.2).

Type the URL you want in the **Link to File or URL** text box and click **OK**. The hyperlink appears in your document or worksheet at the insertion point.

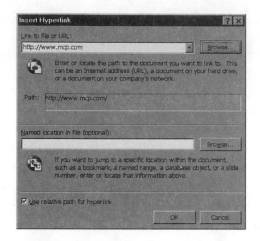

**Figure 6.2** Use the Insert Hyperlink dialog box to place a hyperlink in Word or Excel.

# Inserting Hyperlinks into a PowerPoint Presentation

In PowerPoint, you can assign links to Web addresses (URLs) to a button or to a graphic on a slide. For instance, you might have a button that takes you to your company's home page (the top page at their Internet site) at the bottom of every slide.

Let's say you want to create a Home button on your Slide Master to jump to your Web site's home page (**http://www.mysite.com**) when clicked. Create the button or import the graphic as described in Part 4 in this book, and then perform the following steps:

1. In Slide view, click the button or graphic. Selection handles appear around it.
2. Choose **Slide Show**, **Action Settings**. The Action Settings dialog box appears.
3. Click the **Hyperlink To** option.
4. Open the **Hyperlink To** drop-down list and select **URL**.
5. In the dialog box that appears, type the URL you want to link to (for example, **http://www.mcp.com**).
6. Click **OK** twice to close the dialog boxes.

# Inserting Hyperlinks into an Access Object

There are two ways to add a hyperlink to an Access database. The first is to create a field in a table and set its Data Type as Hyperlink. Then any text that you enter into that field becomes a hyperlink you can click to open a specified Web page.

 **TIP** **Not for Web Use Only** You can hyperlink to a document on your hard disk instead of a Web address if you want. For instance, if you have a supporting document for a record (such as a contract in Word), you can enter the document path in a hyperlink field (for instance, **c:\my documents\contract1.doc**).

The other way to set up a hyperlink is to add it to a form or report. When you do this, the hyperlink is not associated with any particular record, but with the entire form or table. It's very similar to the way you add hyperlinks in Word and Excel. To use this method, follow these steps:

1. Open the form or report in Design view.
2. Click the **Insert Hyperlink** button on the toolbar. The Insert Hyperlink dialog box appears (Figure 6.2).
3. Enter the URL in the **Link to File or URL** text box.
4. Click **OK**. Access inserts the hyperlink in the active section on the form. You can drag it to move it to any position on the form you want, just as you can move any object on a form.

The above method inserts a simple text hyperlink that gives the URL. If you want something fancier, you can create a picture and assign the hyperlink to it. Follow these steps to create a picture that serves as a hyperlink:

1. Insert a picture in the report or form.
2. Right-click the picture and select **Properties** from the shortcut menu that appears.
3. In the Properties dialog box, click the **Format** tab.
4. Type the URL in the **Hyperlink Address** text box (see Figure 6.3).
5. Close the Properties box. Now when you click the picture, it activates the hyperlink.

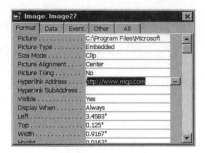

**Figure 6.3**  Specify an URL in the Hyperlink Address text box, and the picture becomes a hyperlinked object.

In this lesson, you learned how to link your Office work to the Internet.

# Index

**776**

# Check out Que® Books on the World Wide Web
## http://www.mcp.com/que

As the biggest software release in computer history, Windows 95 continues to redefine the computer industry. Click here for the latest info on our Windows 95 books

Make computing quick and easy with these products designed exclusively for new and casual users

Examine the latest releases in word processing, spreadsheets, operating systems, and suites

The Internet, The World Wide Web, CompuServe®, America Online®, Prodigy® —it's a world of ever-changing information. Don't get left behind!

Find out about new additions to our site, new bestsellers and hot topics

In-depth information on high-end topics: find the best reference books for databases, programming, networking, and client/server technologies

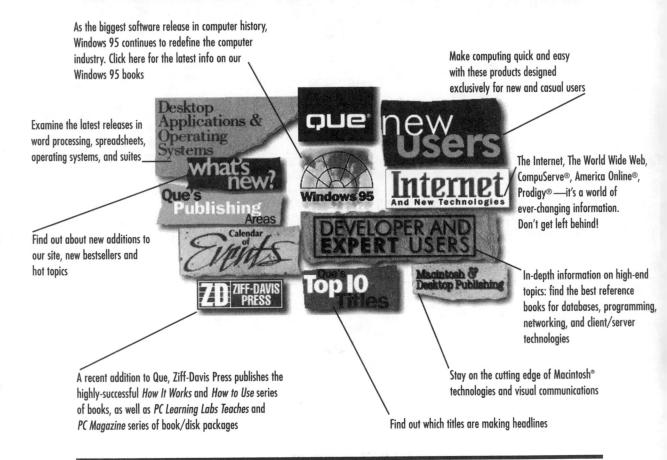

A recent addition to Que, Ziff-Davis Press publishes the highly-successful *How It Works* and *How to Use* series of books, as well as *PC Learning Labs Teaches* and *PC Magazine* series of book/disk packages

Stay on the cutting edge of Macintosh® technologies and visual communications

Find out which titles are making headlines

---

With 6 separate publishing groups, Que develops products for many specific market segments and areas of computer technology. Explore our Web Site and you'll find information on best-selling titles, newly published titles, upcoming products, authors, and much more.

- Stay informed on the latest industry trends and products available
- Visit our online bookstore for the latest information and editions
- Download software from Que's library of the best shareware and freeware

# Complete and Return this Card for a *FREE* Computer Book Catalog

Thank you for purchasing this book! You have purchased a superior computer book written expressly for your needs. To continue to provide the kind of up-to-date, pertinent coverage you've come to expect from us, we need to hear from you. Please take a minute to complete and return this self-addressed, postage-paid form. In return, we'll send you a free catalog of all our computer books on topics ranging from word processing to programming and the internet.

Mr. ☐    Mrs. ☐    Ms. ☐    Dr. ☐

Name (first) ☐☐☐☐☐☐☐☐☐☐☐☐ (M.I.) ☐ (last) ☐☐☐☐☐☐☐☐☐☐☐☐☐☐☐☐

Address ☐☐☐☐☐☐☐☐☐☐☐☐☐☐☐☐☐☐☐☐☐☐☐☐☐☐☐☐☐☐☐☐☐☐☐☐

City ☐☐☐☐☐☐☐☐☐☐☐☐ State ☐☐ Zip ☐☐☐☐☐ ☐☐☐☐

Phone ☐☐☐ ☐☐☐ ☐☐☐☐ Fax ☐☐☐ ☐☐☐ ☐☐☐☐

Company Name ☐☐☐☐☐☐☐☐☐☐☐☐☐☐☐☐☐☐☐☐☐☐☐☐

E-mail address ☐☐☐☐☐☐☐☐☐☐☐☐☐☐☐☐☐☐☐☐☐☐☐☐

## 1. Please check at least (3) influencing factors for purchasing this book.

Front or back cover information on book ☐
Special approach to the content ☐
Completeness of content ☐
Author's reputation ☐
Publisher's reputation ☐
Book cover design or layout ☐
Index or table of contents of book ☐
Price of book ☐
Special effects, graphics, illustrations ☐
Other (Please specify): _____ ☐

## 2. How did you first learn about this book?

Saw in Macmillan Computer Publishing catalog ☐
Recommended by store personnel ☐
Saw the book on bookshelf at store ☐
Recommended by a friend ☐
Received advertisement in the mail ☐
Saw an advertisement in: _____ ☐
Read book review in: _____ ☐
Other (Please specify): _____ ☐

## 3. How many computer books have you purchased in the last six months?

This book only ☐    3 to 5 books ☐
2 books ☐    More than 5 ☐

## 4. Where did you purchase this book?

Bookstore ☐
Computer Store ☐
Consumer Electronics Store ☐
Department Store ☐
Office Club ☐
Warehouse Club ☐
Mail Order ☐
Direct from Publisher ☐
Internet site ☐
Other (Please specify): _____ ☐

## 5. How long have you been using a computer?

☐ Less than 6 months    ☐ 6 months to a year
☐ 1 to 3 years    ☐ More than 3 years

## 6. What is your level of experience with personal computers and with the subject of this book?

|  | With PCs | With subject of book |
|---|---|---|
| New | ☐ | ☐ |
| Casual | ☐ | ☐ |
| Accomplished | ☐ | ☐ |
| Expert | ☐ | ☐ |

Source Code ISBN: 0-7897-0957-0

**7. Which of the following best describes your job title?**

Administrative Assistant ............................... ☐
Coordinator .................................................. ☐
Manager/Supervisor ..................................... ☐
Director ....................................................... ☐
Vice President .............................................. ☐
President/CEO/COO .................................... ☐
Lawyer/Doctor/Medical Professional .......... ☐
Teacher/Educator/Trainer ............................. ☐
Engineer/Technician ..................................... ☐
Consultant .................................................... ☐
Not employed/Student/Retired ..................... ☐
Other (Please specify): _____ ☐

**8. Which of the following best describes the area of the company your job title falls under?**

Accounting .................................................. ☐
Engineering .................................................. ☐
Manufacturing .............................................. ☐
Operations ................................................... ☐
Marketing .................................................... ☐
Sales ........................................................... ☐
Other (Please specify): _____ ☐

**9. What is your age?**

Under 20 ...................................................... ☐
21-29 ........................................................... ☐
30-39 ........................................................... ☐
40-49 ........................................................... ☐
50-59 ........................................................... ☐
60-over ......................................................... ☐

**10. Are you:**

Male .............................................................. ☐
Female ........................................................... ☐

**11. Which computer publications do you read regularly? (Please list)**

_____
_____
_____
_____
_____
_____
_____
_____
_____
_____

*Comments*: _____
_____
_____

Fold here and scotch-tape to mai